Frequently Asked Questions In Quantitative Finance

… including key models, important formulæ, popular contracts, essays and opinions, a history of quantitative finance, sundry lists, the commonest mistakes in quant finance, brainteasers, plenty of straight-talking, the Modellers' Manifesto and lots more

www.wilmott.com

Paul Wilmott

WILEY

A John Wiley and Sons, Ltd., Publication

This edition first published 2009
© 2009 Paul Wilmott

Registered Office
John Wiley & Sons Ltd, The Atrium, Southern Gate, Chichester, West Sussex, PO19 8SQ, United
Kingdom

For details of our global editorial offices, for customers services and for information about how
to apply for permission to reuse the copyright material in this book please see our website at
www.wiley.com.

Library of Congress Cataloging-in-Publication Data

Wilmott, Paul.
  Frequently asked questions in quantitative finance / by Paul Wilmott. — 2nd ed.
      p. cm.
  Includes bibliographical references and index.
  ISBN 978-0-470-74875-6
  1.   Finance—Mathematical models. 2.   Investments—Mathematical models.   3.
Options (Finance)—Mathematical models.   I. Title.
  HG4515.2.W55 2009
  332.601′5118—dc22

                                                          2009027978

A catalogue record for this book is available from the British Library.

ISBN 978-0-470-74875-6

Typeset in 9/10.5 Cheltenham-Book by Laserwords Private Limited, Chennai, India

SKY10080227_072424

To my parents

Paul Wilmott has been called 'the smartest of the quants, he may be the only smart quant' (*Portfolio* magazine/Nassim Nicholas Taleb), 'cult derivatives lecturer' (*Financial Times*), 'expert on quantitative easing,' (Guardian)*, 'the finance industry's Mozart' (*Sunday Business*) and 'financial mathematics guru' (BBC).

.

---

* This was, of course, a typical *Grauniad* mistake.

Contents

Frequently Asked Questions

Preface to the Second Edition

*T*he previous edition of this book was aimed to some extent at those people wanting to get their first job in quantitative finance and perhaps needed something to refresh their memories just as they were going into an interview. In part it was meant to be orthogonal to those interview-prep books that focus almost exclusively on the math. Math is important, but I think it's the easy bit of this business. It's where the math breaks down that I think is crucial, and so there's a lot of that in both the previous edition and this one.

In one respect I couldn't have been more wrong when I said that the last book was for newbies. Recent events have shown that some of those most in need of a refresher in the fundamentals are not necessarily the newbies, but sometimes also the 'experienced' quants, the 'respected' academics and the 'genius' Nobel laureates. I think this book has an additional purpose now if you are going for a job. Yes, take this book with you, but use it to interrogate the interviewer. If he can't answer your questions then don't accept a job from him, his bank might not be around for much longer!

This second edition is not an 'updating.' Nothing in the previous edition is out of date ... And that's not a statement that many quant finance authors can make! One of the themes in my research and writing is that much of quantitative finance is too theoretical, it's far too mathematical, and somewhere along the way common sense has got left behind. In 2000 I wrote that there needed to be a change in modelling methods if there was not to be a "mathematician-led market meltdown." There wasn't, so there was. In 2006 I narrowed this down to credit instruments and credit models. Sadly, money making got in the way of good modelling, and you no doubt know what ensued. But now more and more people are starting to appreciate the importance of getting the level of mathematics right, and this has to be a good thing for the industry. We ran a survey on wilmott.com, our famous "Name and Shame in Our New Blame Game!" in which we asked members to tell us which are the worst finance models. The results are published towards the end of this book so you'll see that common sense and robustness of modelling are on their way back.

To the thankees in the first edition I would like to add Emanuel Derman for allowing me to republish the "Financial Modelers' Manifesto" that we wrote together at the start of 2009.

Some more about the author

Paul Wilmott is still learning the guitar, after 36 years trying. He now knows six chords. His only hobby at which he has been successful is reading, always fiction. But even so, he has been stuck at half way through James Joyce's *Ulysses* for a decade, and has never got beyond the first 10 pages of anything by Salman Rushdie. Paul divides his time between his home in London and airport lounges around the world, where he can often be found nursing a dry martini.

Preface to the First Edition

*T*his book grew out of a suggestion by wilmott.com Member 'bayes' for a Forum (as in 'internet discussion group') dedicated to gathering together answers to the most common quanty questions. We responded positively, as is our wont, and the Wilmott Quantitative Finance FAQs Project was born. This Forum may be found at www.wilmott.com/faq. (There anyone may read the FAQ answers, but to post a message you must be a member. Fortunately, this is entirely free!) The FAQs project is one of the many collaborations between Members of wilmott.com.

As well as being an ongoing online project, the FAQs have inspired the book you are holding. It includes FAQs and their answers and also sections on common models and formulæ, many different ways to derive the Black–Scholes model, the history of quantitative finance, a selection of brainteasers and a couple of sections for those who like lists (there are lists of the most popular quant books and search items on wilmott.com). Right at the end is an excerpt from *Paul and Dominic's Guide to Getting a Quant Job*, this will be of interest to those of you seeking their first quant role.

FAQs in QF is not a shortcut to an in-depth knowledge of quantitative finance. There is no such shortcut. However, it will give you tips and tricks of the trade, and insight, to help you to do your job or to get you through initial job interviews. It will serve as an *aide memoire* to fundamental concepts (including why theory and practice diverge) and some of the basic Black–Scholes formulæ and greeks. The subject is forever evolving, and although the foundations are fairly robust and static there are always going to be new products and models. So, if there are questions you would like to see answered in future editions please drop me an email at paul@wilmott.com.

I would like to thank all Members of the forum for their participation and in particular the following, more prolific, Members for their contributions to the online FAQs and Brainteasers: Aaron, adas, Alan, bayes, Cuchulainn, exotiq, HA, kr, mj, mrbadguy, N, Omar, reza, WaaghBakri and zerdna. Thanks also to DCFC for his advice concerning the book.

I am grateful to Caitlin Cornish, Emily Pears, Graham Russel, Jenny McCall, Sarah Stevens, Steve Smith, Tom Clark and Viv Wickham at John Wiley & Sons Ltd for their continued support, and to Dave Thompson for his entertaining cartoons.

I am also especially indebted to James Fahy for making the Forum happen and run smoothly. Mahalo and aloha to my ever-encouraging wife, Andrea.

About the author

Paul Wilmott is an author, researcher, consultant and trainer in quantitative finance. He owns wilmott.com, is the Editor in Chief of the bimonthly quant magazine *Wilmott* and is the Course Director for the Certificate in Quantitative Finance (cqf.com). He is the author of the student text *Paul Wilmott Introduces Quantitative Finance*, which covers classical quant finance from the ground up, and *Paul Wilmott on Quantitative Finance*, the three-volume research-level epic. Both are also published by John Wiley & Sons, Ltd.

Chapter 1

The Quantitative Finance Timeline

*T*here follows a speedy, roller-coaster of a ride through the official history of quantitative finance, passing through both the highs and lows. Where possible I give dates, name names and refer to the original sources.[1]

1827 *Brown* The Scottish botanist, Robert Brown, gave his name to the random motion of small particles in a liquid. This idea of the random walk has permeated many scientific fields and is commonly used as the model mechanism behind a variety of unpredictable continuous-time processes. The lognormal random walk based on Brownian motion is the classical paradigm for the stock market. See Brown (1827).

1900 *Bachelier* Louis Bachelier was the first to quantify the concept of Brownian motion. He developed a mathematical theory for random walks, a theory rediscovered later by Einstein. He proposed a model for equity prices, a simple normal distribution, and built on it a model for pricing the almost unheard of options. His model contained many of the seeds for later work, but lay 'dormant' for many, many years. It is told that his thesis was not a great success and, naturally, Bachelier's work was not appreciated in his lifetime. See Bachelier (1995).

1905 *Einstein* Albert Einstein proposed a scientific foundation for Brownian motion in 1905. He did some other clever stuff as well. See Stachel (1990).

1911 *Richardson* Most option models result in diffusion-type equations. And often these have to be solved numerically. The two main ways of doing this are Monte Carlo and finite differences (a sophisticated version of the binomial model).

---

[1]A version of this chapter was first published in *New Directions in Mathematical Finance*, edited by Paul Wilmott and Henrik Rasmussen, John Wiley & Sons Ltd, 2002.

The very first use of the finite-difference method, in which a differential equation is discretized into a difference equation, was by Lewis Fry Richardson in 1911, and used to solve the diffusion equation associated with weather forecasting. See Richardson (1922). Richardson later worked on the mathematics for the causes of war. During his work on the relationship between the probability of war and the length of common borders between countries he stumbled upon the concept of fractals, observing that the length of borders depended on the length of the 'ruler.' The fractal nature of turbulence was summed up in his poem "Big whorls have little whorls that feed on their velocity, and little whorls have smaller whorls and so on to viscosity."

1923 Wiener Norbert Wiener developed a rigorous theory for Brownian motion, the mathematics of which was to become a necessary modelling device for quantitative finance decades later. The starting point for almost all financial models, the first equation written down in most technical papers, includes the Wiener process as the representation for randomness in asset prices. See Wiener (1923).

1950s Samuelson The 1970 Nobel Laureate in Economics, Paul Samuelson, was responsible for setting the tone for subsequent generations of economists. Samuelson 'mathematized' both macro and micro economics. He rediscovered Bachelier's thesis and laid the foundations for later option pricing theories. His approach to derivative pricing was via expectations, real as opposed to the much later risk-neutral ones. See Samuelson (1955).

1951 Itô Where would we be without stochastic or Itô calculus? (Some people even think finance is *only* about Itô calculus.) Kiyosi Itô showed the relationship between a stochastic differential equation for some independent variable and the stochastic differential equation for a function of that variable. One of the starting points for classical derivatives theory is the lognormal stochastic differential equation for the evolution of an asset. Itô's lemma tells us the stochastic differential equation for the value of an option on that asset.

In mathematical terms, if we have a Wiener process X with increments dX that are normally distributed with mean zero and variance dt, then the increment of a function $F(X)$ is given by

$$dF = \frac{dF}{dX}dX + \frac{1}{2}\frac{d^2F}{dX^2}dt$$

This is a very loose definition of Itô's lemma but will suffice. See Itô (1951).

1952 Markowitz   Harry Markowitz was the first to propose a modern quantitative methodology for portfolio selection. This required knowledge of assets' volatilities and the correlation between assets. The idea was extremely elegant, resulting in novel ideas such as 'efficiency' and 'market portfolios.' In this Modern Portfolio Theory, Markowitz showed that combinations of assets could have better properties than any individual assets. What did 'better' mean? Markowitz quantified a portfolio's possible future performance in terms of its expected return and its standard deviation. The latter was to be interpreted as its risk. He showed how to optimize a portfolio to give the maximum expected return for a given level of risk. Such a portfolio was said to be 'efficient.' The work later won Markowitz a Nobel Prize for Economics but is problematic to use in practice because of the difficulty in measuring the parameters 'volatility,' and, especially, 'correlation,' and their instability.

1963 Sharpe, Lintner and Mossin   William Sharpe of Stanford, John Lintner of Harvard and Norwegian economist Jan Mossin independently developed a simple model for pricing risky assets. This Capital Asset Pricing Model (CAPM) also reduced the number of parameters needed for portfolio selection from those needed by Markowitz's Modern Portfolio Theory, making asset allocation theory more practical. See Sharpe, Alexander and Bailey (1999), Lintner (1965) and Mossin (1966).

1966 Fama   Eugene Fama concluded that stock prices were unpredictable and coined the phrase 'market efficiency.' Although there are various forms of market efficiency, in a nutshell the idea is that stock market prices reflect all publicly available information, and that no person can gain an edge over another by fair means. See Fama (1966).

1960s Sobol', Faure, Hammersley, Haselgrove and Halton ...   Many people were associated with the definition and development of quasi random number theory or low-discrepancy sequence theory. The subject concerns the distribution of points in an arbitrary number of dimensions in order to cover the space as efficiently as possible, with as few points as possible (see Figure 1.1). The methodology is used in the evaluation of multiple integrals among other things. These ideas would find a use in finance almost three decades later. See Sobol' (1967), Faure (1969), Hammersley & Handscomb (1964), Haselgrove (1961) and Halton (1960).

1968 Thorp   Ed Thorp's first claim to fame was that he figured out how to win at casino Blackjack, ideas that were put into practice by Thorp himself and written about in his best-selling *Beat the Dealer*, the "book that made Las Vegas change its rules." His second claim to fame is that he invented and built, with Claude Shannon, the information theorist, the world's first wearable computer. His third claim to fame is that he used the 'correct' formulæ for pricing options, formulæ that were rediscovered and originally published several years later by the next three people on our list. Thorp used these formulæ to make a fortune for himself and his clients in the first ever quantitative finance-based hedge fund. He proposed dynamic hedging as a way of

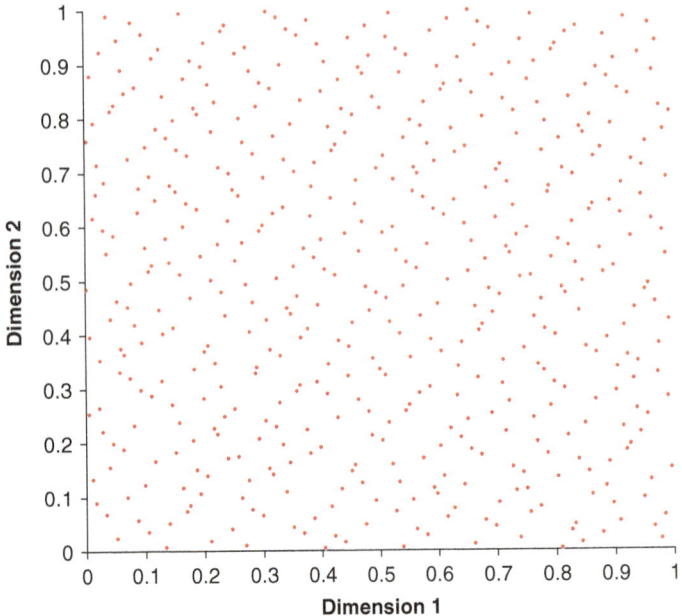

Figure 1.1: They may not look like it, but these dots are distributed deterministically so as to have very useful properties.

removing more risk than static hedging. See Thorp (2002) for the story behind the discovery of the Black–Scholes formulæ.

1973 Black, Scholes and Merton Fischer Black, Myron Scholes and Robert Merton derived the Black–Scholes equation for options in the early seventies, publishing it in two separate papers in 1973 (Black & Scholes, 1973, and Merton, 1973). The date corresponded almost exactly with the trading of call options on the Chicago Board Options Exchange. Scholes and Merton won the Nobel Prize for Economics in 1997. Black had died in 1995.

The Black–Scholes model is based on geometric Brownian motion for the asset price S

$$dS = \mu S \, dt + \sigma S \, dX.$$

The Black–Scholes partial differential equation for the value V of an option is then

$$\frac{\partial V}{\partial t} + \frac{1}{2}\sigma^2 S^2 \frac{\partial^2 V}{\partial S^2} + rS\frac{\partial V}{\partial S} - rV = 0$$

1974 Merton, again In 1974 Robert Merton (Merton, 1974) introduced the idea of modelling the value of a company as a call option on its assets, with the company's debt being related to the strike price and the maturity of the debt being the option's expiration. Thus was born the structural approach to modelling risk of default, for if the option expired out of the money (i.e. assets had less value than the debt at maturity) then the firm would have to go bankrupt.

Credit risk became big, huge, in the 1990s. Theory and practice progressed at rapid speed during this period, urged on by some significant credit-led events, such as the Long Term Capital Management mess. One of the principals of LTCM was Merton who had worked on credit risk two decades earlier. Now the subject really took off, not just along the lines proposed by Merton but also using the Poisson process as the model for the random arrival of an event, such as bankruptcy or default. For a list of key research in this area see Schönbucher (2003).

1977 Boyle Phelim Boyle related the pricing of options to the simulation of random asset paths (Figure 1.2). He showed how to find the fair value of an option by generating lots of possible future paths for an asset and then looking at the average that the option had paid off. The future important

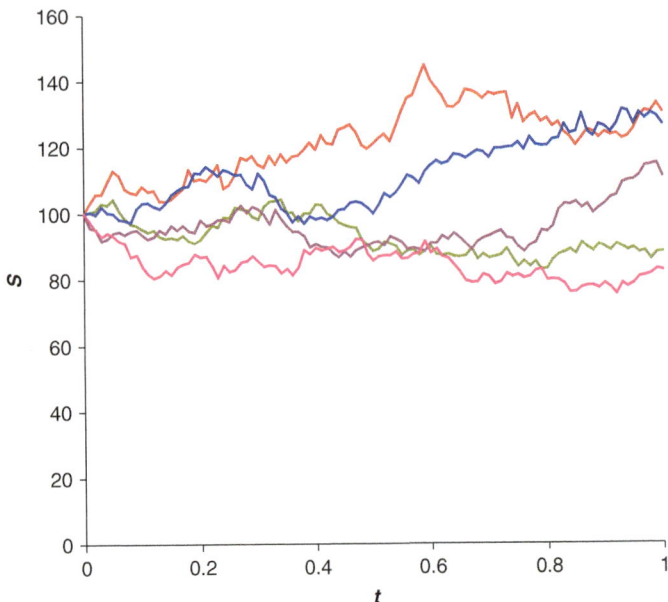

Figure 1.2: Simulations like this can be easily used to value derivatives.

role of Monte Carlo simulations in finance was assured. See Boyle (1977).

1977 Vasicek So far quantitative finance hadn't had much to say about pricing interest rate products. Some people were using equity option formulæ for pricing interest rate options, but a consistent framework for interest rates had not been developed. This was addressed by Vasicek. He started by modelling a short-term interest rate as a random walk and concluded that interest rate derivatives could be valued using equations similar to the Black–Scholes partial differential equation.

Oldrich Vasicek represented the short-term interest rate by a stochastic differential equation of the form

$$dr = \mu(r,t) \; dt + \sigma(r,t) \; dX.$$

The bond pricing equation is a parabolic partial differential equation, similar to the Black–Scholes equation. See Vasicek (1977).

1979 Cox, Ross and Rubinstein   Boyle had shown how to price options via simulations, an important and intuitively reasonable idea, but it was these three, John Cox, Stephen Ross and Mark Rubinstein, who gave option-pricing capability to the masses.

The Black–Scholes equation was derived using stochastic calculus and resulted in a partial differential equation. This was not likely to endear it to the thousands of students interested in a career in finance. At that time these were typically MBA students, not the mathematicians and physicists that are nowadays found on Wall Street. How could MBAs cope? An MBA was a necessary requirement for a prestigious career in finance, but an ability to count beans is not the same as an ability to understand mathematics. Fortunately Cox, Ross and Rubinstein were able to distil the fundamental concepts of option pricing into a simple algorithm requiring only addition, subtraction, multiplication and (twice) division. Even MBAs could now join in the fun. See Cox, Ross & Rubinstein (1979) and Figure 1.3.

1979–81 Harrison, Kreps and Pliska   Until these three came onto the scene quantitative finance was the domain of either economists or applied mathematicians. Mike Harrison and David Kreps, in 1979, showed the relationship between option prices and advanced probability theory, originally in discrete time. Harrison and Stan Pliska in 1981 used the same ideas but in continuous time. From that moment until the mid 1990s applied mathematicians hardly got a look in. Theorem,

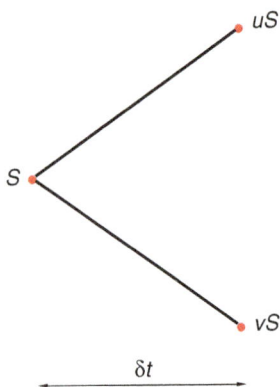

Figure 1.3: The branching structure of the binomial model.

proof everywhere you looked. See Harrison & Kreps (1979) and Harrison & Pliska (1981).

1986 Ho and Lee One of the problems with the Vasicek framework for interest-rate derivative products was that it didn't give very good prices for bonds, the simplest of fixed-income products. If the model couldn't even get bond prices right, how could it hope to correctly value bond options? Thomas Ho and Sang-Bin Lee found a way around this, introducing the idea of yield-curve fitting or calibration. See Ho & Lee (1986).

1992 Heath, Jarrow and Morton Although Ho and Lee showed how to match theoretical and market prices for simple bonds, the methodology was rather cumbersome and not easily generalized. David Heath, Robert Jarrow and Andrew Morton (HJM) took a different approach. Instead of modelling just a short rate and deducing the whole yield curve, they modelled the random evolution of the whole yield curve. The initial yield curve, and hence the value of simple interest rate instruments, was an input to the model. The model cannot easily be expressed in differential equation terms and so relies on either Monte Carlo simulation or tree building. The work was well known via a working paper, but was finally published, and therefore made respectable in Heath, Jarrow & Morton (1992).

1990s Cheyette, Barrett, Moore and Wilmott   When there are many underlyings, all following lognormal random walks, you can write down the value of any European non-path-dependent option as a multiple integral, one dimension for each asset. Valuing such options then becomes equivalent to calculating an integral. The usual methods for quadrature are very inefficient in high dimensions, but simulations can prove quite effective. Monte Carlo evaluation of integrals is based on the idea that an integral is just an average multiplied by a 'volume.' And since one way of estimating an average is by picking numbers at random we can value a multiple integral by picking integrand values at random and summing. With N function evaluations, taking a time of $O(N)$ you can expect an accuracy of $O(1/N^{1/2})$, independent of the number of dimensions. As mentioned above, breakthroughs in the 1960s on low-discrepancy sequences showed how clever, non-random, distributions could be used for an accuracy of $O(1/N)$, to leading order. (There is a weak dependence on the dimension.) In the early 1990s several groups of people were simultaneously working on valuation of multi-asset options. Their work was less of a breakthrough than a transfer of technology.

They used ideas from the field of number theory and applied them to finance. Nowadays, these low-discrepancy sequences are commonly used for option valuation whenever random numbers are needed. A few years after these researchers made their work public, a completely unrelated group at Columbia University successfully patented the work. See Oren Cheyette (1990) and John Barrett, Gerald Moore & Paul Wilmott (1992).

1994 Dupire, Rubinstein, Derman and Kani Another discovery was made independently and simultaneously by three groups of researchers in the subject of option pricing with deterministic volatility. One of the perceived problems with classical option pricing is that the assumption of constant volatility is inconsistent with market prices of exchange-traded instruments. A model is needed that can correctly price vanilla contracts, and then price exotic contracts consistently. The new methodology, which quickly became standard market practice, was to find the volatility as a function of underlying and time that when put into the Black–Scholes equation and solved, usually numerically, gave resulting option prices which matched market prices. This is what is known as an inverse problem: use the 'answer' to find the coefficients in the governing equation. On the plus side, this is not too difficult to do in theory. On the minus side, the practice is much harder, the sought volatility function depending very sensitively on the initial data. From a scientific point of view there is much to be said against the methodology. The resulting volatility structure never matches actual volatility, and even if exotics are priced consistently it is not clear how to best hedge exotics with vanillas in order to minimize any model error. Such concerns seem to carry little weight, since the method is so ubiquitous. As so often happens in finance, once a technique becomes popular it is hard to go against the majority. There is job safety in numbers. See Emanuel Derman & Iraj Kani (1994), Bruno Dupire (1994) and Mark Rubinstein (1994).

1996 Avellaneda and Parás Marco Avellaneda and Antonio Parás were, together with Arnon Levy and Terry Lyons, the creators of the uncertain volatility model for option pricing. It was a great breakthrough for the rigorous, scientific side of finance theory, but the best was yet to come. This model, and many that succeeded it, was nonlinear. Nonlinearity in an option pricing model means that the value of a portfolio of contracts is not necessarily the same as the sum of the values of its constituent parts. An option will have a different value depending on what else is in the portfolio with it, and an exotic will have a different value depending on what it is statically hedged with. Avellaneda and Parás defined an exotic option's value as the highest possible marginal value for that contract when hedged with any or all available exchange-traded contracts. The result was that the method of option pricing also came with its own technique for static hedging with other options. Prior to their work the only result of an option pricing model was its value and its delta, only dynamic hedging was theoretically necessary. With this new concept, theory became a major step closer to practice. Another result of this technique was that the theoretical price of an exchange-traded option exactly matched its market price. The convoluted calibration of volatility surface models was redundant. See Avellaneda & Parás (1996).

1997 Brace, Gatarek and Musiela Although the HJM interest rate model had addressed the main problem with stochastic spot rate models, and others of that ilk, it still had two major drawbacks. It required the existence of a spot rate and it assumed a continuous distribution of forward rates. Alan Brace, Dariusz Gatarek & Marek Musiela (1997) got around both of those difficulties by introducing a model which only relied on a discrete set of rates – ones that actually are traded. As with the HJM model the initial data are the forward rates so that bond prices are calibrated automatically. One specifies a number of random factors, their volatilities and correlations between them, and the requirement of no arbitrage then determines the risk-neutral drifts. Although B, G and M have their names associated with this idea many others worked on it simultaneously.

2000 Li As already mentioned, the 1990s saw an explosion in the number of credit instruments available, and also in the growth of derivatives with multiple underlyings. It's not a great step to imagine contracts depending on the default of many underlyings. Examples of these are the once ubiquitous

Collateralized Debt Obligations (CDOs). But to price such complicated instruments requires a model for the interaction of many companies during the process of default. A probabilistic approach based on copulas was proposed by David Li (2000). The copula approach allows one to join together (hence the word 'copula') default models for individual companies in isolation to make a model for the probabilities of their joint default. The idea was adopted universally as a practical solution to a complicated problem. However with the recent financial crisis the concept has come in for a lot of criticism.

2002 Hagan, Kumar, Lesniewski and Woodward There has always been a need for models that are both fast and match traded prices well. The interest-rate model of Pat Hagan, Deep Kumar, Andrew Lesniewski and Diana Woodward (2002), which has come to be called the SABR (stochastic, α, β, ρ) model, is a model for a forward rate and its volatility, both of which are stochastic. This model is made tractable by exploiting an asymptotic approximation to the governing equation that is highly accurate in practice. The asymptotic analysis simplifies a problem that would otherwise have to be solved numerically. Although asymptotic analysis has been used in financial problems before, for example in modelling transaction costs, this was the first time it really entered mainstream quantitative finance.

August 2007 quantitative finance in disrepute In early August 2007 several hedge funds using quantitative strategies experienced losses on such a scale as to bring the field of quantitative finance into disrepute. From then, and through 2008, trading of complex derivative products in obscene amounts using simplistic mathematical models almost brought the global financial market to its knees: Lend to the less-than-totally-creditworthy for home purchase, repackage these mortgages for selling on from one bank to another, at each stage adding complexity, combine with overoptimistic ratings given to these products by the ratings agencies, with a dash of moral hazard thrown in, base it all on a crunchy base of a morally corrupt compensation scheme, and you have the recipe for the biggest financial collapse in decades. Out of this many people became very, very rich, while in many cases the man in the street lost his life savings. And financial modelling is what made this seem all so simple and safe.

References and Further Reading

Avellaneda, M & Buff, R 1997 Combinatorial implications of nonlinear uncertain volatility models: the case of barrier options. Courant Institute, NYU

Avellaneda, M & Parás, A 1994 Dynamic hedging portfolios for derivative securities in the presence of large transaction costs. *Applied Mathematical Finance* **1** 165–194

Avellaneda, M & Parás, A 1996 Managing the volatility risk of derivative securities: the Lagrangian volatility model. *Applied Mathematical Finance* **3** 21–53

Avellaneda, M, Lévy, A & Parás, A 1995 Pricing and hedging derivative securities in markets with uncertain volatilities. *Applied Mathematical Finance* **2** 73–88

Bachelier, L 1995 *Théorie de la Spéculation*. Jacques Gabay

Barrett, JW, Moore, G & Wilmott, P 1992 Inelegant efficiency. *Risk* magazine **5** (9) 82–84

Black, F & Scholes, M 1973 The pricing of options and corporate liabilities. *Journal of Political Economy* **81** 637–659

Boyle, P 1977 Options: a Monte Carlo approach. *Journal of Financial Economics* **4** 323–338

Brace, A, Gatarek, D & Musiela, M 1997 The market model of interest rate dynamics. *Mathematical Finance* **7** 127–154

Brown, R 1827 *A Brief Account of Microscopical Observations*. London

Cheyette, O 1990 Pricing options on multiple assets. *Advances in Futures and Options Research* **4** 68–91

Cox, JC, Ross, S & Rubinstein M 1979 Option pricing: a simplified approach. *Journal of Financial Economics* **7** 229–263

Derman, E & Kani, I 1994 Riding on a smile. *Risk* magazine **7** (2) 32–39 (February)

Derman, E, Ergener, D & Kani, I 1997 Static options replication. In *Frontiers in Derivatives* (eds Konishi, A & Dattatreya, RE) Irwin

Dupire, B 1993 Pricing and hedging with smiles. Proc AFFI Conf, La Baule June 1993

Dupire, B 1994 Pricing with a smile. *Risk* magazine **7** (1) 18–20 (January)

Fama, E 1965 The behaviour of stock prices. *Journal of Business* **38** 34–105

Faure, H 1969 Résultat voisin d'un théoréme de Landau sur le nombre de points d'un réseau dans une hypersphere. *C.R. Acad. Sci. Paris Sér. A* **269** 383–386

Hagan, P, Kumar, D, Lesniewski, A & Woodward, D 2002 Managing smile risk. *Wilmott* magazine, September

Halton, JH 1960 On the efficiency of certain quasi-random sequences of points in evaluating multi-dimensional integrals. *Num. Maths.* **2** 84–90

Hammersley, JM & Handscomb, DC 1964 *Monte Carlo Methods.* Methuen, London

Harrison, JM & Kreps, D 1979 Martingales and arbitrage in multiperiod securities markets. *Journal of Economic Theory* **20** 381–408

Harrison, JM & Pliska, SR 1981 Martingales and stochastic integrals in the theory of continuous trading. *Stochastic Processes and their Applications* **11** 215–260

Haselgrove, CB 1961 A method for numerical integration. *Mathematics of Computation* **15** 323–337

Heath, D, Jarrow, R & Morton, A 1992 bond pricing and the term structure of interest rates: a new methodology. *Econometrica* **60** 77–105

Ho, T & Lee, S 1986 Term structure movements and pricing interest rate contingent claims. *Journal of Finance* **42** 1129–1142

Itô, K 1951 On stochastic differential equations. *Memoirs of the American Mathematical Society* **4** 1–51

Li, DX 2000 On default correlation: a copula function approach. Risk-Metrics Group

Lintner, J 1965 Security prices, risk, and maximal gains from diversification. *Journal of Finance* **20** 587–615

Markowitz, H 1959 *Portfolio Selection: Efficient Diversification of Investment*. John Wiley & Sons Ltd (www.wiley.com)

Merton, RC 1973 Theory of rational option pricing. *Bell Journal of Economics and Management Science* **4** 141–183

Merton, RC 1974 On the pricing of corporate debt: the risk structure of interest rates. *Journal of Finance* **29** 449–470

Merton, RC 1992 *Continuous-Time Finance*. Blackwell

Mossin, J 1966 Equilibrium in a capital asset market. *Econometrica* **34** 768–783

Niederreiter, H 1992 *Random Number Generation and Quasi-Monte Carlo Methods*. SIAM

Ninomiya, S & Tezuka, S 1996 Toward real-time pricing of complex financial derivatives. *Applied Mathematical Finance* **3** 1–20

Paskov 1996 New methodologies for valuing derivatives. In *Mathematics of Derivative Securities* (eds Pliska, SR & Dempster, M)

Paskov, SH & Traub, JF 1995 Faster valuation of financial derivatives. *Journal of Portfolio Management* Fall 113–120

Richardson, LF 1922 *Weather Prediction by Numerical Process*. Cambridge University Press

Rubinstein, M 1994 Implied binomial trees. *Journal of Finance* **69** 771–818

Samuelson, P 1955 Brownian motion in the stock market. Unpublished

Schönbucher, PJ 2003 *Credit Derivatives Pricing Models*. John Wiley & Sons Ltd

Sharpe, WF, Alexander, GJ & Bailey, JV 1999 *Investments*. Prentice–Hall

Sloan, IH & Walsh, L 1990 A computer search of rank two lattice rules for multidimensional quadrature. *Mathematics of Computation* **54** 281–302

Sobol', IM 1967 On the distribution of points in cube and the approximate evaluation of integrals. *USSR Computational Mathematics and Mathematical Physics* **7** 86–112

Stachel, J (ed.) 1990 *The Collected Papers of Albert Einstein.* Princeton University Press

Thorp, EO 1962 *Beat the Dealer.* Vintage

Thorp, EO 2002 *Wilmott* magazine, various papers

Thorp, EO & Kassouf, S 1967 *Beat the Market.* Random House

Traub, JF & Wozniakowski, H 1994 Breaking intractability. *Scientific American* January 102–107

Vasicek, OA 1977 An equilibrium characterization of the term structure. *Journal of Financial Economics* **5** 177–188

Wiener, N 1923 Differential space. *Journal of Mathematics and Physics* **58** 131–174

And Now a Brief Unofficial History!

Espen Gaarder Haug, as well as being an option trader, author, lecturer, researcher, gardener, soldier, and collector of option-pricing formulæ, is also a historian of derivatives theory. In his excellent book *Derivatives: Model on Models* (John Wiley and Sons Ltd, 2007) he gives the 'alternative' history of derivatives, a history often ignored for various reasons. He also keeps us updated on his findings via his blog http://www.wilmott.com/blogs/collector. Here are a few of the many interesting facts Espen has unearthed.

1688 de la Vega Possibly a reference to put–call parity. But then possibly not. De la Vega's language is not particularly precise.

1900s Higgins and Nelson They appear to have some grasp of delta hedging and put–call parity.

1908 Bronzin Publishes a book that includes option formulæ, and seems to be using risk neutrality. But the work is rapidly forgotten!

1915 Mitchell, 1926 Oliver and 1927 Mills   They all described the high-peak/fat-tails in empirical price data.

1956 Kruizenga and 1961 Reinach   They definitely describe put–call parity. Reinach explains 'conversion,' which is what we know as put–call parity, he also understands that it does not necessarily apply for American options.

1962 Mandelbrot   In this year Benoit Mandelbrot wrote his famous paper on the distribution of cotton price returns, observing their fat tails.

1970 Arnold Bernhard & Co   They describe market-neutral delta hedging of convertible bonds and warrants. And show how to numerically find an approximation to the delta.

For more details about the underground history of derivatives see Espen's excellent book (2007).

References and Further Reading

Haug, EG 2007 *Derivatives: Models on Models*, John Wiley & Sons, Ltd.

Mandelbrot, B & Hudson, R 2004 *The (Mis)Behaviour of Markets: A Fractal View of Risk, Ruin and Reward*. Profile Books

Chapter 2

FAQs

What are the Different Types of Mathematics Found in Quantitative Finance?

Short answer
The fields of mathematics most used in quantitative finance are those of probability theory and differential equations. And, of course, numerical methods are usually needed for producing numbers.

Example
The classical model for option pricing can be written as a partial differential equation. But the same model also has a probabilistic interpretation in terms of expectations.

Long answer
The real-world subject of quantitative finance uses tools from many branches of mathematics. And financial modelling can be approached in a variety of different ways. For some strange reason the advocates of different branches of mathematics get quite emotional when discussing the merits and demerits of their methodologies and those of their 'opponents.' Is this a territorial thing? What are the pros and cons of martingales and differential equations? What is all this fuss, and will it end in tears before bedtime?

Here's a list of the various approaches to modelling and a selection of useful tools. The distinction between a 'modelling approach' and a 'tool' will start to become clear.

Modelling approaches:

- Probabilistic
- Deterministic

- Discrete: difference equations
- Continuous: differential equations

Useful tools:

- Simulations
- Discretization methods
- Approximations
- Asymptotic analysis
- Series solutions
- Green's functions

While these are not exactly arbitrary lists, they are certainly open to some criticism or addition. Let's first take a look at the modelling approaches.

Probabilistic One of the main assumptions about the financial markets, at least as far as quantitative finance goes, is that asset prices are random. We tend to think of describing financial variables as following some random path, with parameters describing the growth of the asset and its degree of randomness. We effectively model the asset path via a specified rate of growth, on average, and its deviation from that average. This approach to modelling has had the greatest impact over the last 30 years, leading to the explosive growth of the derivatives markets.

Deterministic The idea behind this approach is that our model will tell us everything about the future. Given enough data, and a big enough brain, we can write down some equations or an algorithm for predicting the future. Interestingly, the subjects of dynamical systems and chaos fall into this category. And, as you know, chaotic systems show such sensitivity to initial conditions that predictability is in practice impossible. This is the 'butterfly effect,' that a butterfly flapping its wings in Brazil will 'cause' rainfall over Manchester. (And what doesn't!) A topic popular in the early 1990s, this has not lived up to its promises in the financial world.

Discrete/Continuous Whether probabilistic or deterministic, the eventual model you write down can be discrete or continuous. Discrete means that asset prices and/or time can only be incremented in finite chunks, whether a dollar or a cent, a year or a day. Continuous means that no such lower increment exists. The mathematics of continuous processes is often easier than that of discrete ones. But then when it comes to number crunching you have in any case to turn a continuous model into a discrete one.

In discrete models we end up with difference equations. An example of this is the binomial model for option pricing. Time progresses in finite amounts, the time step. In continuous models we end up with differential equations. The equivalent of the binomial model in discrete space is the Black–Scholes model, which has continuous asset price and continuous time. Whether binomial or Black–Scholes, both of these models come from the probabilistic assumptions about the financial world.

Now let's take a look at some of the tools available.

Simulations If the financial world is random then we can experiment with the future by running simulations. For example, an asset price may be represented by its average growth and its risk, so let's simulate what could happen in the future to this random asset. If we were to take such an approach we would want to run many, many simulations. There'd be little point in running just the one; we'd like to see a range of possible future scenarios.

Simulations can also be used for non-probabilistic problems. Just because of the similarities between mathematical equations, a model derived in a deterministic framework may have a probabilistic interpretation.

Discretization methods   The complement to simulation methods, and there are many types of these. The best known are the finite-difference methods which are discretizations of continuous models such as Black–Scholes.

Depending on the problem you are solving, and unless it's very simple, you will probably go down the simulation or finite-difference routes for your number crunching.

Approximations   In modelling we aim to come up with a solution representing something meaningful and useful, such as an option price. Unless the model is really simple, we may not be able to solve it easily. This is where approximations come in. A complicated model may have approximate solutions. And these approximate solutions might be good enough for our purposes.

Asymptotic analysis   This is an incredibly useful technique, used in most branches of applicable mathematics, but until recently almost unknown in finance. The idea is simple: find approximate solutions to a complicated problem by exploiting parameters or variables that are either large or small, or special in some way. For example, there are simple approximations for vanilla option values close to expiry.

Series solutions   If your equation is linear (and they almost all are in quantitative finance) then you might be able to solve a particular problem by adding together the solutions of other problems. Series solutions are when you decompose the solution into a (potentially infinite) sum of simple functions, such as sines and cosines, or a power series. This is the case, for example, with barrier options having two barriers, one below the current asset price and the other above.

Green's functions This is a very special technique that only works in certain situations. The idea is that solutions to some difficult problems can be built up from solutions to special cases of a similar problem.

References and Further Reading

Joshi, M 2003 *The Concepts and Practice of Mathematical Finance*. Cambridge University Press.

Wilmott, P 2006 *Paul Wilmott on Quantitative Finance*, second edition. John Wiley & Sons Ltd.

Wilmott, P 2007 *Paul Wilmott Introduces Quantitative Finance*, second edition. John Wiley & Sons Ltd.

What is Arbitrage?

Short answer
Arbitrage is making a sure profit in excess of the risk-free rate of return. In the language of quantitative finance we can say that an arbitrage opportunity is a portfolio of zero value today which is of positive value in the future with positive probability, and of negative value in the future with zero probability.

The assumption that there are no arbitrage opportunities in the market is fundamental to classical finance theory. This idea is popularly known as 'there's no such thing as a free lunch.'

Example
An at-the-money European call option with a strike of $100 and an expiration of six months is worth $8. A European put with the same strike and expiration is worth $6. There are no dividends on the stock and a six-month zero-coupon bond with a principal of $100 is worth $97.

Buy the call and a bond, sell the put and the stock, which will bring in $-8-97+6+100 = 1. At expiration this portfolio will be worthless regardless of the final price of the stock. You will make a profit of $1 with no risk. This is arbitrage. It is an example of the violation of ***put–call parity***.

Long answer
The principle of no arbitrage is one of the foundations of classical finance theory. In derivatives theory it is assumed during the derivation of the binomial model option-pricing algorithm and in the Black–Scholes model. In these cases it is rather more complicated than the simple example given above. In the above example we set up a portfolio that gave us an immediate profit, and that portfolio did not have to

be touched until expiration. This is a case of a static arbitrage. Another special feature of the above example is that it does not rely on any assumptions about how the stock price behaves. So the example is that of model-independent arbitrage. However, when deriving the famous option-pricing models we rely on a dynamic strategy, called delta hedging, in which a portfolio consisting of an option and stock is constantly adjusted by purchase or sale of stock in a very specific manner.

Now we can see that there are several types of arbitrage that we can think of. Here is a list and description of the most important.

- A static arbitrage is an arbitrage that does not require rebalancing of positions
- A dynamic arbitrage is an arbitrage that requires trading instruments in the future, generally contingent on market states
- A statistical arbitrage is not an arbitrage but simply a likely profit in excess of the risk-free return (perhaps even suitably adjusted for risk taken) as predicted by past statistics
- Model-independent arbitrage is an arbitrage which does not depend on any mathematical model of financial instruments to work. For example, an exploitable violation of put–call parity or a violation of the relationship between spot and forward prices, or between bonds and swaps
- Model-dependent arbitrage does require a model. For example, options mispriced because of incorrect volatility estimate. To profit from the arbitrage you need to delta hedge, and that requires a model

Not all apparent arbitrage opportunities can be exploited in practice. If you see such an opportunity in quoted prices on a screen in front of you then you are likely to find that when you try to take advantage of them they just evaporate. Here are several reasons for this.

- Quoted prices are wrong or not tradeable
- Option and stock prices were not quoted synchronously
- There is a bid–offer spread you have not accounted for
- Your model is wrong, or there is a risk factor you have not accounted for

References and Further Reading

Merton, RC 1973 Theory of rational option pricing. *Bell Journal of Economics and Management Science* **4** 141–183

Wilmott, P 2007 *Paul Wilmott Introduces Quantitative Finance*, second edition. John Wiley & Sons Ltd

What is Put–Call Parity?

Short answer
Put–call parity is a relationship between the prices of a European-style call option and a European-style put option, as long as they have the same strike and expiration:

Call price − Put price = Stock price

− Strike price (present valued from expiration).

Example Stock price is $98, a European call option struck at $100 with an expiration of nine months has a value of $9.07. The nine-month, continuously compounded, interest rate is 4.5%. What is the value of the put option with the same strike and expiration?

By rearranging the above expression we find

$$\text{Put price} = 9.07 - 98 + 100 \, e^{-0.045 \times 0.75} = 7.75.$$

The put must therefore be worth $7.75.

Long answer
This relationship,

$$C - P = S - K \, e^{-r(T-t)},$$

between European calls (value C) and puts (value P) with the same strike (K) and expiration (T) valued at time t is a result of a simple arbitrage argument. If you buy a call option, at the same time write a put, and sell stock short, what will your payoff be at expiration? If the stock is above the strike at expiration you will have $S - K$ from the call, 0 from the put and $-S$ from the stock. A total of $-K$. If the stock is below the strike at expiration you will have 0 from the call, $-S$ again from the stock, and $-(K - S)$ from the short put. Again a total of $-K$. So, whatever the stock price is at expiration this portfolio will always be worth $-K$, a guaranteed amount. Since this amount is guaranteed we can discount it back to the present. We must have

$$C - P - S = -K\,e^{-r(T-t)}.$$

This is put–call parity.

Another way of interpreting put–call parity is in terms of implied volatility. Calls and puts with the same strike and expiration must have the same implied volatility.

The beauty of put–call parity is that it is a model-independent relationship. To value a call on its own we need a model for the stock price, in particular its volatility. The same is true for valuing a put. But to value a portfolio consisting of a long call and a short put (or vice versa), no model is needed. Such model-independent relationships are few and far between in finance. The relationship between forward and spot prices is one, and the relationships between bonds and swaps is another.

In practice options don't have a single price, they have two prices, a bid and an offer (or ask). This means that when looking for violations of put–call parity you must use bid (offer) if you are going short (long) the options. This makes the calculations a little bit messier. If you think in terms of implied volatility then it's much easier to spot violations of put–call parity. You must look for non-overlapping implied volatility ranges. For example, suppose that the bid/offer on a call is 22%/25% in implied volatility terms and that on a put (same strike and expiration) is 21%/23%. There is an overlap between these two ranges (22–23%) and so no arbitrage opportunity. However, if the put prices were 19%/21% then there would be a violation of put–call parity and hence an easy arbitrage opportunity. Don't expect to find many (or, indeed, any) of such simple free-money opportunities in practice though. If you do find such an arbitrage then it usually disappears by the time you put the trade on. See Kamara and Miller (1995) for details of the statistics of no-arbitrage violations.

When there are dividends on the underlying stock during the life of the options, we must adjust the equation to allow for this. We now find that

$C - P = S -$ Present value of all dividends $- E\,e^{-r(T-t)}$.

This, of course, assumes that we know what the dividends will be.

If interest rates are not constant then just discount the strike back to the present using the value of a zero-coupon bond with maturity the same as the expiration of the option. Dividends should similarly be discounted.

When the options are American, put–call parity does not hold, because the short position could be exercised against you, leaving you with some exposure to the stock price. Therefore you don't know what you will be worth at expiration. In the absence of dividends it is theoretically never optimal to exercise an American call before expiration, whereas an American put should be exercised if the stock falls low enough.

References and Further Reading

Kamara, A & Miller, T 1995 Daily and Intradaily Tests of European Put–Call Parity. *Journal of Financial and Quantitative Analysis*, December 519–539.

What is the Central Limit Theorem and What are its Implications for Finance?

Short answer

The distribution of the average of a lot of random numbers will be normal (also known as Gaussian) even when the individual numbers are not normally distributed.

Example

Play a dice game where you win $10 if you throw a six, but lose $1 if you throw anything else. The distribution of your profit after one coin toss is clearly not normal, it's bimodal and skewed, but if you play the game thousands of times your total profit will be approximately normal.

Long answer

Let $X_1, X_2, \ldots, X_n$ be a sequence of random variables which are independent and identically distributed (i.i.d.), with finite mean, m and standard deviation s. The sum

$$S_n = \sum_{i=1}^{n} X_i$$

has mean mn and standard deviation $s\sqrt{n}$. The Central Limit Theorem says that as n gets larger the distribution of S_n tends to the normal distribution. More accurately, if we work with the scaled quantity

$$\overline{S}_n = \frac{S_n - mn}{s\sqrt{n}}$$

then the distribution of $\overline{S}_n$ converges to the normal distribution with zero mean and unit standard deviation as n tends to infinity. The cumulative distribution for $\overline{S}_n$ approaches that for the standardized normal distribution.

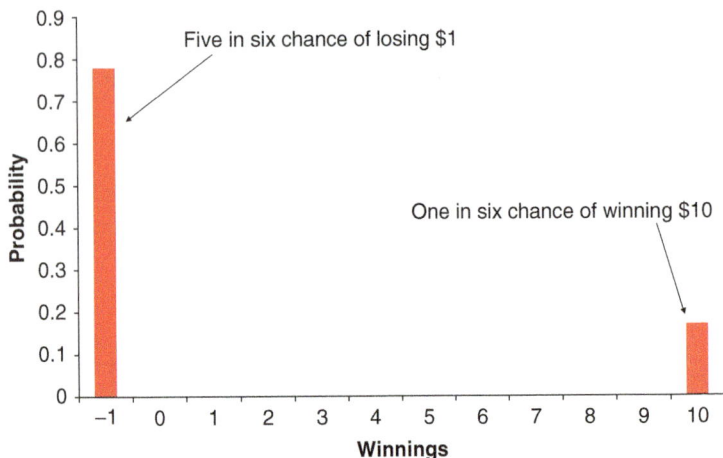

Figure 2.1: Probabilities in a simple coin-tossing experiment: one toss.

Figure 2.1 shows the distribution for the above coin-tossing experiment.

Now here's what your total profit will be like after one thousand tosses (Figure 2.2). Your expected profit after one toss is

$$\frac{1}{6} \times 10 + \frac{5}{6} \times (-1) = \frac{5}{6} \approx 0.833.$$

Your variance is therefore

$$\frac{1}{6} \times \left(10 - \frac{5}{6}\right)^2 + \frac{5}{6} \times \left(-1 - \frac{5}{6}\right)^2 = \frac{605}{54},$$

so a standard deviation of $\sqrt{605/54} \approx 1.097$. After one thousand tosses your expected profit is

$$1,000 \times \frac{5}{6} \approx 833.3$$

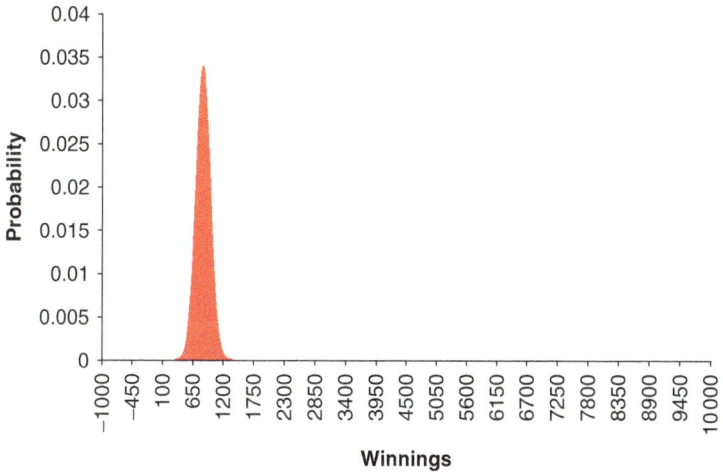

Figure 2.2: Probabilities in a simple coin-tossing experiment: one thousand tosses.

and your standard deviation is

$$\sqrt{1{,}000 \times \frac{605}{54}} \approx 34.7$$

See how the standard deviation has grown much less than the expectation. That's because of the square-root rule.

In finance we often assume that equity returns are normally distributed. We could argue that this ought to be the case by saying that returns over any finite period, one day, say, are made up of many, many trades over smaller time periods, with the result that the returns over the finite timescale are normal thanks to the Central Limit Theorem. The same argument could be applied to the daily changes in exchange rate rates, or interest rates, or risk of default, etc. We find ourselves using the normal distribution quite naturally for many financial processes.

As often with mathematical 'laws' there is the 'legal' small print, in this case the conditions under which the Central Limit Theorem applies. These are as follows.

- The random numbers must all be drawn from the same distribution
- The draws must all be independent
- The distribution must have finite mean and standard deviation.

Of course, financial data may not satisfy all of these, or indeed, any. In particular, it turns out that if you try to fit equity returns data with non-normal distributions you often find that the best distribution is one that has infinite variance. Not only does it complicate the nice mathematics of normal distributions and the Central Limit Theorem, it also results in infinite volatility. This is appealing to those who want to produce the best models of financial reality but does rather spoil many decades of financial theory and practice based on volatility as a measure of risk, for example.

However, you can get around these three restrictions to some extent and still get the Central Limit Theorem, or something very much like it. For example, you don't need to have completely identical distributions. As long as none of the random variables has too much more impact on the average than the others then it still works. You are even allowed to have some weak dependence between the variables.

A generalization that is important in finance applies to distributions with infinite variance. If the tails of the individual distributions have a power-law decay, $|x|^{-1-\alpha}$ with $0 < \alpha < 2$, then the average will tend to a stable Lévy distribution.

If you add random numbers and get normal, what happens when you multiply them? To answer this question we must think in terms of logarithms of the random numbers.

Logarithms of random numbers are themselves random (let's stay with logarithms of strictly positive numbers). So if you add up lots of logarithms of random numbers you will get a normal distribution. But, of course, a sum of logarithms is just the logarithm of a product, therefore the logarithm of the product must be normal, and this is the definition of lognormal: the product of positive random numbers converges to lognormal.

This is important in finance because a stock price after a long period can be thought of as its value on some starting day multiplied by lots of random numbers, each representing a random return. So whatever the distribution of returns is, the logarithm of the stock price will be normally distributed. We tend to assume that equity returns are normally distributed, and equivalently, equities themselves are lognormally distributed.

References and Further Reading

Feller, W 1968 *An Introduction to Probability Theory and Its Applications*, third edition. John Wiley & Sons Inc, New York

How is Risk Defined in Mathematical Terms?

Short answer
In layman's terms, risk is the possibility of harm or loss. In finance it refers to the possibility of a monetary loss associated with investments.

Example
The most common measure of risk is simply standard deviation of portfolio returns. The higher this is, the more randomness in a portfolio, and this is seen as a bad thing.

Long answer
Financial risk comes in many forms:

- **Market risk**: The possibility of loss due to movements in the market, either as a whole or specific investments
- **Credit risk**: The possibility of loss due to default on a financial obligation
- **Model risk**: The possibility of loss due to errors in mathematical models, often models of derivatives. Since these models contain parameters, such as volatility, we can also speak of parameter risk, volatility risk, etc.
- **Operational risk**: The possibility of loss due to people, procedures or systems. This includes human error and fraud
- **Legal risk**: The possibility of loss due to legal action or the meaning of legal contracts

Before looking at the mathematics of risk we should understand the difference between risk, randomness and uncertainty, all of which are important.

When measuring risk we often use probabilistic concepts. But this requires having a distribution for the randomness in investments, a probability density function, for example. With enough data or a decent enough model we may have a good idea about the distribution of returns. However, without the data, or when embarking into unknown territory we may be completely in the dark as to probabilities. This is especially true when looking at scenarios which are incredibly rare, or have never even happened before. For example, we may have a good idea of the results of an alien invasion, after all, many scenarios have been explored in the movies, but what is the probability of this happening? When you do not know the probabilities then you have what Knight (1921) termed 'uncertainty.'

We can categorize these issues, following Knight, as follows.

1. For 'risk' the probabilities that specified events will occur in the future are measurable and known, i.e. there is randomness but with a known probability distribution. This can be further divided.
   (a) *a priori* risk, such as the outcome of the roll of a fair die
   (b) estimable risk, where the probabilities can be estimated through statistical analysis of the past, for example, the probability of a one-day fall of 10% in the S&P index
2. With 'uncertainty' the probabilities of future events cannot be estimated or calculated.

In finance we tend to concentrate on risk with probabilities we estimate, we then have all the tools of statistics and probability for quantifying various aspects of that risk. In some financial models we do attempt to address the uncertain. For example, the uncertain volatility work of Avellaneda *et al.* (1995). Here volatility is uncertain, is allowed to lie within a specified range, but the probability of volatility having any value is not given. Instead of working with probabilities we now work with worst-case scenarios. Uncertainty is therefore more associated with the idea of stress-testing portfolios.

CrashMetrics is another example of worst-case scenarios and uncertainty.

A starting point for a mathematical definition of risk is simply as standard deviation. This is sensible because of the results of the **Central Limit Theorem** (CLT), that if you add up a large number of investments what matters as far as the statistical properties of the portfolio are just the expected return and the standard deviation of individual investments, and the resulting portfolio returns are normally distributed. The normal distribution being symmetrical about the mean, the potential downside can be measured in terms of the standard deviation.

However, this is only meaningful if the conditions for the CLT are satisfied. For example, if we only have a small number of investments, or if the investments are correlated, or if they don't have finite variance, then standard deviation may not be relevant.

Another mathematical definition of risk is semivariance, in which only downside deviations are used in the calculation. This definition is used in the **Sortino** performance measure.

Artzner *et al.* (1997) proposed a set of properties that a measure of risk should satisfy for it to be sensible. Such risk measures are called **coherent**.

References and Further Reading

Artzner, P, Delbaen, F, Eber, J-M & Heath, D 1997 Thinking coherently. *Risk* magazine **10** (11) 68–72.

Avellaneda, M & Parás, A 1996 Managing the volatility risk of derivative securities: the Lagrangian volatility model. *Applied Mathematical Finance* **3** 21–53

Avellaneda, M, Levy, A & Parás, A 1995 Pricing and hedging derivative securities in markets with uncertain volatilities. *Applied Mathematical Finance* **2** 73–88

Knight, FH 1921 *Risk, Uncertainty, and Profit*. Hart, Schaffner, and Marx. Prize Essays, no. 31. Boston and New York: Houghton Mifflin

Wilmott, P 2006 *Paul Wilmott on Quantitative Finance*, second edition. John Wiley & Sons Ltd.

What is Value at Risk and How is it Used?

Short answer

Value at Risk, or VaR for short, is a measure of the amount that could be lost from a position, portfolio, desk, bank, etc. VaR is generally understood to mean the maximum loss an investment could incur at a given confidence level over a specified time horizon. There are other risk measures used in practice but this is the simplest and most common.

Example

An equity derivatives hedge fund estimates that its Value at Risk over one day at the 95% confidence level is $500,000. This is interpreted as one day out of 20 the fund expects to lose more than half a million dollars.

Long answer

VaR calculations often assume that returns are normally distributed over the time horizon of interest. Inputs for a VaR calculation will include details of the portfolio composition, the time horizon, and parameters governing the distribution of the underlyings. The latter set of parameters includes average growth rate, standard deviations (volatilities) and correlations. (If the time horizon is short you can ignore the growth rate, as it will only have a small effect on the final calculation.)

With the assumption of normality, VaR is calculated by a simple formula if you have a simple portfolio, or by simulations if you have a more complicated portfolio. The difference between simple and complicated is essentially the difference between portfolios without derivatives and those with. If your portfolio only contains linear instruments then calculations involving normal distributions, standard deviations, etc., can all be done analytically. This is also the case if the time horizon is short so that derivatives can be approximated by a position of delta in the underlying.

The simulations can be quite straightforward, albeit rather time consuming. Simulate many realizations of all of the underlyings up to the time horizon using traditional Monte Carlo methods. For each realization calculate the portfolio's value. This will give you a distribution of portfolio values at the time horizon. Now look at where the tail of the distribution begins, the left-hand 5% tail if you want 95% confidence, or the 1% tail if you are working to 99%, etc.

If you are working entirely with normal distributions then going from one confidence level to another is just a matter of looking at a table of numbers for the standardized normal distribution (see Table 2.1). As long as your time horizon is sufficiently short for the growth to be unimportant you can use the square-root rule to go from one time horizon to another. (The VaR will scale with the square root of the time horizon; this assumes that the portfolio return is also normally distributed.)

Table 2.1: Degree of confidence and the relationship with deviation from the mean.

Degree of confidence	Number of standard deviations from the mean
99%	2.326342
98%	2.053748
97%	1.88079
96%	1.750686
95%	1.644853
90%	1.281551

An alternative to using a parameterized model for the under-lyings is to simulate straight from historical data, bypassing the normal distribution assumption altogether.

VaR is a very useful concept in practice for the following reasons:

- VaR is easily calculated for individual instruments, entire portfolios, or at any level right up to an entire bank or fund
- You can adjust the time horizon depending on your trading style. If you hedge every day you may want a one-day horizon; if you buy and hold for many months, then a longer horizon would be relevant
- It can be broken down into components, so you can examine different classes of risk, or you can look at the marginal risk of adding new positions to your book
- It can be used to constrain positions of individual traders or entire hedge funds
- It is easily understood, by management, by investors, by people who are perhaps not that technically sophisticated

Of course, there are also valid criticisms as well:

- It does not tell you what the loss will be beyond the VaR value
- VaR is concerned with typical market conditions, not the extreme events
- It uses historical data, 'like driving a car by looking in the rear-view mirror only'
- Within the time horizon positions could change dramatically (due to normal trading or due to hedging or expiration of derivatives).

A common criticism of traditional VaR has been that it does not satisfy all of certain commonsense criteria. Artzner *et al.* (1997) specify criteria that make a risk measure **coherent**. And VaR as described above is not coherent.

Prudence would suggest that other risk-measurement methods are used in conjunction with VaR including, but not limited to, stress testing under different real and hypothetical scenarios, including the stressing of volatility especially for portfolios containing derivatives.

References and Further Reading

Artzner, P, Delbaen, F, Eber, J-M & Heath, D 1997 Thinking coherently. *Risk* magazine **10** (11) 68–72

What is Extreme Value Theory?

Short answer

Extreme Value Theory (EVT) is the mathematics behind extreme events. Some important results have analogies with the Central Limit Theorem, but instead of being about averages they are about extremes. Of course, whether one should even be talking about probabilities when talking about crashes is another matter. It's probably safer to look at worst-case scenarios.

Example

(Taken from McNeil, 1998.) Fit a Frechet distribution to the 28 annual maxima of the SP500 index returns from 1960 to October 16th 1987, the business day before the '87 crash. In this dataset the largest fall was 'just' 6.7%. Now calculate the probability of various returns. For example, a 50-year return level is the level which on average should only be exceeded in one year every 50 years. The Frechet distribution gives the result as 24%. One business day later the index falls 20.4%.

Long answer

Modern techniques for estimating tail risk use Extreme Value Theory. The idea is to more accurately represent the outer limits of returns distributions since this is where the most important risk is. Throw normal distributions away, their tails are far too thin to capture the frequent market crashes (and rallies).

One important EVT result concerns the distribution of maxima and minima and is used in calculations such as in the example above.

If X_i are independent, identically distributed random variables and

$$x = \max(X_1, X_2, \ldots, X_n)$$

then the distribution of x converges to

$$\frac{1}{\sigma}\left(1 + \xi\frac{\xi(x-\mu)}{\sigma}\right)^{-1/\xi-1}\exp\left(-\left(1+\frac{\xi(x-\mu)}{\sigma}\right)^{-1/\xi}\right).$$

When $\xi = 0$ this is a Gumbel distribution, $\xi < 0$ a Weibull and $\xi > 0$ a Frechet. Frechet is the one of interest in finance because it is associated with fat tails.

The role of theorems about extremes is similar to that of the **Central Limit Theorem** for sums/averages.

References and Further Reading

McNeil, A 1998 On extremes and crashes. *Risk* magazine January 99

What is CrashMetrics?

Short answer

CrashMetrics is a stress-testing methodology for evaluating portfolio performance in the event of extreme movements in financial markets. Like **CAPM** it relates moves in individual stocks to the moves in one or more indices but only during large moves. It is applicable to portfolios of equities and equity derivatives.

Example

Your portfolio contains many individual stocks and many derivatives of different types. It is perfectly constructed to profit from your view on the market and its volatility. But what if there is a dramatic fall in the market, perhaps 5%? What will the effect be on your P&L? And if the fall is 10%, 20%...?

Long answer

CrashMetrics is a very simple risk-management tool for examining the effects of a large move in the market as a whole. It is therefore of use for studying times when diversification does not work.

If your portfolio consists of a single underlying equity and its derivatives, then the change in its value during a crash, $\delta\Pi$, can be written as

$$\delta\Pi = F(\delta S),$$

where $F(\cdot)$ is the 'formula' for the portfolio, meaning option-pricing formulæ for all of the derivatives and equity in the portfolio, and δS is the change in the underlying.

In CrashMetrics the risk in this portfolio is measured as the worst case over some range of equity moves:

$$\text{Worst-case loss} = \min_{-\delta S^- \leq \delta S \leq \delta S^+} F(\delta S).$$

This is the number that would be quoted as the possible downside during a dramatic move in the market. This downside can be reduced by adding derivatives to the portfolio in an optimal fashion. This is called **Platinum Hedging**. For example, if you want to use some out-of-the-money puts to make this worst case not so bad, then you could optimize by choosing λ so that the worst case of

$$F(\delta S) + \lambda F^*(\delta S) - |\lambda|C$$

represents an acceptable level of downside risk. Here $F^*(\cdot)$ is the 'formula' for the change in value of the hedging contract, C is the 'cost' associated with each hedging contract and λ is the quantity of the contract which is to be determined. In practice there would be many such hedging contracts, not necessarily just an out-of-the-money put, so you would sum over all of them and then optimize.

CrashMetrics deals with any number of underlyings by exploiting the high degree of correlation between equities during extreme markets. We can relate the return on the ith stock to the return on a representative index, x, during a crash by

$$\frac{\delta S_i}{S_i} = \kappa_i x,$$

where κ_i is a constant **crash coefficient**. For example, if the kappa for stock XYZ is 1.2 it means that when the index falls by 10% XYZ will fall by 12%. The crash coefficient therefore allows a portfolio with many underlyings to be interpreted during a crash as a portfolio on a single underlying, the index. We therefore consider the worst case of

$$\delta \Pi = F(\delta S_1, \ldots, \delta S_N) = F(\kappa_1 x S_1, \ldots, \kappa_N x S_N)$$

as our measure of downside risk. Note that this is really just a function of the one variable x and so it is very easy to plot the change in the portfolio against x, the retun on the index.

Again Platinum Hedging can be applied when we have many underlyings. We must consider the worst case of

$$\delta \Pi = F(\kappa_1 x S_1, \ldots, \kappa_N x S_N) + \sum_{k=1}^{M} \lambda_k F_k(\kappa_1 x S_1, \ldots, \kappa_N x S_N)$$
$$- \sum_{k=1}^{M} |\lambda_k| \, C_k,$$

where F is the original portfolio and the F_ks are the M available hedging contracts.

CrashMetrics is very robust because

- it does not use unstable parameters such as volatilities or correlations
- it does not rely on probabilities, instead considers worst cases.

CrashMetrics is a good risk tool because

- it is very simple and fast to implement
- it can be used to optimize portfolio insurance against market crashes

CrashMetrics is used for

- analysing derivatives portfolios under the threat of a crash
- optimizing portfolio insurance
- reporting risk
- providing trading limits to avoid intolerable performance during a crash.

References and Further Reading

Hua, P & Wilmott, P 1997 Crash courses. *Risk* magazine **10** (6) 64–67

Wilmott, P 2006 *Paul Wilmott on Quantitative Finance*, second edition. John Wiley & Sons Ltd

What is a Coherent Risk Measure and What are its Properties?

Short answer

A risk measure is coherent if it satisfies certain simple, mathematical properties. One of these properties, which some popular measures do *not* possess is sub-additivity, that adding together two risky portfolios cannot increase the measure of risk.

Example

Artzner *et al.* (1997) give a simple example of traditional VaR which violates this, and illustrates perfectly the problems of measures that are not coherent. Portfolio X consists only of a far out-of-the-money put with one day to expiry. Portfolio Y consists only of a far out-of-the-money call with one day to expiry. Let us suppose that each option has a probability of 4% of ending up in the money. For each option individually, at the 95% confidence level the one-day traditional VaR is effectively zero. Now put the two portfolios together and there is a 92% chance of not losing anything, 100% less two lots of 4%. So at the 95% confidence level there will be a significant VaR. Putting the two portfolios together has in this example increased the risk. 'A merger does not create extra risk' (Artzner *et al.* 1997).

Long answer

A common criticism of traditional VaR has been that it does not satisfy all of certain commonsense criteria. Artzner *et al.* (1997) defined the following set of sensible criteria that a measure of risk, $\rho(X)$ where X is a set of outcomes, should satisfy. These are as follows:

1. *Sub-additivity*: $\rho(X + Y) \leq \rho(X) + \rho(Y)$. This just says that if you add two portfolios together the total risk can't get any worse than adding the two risks separately. Indeed,

there may be cancellation effects or economies of scale that will make the risk better.

2. *Monotonicity*: If $X \leq Y$ for each scenario then $\rho(X) \geq \rho(Y)$. If one portfolio has better values than another under all scenarios then its risk will be better.

3. *Positive homogeneity*: For all $\lambda > 0$, $\rho(\lambda X) = \lambda \rho(X)$. Double your portfolio then you double your risk.

4. *Translation invariance*: For all constant c, $\rho(X + c) = \rho(X) - c$. Think of just adding cash to a portfolio; this would come off your risk.

A risk measure that satisfies all of these is called **coherent**. The traditional, simple VaR measure is not coherent since it does not satisfy the sub-additivity condition. Sub-additivity is an obvious requirement for a risk measure, otherwise there would be no risk benefit to adding uncorrelated new trades into a book. If you have two portfolios X and Y then this benefit can be defined as

$$\rho(X) + \rho(Y) - \rho(X + Y).$$

Sub-additivity says that this can only be non-negative.

Lack of sub-additivity in a risk measure and that can be exploited can lead to a form of regulatory arbitrage. All a bank has to do is create subsidiary firms, in a reverse form of the above example, to save regulatory capital.

With a coherent measure of risk, specifically because of its sub-additivity, one can simply add together risks of individual portfolios to get a conservative estimate of the total risk.

Coherent measures A popular measure that is coherent is **Expected Shortfall**. This is calculated as the average of all the P&Ls making up the tail percentile of interest. Suppose we are working with the 5% percentile, rather than quoting this number (this would be traditional VaR) instead calculate the average of all the P&Ls in this 5% tail.

Attribution Having calculated a coherent measure of risk, one often wants to attribute this to smaller units. For example, a desk has calculated its risk and wants to see how much each trader is responsible for. Similarly, one may want to break down the risk into contributions from each of the greeks in a derivatives portfolio. How much risk is associated with direction of the market, and how much is associated with volatility exposure, for example.

References and Further Reading

Acerbi, C & Tasche, D On the coherence of expected shortfall. www-m1.mathematik.tu-muenchen.de/m4/Papers/Tasche/shortfall.pdf

Artzner, P, Delbaen, F, Eber, J-M & Heath, D 1997 Thinking coherently. *Risk* magazine **10** (11) 68–72

What is Modern Portfolio Theory?

Short answer
The Modern Portfolio Theory (MPT) of Harry Markowitz (1952) introduced the analysis of portfolios of investments by considering the expected return and risk of individual assets and, crucially, their interrelationship as measured by correlation. Prior to this investors would examine investments individually, build up portfolios of favoured stocks, and not consider how they related to each other. In MPT diversification plays an important role.

Example
Should you put all your money in a stock that has low risk but also low expected return, or one with high expected return but which is far riskier? Or perhaps divide your money between the two. Modern Portfolio Theory addresses this question and provides a framework for quantifying and understanding risk and return.

Long answer
In MPT the return on individual assets are represented by normal distributions with certain mean and standard deviation over a specified period. So one asset might have an annualized expected return of 5% and an annualized standard deviation (volatility) of 15%. Another might have an expected return of -2% and a volatility of 10%. Before Markowitz, one would only have invested in the first stock, or perhaps sold the second stock short. Markowitz showed how it might be possible to better both of these simplistic portfolios by taking into account the correlation between the returns on these stocks.

In the MPT world of N assets there are $2N + N(N-1)/2$ parameters: expected return, one per stock; standard deviation, one per stock; correlations, between any two stocks (choose two from N without replacement, order unimportant). To Markowitz all investments and all portfolios should be compared and contrasted via a plot of expected return versus risk, as measured by standard deviation. If we write μ_A to represent the expected return from investment or portfolio A (and similarly for B, C, etc.) and σ_B for its standard deviation then investment/portfolio A is at least as good as B if

$$\mu_A \geq \mu_B \quad \text{and} \quad \sigma_A \leq \sigma_B.$$

The mathematics of risk and return is very simple. Consider a portfolio, Π, of N assets, with W_i being the fraction of wealth invested in the ith asset. The expected return is then

$$\mu_\Pi = \sum_{i=1}^{N} W_i \mu_i$$

and the standard deviation of the return, the risk, is

$$\sigma_\Pi = \sqrt{\sum_{i=1}^{N} \sum_{j=1}^{N} W_i W_j \rho_{ij} \sigma_i \sigma_j}$$

where ρ_{ij} is the correlation between the ith and jth investments, with $\rho_{ii} = 1$.

Markowitz showed how to optimize a portfolio by finding the W's giving the portfolio the greatest expected return for a prescribed level of risk. The curve in the risk-return space with the largest expected return for each level of risk is called the **efficient frontier**.

According to the theory, no one should hold portfolios that are not on the efficient frontier. Furthermore, if you introduce a risk-free investment into the universe of assets, the efficient frontier becomes the tangential line shown in Figure 2.3. This line is called the **Capital Market Line** and the portfolio at the point at which it is tangential is called the **Market Portfolio**. Now, again according to the theory, no one ought to hold any portfolio of assets other than the risk-free investment and the Market Portfolio.

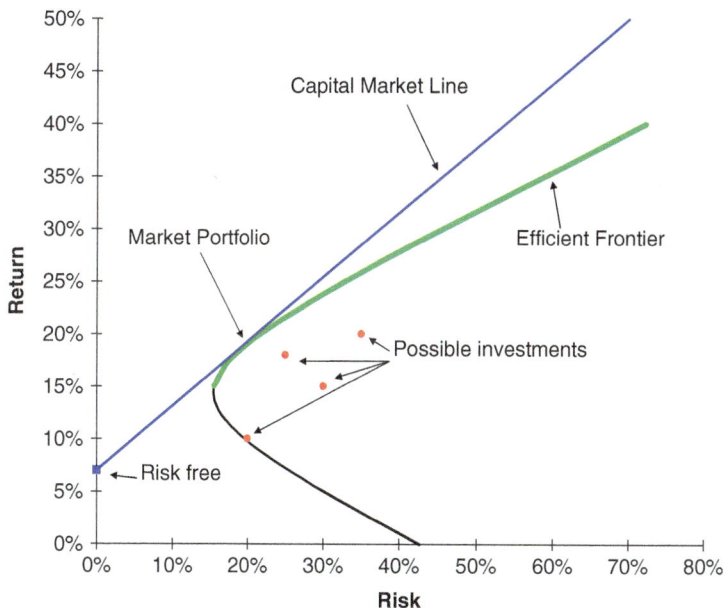

Figure 2.3: Reward versus risk, a selection of risky assets and the efficient frontier (bold green).

Harry Markowitz, together with Merton Miller and William Sharpe, was awarded the Nobel Prize for Economic Science in 1990.

References and Further Reading

Ingersoll, JE Jr 1987 *Theory of Financial Decision Making*. Rowman & Littlefield

Markowitz, HM 1952 Portfolio selection. *Journal of Finance* **7** (1) 77–91

What is the Capital Asset Pricing Model?

Short answer

The Capital Asset Pricing Model (CAPM) relates the returns on individual assets or entire portfolios to the return on the market as a whole. It introduces the concepts of specific risk and systematic risk. **Specific risk** is unique to an individual asset, **systematic risk** is that associated with the market. In CAPM investors are compensated for taking systematic risk but not for taking specific risk. This is because specific risk can be diversified away by holding many different assets.

Example

A stock has an expected return of 15% and a volatility of 20%. But how much of that risk and return are related to the market as a whole? The less that can be attributed to the behaviour of the market, the better will that stock be for diversification purposes.

Long answer

CAPM simultaneously simplified Markowitz's **Modern Portfolio Theory** (MPT), made it more practical and introduced the idea of specific and systematic risk. Whereas MPT has arbitrary correlation between all investments, CAPM, in its basic form, only links investments via the market as a whole. CAPM is an example of an equilibrium model, as opposed to a no-arbitrage model such as Black–Scholes.

The mathematics of CAPM is very simple. We relate the random return on the ith investment, R_i, to the random return on the market as a whole (or some representative index), R_M by

$$R_i = \alpha_i + \beta_i R_M + \epsilon_i.$$

The ϵ_i is random with zero mean and standard deviation e_i, and uncorrelated with the market return R_M and the other

ϵ_j. There are three parameters associated with each asset, α_i, β_i and e_i. In this representation we can see that the return on an asset can be decomposed into three parts: a constant drift; a random part common with the index; a random part uncorrelated with the index, ϵ_i. The random part ϵ_i is unique to the ith asset. Notice how all the assets are related to the index but are otherwise completely uncorrelated.

Let us denote the expected return on the index by μ_M and its standard deviation by σ_M. The expected return on the ith asset is then

$$\mu_i = \alpha_i + \beta_i \mu_M$$

and the standard deviation

$$\sigma_i = \sqrt{\beta_i^2 \sigma_M^2 + e_i^2}.$$

If we have a portfolio of such assets then the return is given by

$$\frac{\delta \Pi}{\Pi} = \sum_{i=1}^{N} W_i R_i = \left(\sum_{i=1}^{N} W_i \alpha_i \right) + R_M \left(\sum_{i=1}^{N} W_i \beta_i \right) + \sum_{i=1}^{N} W_i \epsilon_i.$$

From this it follows that

$$\mu_\Pi = \left(\sum_{i=1}^{N} W_i \alpha_i \right) + E[R_M] \left(\sum_{i=1}^{N} W_i \beta_i \right).$$

Writing

$$\alpha_\Pi = \sum_{i=1}^{N} W_i \alpha_i \quad \text{and} \quad \beta_\Pi = \sum_{i=1}^{N} W_i \beta_i,$$

we have

$$\mu_\Pi = \alpha_\Pi + \beta_\Pi E[R_M] = \alpha_\Pi + \beta_\Pi \mu_M.$$

Similarly the risk in Π is measured by

$$\sigma_\Pi = \sqrt{\sum_{i=1}^{N} \sum_{j=1}^{N} W_i W_j \beta_i \beta_j \sigma_M^2 + \sum_{i=1}^{N} W_i^2 e_i^2}.$$

Note that if the weights are all about the same, N^{-1}, then the final terms inside the square root are also $O(N^{-1})$. Thus this expression is, to leading order as $N \to \infty$,

$$\sigma_\Pi = \left| \sum_{i=1}^{N} W_i \beta_i \right| \sigma_M = |\beta_\Pi| \sigma_M.$$

Observe that the contribution from the uncorrelated ϵs to the portfolio vanishes as we increase the number of assets in the portfolio; this is the risk associated with the diversifiable risk. The remaining risk, which is correlated with the index, is the undiversifiable systematic risk.

Multi-index versions of CAPM can be constructed. Each index being representative of some important financial or economic variable.

The parameters alpha and beta are also commonly referred to in the hedge-fund world. Performance reports for trading strategies will often quote the alpha and beta of the strategy. A good strategy will have a high, positive alpha with a beta close to zero. With beta being small you would expect performance to be unrelated to the market as a whole and with large, positive alpha you would expect good returns whichever way the market was moving. Small beta also means that a strategy should be a valuable addition to a portfolio because of its beneficial diversification.

Sharpe shared the 1990 Nobel Prize in Economics with Harry Markowitz and Merton Miller.

References and Further Reading

Lintner, J 1965 The valuation of risk assets and the selection of risky investments in stock portfolios and capital budgets. *Review of Economics and Statistics* **47**

Mossin, J 1966 Equilibrium in a Capital Asset Market. *Econometrica* **34** 768–783

Sharpe, WF 1964 Capital asset prices: a theory of market equilibrium under conditions of risk. *Journal of Finance* **19** (3) 425–442

Tobin, J 1958 Liquidity preference as behavior towards risk. *Review of Economic Studies* **25**

What is Arbitrage Pricing Theory?

Short answer
The Arbitrage Pricing Theory (APT) of Stephen Ross (1976) represents the returns on individual assets as a linear combination of multiple random factors. These random factors can be fundamental factors or statistical. For there to be no arbitrage opportunities there must be restrictions on the investment processes.

Example
Suppose that there are five dominant causes of randomness across investments. These five factors might be market as a whole, inflation, oil prices, etc. If you are asked to invest in six different, well-diversified portfolios then either one of these portfolios will have approximately the same risk and return as a suitable combination of the other five, or there will be an arbitrage opportunity.

Long answer
Modern Portfolio Theory represents each asset by its own random return and then links the returns on different assets via a correlation matrix. In the **Capital Asset Pricing Model** returns on individual assets are related to returns on the market as a whole together with an uncorrelated stock-specific random component. In Arbitrage Pricing Theory returns on investments are represented by a linear combination of multiple random factors, with associated factor weighting. Portfolios of assets can also be decomposed in this way. Provided the portfolio contains a sufficiently large number of assets, then the stock-specific component can be ignored. Being able to ignore the stock-specific risk is the key to the 'A' in 'APT.'

We write the random return on the ith asset as

$$R_i = \alpha_i + \sum_{j=1}^{n} \beta_{ji}\overline{R}_j + \epsilon_i,$$

where the $\overline{R}_j$ are the factors, the α's and β's are constants and ϵ_i is the stock-specific risk. A portfolio of these assets has return

$$\sum_{i=1}^{N} a_i R_i = \sum_{i=1}^{N} a_i \alpha_i + \sum_{j=1}^{n} \left(\sum_{i=1}^{N} a_i \beta_{ji} \right) \overline{R}_j + \cdots,$$

where the '$\cdots$' can be ignored if the portfolio is well diversified.

Suppose we think that five factors are sufficient to represent the economy. We can therefore decompose any portfolio into a linear combination of these five factors, plus some supposedly negligible stock-specific risks. If we are shown six diversified portfolios we can decompose each into the five random factors. Since there are more portfolios than factors we can find a relationship between (some of) these portfolios, effectively relating their values, otherwise there would be an arbitrage. Note that the arbitrage argument is an approximate one, relating diversified portfolios, on the assumption that the stock-specific risks are negligible compared with the factor risks.

In practice we can choose the factors to be macroeconomic or statistical. Here are some possible macroeconomic variables.

- an index level
- GDP growth
- an interest rate (or two)
- a default spread on corporate bonds
- an exchange rate.

Statistical variables come from an analysis of a covariance of asset returns. From this one extracts the factors by some suitable decomposition.

The main differences between CAPM and APT is that CAPM is based on equilibrium arguments to get to the concept of the **Market Portfolio**, whereas APT is based on a simple approximate arbitrage argument. Although APT talks about arbitrage, this must be contrasted with the arbitrage arguments we see in spot versus forward and in option pricing. These are genuine exact arbitrages (albeit the latter being model dependent). In APT the arbitrage is only approximate.

References and Further Reading

Ross, S 1976 The arbitrage theory of Capital Asset Pricing. *Journal of Economic Theory* **13** 341–360

What is Maximum Likelihood Estimation?

Short answer

Maximum Likelihood Estimation (MLE) is a statistical technique for estimating parameters in a probability distribution. We choose parameters that maximize the *a priori* probability of the final outcome actually happening.

Example

You have three hats containing normally distributed random numbers. One hat's numbers have a mean of zero and a standard deviation of 0.1. This is hat A. Another hat's numbers have a mean of zero and a standard deviation of 1. This is hat B. The final hat's numbers have a mean of zero and a standard deviation of 10. This is hat C. You don't know which hat is which.

You pick a number out of one hat. It is −2.6. Which hat do you think it came from? MLE can help you answer this question.

Long answer

A large part of statistical modelling concerns finding model parameters. One popular way of doing this is Maximum Likelihood Estimation.

The method is easily explained by a very simple example. You are attending a maths conference. You arrive by train at the city hosting the event. You take a taxi from the train station to the conference venue. The taxi number is 20,922. How many taxis are there in the city?

This is a parameter estimation problem. Getting into a specific taxi is a probabilistic event. Estimating the number of taxis in the city from that event is a question of assumptions and statistical methodology.

For this problem the obvious assumptions to make are:

1. Taxi numbers are strictly positive integers
2. Numbering starts at 1
3. No number is repeated
4. No number is skipped.

We will look at the probability of getting into taxi number 20,922 when there are N taxis in the city. This couldn't be simpler, the probability of getting into any specific taxi is

$$\frac{1}{N}.$$

Which N maximizes the probability of getting into taxi number 20,922? The answer is

$$N = 20,922.$$

This example explains the concept of MLE: *Choose parameters that maximize the probability of the outcome actually happening.*

Another example, more closely related to problems in quantitative finance, is the hat example above. You have three hats containing normally distributed random numbers. One hat's numbers have a mean of zero and a standard deviation of 0.1. This is hat A. Another hat's numbers have a mean of zero and a standard deviation of 1. This is hat B. The final hat's numbers have a mean of zero and a standard deviation of 10. This is hat C.

You pick a number out of one hat, it is -2.6. Which hat do you think it came from?

The 'probability' of picking the number -2.6 from hat A (having a mean of zero and a standard deviation of 0.1) is

$$\frac{1}{\sqrt{2\pi}\ 0.1}\ \exp\left(-\frac{2.6^2}{2 \times 0.1^2}\right) = 6\ 10^{-147}.$$

Very, very unlikely!

(N.B. The word 'probability' is in inverted commas to emphasize the fact that this is the value of the probability density function, not the actual probability. The probability of picking exactly -2.6 is, of course, zero.)

The 'probability' of picking the number -2.6 from hat B (having a mean of zero and a standard deviation of 1) is

$$\frac{1}{\sqrt{2\pi}\ 1} \exp\left(-\frac{2.6^2}{2 \times 1^2}\right) = 0.014,$$

and from hat C (having a mean of zero and a standard deviation of 10)

$$\frac{1}{\sqrt{2\pi}\ 10} \exp\left(-\frac{2.6^2}{2 \times 10^2}\right) = 0.039.$$

We would conclude that hat C is the most likely, since it has the highest probability for picking the number -2.6.

We now pick a second number from the same hat. It is 0.37. This looks more likely to have come from hat B. Table 2.2 shows the probabilities.

The second column represents the probability of drawing the number -2.6 from each of the hats; the third column represents the probability of drawing 0.37 from each of the hats; and the final column is the joint probability, that is, the probability of drawing both numbers from each of the hats.

Table 2.2: Probabilities and hats.

Hat	-2.6	0.37	Joint
A	6×10^{-147}	0.004	2×10^{-149}
B	0.014	0.372	0.005
C	0.039	0.040	0.002

Using the information about *both* draws, we can see that the most likely hat is now B.

Now let's make this into precisely a quant finance problem.

Find the volatility

You have one hat containing normally distributed random numbers, with a mean of zero and a standard deviation of σ which is unknown. You draw N numbers ϕ_i from this hat. Estimate σ.

Q. What is the 'probability' of drawing ϕ_i from a Normal distribution with mean zero and standard deviation σ?

A. It is

$$\frac{1}{\sqrt{2\pi}\sigma}e^{-\frac{\phi_i^2}{2\sigma^2}}.$$

Q. What is the 'probability' of drawing all of the numbers $\phi_1, \phi_2, \ldots, \phi_N$ from independent Normal distributions with mean zero and standard deviation σ?

A. It is

$$\prod_{i=1}^{N}\frac{1}{\sqrt{2\pi}\sigma}e^{-\frac{\phi_i^2}{2\sigma^2}}.$$

Now choose the σ that maximizes this quantity. This is easy. First take logarithms of this expression, and then differentiate with respect to σ and set result equal to zero:

$$\frac{d}{d\sigma}\left(-N\ln(\sigma) - \frac{1}{2\sigma^2}\sum_{i=1}^{N}\phi_i^2\right) = 0.$$

(A multiplicative factor has been ignored here.) That is:

$$-\frac{N}{\sigma} + \frac{1}{\sigma^3}\sum_{i=1}^{N}\phi_i^2 = 0.$$

Therefore, our best guess for σ is given by

$$\sigma^2 = \frac{1}{N}\sum_{i=1}^{N}\phi_i^2.$$

You should recognize this as a measure of the variance.

Quants' salaries

Figure 2.4 shows the results of a 2004 survey on www.wilmott.com concerning the salaries of quants using the Forum (or rather, those answering the question!). This distribution looks vaguely lognormal, with distribution

$$\frac{1}{\sqrt{2\pi}\sigma E}\exp\left(-\frac{(\ln E - \ln E_0)^2}{2\sigma^2}\right),$$

**If you are a professional 'quant,'
how much do you earn?**

Last year I earned:

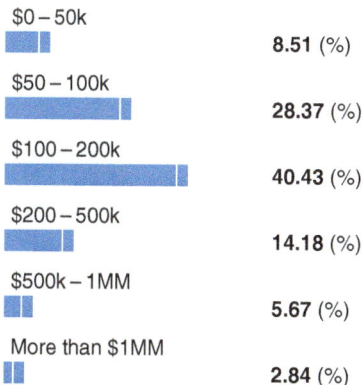

$0 – 50k

8.51 (%)

$50 – 100k

28.37 (%)

$100 – 200k

40.43 (%)

$200 – 500k

14.18 (%)

$500k – 1MM

5.67 (%)

More than $1MM

2.84 (%)

Figure 2.4: Distribution of quants' salaries.

where E is annual earnings, σ is the standard deviation and E_0 the mean. We can use MLE find σ and E_0.

It turns out that the mean $E_0 = \$133,284$, with $\sigma = 0.833$.

References and Further Reading

Eliason, SR 1993 *Maximum Likelihood Estimation: Logic and Practice.* Sage

What is Cointegration?

Short answer
Two time series are cointegrated if a linear combination has constant mean and standard deviation. In other words, the two series never stray too far from one another. Cointegration is a useful technique for studying relationships in multivariate time series, and provides a sound methodology for modelling both long-run and short-run dynamics in a financial system.

Example
Suppose you have two stocks S_1 and S_2 and you find that $S_1 - 3\,S_2$ is stationary, so that this combination never strays too far from its mean. If one day this 'spread' is particularly large then you would have sound statistical reasons for thinking the spread might shortly reduce, giving you a possible source of statistical arbitrage profit. This can be the basis for **pairs trading**.

Long answer
The correlations between financial quantities are notoriously unstable. Nevertheless correlations are regularly used in almost all multivariate financial problems. An alternative statistical measure to correlation is cointegration. This is probably a more robust measure of the linkage between two financial quantities but as yet there is little derivatives theory based on the concept.

Two stocks may be perfectly correlated over short timescales yet diverge in the long run, with one growing and the other decaying. Conversely, two stocks may follow each other, never being more than a certain distance apart, but with any correlation, positive, negative or varying. If we are delta hedging then maybe the short timescale correlation matters, but not if we are holding stocks for a long time in an unhedged portfolio. To see whether two stocks stay close together we need a definition of **stationarity**. A time series is stationary if it has finite and constant mean, standard deviation and autocorrelation function. Stocks, which tend to grow, are not stationary. In a sense, stationary series do not wander too far from their mean.

Testing for the stationarity of a time series X_t involves a linear regression to find the coefficients a, b and c in

$$X_t = aX_{t-1} + b + ct.$$

If it is found that $|a| > 1$ then the series is unstable. If $-1 \leq a < 1$ then the series is stationary. If $a = 1$ then the series is non-stationary. As with all things statistical, we can only say that our value for a is accurate with a certain degree of confidence. To decide whether we have got a stationary or non-stationary series requires us to look at the Dickey–Fuller statistic to estimate the degree of confidence in our result. So far, so good, but from this point on the subject of cointegration gets complicated.

How is this useful in finance? Even though individual stock prices might be non stationary it is possible for a linear combination (i.e. a portfolio) to be stationary. Can we find λ_i, with $\sum_{i=1}^{N} \lambda_i = 1$, such that

$$\sum_{i=1}^{N} \lambda_i S_i$$

is stationary? If we can, then we say that the stocks are cointegrated.

For example, suppose we find that the S&P500 index is cointegrated with a portfolio of 15 stocks. We can then use these fifteen stocks to **track the index**. The error in this tracking portfolio will have constant mean and standard deviation, so should not wander too far from its average. This is clearly easier than using all 500 stocks for the tracking (when, of course, the tracking error would be zero).

We don't have to track the index, we could track anything we want, such as $e^{0.2t}$ to choose a portfolio that gets a 20% return. We could analyse the cointegration properties of two related stocks, Nike and Reebok, for example, to look for relationships. This would be pairs trading. Clearly there are similarities with MPT and CAPM in concepts such as means and standard deviations. The important difference is that cointegration assumes far fewer properties for the individual time series. Most importantly, volatility and correlation do not appear explicitly.

Another feature of cointegration is **Granger causality** which is where one variable leads and another lags. This is of help in explaining why there is any dynamic relationship between several financial quantities.

References and Further Reading

Alexander, CO 2001 *Market Models*. John Wiley & Sons Ltd

Engle, R & Granger, C 1987 Cointegration and error correction: representation, estimation and testing. *Econometrica* **55** 251–276

What is the Kelly Criterion?

Short answer
The Kelly criterion is a technique for maximizing expected growth of assets by optimally investing a fixed fraction of your wealth in a series of investments. The idea has long been used in the world of gambling.

Example
You own a biased coin that will land heads up with probability $p > \frac{1}{2}$. You find someone willing to bet any amount against you at evens. They are willing to bet any number of times. Clearly you can make a lot of money with this special coin. You start with \$1,000. How much of this should you bet?

Long answer
Let's work with the above example. The first observation is that you should bet an amount proportional to how much you have. As you win and your wealth grows you will bet a larger amount. But you shouldn't bet too much. If you bet all \$1,000 you will eventually toss a tail and lose everything and will be unable to continue. If you bet too little then it will take a long time for you to make a decent amount.

The **Kelly criterion** is to bet a certain fraction of your wealth so as to maximize your expected growth of wealth.

We use ϕ to denote the random variable taking value 1 with probability p and -1 with probability $1 - p$ and f to denote the fraction of our wealth that we bet. The growth of wealth after each toss of the coin is then the random amount

$$\ln(1 + f\phi).$$

The expected growth rate is

$$p \ln(1 + f) + (1 - p) \ln(1 - f).$$

This function is plotted in Figure 2.5 for $p = 0.55$.

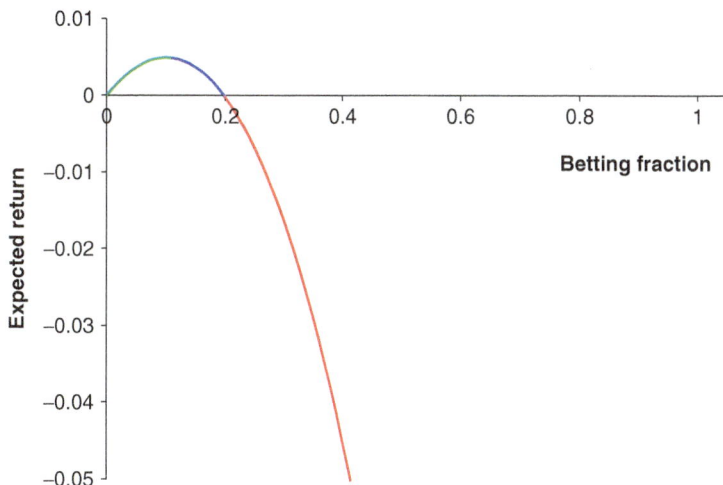

Figure 2.5: Expected return *versus* betting fraction.

This expected growth rate is maximized by the choice

$$f = 2p - 1.$$

This is the **Kelly fraction**.

A betting fraction of less than this would be a conservative strategy. Anything to the right will add volatility to returns, and decrease the expected returns. Too far to the right and the expected return becomes negative.

This money management principle can be applied to any bet or investment, not just the coin toss. More generally, if the investment has an expected return of μ and a standard deviation $\sigma \gg \mu$ then the expected growth for an investment fraction of f is

$$E[\ln(1 + f\phi)]$$

which can be approximated by **Taylor series**

$$f\phi - \frac{1}{2}f^2\phi^2 + \dots.$$

The Kelly fraction, which comes from maximizing this expression, is therefore

$$f = \frac{\mu}{\sigma^2}.$$

In practice, because the mean and standard deviation are rarely known accurately, one would err on the side of caution and bet a smaller fraction. A common choice is **half Kelly**.

Other money management strategies are, of course, possible, involving target wealth, probability of ruin, etc.

References and Further Reading

Kelly, JL 1956 *A new interpretation of information rate*. Bell Systems Technical Journal **35** 917–926

Poundstone, W 2005 *Fortune's Formula*. Hill & Wang

Why Hedge?

Short answer
'Hedging' in its broadest sense means the reduction of
risk by exploiting relationships or correlation (or lack of
correlation) between various risky investments. The purpose
behind hedging is that it can lead to an improved risk/return.
In the classical **Modern Portfolio Theory** framework, for
example, it is usually possible to construct many portfolios
having the same expected return but with different variance
of returns ('risk'). Clearly, if you have two portfolios with
the same expected return the one with the lower risk is the
better investment.

Example
You buy a call option, it could go up or down in value
depending on whether the underlying go up or down. So now
sell some stock short. If you sell the right amount short then
any rises or falls in the stock position will balance the falls
or rises in the option, reducing risk.

Long answer
To help to understand why one might hedge it is useful to
look at the different types of hedging.

The two main classifications   Probably the most important distinction between types of hedging is between model-independent
and model-dependent hedging strategies.

- **Model-independent hedging**: An example of such hedging
  is **put–call parity**. There is a simple relationship between
  calls and puts on an asset (when they are both European
  and with the same strikes and expiries), the underlying
  stock and a zero-coupon bond with the same maturity.
  This relationship is completely independent of how the
  underlying asset changes in value. Another example is
  spot-forward parity. In neither case do we have to specify

the dynamics of the asset, not even its volatility, to find a possible hedge. Such model-independent hedges are few and far between.

- **Model-dependent hedging**: Most sophisticated finance hedging strategies depend on a model for the underlying asset. The obvious example is the hedging used in the Black–Scholes analysis that leads to a whole theory for the value of derivatives. In pricing derivatives we typically need to at least know the volatility of the underlying asset. If the model is wrong then the option value and any hedging strategy could also be wrong.

Delta hedging One of the building blocks of derivatives theory is delta hedging. This is the theoretically perfect elimination of all risk by using a very clever hedge between the option and its underlying. Delta hedging exploits the perfect correlation between the changes in the option value and the changes in the stock price. This is an example of 'dynamic' hedging; the hedge must be continually monitored and frequently adjusted by the sale or purchase of the underlying asset. Because of the frequent rehedging, any dynamic hedging strategy is going to result in losses due to transaction costs. In some markets this can be very important.

The 'underlying' in a delta-hedged portfolio could be a traded asset, a stock for example, or it could be another random quantity that determines a price such as a risk of default. If you have two instruments depending on the same risk of default, you can calculate the sensitivities, the deltas, of their prices to this quantity and then buy the two instruments in amounts inversely proportional to these deltas (one long, one short). This is also delta hedging.

If two underlyings are very highly correlated you can use one as a proxy for the other for hedging purposes. You would then only be exposed to basis risk. Be careful with this because there may be times when the close relationship breaks down.

If you have many financial instruments that are uncorrelated with each other then you can construct a portfolio with much less risk than any one of the instruments individually. With such a large portfolio you can theoretically reduce risk to negligible levels. Although this isn't strictly hedging it achieves the same goal.

Gamma hedging To reduce the size of each rehedge and/or to increase the time between rehedges, and thus reduce costs, the technique of gamma hedging is often employed. A portfolio that is delta hedged is insensitive to movements in the underlying as long as those movements are quite small. There is a small error in this due to the convexity of the port-folio with respect to the underlying. Gamma hedging is a more accurate form of hedging that theoretically eliminates these second-order effects. Typically, one hedges one, exotic, say, contract with a vanilla contract and the underlying. The quantities of the vanilla and the underlying are chosen so as to make both the portfolio delta and the portfolio gamma instantaneously zero.

Vega hedging The prices and hedging strategies are only as good as the model for the underlying. The key parameter that determines the value of a contract is the volatility of the underlying asset. Unfortunately, this is a very difficult parameter to measure. Nor is it usually a constant as assumed in the simple theories. Obviously, the value of a contract depends on this parameter, and so to ensure that a portfolio value is insensitive to this parameter we can vega hedge. This means that we hedge one option with both the underlying and another option in such a way that both the delta and the vega, the sensitivity of the portfolio value to volatility, are zero. This is often quite satisfactory in practice but is usually theoretically inconsistent; we should not use a constant volatility (basic Black–Scholes) model to calculate sensitivities to parameters that are assumed not to vary. The distinction between variables (underlying asset price and time) and parameters (volatility, dividend yield, interest rate) is extremely important here. It is justifiable to rely on sensitivities of prices to variables, but usually not sensitivity to parameters. To get around this problem it is possible to independently model volatility, etc., as variables themselves. In such a way it is possible to build up a consistent theory.

Static hedging   There are quite a few problems with delta hedging, on both the practical and the theoretical side. In practice, hedging must be done at discrete times and is costly. Sometimes one has to buy or sell a prohibitively large number of the underlying in order to follow the theory. This is a problem with barrier options and options with discontinuous payoff. On the theoretical side, the model for the underlying is not perfect, at the very least we do not know parameter values accurately. Delta hedging alone leaves us very exposed to the model, this is model risk. Many of these problems can be reduced or eliminated if we follow a strategy of static hedging as well as delta hedging; buy or sell more liquid traded contracts to reduce the cashflows in the original contract. The static hedge is put into place now, and left until expiry. In the extreme case where an exotic contract has all of its cashflows matched by cashflows from traded options then its value is given by the cost of setting up the static hedge; a model is not needed. (But then the option wasn't exotic in the first place.)

Superhedging   In incomplete markets you cannot eliminate all risk by classical dynamic delta hedging. But sometimes you can superhedge meaning that you construct a portfolio that has a positive payoff whatever happens to the market. A simple example of this would be to superhedge a short call position by buying one of the stock, and never rebalancing. Unfortunately, as you can probably imagine, and certainly as in this example, superhedging might give you prices that differ vastly from the market.

Margin hedging Often what causes banks, and other institutions, to suffer during volatile markets is not the change in the paper value of their assets but the requirement to suddenly come up with a large amount of cash to cover an unexpected margin call. Examples where margin has caused significant damage are Metallgesellschaft and Long Term Capital Management. Writing options is very risky. The downside of buying an option is just the initial premium, the upside may be unlimited. The upside of writing an option is limited, but the downside could be huge. For this reason, to cover the risk of default in the event of an unfavourable outcome, the clearing houses that register and settle options insist on the deposit of a margin by the writers of options. Margin comes in two forms: the initial margin and the maintenance margin. The initial margin is the amount deposited at the initiation of the contract. The total amount held as margin must stay above a prescribed maintenance margin. If it ever falls below this level then more money (or equivalent in bonds, stocks, etc.) must be deposited. The amount of margin that must be deposited depends on the particular contract. A dramatic market move could result in a sudden large margin call that may be difficult to meet. To prevent this situation it is possible to margin hedge. That is, set up a portfolio such that a margin calls on one part of the portfolio are balanced by refunds from other parts. Usually over-the-counter contracts have no associated margin requirements and so won't appear in the calculation.

Crash (Platinum) hedging The final variety of hedging is specific to extreme markets. Market crashes have at least two obvious effects on our hedging. First of all, the moves are so large and rapid that they cannot be traditionally delta hedged. The convexity effect is not small. Second, normal market correlations become meaningless. Typically all correlations become one (or minus one). Crash or Platinum hedging exploits the latter effect in such a way as to minimize the worst possible outcome for the portfolio. The method, called **CrashMetrics**, does not rely on parameters such as volatilities and so is a very robust hedge. Platinum hedging comes in two types: hedging the paper value of the portfolio and hedging the margin calls.

References and Further Reading

Taleb, NN 1997 *Dynamic Hedging*. John Wiley & Sons Ltd

Wilmott, P 2006 *Paul Wilmott on Quantitative Finance*, second edition. John Wiley & Sons Ltd

What is Marking to Market and How Does it Affect Risk Management in Derivatives Trading?

Short answer

Marking to market means valuing an instrument at the price at which it is currently trading in the market. If you buy an option because you believe it is undervalued then you will not see any profit appear immediately, you will have wait until the market value moves into line with your own estimate. With an option this may not happen until expiration. When you hedge options you have to choose whether to use a delta based on the implied volatility or your own estimate of volatility. If you want to avoid fluctuations in your mark-to-market P&L you will hedge using the implied volatility, even though you may believe this volatility to be incorrect.

Example

A stock is trading at $47, but you think it is seriously undervalued. You believe that the value should be $60. You buy the stock. How much do you tell people your little 'portfolio' is worth? $47 or $60? If you say $47 then you are marking to market, if you say $60 you are marking to (your) model. Obviously this is open to serious abuse and so it is usual, and often a regulatory requirement, to quote the mark-to-market value. If you are right about the stock value then the profit will be realized as the stock price rises. Patience, my son.

Long answer

If instruments are liquid, exchange traded, then marking to market is straightforward. You just need to know the most recent market-traded price. Of course, this doesn't stop you also saying what you believe the value to be, or the profit you expect to make. After all, you presumably entered the trade because you thought you would make a gain.

Hedge funds will tell their investors their Net Asset Value based on the mark-to-market values of the liquid instruments in their portfolio. They may estimate future profit, although this is a bit of a hostage to fortune.

With futures and short options there are also margins to be paid, usually daily, to a clearing house as a safeguard against credit risk. So if prices move against you, you may have to pay a maintenance margin. This will be based on the prevailing market values of the futures and short options. (There is no margin on long options positions because they are paid for up front, from which point the only way is up.)

Marking to market of exchange-traded instruments is clearly very straightforward. But what about exotic or over-the-counter (OTC) contracts? These are not traded actively, they may be unique to you and your counterparty. These instruments have to be **marked to model**. And this obviously raises the question of which model to use. Usually in this context the 'model' means the volatility, whether in equity markets, FX or fixed income. So the question about which model to use becomes a question about which volatility to use. With credit instruments the model often boils down to a number for risk of default.

Here are some possible ways of marking OTC contracts.

- The trader uses his own volatility. Perhaps his best forecast going forward. This is very easy to abuse, it is very easy to rack up an imaginary profit this way. Whatever volatility is used it cannot be too far from the market's implied volatilities on liquid options with the same underlying.
- Use prices obtained from brokers. This has the advantage of being real, tradeable prices, and unprejudiced. The main drawback is that you can't be forever calling brokers for prices with no intention of trading. They get very annoyed. And they won't give you tickets to Wimbledon anymore.

- Use a volatility model that is calibrated to vanillas. This has the advantage of giving prices that are consistent with the information in the market, and are therefore arbitrage free. Although there is always the question of which volatility model to use, deterministic, stochastic, etc., so 'arbitrage freeness' is in the eye of the modeller. It can also be time consuming to have to crunch prices frequently.

One subtlety concerns the marking method and the hedging of derivatives. Take the simple case of a vanilla equity option bought because it is considered cheap. There are potentially three different volatilities here: implied volatility; forecast volatility; hedging volatility. In this situation the option, being exchange traded, would probably be marked to market using the implied volatility, but the ultimate profit will depend on the realized volatility (let's be optimistic and assume it is as forecast) and also how the option is hedged. Hedging using implied volatility in the delta formula theoretically eliminates the otherwise random fluctuations in the mark-to-market value of the hedged option portfolio, but at the cost of making the final profit path dependent, directly related to realized gamma along the stock's path.

By marking to market, or using a model-based marking that is as close to this as possible, your losses will be plain to see. If your theoretically profitable trade is doing badly you will see your losses mounting up. You may be forced to close your position if the loss gets to be too large. Of course, you may have been right in the end, just a bit out in the timing. The loss could have reversed, but if you have closed out your position previously then tough. Having said that, human nature is such that people tend to hold onto losing positions too long on the assumption that they will recover, yet close out winning positions too early. Marking to market will therefore put some rationality back into your trading.

References and Further Reading

Wilmott, P 2006 *Paul Wilmott on Quantitative Finance*, second edition. John Wiley & Sons Ltd

What is the Efficient Markets Hypothesis?

Short answer

An efficient market is one where it is impossible to beat the market because all information about securities is already reflected in their prices.

Example

Or rather a counter-example, "I'd be a bum in the street with a tin cup if the markets were efficient," Warren Buffett.

Long answer

The concept of market efficiency was proposed by Eugene Fama in the 1960s. Prior to that it had been assumed that excess returns could be made by careful choice of investments. Here and in the following the references to 'excess returns' refers to profit above the risk-free rate not explained by a risk premium, i.e. the reward for taking risk. Fama argued that since there are so many active, well-informed and intelligent market participants securities will be priced to reflect all available information. Thus was born the idea of the efficient market, one where it is impossible to beat the market.

There are three classical forms of the **Efficient Markets Hypothesis** (EMH). These are weak form, semi-strong form and strong form.

- **Weak-form efficiency**: In weak-form efficiency excess returns cannot be made by using investment strategies based on historical prices or other historical financial data. If this form of efficiency is true then it will not be possible to make excess returns by using methods such as technical analysis. A trading strategy incorporating historical data, such as price and volume information, will not systematically outperform a buy-and-hold strategy. It is often said that current prices accurately incorporate all historical information, and that current prices are the best estimate of the value of the investment. Prices will respond to news, but if this news is random then price changes will also be random. Technical analysis will not be profitable.

- **Semi-strong form efficiency**: In the semi-strong form of the EMH a trading strategy incorporating current publicly available fundamental information (such as financial statements) and historical price information will not systematically outperform a buy-and-hold strategy. Share prices adjust instantaneously to publicly available new information, and no excess returns can be earned by using that information. Fundamental analysis will not be profitable.
- **Strong-form efficiency**: In strong-form efficiency share prices reflect all information, public and private, fundamental and historical, and no one can earn excess returns. Inside information will not be profitable.

Of course, tests of the EMH should always allow for transaction costs associated with trading and the internal efficiency of trade execution.

A weaker cousin of EMH is the **Adaptive Market Hypothesis** of Andrew Lo. This idea is related to behavioural finance and proposes that market participants adapt to changing markets, information, models, etc., in such a way as to lead to market efficiency but in the meantime there may well be exploitable opportunities for excess returns. This is commonly seen when new contracts, exotic derivatives, are first created leading to a short period of excess profit before the knowledge diffuses and profit margins shrink. The same is true of previously neglected sources of convexity and therefore value. A profitable strategy can exist for a while but perhaps others find out about it, or because of the exploitation of the profit opportunity, either way that efficiency disappears.

The Grossman–Stiglitz paradox says that if a market were efficient, reflecting all available information, then there would be no incentive to acquire the information on which prices are based. Essentially the job has been done for everyone. This is seen when one calibrates a model to market prices of derivatives, without ever studying the statistics of the underlying process.

The validity of the EMH, whichever form, is of great importance because it determines whether anyone can outperform the market, or whether successful investing is all about luck. EMH does not require investors to behave rationally, only that in response to news or data there will be a sufficiently large random reaction that an excess profit cannot be made. Market bubbles, for example, do not invalidate EMH provided they cannot be exploited.

There have been many studies of the EMH, and the validity of its different forms. Many early studies concluded in favour of the weak form. Bond markets and large-capitalization stocks are thought to be highly efficient, smaller stocks less so. Because of different quality of information among investors and because of an emotional component, real estate is thought of as being quite inefficient.

References and Further Reading

Fama, EF 1965 Random Walks in Stock Market Prices. *Financial Analysts Journal* September/October

Lo, A 2004 The Adaptive Markets Hypothesis: market efficiency from an evolutionary perspective. *Journal of Portfolio Management* **30** 15–29

What are the Most Useful Performance Measures?

Short answer
Performance measures are used to quantify the results of a trading strategy. They are usually adjusted for risk. The most popular is the Sharpe ratio.

Example
One stock has an average growth of 10% per annum, another is 30% per annum. You'd rather invest in the second, right? What if I said that the first had a volatility of only 5%, whereas the second was 20%, does that make a difference?

Long answer
Performance measures are used to determine how successful an investment strategy has been. When a hedge fund or trader is asked about past performance the first question is usually "What was your return?" Later maybe "What was your worst month?" These are both very simple measures of performance. The more sensible measures make allowance for the risk that has been taken, since a high return with low risk is much better than a high return with a lot of risk.

Sharpe ratio   The Sharpe ratio is probably the most important non-trivial risk-adjusted performance measure. It is calculated as

$$\text{Sharpe ratio} = \frac{\mu - r}{\sigma}$$

where μ is the return on the strategy over some specified period, r is the risk-free rate over that period and σ is the standard deviation of returns. The Sharpe ratio will be quoted in annualized terms. A high Sharpe ratio is intended to be a sign of a good strategy.

If returns are normally distributed then the Sharpe ratio is related to the probability of making a return in excess of the risk-free rate. In the expected return versus risk diagram of **Modern Portfolio Theory** the Sharpe ratio is the slope of the line joining each investment to the risk-free investment. Choosing the portfolio that maximizes the Sharpe ratio will give you the **Market Portfolio**. We also know from the **Central Limit Theorem** that if you have many different investments all that matters is the mean and the standard deviation. So as long as the CLT is valid the Sharpe ratio makes sense.

The Sharpe ratio has been criticized for attaching equal weight to upside 'risk' as downside risk since the standard deviation incorporates both in its calculation. This may be important if returns are very skewed.

Modigliani–Modigliani measure The Modigliani–Modigliani or M2 measure is a simple linear transformation of the Sharpe ratio:

$$M2 = r + v \times \text{Sharpe}$$

where v is the standard deviation of returns of the relevant benchmark. This is easily interpreted as the return you would expect from your portfolio is it were (de)leveraged to have the same volatility as the benchmark.

Sortino ratio The Sortino ratio is calculated in the same way as the Sharpe ratio except that it uses the square root of the semi-variance as the denominator measuring risk. The semi-variance is measured in the same way as the variance except that all data points with positive return are replaced with zero, or with some target value.

This measure ignores upside 'risk' completely. However, if returns are expected to be normally distributed the semi-variance will be statistically noisier than the variance because fewer data points are used in its calculation.

Treynor ratio   The Treynor or **Reward-to-variability ratio** is another Sharpe-like measure, but now the denominator is the systematic risk, measured by the portfolio's beta, (see **Capital Asset Pricing Model**), instead of the total risk:

$$\text{Treynor ratio} = \frac{\mu - r}{\beta}.$$

In a well-diversified portfolio Sharpe and Treynor are similar, but Treynor is more relevant for less diversified portfolios or individual stocks.

Information ratio   The Information ratio is a different type of performance measure in that it uses the idea of tracking error. The numerator is the return in excess of a benchmark again, but the denominator is the standard deviation of the differences between the portfolio returns and the benchmark returns, the **tracking error**.

$$\text{Information ratio} = \frac{\mu - r}{\text{Tracking error}}.$$

This ratio gives a measure of the value added by a manager relative to their benchmark.

References and Further Reading

Modigliani, F & Modigliani, L 1997 Risk-adjusted performance. *Journal of Portfolio Management* **23** (2) 45–54

Sharpe, WF 1966 Mutual Fund Performance. *Journal of Business* January, 119–138

Sortino FA & van der Meer, R 1991 Downside risk. *Journal of Portfolio Management* 27–31

Treynor, JL 1966 How to rate management investment funds. *Harvard Business Review* **43** 63–75

What is a Utility Function and How is it Used?

Short answer
A utility function represents the 'worth,' 'happiness' or 'satisfaction' associated with goods, services, events, outcomes, levels of wealth, etc. It can be used to rank outcomes, to aggregate 'happiness' across individuals and to value games of chance.

Example
You own a valuable work of art; you are going to put it up for auction. You don't know how much you will make but the auctioneer has estimated the chances of achieving certain amounts. Someone then offers you a guaranteed amount provided you withdraw the painting from the auction. Should you take the offer or take your chances? Utility theory can help you make that decision.

Long answer
The idea is not often used in practice in finance but is common in the literature, especially economics literature. The **utility function** allows the ranking of the otherwise incomparable, and is used to explain people's actions; rational people are supposed to act so as to increase their utility.

When a meaningful numerical value is used to represent utility this is called **cardinal utility**. One can then talk about one thing having three times the utility of another, and one can compare utility from person to person. If the ordering of utility is all that matters (so that one is only concerned with ranking of preferences, not the numerical value) then this is called **ordinal utility**.

If we denote a utility function by $U(W)$ where W is the 'wealth,' then one would expect utility functions to have certain commonsense properties. In the following a prime (') denotes differentiation with respect to W.

- The function $U(W)$ can vary among investors, each will have a different attitude to risk for example.
- $U'(W) \geq 0$: more is preferred to less. If it is a strict inequality then satiation is not possible, the investor will always prefer more than he has. This slope measures the marginal improvement in utility with changes in wealth.
- Usually $U''(W) < 0$: the utility function is strictly concave. Since this is the rate of change of the marginal 'happiness,' it gets harder and harder to increase happiness as wealth increases. An investor with a concave utility function is said to be **risk averse**. This property is often referred to as the law of diminishing returns.

The final point in the above leads to definitions for measurement of **risk aversion**. The **absolute risk aversion function** is defined as

$$A(W) = -\frac{U''(W)}{U'(W)}.$$

The **relative risk aversion function** is defined as

$$R(W) = -\frac{WU''(W)}{U'(W)} = WA(W).$$

Utility functions are often used to analyse random events. Suppose a monetary amount is associated with the number of spots on a rolled dice. You could calculate the expected winnings as the average of all of the six amounts. But what if the amounts were \$1, \$2, \$3, \$4, \$5 and \$6,000,000? Would the average, \$1,000,002.5, be meaningful? Would you be willing to pay \$1,000,000 to enter this as a bet? After all, you expect to make a profit. A more sensible way of valuing this game might be to look at the utility of each of the six outcomes, and then average the utility. This leads on to the idea of certainty equivalent wealth.

When the wealth is random, and all outcomes can be assigned a probability, one can ask what amount of certain wealth has the same utility as the expected utility of the unknown outcomes. Simply solve

$$U(W_c) = E[U(W)].$$

The quantity of wealth W_c that solves this equation is called the **certainty equivalent wealth**. One is therefore indifferent between the average of the utilities of the random outcomes and the guaranteed amount W_c. As an example, consider the above dice-rolling game, supposing our utility function is $U(W) = -\frac{1}{\eta}e^{-\eta W}$. With $\eta = 1$ we find that the certainty equivalent is \$2.34. So we would pay this amount or less to play

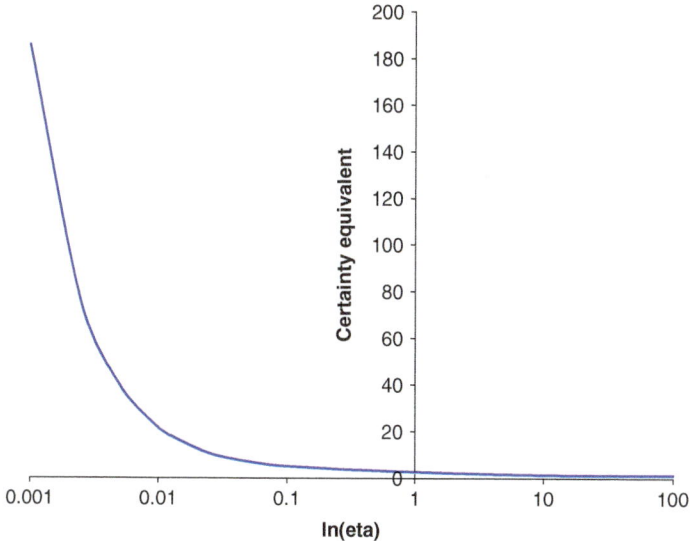

Figure 2.6: Certainty equivalent as a function of the risk-aversion parameter for example in the text.

the game. Figure 2.6 shows a plot of the certainty equivalent for this example as a function of the risk-aversion parameter η. Observe how this decreases the greater the risk aversion.

References and Further Reading

Ingersoll, JE Jr 1987 *Theory of Financial Decision Making*. Rowman & Littlefield

What is the Difference between a Quant and an Actuary?

Short answer
The answer is 'Lots.' They can both learn a lot from each other.

Example
Actuaries work more than quants with historical data and that data tends to be more stable. Think of mortality statistics. Quants often project forward using information contained in a snapshot of option prices.

Long answer
(Note: The following was published in *The Actuary* in September 2008.)

Those working in the two fields of actuarial science and quantitative finance have not always been totally appreciative of each others' skills. Actuaries have been dealing with randomness and risk in finance for centuries. Quants are the relative newcomers, with all their fancy stochastic mathematics. Rather annoyingly for actuaries, quants come along late in the game and thanks to one piece of insight in the early '70s completely change the face of the valuation of risk. The insight I refer to is the concept of dynamic hedging, first published by Black, Scholes and Merton in 1973. Before 1973 derivatives were being valued using the 'actuarial method,' i.e. in a sense relying, as actuaries always have, on the Central Limit Theorem. Since 1973 and the publication of the famous papers, all that has been made redundant. Quants have ruled the financial roost.

But this might just be the time for actuaries to fight back.

I am putting the finishing touches to this article a few days after the first anniversary of the 'day that quant died.' In early August 2007 a number of high-profile and previously successful quantitative hedge funds suffered large losses. People said that their models 'just stopped working.' The year since has been occupied with a lot of soul searching by quants; how could this happen when they've got such incredible models?

In my view the main reason why quantitative finance is in a mess is because of complexity and obscurity. Quants are making their models increasingly complicated, in the belief that they are making improvements. This is not the case. More often than not each 'improvement' is a step backwards. If this were a proper hard science then there would be a reason for trying to perfect models. But finance is not a hard science, one in which you can conduct experiments for which the results are repeatable. Finance, thanks to it being underpinned by human beings and their wonderfully irrational behaviour, is forever changing. It is therefore much better to focus your attention on making the models robust and transparent rather than ever more intricate. As I mentioned in a recent wilmott.com blog, there is a maths sweet spot in quant finance. The models should not be too elementary so as to make it impossible to invent new structured products, but nor should they be so abstract as to be easily misunderstood by all except their inventor (and sometimes even by him), with the obvious and financially dangerous consequences. I teach on the Certificate in Quantitative Finance and in that our goal is to make quant finance practical, understandable and, above all, safe.

When banks sell a contract they do so assuming that it is going to make a profit. They use their complex models, with sophisticated numerical solutions, to come up with the perfect value. Having gone to all that effort for that contract they then throw it into the same pot as all the others and risk manage *en masse*. The funny thing is that they never know whether each individual contract has 'washed its own face.' Sure they know whether the pot has made money; their bonus is tied to it. But each contract? It makes good sense to risk manage all contracts together but it doesn't make sense to go to such obsessive detail in valuation when ultimately it's the portfolio that makes money, especially when the basic models are so dodgy. The theory of quant finance and the practice diverge. Money is made by portfolios, not by individual contracts.

In other words, quants make money from the Central Limit Theorem, just like actuaries, it's just that quants are loath to admit it! Ironic.

It's about time that actuaries got more involved in quantitative finance. They could bring some common sense back into this field. We need models which people can understand and a greater respect for risk. Actuaries and quants have complementary skill sets. What high finance needs now are precisely those skills that actuaries have, a deep understanding of statistics, a historical perspective, and a willingness to work with data.

References and Further Reading

Visit www.actuarialwiki.org for information about the actuarial industry.

What is a Wiener Process/Brownian Motion and What are its Uses in Finance?

Short answer

The Wiener process or Brownian motion is a stochastic process with stationary independent normally distributed increments and which also has continuous sample paths. It is the most common stochastic building block for random walks in finance.

Example

Pollen in water, smoke in a room, pollution in a river, are all examples of Brownian motion. And this is the common model for stock prices as well.

Long answer

Brownian motion (BM) is named after the Scottish botanist who first described the random motions of pollen grains suspended in water. The mathematics of this process were formalized by Bachelier, in an option-pricing context, and by Einstein. The mathematics of BM is also that of heat conduction and diffusion.

Mathematically, BM is a continuous, stationary, stochastic process with independent normally distributed increments. If W_t is the BM at time t then for every t, $\tau \geq 0$, $W_{t+\tau} - W_t$ is independent of $\{W_u : 0 \leq u \leq t\}$, and has a normal distribution with zero mean and variance τ.

The important properties of BM are as follows:

- **Finiteness**: the scaling of the variance with the time step is crucial to BM remaining finite.

- **Continuity**: the paths are continuous, there are no discontinuities. However, the path is fractal, and not differentiable anywhere.
- **Markov**: the conditional distribution of W_t given information up until $\tau < t$ depends only on W_τ.
- **Martingale**: given information up until $\tau < t$ the conditional expectation of W_t is W_τ.
- **Quadratic variation**: if we divide up the time 0 to t in a partition with $n+1$ partition points $t_i = it/n$ then

$$\sum_{j=1}^{n} \left(W_{t_j} - W_{t_{j-1}} \right)^2 \to t.$$

- **Normality**: Over finite time increments t_{i-1} to t_i, $W_{t_i} - W_{t_{i-1}}$ is normally distributed with mean zero and variance $t_i - t_{i-1}$.

You'll see this 'W' in the form dW as the stochastic increment term in stochastic differential equations. It might also appear as dX or dB, different authors using different letters, and sometimes with a time subscript. But these are all the same thing!

It's often easiest just to think of dW as being a random number drawn from a normal distribution with the properties: $E[dW] = 0$ and $E[dW^2] = dt$.

BM is a very simple yet very rich process, extremely useful for representing many random processes especially those in finance. Its simplicity allows calculations and analysis that would not be possible with other processes. For example, in option pricing it results in simple closed-form formulæ for the prices of vanilla options. It can be used as a building block for random walks with characteristics beyond those of BM itself. For example, it is used in the modelling of interest rates via mean-reverting random walks. Higher-dimensional versions of BM can be used to represent multi-factor random walks, such as stock prices under stochastic volatility.

One of the unfortunate features of BM is that it gives returns distributions with tails that are unrealistically shallow. In practice, asset returns have tails that are much fatter than those given by the normal distribution of BM. There is even some evidence that the distribution of returns has infinite second moment. Despite this, and the existence of financial theories that do incorporate such fat tails, BM motion is easily the most common model used to represent random walks in finance.

References and Further Reading

Bachelier, L 1995 *Théorie de la Spéculation*. Jacques Gabay

Brown, R 1827 *A Brief Account of Microscopical Observations*. London

Stachel, J (ed.) 1990 *The Collected Papers of Albert Einstein*. Princeton University Press

Wiener, N 1923 Differential space. *Journal of Mathematics and Physics* **58** 131–174

What is Jensen's Inequality and What is its Role in Finance?

Short answer

Jensen's Inequality states[1] that if $f(\cdot)$ is a convex function and x is a random variable then

$$E\left[f(x)\right] \geq f\left(E[x]\right).$$

This justifies why non-linear instruments, options, have inherent value.

Example

You roll a die, square the number of spots you get, you win that many dollars. For this exercise $f(x)$ is x^2 a convex function. So $E\left[f(x)\right]$ is $1 + 4 + 9 + 16 + 25 + 36 = 91$ divided by 6, so 15 1/6. But $E[x]$ is 3 1/2 so $f\left(E[x]\right)$ is 12 1/4.

Long answer

A function $f(\cdot)$ is **convex** on an interval if for every x and y in that interval

$$f(\lambda x + (1 - \lambda)y) \leq \lambda f(x) + (1 - \lambda)f(y)$$

for any $0 \leq \lambda \leq 1$. Graphically this means that the line joining the points $(x, f(x))$ and $(y, f(y))$ is nowhere lower than the curve. (Concave is the opposite, simply $-f$ is convex.)

Jensen's Inequality and convexity can be used to explain the relationship between randomness in stock prices and the value inherent in options, the latter typically having some convexity.

Suppose that a stock price S is random and we want to consider the value of an option with payoff $P(S)$. We could calculate the expected stock price at expiration as $E[S_T]$, and

---

[1] This is the probabilistic interpretation of the inequality.

then the payoff at that expected price $P(E[S_T])$. Alternatively, we could look at the various option payoffs and then calculate the expected payoff as $E[P(S_T)]$. The latter makes more sense, and is indeed the correct way to value options, provided the expectation is with respect to the **risk-neutral** stock price. If the payoff is convex then

$$E[P(S_T)] \geq P(E[S_T]).$$

We can get an idea of how much greater the left-hand side is than the right-hand side by using a Taylor series approximation around the mean of S. Write

$$S = \overline{S} + \epsilon,$$

where $\overline{S} = E[S]$, so $E[\epsilon] = 0$. Then

$$
\begin{aligned}
E\left[f(S)\right] = E\left[f(\overline{S} + \epsilon)\right] &= E\left[f(\overline{S}) + \epsilon f'(\overline{S}) + \frac{1}{2}\epsilon^2 f''(\overline{S}) + \cdots\right] \\
&\approx f(\overline{S}) + \frac{1}{2}f''(\overline{S})E\left[\epsilon^2\right] \\
&= f(E[S]) + \frac{1}{2}f''(E[S])E\left[\epsilon^2\right].
\end{aligned}
$$

Therefore the left-hand side is greater than the right by approximately

$$\frac{1}{2}f''(E[S])\, E\left[\epsilon^2\right].$$

This shows the importance of two concepts:

- $f''(E[S])$: The **convexity** of an option. As a rule this adds value to an option. It also means that any intuition we may get from linear contracts (forwards and futures) might not be helpful with non-linear instruments such as options.
- $E\left[\epsilon^2\right]$: Randomness in the underlying, and its **variance**. Modelling randomness is the key to modelling options.

The lesson to learn from this is that whenever a contract has convexity in a variable or parameter, and that variable or parameter is random, then allowance must be made for this in the pricing. To do this correctly requires a knowledge of the amount of convexity and the amount of randomness.

References and Further Reading

Wilmott, P 2006 *Paul Wilmott on Quantitative Finance*, second edition. John Wiley & Sons Ltd

What is Itô's Lemma?

Short answer

Itô's lemma is a theorem in stochastic calculus. It tells you that if you have a random walk, in y, say, and a function of that randomly walking variable, call it $f(y, t)$, then you can easily write an expression for the random walk in f. A function of a random variable is itself random in general.

Example

The obvious example concerns the random walk

$$dS = \mu S\, dt + \sigma S\, dX$$

commonly used to model an equity price or exchange rate, S. What is the stochastic differential equation for the logarithm of S, $\ln S$?

The answer is

$$d(\ln S) = \left(\mu - \frac{1}{2}\sigma^2\right)\, dt + \sigma\, dX.$$

Long answer

Let's begin by stating the theorem. Given a random variable y satisfying the stochastic differential equation

$$dy = a(y, t)\, dt + b(y, t)\, dX,$$

where dX is a Wiener process, and a function $f(y, t)$ that is differentiable with respect to t and twice differentiable with respect to y, then f satisfies the following stochastic differential equation

$$df = \left(\frac{\partial f}{\partial t} + a(y, t)\frac{\partial f}{\partial y} + \frac{1}{2}b(y, t)^2\frac{\partial^2 f}{\partial y^2}\right)\, dt + b(y, t)\frac{\partial f}{\partial y}\, dX.$$

Itô's lemma is to stochastic variables what **Taylor series** is to deterministic. You can think of it as a way of expanding functions in a series in dt, just like Taylor series. If it helps to think of it this way then you must remember the simple rules of thumb as follows:

1. Whenever you get dX^2 in a Taylor series expansion of a stochastic variable you must replace it with dt.
2. Terms that are $O(dt^{3/2})$ or smaller must be ignored. This means that dt^2, dX^3, $dt\, dX$, etc. are too small to keep.

It is difficult to overstate the importance of Itô's lemma in quantitative finance. It is used in many of the derivations of the Black–Scholes option-pricing model and the equivalent models in the fixed-income and credit worlds. If we have a random walk model for a stock price S and an option on that stock, with value $V(S,t)$, then Itô's lemma tells us how the option price changes with changes in the stock price. From this follows the idea of hedging, by matching random fluctuations in S with those in V. This is important both in the theory of derivatives pricing and in the practical management of market risk.

Even if you don't know how to prove Itô's lemma you must be able to quote it and use the result.

Sometimes we have a function of more than one stochastic quantity. Suppose that we have a function $f(y_1, y_2, \ldots, y_n, t)$ of n stochastic quantities and time such that

$$dy_i = a_i(y_1, y_2, \ldots, y_n, t)\, dt + b_i(y_1, y_2, \ldots, y_n, t)\, dX_i,$$

where the n Wiener processes dX_i have correlations ρ_{ij}, then

$$df = \left(\frac{\partial f}{\partial t} + \sum_{i=1}^{n} a_i \frac{\partial f}{\partial y_i} + \frac{1}{2} \sum_{i=1}^{n} \sum_{j=1}^{n} \rho_{ij} b_i b_j \frac{\partial^2 f}{\partial y_i\, \partial y_j} \right) dt \\ + \sum_{i=1}^{n} b_i \frac{\partial f}{\partial y_i}\, dX_i.$$

We can understand this (if not entirely legitimately derive it) via Taylor series by using the rules of thumb

$$dX_i^2 = dt \quad \text{and} \quad dX_i dX_j = \rho_{ij} dt.$$

Another extension that is often useful in finance is to incorporate jumps in the independent variable. These are usually modelled by a Poisson process. This is dq such that $dq = 1$ with probability $\lambda \, dt$ and is 0 with probability $1 - \lambda \, dt$. Returning to the single independent variable case for simplicity, suppose y satisfies

$$dy = a(y, t) \, dt + b(y, t) \, dX + J(y, t) \, dq$$

where dq is a Poisson process and J is the size of the jump or discontinuity in y (when $dq = 1$) then

$$df = \left(\frac{\partial f}{\partial t} + a(y, t) \frac{\partial f}{\partial y} + \frac{1}{2} b(y, t)^2 \frac{\partial^2 f}{\partial y^2} \right) \, dt$$
$$+ b(y, t) \frac{\partial f}{\partial y} \, dX + (f(y + J(y, t)) - f(y, t)) \, dq.$$

And this is Itô in the presence of jumps.

References and Further Reading

Joshi, M 2003 *The Concepts and Practice of Mathematical Finance*. CUP

Neftci, S 1996 *An Introduction to the Mathematics of Financial Derivatives*. Academic Press

Wilmott, P 2007 *Paul Wilmott Introduces Quantitative Finance*, second edition. John Wiley & Sons Ltd

Why Does Risk-Neutral Valuation Work?

Short answer

Risk-neutral valuation means that you can value options in terms of their expected payoffs, discounted from expiration to the present, assuming that they grow on average at the risk-free rate.

Option value = Expected present value of payoff

(under a risk-neutral random walk).

Therefore the real rate at which the underlying grows on average doesn't affect the value. Of course, the volatility, related to the standard deviation of the underlying's return, does matter. In practice, it's usually much, much harder to estimate this average growth than the volatility, so we are rather spoiled in derivatives, that we only need to estimate the relatively stable parameter, volatility.[2] The reason that this is true is that by hedging an option with the underlying we remove any exposure to the direction of the stock, whether it goes up or down ceases to matter. By eliminating risk in this way we also remove any dependence on the value of risk. End result is that we may as well imagine we are in a world in which no one values risk at all, and all tradeable assets grow at the risk-free rate on average.

For any derivative product, as long as we can hedge it dynamically and perfectly (supposing we can as in the case of known, deterministic volatility and no defaults) the hedged portfolio loses its randomness and behaves like a bond.

---

[2]I should emphasize the word 'relatively.' Volatility does vary in reality, but probably not as much as the growth rate.

Example

A stock whose value is currently $44.75 is growing on average by 15% per annum. Its volatility is 22%. The interest rate is 4%. You want to value a call option with a strike of $45, expiring in two months' time. What can you do?

First of all, the 15% average growth is totally irrelevant. The stock's growth and therefore its real direction does not affect the value of derivatives. What you can do is simulate many, many future paths of a stock with an average growth of 4% per annum, since that is the risk-free interest rate, and a 22% volatility, to find out where it may be in two months' time. Then calculate the call payoff for each of these paths. Present value each of these back to today, and calculate the average over all paths. That's your option value. (For this simple example of the call option there is a formula for its value, so you don't need to do all these simulations. And in that formula you'll see an *r* for the risk-free interest rate, and no mention of the real drift rate.)

Long answer

Risk-neutral valuation of derivatives exploits the perfect correlation between the changes in the value of an option and its underlying asset. As long as the underlying is the only random factor then this correlation should be perfect. So if an option goes up in value with a rise in the stock then a long option and sufficiently short stock position shouldn't have any random fluctuations, therefore the stock hedges the option. The resulting portfolio is risk free.

Of course, you need to know the correct number of the stock to sell short. That's called the 'delta' and usually comes from a model. Because we usually need a mathematical model to calculate the delta, and because quantitative finance models are necessarily less than perfect, the theoretical elimination of risk by delta hedging is also less than perfect in practice. There are several such imperfections with risk-neutral valuation. First, it requires continuous rebalancing of the hedge.

Delta is constantly changing so you must always be buying or selling stock to maintain a risk-free position. Obviously, this is not possible in practice. Second, it hinges on the accuracy of the model. The underlying has to be consistent with certain assumptions, such as being Brownian motion without any jumps, and with known volatility.

One of the most important side effects of risk-neutral pricing is that we can value derivatives by doing simulations of the risk-neutral path of underlyings, to calculate payoffs for the derivatives. These payoffs are then discounted to the present, and finally averaged. This average that we find is the contract's fair value.

Here are some further explanations of risk-neutral pricing.

Explanation 1: If you hedge correctly in a Black–Scholes world then all risk is eliminated. If there is no risk then we should not expect any compensation for risk. We can therefore work under a measure in which everything grows at the risk-free interest rate.

Explanation 2: If the model for the asset is $dS = \mu S \, dt + \sigma S \, dX$ then the μs cancel in the derivation of the Black–Scholes equation.

Explanation 3: Two measures are equivalent if they have the same sets of zero probability. Because zero probability sets don't change, a portfolio is an arbitrage under one measure if and only if it is one under all equivalent measures. Therefore a price is non-arbitrageable in the real world if and only if it is non-arbitrageable in the risk-neutral world. The risk-neutral price is always non-arbitrageable. If everything has a discounted asset price process which is a martingale then there can be no arbitrage. So if we change to a measure in which all the fundamental assets, for example the stock and bond, are martingales after discounting, and then define the option price to be the discounted expectation making it into a martingale too, we have that everything is a martingale in the risk-neutral world. Therefore there is no arbitrage in the real world.

Explanation 4: If we have calls with a continuous distribution of strikes from zero to infinity then we can synthesize arbitrarily well any payoff with the same expiration. But these calls define the risk-neutral probability density function for that expiration, and so we can interpret the synthesized option in terms of risk-neutral random walks. When such a static replication is possible then it is model independent, we can price complex derivatives in terms of vanillas. (Of course, the continuous distribution requirement does spoil this argument to some extent.)

It should be noted that risk-neutral pricing only works under assumptions of continuous hedging, zero transaction costs, continuous asset paths, etc. Once we move away from this simplifying world we may find that it doesn't work.

References and Further Reading

Joshi, M 2003 *The Concepts and Practice of Mathematical Finance*. Cambridge University Press

Neftci, S 1996 *An Introduction to the Mathematics of Financial Derivatives*. Academic Press

What is Girsanov's Theorem, and Why is it Important in Finance?

Short answer
Girsanov's theorem is the formal concept underlying the change of measure from the real world to the risk-neutral world. We can change from a Brownian motion with one drift to a Brownian motion with another.

Example
The classical example is to start with

$$dS = \mu S \, dt + \sigma S \, dW_t$$

with W being Brownian motion under one measure (the real-world measure) and converting it to

$$dS = rS \, dt + \sigma S \, d\tilde{W}_t$$

under a different, the risk-neutral, measure.

Long answer
First a statement of the theorem. Let W_t be a Brownian motion with measure $\mathbb{P}$ and sample space Ω. If γ_t is a previsible process satisfying the constraint $E_{\mathbb{P}} \left[\exp\left(\frac{1}{2} \int_0^T \gamma_t^2 \right) \right] < \infty$ then there exists an equivalent measure $\mathbb{Q}$ on Ω such that

$$\tilde{W}_t = W_t + \int_0^t \gamma_s ds$$

is a Brownian motion.

It will be helpful if we explain some of the more technical terms in this theorem.

- **Sample space**: All possible future states or outcomes.
- **(Probability) Measure**: In layman's terms, the measure gives the probabilities of each of the outcomes in the sample space.

- **Previsible**: A previsible process is one that only depends on the previous history.
- **Equivalent**: Two measures are equivalent if they have the same sample space and the same set of 'possibilities.' Note the use of the word possibilities instead of probabilities. The two measures can have different probabilities for each outcome but must agree on what is possible.

Another way of writing the above is in differential form

$$d\tilde{W}_t = dW_t + \gamma_t \, dt.$$

One important point about Girsanov's theorem is its converse, that every equivalent measure is given by a drift change. This implies that in the Black–Scholes world there is only the one equivalent risk-neutral measure. If this were not the case then there would be multiple arbitrage-free prices.

For many problems in finance Girsanov theorem is not necessarily useful. This is often the case in the world of equity derivatives. Straightforward Black–Scholes does not require any understanding of Girsanov. Once you go beyond basic Black–Scholes it becomes more useful. For example, suppose you want to derive the valuation partial differential equations for options under stochastic volatility. The stock price follows the real-world processes, $\mathbb{P}$,

$$dS = \mu S \, dt + \sigma S \, dX_1$$

and

$$d\sigma = a(S, \sigma, t)dt + b(S, \sigma, t)dWX_2,$$

where dX_1 and dX_2 are correlated Brownian motions with correlation $\rho(S, \sigma, t)$.

Using Girsanov you can get the governing equation in three steps:

1. Under a pricing measure $\mathbb{Q}$, Girsanov plus the fact that S is traded implies that

$$dX_1 = d\tilde{X}_1 - \frac{\mu - r}{\sigma}dt$$

and

$$dX_2 = d\tilde{X}_2 - \lambda(S, \sigma, t)\,dt,$$

where λ is the market price of volatility risk.

2. Apply Itô's formula to the discounted option price $V(S, \sigma, t) = e^{-r(T-t)}F(S, \sigma, t)$, expanding under $\mathbb{Q}$, using the formulæ for dS and dV obtained from the Girsanov transformation

3. Since the option is traded, the coefficient of the dt term in its Itô expansion must also be zero; this yields the relevant equation

Girsanov and the idea of change of measure are particularly important in the fixed-income world where practitioners often have to deal with many different measures at the same time, corresponding to different maturities. This is the reason for the popularity of the BGM model and its ilk.

References and Further Reading

Joshi, M 2003 *The Concepts and Practice of Mathematical Finance*. Cambridge University Press

Lewis, A 2000 *Option Valuation under Stochastic Volatility*. Finance Press

Neftci, S 1996 *An Introduction to the Mathematics of Financial Derivatives*. Academic Press

What are the Greeks?

Short answer

The 'greeks' are the sensitivities of derivatives prices to underlyings, variables and parameters. They can be calculated by differentiating option values with respect to variables and/or parameters, either analytically, if you have a closed-form formula, or numerically.

Example

Delta, $\Delta = \frac{\partial V}{\partial S}$, is the sensitivity of an option price to the stock price. Gamma, $\Gamma = \frac{\partial^2 V}{\partial S^2}$, is the second derivative of the option price to the underlying stock, it is the sensitivity of the delta to the stock price. These two examples are called greek because they are members of the Greek alphabet. Some sensitivities, such as vega $= \frac{\partial V}{\partial \sigma}$, are still called 'greek' even though they aren't in the Greek alphabet.

Long answer

Delta The delta, Δ, of an option or a portfolio of options is the sensitivity of the option or portfolio to the underlying. It is the rate of change of value with respect to the asset:

$$\Delta = \frac{\partial V}{\partial S}.$$

Speculators take a view on the direction of some quantity such as the asset price and implement a strategy to take advantage of their view. If they own options then their exposure to the underlying is, to a first approximation, the same as if they own delta of the underlying.

Those who are not speculating on direction of the underlying will hedge by buying or selling the underlying, or another option, so that the portfolio delta is zero. By doing this they eliminate market risk.

Typically the delta changes as stock price and time change, so to maintain a **delta-neutral** position the number of assets held requires continual readjustment by purchase or sale of the stock. This is called **rehedging** or **rebalancing** the portfolio, and is an example of **dynamic hedging**.

Sometimes going short the stock for hedging purposes requires the borrowing of the stock in the first place. (You then *sell* what you have *borrowed*, buying it back later.) This can be costly, you may have to pay a repo rate, the equivalent of an interest rate, on the amount borrowed.

Gamma The gamma, Γ, of an option or a portfolio of options is the second derivative of the position with respect to the underlying:

$$\Gamma = \frac{\partial^2 V}{\partial S^2}.$$

Since gamma is the sensitivity of the delta to the underlying it is a measure of by how much or how often a position must be rehedged in order to maintain a delta-neutral position. If there are costs associated with buying or selling stock, the bid–offer spread, for example, then the larger the gamma the larger the cost or friction caused by dynamic hedging.

Because costs can be large and because one wants to reduce exposure to model error it is natural to try to minimize the need to rebalance the portfolio too frequently. Since gamma is a measure of sensitivity of the hedge ratio Δ to the movement in the underlying, the hedging requirement can be decreased by a **gamma-neutral** strategy. This means buying or selling more *options*, not just the underlying.

Theta The theta, Θ, is the rate of change of the option price with time.

$$\Theta = \frac{\partial V}{\partial t}.$$

The theta is related to the option value, the delta and the gamma by the Black–Scholes equation.

Speed The speed of an option is the rate of change of the gamma with respect to the stock price.

$$\text{Speed} \ = \frac{\partial^3 V}{\partial S^3}.$$

Traders use the gamma to estimate how much they will have to rehedge by if the stock moves. The stock moves by \$1 so the delta changes by whatever the gamma is. But that's only an approximation. The delta may change by more or less than this, especially if the stock moves by a larger amount, or the option is close to the strike and expiration. Hence the use of speed in a higher-order Taylor series expansion.

Vega The vega, sometimes known as zeta or kappa, is a very important but confusing quantity. It is the sensitivity of the option price to volatility.

$$\text{Vega} \ = \frac{\partial V}{\partial \sigma}.$$

This is completely different from the other greeks since it is a derivative with respect to a *parameter* and not a *variable*. This can be important. It is perfectly acceptable to consider sensitivity to a variable, which does vary, after all. However, it can be dangerous to measure sensitivity to something, such as volatility, which is a parameter and may, for example, have been assumed to be constant. That would be internally inconsistent. (See **bastard greeks**.)

As with gamma hedging, one can vega hedge to reduce sensitivity to the volatility. This is a major step towards eliminating some model risk, since it reduces dependence on a quantity that is not known very accurately.

There is a downside to the measurement of vega. It is only really meaningful for options having single-signed gamma everywhere. For example, it makes sense to measure vega for calls and puts but not binary calls and binary puts. The reason for this is that call and put values (and options with single-signed gamma) have values that are monotonic in the volatility: increase the volatility in a call and its value increases everywhere. Contracts with a gamma that changes sign may have a vega measured at zero because as we increase the volatility the price may rise somewhere and fall somewhere else. Such a contract is very exposed to volatility risk but that risk is not measured by the vega.

Rho ρ, is the sensitivity of the option value to the interest rate used in the Black–Scholes formulæ:

$$\rho = \frac{\partial V}{\partial r}.$$

In practice one often uses a whole term structure of interest rates, meaning a time-dependent rate $r(t)$. Rho would then be the sensitivity to the level of the rates assuming a parallel shift in rates at all times. (But see bastard greeks again.)

Rho can also be sensitivity to dividend yield, or foreign interest rate in a foreign exchange option.

Charm The charm is the sensitivity of delta to time.

$$\frac{\partial^2 V}{\partial S\, \partial t}.$$

This is useful for seeing how your hedge position will change with time, for example, up until the next time you expect to hedge. This can be important near expiration.

Colour The colour is the rate of change of gamma with time.

$$\frac{\partial^3 V}{\partial S^2\, \partial t}.$$

Vanna   The Vanna is the sensitivity of delta to volatility.

$$\frac{\partial^2 V}{\partial S \, \partial \sigma}.$$

This is used when testing sensitivity of hedge ratios to volatility. It can be misleading at places where gamma is small.

Vomma or Volga   The Vomma or Volga is the second derivative of the option value with respect to volatility.

$$\frac{\partial^2 V}{\partial \sigma^2}.$$

Because of **Jensen's Inequality**, if volatility is stochastic the Vomma/Volga measures convexity due to random volatility and so gives you an idea of how much to add (or subtract) from an option's value.

Shadow greeks   The above greeks are defined in terms of partial derivatives with respect to underlying, time, volatility, etc. *while holding the other variables/parameters fixed*. That is the definition of a partial derivative.[3] But, of course, the variables/parameters might, in practice, move together. For example, a fall in the stock price might be accompanied by an increase in volatility. So one can measure sensitivity as both the underlying and volatility move together. This is called a shadow greek and is just like the concept of a total derivative in, for example, fluid mechanics where one might follow the path of a fluid particle.

---

[3]Here derivative has its mathematical meaning of that which is differentiated not its financial meaning as an option.

References and Further Reading

Taleb, NN 1997 *Dynamic Hedging*. John Wiley & Sons Ltd

Wilmott, P 2007 *Paul Wilmott Introduces Quantitative Finance*, second edition. John Wiley & Sons Ltd

Why do Quants like Closed-Form Solutions?

Short answer
Because they are fast to compute and easy to understand.

Example
The Black–Scholes formulæ are simple and closed form and often used despite people knowing that they have limitations, and despite being used for products for which they were not originally intended.

Long answer
There are various pressures on a quant when it comes to choosing a model. What he'd really like is a model that is

- **robust**: small changes in the random process for the underlying don't matter too much
- **fast**: prices and the greeks have to be quick to compute for several reasons, so that the trade gets done and you don't lose out to a competitor, and so that positions can be managed in real time as just one small part of a large portfolio
- **accurate**: in a scientific sense the prices ought to be good, perhaps matching historical data; this is different from robust, of course
- **easy to calibrate**: banks like to have models that match traded prices of simple contracts

There is some overlap in these. Fast may also mean easy to calibrate, but not necessarily. Accurate and robust might be similar, but again, not always.

From the scientific point of view the most important of these is accuracy. The least important is speed. To the scientist the question of calibration becomes one concerning the existence of arbitrage. If you are a hedge fund looking for prop trading opportunities with vanillas then calibration is precisely what you *don't* want to do. And robustness would be nice, but maybe the financial world is so unstable that models can never be robust.

To the practitioner he needs to be able to price quickly to get the deal done and to manage the risk. If he is in the business of selling exotic contracts then he will invariably be calibrating, so that he can say that his prices are consistent with vanillas. As long as the model isn't too inaccurate or sensitive, and he can add a sufficient profit margin, then he will be content. So to the practitioner speed and ability to calibrate to the market are the most important.

The scientist and the practitioner have conflicting interests. And the practitioner usually wins.

And what could be faster than a closed-form solution? This is why practitioners tend to favour closed forms. They also tend to be easier to understand intuitively than a numerical solution. The Black–Scholes formulæ are perfect for this, having a simple interpretation in terms of expectations, and using the cumulative distribution function for the Gaussian distribution.

Such is the desire for simple formulæ that people often use the formulæ for the wrong product. Suppose you want to price certain Asian options based on an arithmetic average. To do this properly in the Black–Scholes world you would do this by solving a three-dimensional partial differential equation or by Monte Carlo simulation. But if you pretend that the averaging is geometric and not arithmetic then often there are simple closed-form solutions. So use those, even though they must be wrong. The point is that they will probably be less wrong than other assumptions you are making, such as what future volatility will be.

Of course, the definition of closed form is to some extent in the eye of the beholder. If an option can be priced in terms of an infinite sum of hypergeometric functions does that count? Some Asian options can be priced that way. Or what about a closed form involving a subtle integration in the complex plane that must ultimately be done numerically? That is the Heston stochastic volatility model.

If closed form is so appreciated, is it worth spending much time seeking them out? Probably not. There are always new products being invented and new pricing models being devised, but they are unlikely to be of the simple type that can be solved explicitly. Chances are that you will either have to solve these numerically, or approximate them by something not too dissimilar. Approximations such as Black '76 are probably your best chance of finding closed-form solutions for new products these days.

References and Further Reading

Black F 1976 The pricing of commodity contracts. *Journal of Financial Economics* **3** 167–179

Haug, EG 2003 Know your weapon, Parts 1 and 2. *Wilmott* magazine, May and July

Haug, EG 2006 *The Complete Guide to Option Pricing Formulas*. McGraw–Hill

Lewis, A 2000 *Option Valuation under Stochastic Volatility*. Finance Press

What are the Forward and Backward Equations?

Short answer

Forward and backward equations usually refer to the differential equations governing the transition probability density function for a stochastic process. They are diffusion equations and must therefore be solved in the appropriate direction in time, hence the names.

Example

An exchange rate is currently 1.88. What is the probability that it will be over 2 by this time next year? If you have a stochastic differential equation model for this exchange rate then this question can be answered using the equations for the transition probability density function.

Long answer

Let us suppose that we have a random variable y evolving according to a quite general, one-factor stochastic differential equation

$$dy = A(y,t) \, dt + B(y,t) \, dX.$$

Here A and B are both arbitrary functions of y and t.

Many common models can be written in this form, including the lognormal asset random walk, and common spot interest rate models.

The **transition probability density function** $p(y,t;y',t')$ is the function of four variables defined by

$$\text{Prob}(a < y < b \text{ at time } t'|y \text{ at time } t) = \int_a^b p(y,t;y',t') \, dy'.$$

This simply means the probability that the random variable y lies between a and b at time t' in the future, given that it started out with value y at time t. You can think of y and t

as being current or starting values with y' and t' being future values.

The transition probability density function $p(y, t; y', t')$ satisfies two equations, one involving derivatives with respect to the future state and time (y' and t') and called the forward equation, and the other involving derivatives with respect to the current state and time (y and t) and called the backward equation. These two equations are parabolic partial differential equations not dissimilar to the Black–Scholes equation.

The forward equation
Also known as the **Fokker–Planck** or **forward Kolmogorov equation** this is

$$\frac{\partial p}{\partial t'} = \frac{1}{2} \frac{\partial^2}{\partial y'^2} (B(y', t')^2 p) - \frac{\partial}{\partial y'} (A(y', t') p).$$

This forward parabolic partial differential equation requires initial conditions at time t and to be solved for $t' > t$.

Example An important example is that of the distribution of equity prices in the future. If we have the random walk

$$dS = \mu S \, dt + \sigma S \, dX$$

then the forward equation becomes

$$\frac{\partial p}{\partial t'} = \frac{1}{2} \frac{\partial^2}{\partial S'^2} (\sigma^2 S'^2 p) - \frac{\partial}{\partial S'} (\mu S' p).$$

A special solution of this representing a variable that begins with certainty with value S at time t is

$$p(S, t; S', t') = \frac{1}{\sigma S' \sqrt{2\pi(t' - t)}} e^{-\left(\ln(S/S') + (\mu - \frac{1}{2}\sigma^2)(t' - t)\right)^2 / 2\sigma^2(t' - t)}.$$

This is plotted as a function of both S' and t' in Figure 2.7.

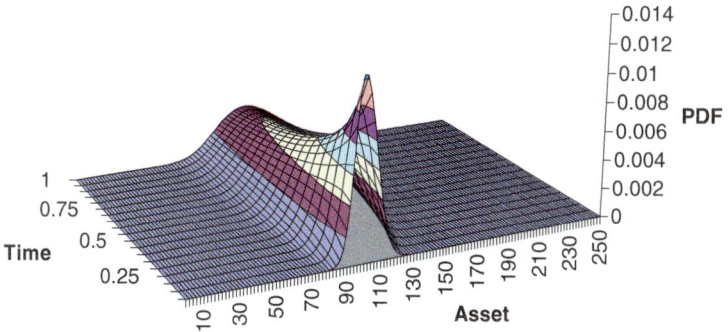

Figure 2.7: The probability density function for the lognormal random walk evolving through time.

The backward equation
Also known as the **backward Kolmogorov equation** this is

$$\frac{\partial p}{\partial t} + \frac{1}{2}B(y,t)^2 \frac{\partial^2 p}{\partial y^2} + A(y,t)\frac{\partial p}{\partial y} = 0.$$

This must be solved backwards in t with specified final data. For example, if we wish to calculate the expected value of some function $F(S)$ at time T we must solve this equation for the function $p(S,t)$ with

$$p(S,T) = F(S).$$

Option prices
If we have the lognormal random walk for S, as above, and we transform the dependent variable using a discount factor according to

$$p(S,t) = e^{r(T-t)}V(S,t),$$

then the backward equation for p becomes an equation for V which is identical to the Black–Scholes partial differential equation. Identical but for one subtlety, the equation contains a μ where Black–Scholes contains r. We can conclude that the fair value of an option is the present value of the expected payoff at expiration under a risk-neutral random walk for the underlying. Risk neutral here means replace μ with r.

References and Further Reading

Feller, W 1950 *Probability Theory and Its Applications*. John Wiley & Sons Inc.

Wilmott, P 2006 *Paul Wilmott on Quantitative Finance*, second edition. John Wiley & Sons Ltd

What is the Black–Scholes Equation?

Short answer
The Black–Scholes equation is a differential equation for the value of an option as a function of the underlying asset and time.

Example
The basic equation is

$$\frac{\partial V}{\partial t} + \frac{1}{2}\sigma^2 S^2 \frac{\partial^2 V}{\partial S^2} + rS\frac{\partial V}{\partial S} - rV = 0,$$

where $V(S,t)$ is the option value as a function of asset price S and time t.

There have been many extensions to this model, some people call them 'improvements.' But these extensions are all trivial compared with the breakthrough in modelling that was the original equation.

Long answer
Facts about the Black–Scholes equation:

- The equation follows from certain assumptions and from a mathematical and financial argument that involves hedging.
- The equation is linear and homogeneous (we say 'there is no right-hand side,' i.e. no non-V terms) so that you can value a portfolio of derivatives by summing the values of the individual contracts.
- It is a partial differential equation because it has more than one independent variable, here S and t.
- It is of parabolic type, meaning that one of the variables, t, only has a first-derivative term, and the other S has a second-derivative term.
- It is of backward type, meaning that you specify a final condition representing the option payoff at expiry and then solve backwards in time to get the option value now. You

can tell it's backward by looking at the sign of the t-derivative term and the second S-derivative term, when on the same side of the equals sign they are both the same sign. If they were of opposite signs then it would be a forward equation.

- The equation is an example of a diffusion equation or heat equation. Such equations have been around for nearly two hundred years and have been used to model all sorts of physical phenomena.
- The equation requires specification of two parameters, the risk-free interest rate and the asset volatility. The interest rate is easy enough to measure, and the option value isn't so sensitive to it anyway. But the volatility is another matter, rather harder to forecast accurately.
- Because the main uncertainty in the equation is the volatility one sometimes thinks of the equation less as a valuation tool and more as a way of understanding the relationship between options and volatility.
- The equation is easy to solve numerically, by finite-difference or Monte Carlo methods, for example.
- The equation can be generalized to allow for dividends, other payoffs, stochastic volatility, jumping stock prices, etc.

And then there are the Black–Scholes *formulæ* which are solutions of the equation in special cases, such as for calls and puts.

The equation contains four terms:

$\dfrac{\partial V}{\partial t} =$ time decay, how much the option value changes by

if the stock price doesn't change

$\dfrac{1}{2}\sigma^2 S^2 \dfrac{\partial^2 V}{\partial S^2} =$ convexity term, how much a hedged position

makes on average from stock moves

$rS\dfrac{\partial V}{\partial S} =$ drift term allowing for the growth in the stock at the risk-free rate

and

$-rV =$ the discounting term, since the payoff is received at expiration but you are valuing the option now.

References and Further Reading

Black, F & Scholes, M 1973 The pricing of options and corporate liabilities. *Journal of Political Economy* **81** 637–659

Which Numerical Method should I Use and When?

Short answer

The three main numerical methods in common use are Monte Carlo, finite difference and numerical quadrature. (I'm including the binomial method as just a simplistic version of finite differences.) Monte Carlo is great for complex path dependency and high dimensionality, and for problems which cannot easily be written in differential equation form. Finite difference is best for low dimensions and contracts with decision features such as early exercise, ones which have a differential equation formulation. Numerical quadrature is for when you can write the option value as a multiple integral.

Example

You want to price a fixed-income contract using the BGM model. Which numerical method should you use? BGM is geared up for solution by simulation, so you would use a Monte Carlo simulation.

You want to price an option which is paid for in instalments, and you can stop paying and lose the option at any time if you think it's not worth keeping up the payments. This may be one for finite-difference methods since it has a decision feature.

You want to price a European, non-path-dependent contract on a basket of equities. This may be recast as a multiple integral and so you would use a quadrature method.

Long answer

Finite-difference methods

Finite-difference methods are designed for finding numerical solutions of differential equations. Since we work with a mesh, not unlike the binomial method, we will find the contract value at all points is stock price-time space. In quantitative finance that differential equation is almost always of diffusion or parabolic type. The only real difference between the partial differential equations are the following:

- Number of dimensions
- Functional form of coefficients
- Boundary/final conditions
- Decision features
- Linear or non-linear.

Number of dimensions Is the contract an option on a single underlying or many? Is there any strong path dependence in the payoff? Answers to these questions will determine the number of dimensions in the problem. At the very least we will have two dimensions: S or r, and t. Finite-difference methods cope extremely well with smaller number of dimensions, up to four, say. Above that they get rather time consuming.

Functional form of coefficients The main difference between an equity option problem and a single-factor interest rate option problem is in the functional form of the drift rate and the volatility. These appear in the governing partial differential equations as coefficients. The standard model for equities is the lognormal model, but there are many more 'standard' models in fixed income. Does this matter? No, not if you are solving the equations numerically, only if you are trying to find a closed-form solution in which case the simpler the coefficients the more likely you are to find a closed-form solution.

Boundary/final conditions In a numerical scheme the difference between a call and a put is in the final condition. You tell the finite-difference scheme how to start. And in finite-difference schemes in finance we start at expiration and work towards the present. Boundary conditions are where we tell the scheme about things like knock-out barriers.

Decision features Early exercise, instalment premiums, chooser features, are all examples of embedded decisions seen in exotic contracts. Coping with these numerically is quite straightforward using finite-difference methods, making these numerical techniques the natural ones for such contracts. The difference between a European and an American option is about three lines of code in a finite-difference program and less than a minute's coding.

Linear or non-linear Almost all quant finance models are linear, so that you can solve for a portfolio of options by solving each contract at a time and adding. Some more modern models are nonlinear. Linear or nonlinear doesn't make that much difference when you are solving by finite-difference methods. So choosing this method gives you a lot of flexibility in the type of model you can use.

Efficiency
Finite differences are very good at coping with low dimensions, and are the method of choice if you have a contract with embedded decisions. They are excellent for non-linear differential equations.

The time taken to price an option and calculate the sensitivities to underlying(s) and time using the explicit finite-difference method will be

$$O(M\epsilon^{-1-d/2}),$$

where M is the number of different options in the portfolio and we want an accuracy of ϵ, and d is the number of dimensions other than time. So if we have a non-path-dependent option on a single underlying then $d = 1$. Note that we may need one piece of code per option, hence M in the above.

Programme of study
If you are new to finite-difference methods and you really want to study them, here is a suggested programme of study.

- **Explicit method/European calls, puts and binaries**: To get started you should learn the explicit method as applied to the Black–Scholes equation for a European option. This is very easy to program and you won't make many mistakes.
- **Explicit method/American calls, puts and binaries**: Not much harder is the application of the explicit method to American options.
- **Crank–Nicolson/European calls, puts and binaries**: Once you've got the explicit method under your belt you should learn the Crank–Nicolson implicit method. This is harder to program, but you will get a better accuracy.
- **Crank–Nicolson/American calls, puts and binaries**: There's not much more effort involved in pricing American-style options than in the pricing of European-style options.
- **Explicit method/path-dependent options**: By now you'll be quite sophisticated and it's time to price a path-dependent contract. Start with an Asian option with discrete sampling, and then try a continuously-sampled Asian. Finally, try your hand at lookbacks.
- **Interest rate products**: Repeat the above programme for non-path-dependent and then path-dependent interest rate products. First price caps and floors and then go on to the index amortizing rate swap.
- **Two-factor explicit**: To get started on two-factor problems price a convertible bond using an explicit method, with both the stock and the spot interest rate being stochastic.
- **Two-factor implicit**: The final stage is to implement the implicit two-factor method as applied to the convertible bond.

Monte Carlo methods

Monte Carlo methods simulate the random behaviour underlying the financial models. So, in a sense they get right to the heart of the problem. Always remember, though, that when pricing you must simulate the risk-neutral random walk(s), the value of a contract is then the expected present value of all cashflows. When implementing a Monte Carlo method look out for the following:

- Number of dimensions
- Functional form of coefficients
- Boundary/final conditions
- Decision features
- Linear or non-linear.

again!

Number of dimensions For each random factor you will have to simulate a time series. It will obviously take longer to do this, but the time will only be proportional to number of factors, which isn't so bad. This makes Monte Carlo methods ideal for higher dimensions when the finite-difference methods start to crawl.

Functional form of coefficients As with the finite-difference methods it doesn't matter too much what the drift and volatility functions are in practice, since you won't be looking for closed-form solutions.

Boundary/final conditions These play a very similar role as in finite differences. The final condition is the payoff function and the boundary conditions are where we implement trigger levels etc.

Decision features When you have a contract with embedded decisions the Monte Carlo method becomes cumbersome. This is easily the main drawback for simulation methods. When we use the Monte Carlo method we only find the option value at today's stock price and time. But to correctly price an American option, say, we need to know what the option value *would be* at every point in stock price-time space. We don't typically find this as part of the Monte Carlo solution.

Linear or non-linear Simulation methods also cope poorly with non-linear models. Some models just don't have a useful interpretation in terms of probabilities and expectations so you wouldn't expect them to be amenable to solution by methods based on random simulations.

Efficiency
If we want an accuracy of ϵ and we have d underlyings then the calculation time is

$$O(d\epsilon^{-3}).$$

It will take longer to price the greeks, but, on the positive side, we can price many options at the same time for almost no extra time cost.

Programme of study
Here is a programme of study for the Monte Carlo path-simulation methods.

- **European calls, puts and binaries on a single equity**: Simulate a single stock path, the payoff for an option, or even a portfolio of options, calculate the expected payoff and present value to price the contract.
- **Path-dependent option on a single equity**: Price a barrier, Asian, lookback, etc.
- **Options on many stocks**: Price a multi-asset contract by simulating correlated random walks. You'll see how time taken varies with number of dimensions.
- **Interest rate derivatives, spot rate model**: This is not that much harder than equities. Just remember to present value along each realized path of rates *before* taking the expectation across all paths.
- **HJM model**: Slightly more ambitious is the HJM interest rate model. Use a single factor, then two factors, etc.
- **BGM model**: A discrete version of HJM.

Numerical integration

Occasionally one can write down the solution of an option-pricing problem in the form of a multiple integral. This is because you can interpret the option value as an expectation of a payoff, and an expectation of the payoff is mathematically just the integral of the product of that payoff function and a probability density function. This is only possible in special cases. The option has to be European, the underlying stochastic differential equation must be explicitly integrable (so the lognormal random walk is perfect for this) and the payoff shouldn't usually be path dependent. So if this is possible then pricing is easy... you have a formula. The only difficulty comes in turning this formula into a number. And that's the subject of numerical integration or quadrature. Look out for the following.

• Can you write down the value of an option as an integral?

That's it in a nutshell.

Efficiency

There are several numerical quadrature methods. But the two most common are based on random number generation again. One uses normally distributed numbers and the other uses what are called low-discrepancy sequences. The low-discrepancy numbers are clever in that they appear superficially to be random but don't have the inevitable clustering that truly random numbers have.

Using the simple normal numbers, if you want an accuracy of ϵ and you are pricing M options the time taken will be

$$O(M\epsilon^{-2}).$$

If you use the low-discrepancy numbers the time taken will be

$$O(M\epsilon^{-1}).$$

You can see that this method is very fast, unfortunately it isn't often applicable.

Programme of study
Here is a programme of study for the numerical quadrature methods.

- **European calls, puts and binaries on a single equity using normal numbers**: Very simple. You will be evaluating a single integral.
- **European calls, puts and binaries on several underlying lognormal equities, using normal numbers**: Very simple again. You will be evaluating a multiple integral.
- **Arbitrary European, non-path-dependent payoff, on several underlying lognormal equities, using normal numbers**: You'll only have to change a single function.
- **Arbitrary European, non-path-dependent payoff, on several underlying lognormal equities, using low-discrepancy numbers**: Just change the source of the random numbers in the previous code.

Summary

Table 2.3: Pros and cons of different methods.

Subject	FD	MC	Quad.
Low dimensions	Good	Inefficient	Good
High dimensions	Slow	Excellent	Good
Path dependent	Depends	Excellent	Not good
Greeks	Excellent	Not good	Excellent
Portfolio	Inefficient	Very good	Very good
Decisions	Excellent	Poor	Very poor
Non-linear	Excellent	Poor	Very poor

References and Further Reading

Wilmott, P 2006 *Paul Wilmott on Quantitative Finance*, second edition. John Wiley & Sons Ltd

What is Monte Carlo Simulation?

Short answer

Monte Carlo simulations are a way of solving probabilistic problems by numerically 'imagining' many possible scenarios or games so as to calculate statistical properties such as expectations, variances or probabilities of certain outcomes. In finance we use such simulations to represent the future behaviour of equities, exchange rates, interest rates, etc., so as to either study the possible future performance of a portfolio or to price derivatives.

Example

We hold a complex portfolio of investments, we would like to know the probability of losing money over the next year since our bonus depends on our making a profit. We can estimate this probability by simulating how the individual components in our portfolio might evolve over the next year. This requires us to have a model for the random behaviour of each of the assets, including the relationship or correlation between them, if any.

Some problems which are completely deterministic can also be solved numerically by running simulations, most famously finding a value for π.

Long answer

It is clear enough that probabilistic problems can be solved by simulations. What is the probability of tossing heads with a coin, just toss the coin often enough and you will find the answer. More on this and its relevance to finance shortly. But many deterministic problems can also be solved this way, provided you can find a probabilistic equivalent of the deterministic problem. A famous example of this is Buffon's needle, a problem and solution dating back to 1777. Draw parallel lines on a table one inch apart. Drop a needle, also one inch long, onto this table. Simple trigonometry will show you that the probability of the needle touching one of the lines is $2/\pi$. So conduct many such experiments to get an approximation to π. Unfortunately because of the probabilistic nature of this method you will have to drop the needle many billions of times to find π accurate to half a dozen decimal places.

There can also be a relationship between certain types of differential equation and probabilistic methods. Stanislaw Ulam, inspired by a card game, invented this technique while working on the Manhattan Project towards the development of nuclear weapons. The name 'Monte Carlo' was given to this idea by his colleague Nicholas Metropolis.

Monte Carlo simulations are used in financial problems for solving two types of problems:

- Exploring the statistical properties of a portfolio of investments or cashflows to determine quantities such as expected returns, risk, possible downsides, probabilities of making certain profits or losses, etc.
- Finding the value of derivatives by exploiting the theoretical relationship between option values and expected payoff under a risk-neutral random walk.

Exploring portfolio statistics The most successful quantitative models represent investments as random walks. There is a whole mathematical theory behind these models, but to appreciate the role they play in portfolio analysis you just need to understand three simple concepts.

First, you need an algorithm for how the most basic investments evolve randomly. In equities this is often the lognormal random walk. (If you know about the real/risk-neutral distinction then you should know that you will be using the real random walk here.) This can be represented on a spreadsheet or in code as how a stock price changes from one period to the next by adding on a random return. In the fixed-income world you may be using the BGM model to model how interest rates of various maturities evolve. In credit you may have a model that models the random bankruptcy of a company. If you have more than one such investment that you must model then you will also need to represent any interrelationships between them. This is often achieved by using correlations.

Once you can perform such simulations of the basic investments then you need to have models for more complicated contracts that depend on them, these are the options/derivatives/contingent claims. For this you need some theory, derivatives theory. This the second concept you must understand.

Finally, you will be able to simulate many thousands, or more, future scenarios for your portfolio and use the results to examine the statistics of this portfolio. This is, for example, how classical **Value at Risk** can be estimated, among other things.

Pricing derivatives We know from the results of **risk-neutral pricing** that in the popular derivatives theories the value of an option can be calculated as the present value of the expected payoff under a risk-neutral random walk. And calculating expectations for a single contract is just a simple example of the above-mentioned portfolio analysis, but just for a single option and using the risk-neutral instead of the real random walk. Even though the pricing models can often be written as deterministic partial differential equations they can be solved in a probabilistic way, just as Stanislaw Ulam noted for other, non-financial, problems. This pricing methodology for derivatives was first proposed by the actuarially trained Phelim Boyle in 1977.

Whether you use Monte Carlo for probabilistic or deterministic problems the method is usually quite simple to implement in basic form and so is extremely popular in practice.

References and Further Reading

Boyle, P 1977 Options: a Monte Carlo approach. *Journal of Financial Economics* **4** 323–338

Glasserman, P 2003 *Monte Carlo Methods in Financial Engineering.* Springer Verlag

Jäckel, P 2002 *Monte Carlo Methods in Finance.* John Wiley & Sons Ltd

What is the Finite-Difference Method?

Short answer
The finite-difference method is a way of approximating *differential* equations, in continuous variables, into *difference* equations, in discrete variables, so that they may be solved numerically. It is a method particularly useful when the problem has a small number of dimensions, that is, independent variables.

Example
Many financial problems can be cast as partial differential equations. Usually these cannot be solved analytically and so they must be solved numerically.

Long answer
Financial problems starting from stochastic differential equations as models for quantities evolving randomly, such as equity prices or interest rates, are using the language of calculus. In calculus we refer to gradients, rates of change, slopes, sensitivities. These mathematical 'derivatives' describe how fast a dependent variable, such as an option value, changes as one of the independent variables, such as an equity price, changes. These sensitivities are technically defined as the ratio of the infinitesimal change in the dependent variable to the infinitesimal change in the independent. And we need an infinite number of such infinitesimals to describe an entire curve. However, when trying to calculate these slopes numerically, on a computer, for example, we cannot deal with infinites and infinitesimals, and have to resort to approximations.

Technically, a definition of the delta of an option is

$$\Delta = \frac{\partial V}{\partial S} = \lim_{h \to 0} \frac{V(S+h,t) - V(S-h,t)}{2h}$$

where $V(S,t)$ is the option value as a function of stock price, S, and time, t. Of course, there may be other independent variables. The limiting procedure in the above is the clue to how to approximate such derivatives based on continuous variables by differences based on discrete variables.

The first step in the finite-difference methods is to lay down a grid, such as the one shown in Figure 2.8.

The grid typically has equally spaced asset points, and equally spaced time steps, although in more sophisticated

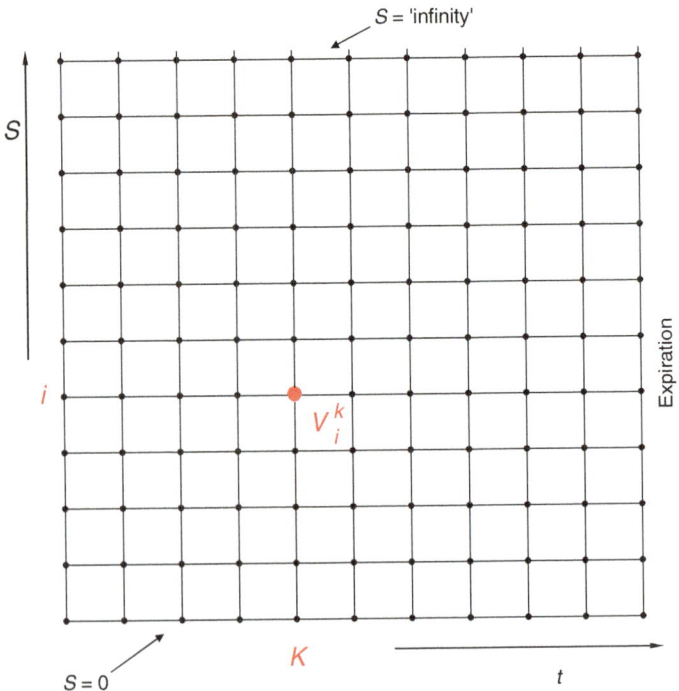

Figure 2.8: The finite-difference grid.

schemes these can vary. Our task will be to find numerically an approximation to the option values at each of the nodes on this grid.

The classical option pricing differential equations are written in terms of the option function, $V(S, t)$, say, a single derivative with respect to time, $\frac{\partial V}{\partial t}$, the option's theta, the first derivative with respect to the underlying, $\frac{\partial V}{\partial S}$, the option's delta, and the second derivative with respect to the underlying, $\frac{\partial^2 V}{\partial S^2}$, the option's gamma. I am explicitly assuming we have an equity or exchange rate as the underlying in these examples. In the world of fixed income we might have similar equations but just read interest rate, r, for underlying, S, and the ideas carry over.

A simple discrete approximation to the partial derivative for theta is

$$\theta = \frac{\partial V}{\partial t} \approx \frac{V(S, t) - V(S, t - \delta t)}{\delta t}$$

where δt is the time step between grid points. Similarly,

$$\Delta = \frac{\partial V}{\partial S} \approx \frac{V(S + \delta S, t) - V(S - \delta S, t)}{2\,\delta S}$$

where δS is the asset step between grid points. There is a subtle difference between these two expressions. Note how the time derivative has been discretized by evaluating the function V at the 'current' S and t, and also one time step before. But the asset derivative uses an approximation that straddles the point S, using $S + \delta S$ and $S - \delta S$. The first type of approximation is called a one-sided difference, the second is a central difference. The reasons for choosing one type of approximation over another are to do with stability and accuracy. The central difference is more accurate than a one-sided difference and tends to be preferred for the delta approximation, but when used for the time derivative it can lead to instabilities in the numerical scheme. (Here I am going to describe the explicit finite-difference scheme, which is the easiest such scheme, but is one which suffers from being unstable if the wrong time discretization is used.)

The central difference for the gamma is

$$\Gamma = \frac{\partial^2 V}{\partial S^2} \approx \frac{V(S + \delta S, t) - 2\ V(S, t) + V(S - \delta S, t)}{\delta S^2}.$$

Slightly changing the notation so that V_i^k is the option value approximation at the ith asset step and kth time step, we can write

$$\theta \approx \frac{V_i^k - V_i^{k-1}}{\delta t}, \ \ \Delta \approx \frac{V_{i+1}^k - V_{i-1}^k}{2\ \delta S} \text{ and } \Gamma \approx \frac{V_{i+1}^k - 2V_i^k + V_{i-1}^k}{\delta S^2}.$$

Finally, plugging the above, together with $S = i\ \delta S$, into the Black–Scholes equation gives the following discretized version of the equation:

$$\frac{V_i^k - V_i^{k-1}}{\delta t} + \frac{1}{2}\sigma^2 i^2 \delta S^2 \ \frac{V_{i+1}^k - 2V_i^k + V_{i-1}^k}{\delta S^2}$$
$$+ ri\ \delta S\ \frac{V_{i+1}^k - V_{i-1}^k}{2\ \delta S} - rV_i^k = 0.$$

This can easily be rearranged to give V_i^{k-1} in terms of V_{i+1}^k, V_i^k and V_{i-1}^k, as shown schematically in Figure 2.9.

In practice we know what the option value is as a function of S, and hence i, at expiration. And this allows us to work backwards from expiry to calculate the option value today, one time step at a time.

The above is the most elementary form of the finite-difference methods, there are many other more sophisticated versions.

The advantages of the finite-difference methods are in their speed for low-dimensional problems, those with up to three sources of randomness. They are also particularly good when the problem has decision features such as early exercise

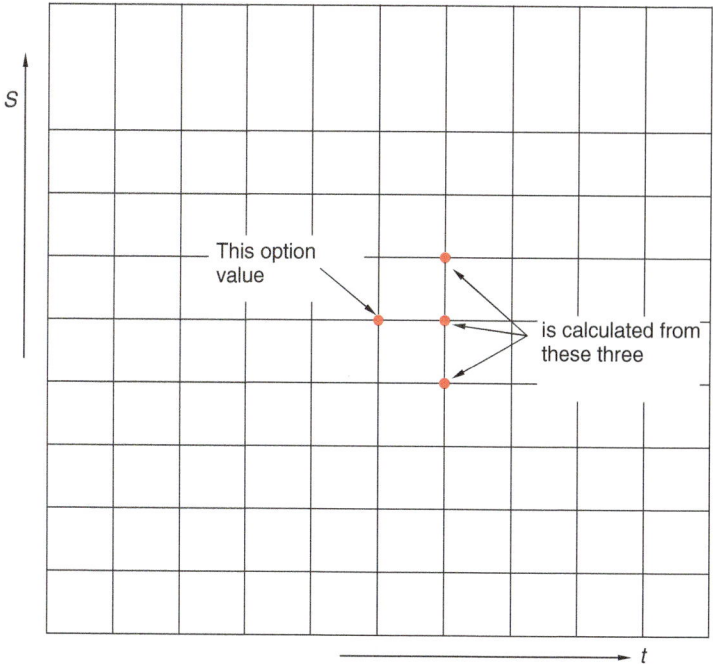

Figure 2.9: The relationship between option values in the explicit method.

because at each node we can easily check whether the option price violates arbitrage constraints.

References and Further Reading

Wilmott, P 2006 *Paul Wilmott on Quantitative Finance*, second edition. John Wiley & Sons Ltd

What is a Poisson Process and What are its Uses in Finance?

Short answer
The Poisson process is a model for a discontinuous random variable. Time is continuous, but the variable is discrete. The variable can represent a 'jump' in a quantity or the occurrence of an 'event.'

Example
The Poisson process is used to model radioactive decay. In finance it can be used to model default or bankruptcy, or to model jumps in stock prices.

Long answer
The most important stochastic process in quantitative finance is **Brownian Motion** (the Wiener process) used to model continuous asset paths. The next most useful stochastic process is the Poisson process. It is used to model discontinuous jumps in an asset price or to model events such as bankruptcy.

A Poisson process dq is defined by the limit as dt goes to zero of

$$dq = \begin{cases} 0 & \text{with probability } 1 - \lambda\, dt \\ 1 & \text{with probability } \lambda\, dt. \end{cases}$$

There is therefore a probability $\lambda\, dt$ of a jump in q in the time step dt. The parameter λ is called the **intensity** of the Poisson process, it is a parameter, possibly time dependent, or dependent on other variables in a model, that represents the likelihood of the jump.

When a model has both a Wiener process dX term and a Poisson process dq term it is called a **jump-diffusion model**.

If the Poisson process is used to model events, such as the arrival of buses at a bus-stop, then we can answer questions about the number of buses arriving with a certain time using the following result:

$$P(q(t) = n) = e^{-\lambda t}\frac{(\lambda t)^n}{n!}.$$

This is the probability of exactly n buses having arrived (or there having been n asset price jumps) in a time t.

References and Further Reading

Ross, SM 1995 *Stochastic Processes*. John Wiley & Sons Ltd

What is a Jump-Diffusion Model and How does it Affect Option Values?

Short answer

Jump-diffusion models combine the continuous Brownian motion seen in Black–Scholes models (the diffusion) with prices that are allowed to jump discontinuously. The timing of the jump is usually random, and this is represented by a Poisson process. The size of the jump can also be random. As you increase the frequency of the jumps (all other parameters remaining the same), the values of calls and puts increase. The prices of binaries, and other options, can go either up or down.

Example

A stock follows a lognormal random walk. Every month you roll a dice. If you roll a one then the stock price jumps discontinuously. The size of this jump is decided by a random number you draw from a hat. (This is not a great example because the Poisson process is a continuous process, not a monthly event.)

Long answer

A **Poisson process** can be written as dq where dq is the jump in a random variable q during time t to $t + dt$. dq is 0 with probability $1 - \lambda \, dt$ and 1 with probability $\lambda \, dt$. Note how the probability of a jump scales with the time period over which the jump may happen, dt. The scale factor λ is known as the **intensity** of the process, the larger λ the more frequent the jumps.

This process can be used to model a discontinuous financial random variable, such as an equity price, volatility or an interest rate. Although there have been research papers on pure jump processes as financial models it is more usual to combine jumps with classical **Brownian motion**. The model for equities, for example, is often taken to be

$$dS = \mu S \, dt + \sigma S \, dX + (J - 1)S \, dq.$$

dq is as defined above, with intensity λ, $J - 1$ is the jump size, usually taken to be random as well. Jump-diffusion models can do a good job of representing the real-life phenomenon of discontinuity in variables, and capturing the fat tails seen in returns data.

The model for the underlying asset results in a model for option prices. This model will be an integro-differential equation, typically, with the integral term representing the probability of the stock jumping a finite distance discontinuously. Unfortunately, markets with jumps of this nature are incomplete, meaning that options cannot be hedged to eliminate risk. In order to derive option-pricing equations one must therefore make some assumptions about risk preferences or introduce more securities with which to hedge.

Robert Merton was the first to propose jump-diffusion models. He derived the following equation for equity option values

$$\frac{\partial V}{\partial t} + \frac{1}{2}\sigma^2 S^2 \frac{\partial^2 V}{\partial S^2} + rS\frac{\partial V}{\partial S} - rV$$
$$+ \lambda E\left[V(JS,t) - V(S,t)\right] - \lambda \frac{\partial V}{\partial S}SE\left[J - 1\right] = 0.$$

$E[\cdot]$ is the expectation taken over the jump size. In probability terms this equation represents the expected value of the discounted payoff. The expectation being over the risk-neutral measure for the diffusion but the real measure for the jumps.

There is a simple solution of this equation in the special case that the logarithm of J is Normally distributed. If the logarithm of J is Normally distributed with standard deviation σ' and if we write

$$k = E[J - 1]$$

then the price of a European non-path-dependent option can be written as

$$\sum_{n=0}^{\infty} \frac{1}{n!} e^{-\lambda'(T-t)} (\lambda'(T-t))^n V_{BS}(S, t; \sigma_n, r_n).$$

In the above

$$\lambda' = \lambda(1+k), \quad \sigma_n^2 = \sigma^2 + \frac{n\sigma'^2}{T-t}$$

and

$$r_n = r - \lambda k + \frac{n \ln(1+k)}{T-t},$$

and V_{BS} is the Black–Scholes formula for the option value in the absence of jumps. This formula can be interpreted as the sum of individual Black–Scholes values each of which assumes that there have been n jumps, and they are weighted according to the probability that there will have been n jumps before expiry.

Jump-diffusion models can do a good job of capturing steepness in volatility skews and smiles for short-dated option, something that other models, such as stochastic volatility, have difficulties in doing.

References and Further Reading

Cox, J & Ross, S 1976 Valuation of options for alternative stochastic processes. *Journal of Financial Economics* **3** 145–166

Kingman, JFC 1995 *Poisson Processes*. Oxford Science Publications

Lewis, A series of articles in *Wilmott* magazine, September 2002 to August 2004

Merton, RC 1976 Option pricing when underlying stock returns are discontinuous. *Journal of Financial Economics* **3** 125–144

What is Meant by 'Complete' and 'Incomplete' Markets?

Short answer

A complete market is one in which a derivative product can be artificially made from more basic instruments, such as cash and the underlying asset. This usually involves dynamically rebalancing a portfolio of the simpler instruments, according to some formula or algorithm, to replicate the more complicated product, the derivative. Obviously, an incomplete market is one in which you can't replicate the option with simpler instruments.

Example

The classic example is replicating an equity option, a call, say, by continuously buying or selling the equity so that you always hold the amount

$$\Delta = e^{-D(T-t)}N(d_1),$$

in the stock, where

$$N(x) = \frac{1}{\sqrt{2\pi}} \int_{-\infty}^{x} e^{-\frac{1}{2}\phi^2} d\phi$$

and

$$d_1 = \frac{\ln(S/E) + (r - D + \frac{1}{2}\sigma^2)(T - t)}{\sigma\sqrt{T - t}}.$$

Long answer

A slightly more mathematical, yet still quite easily understood, description is to say that a complete market is one for which there exist the same number of linearly independent securities as there are states of the world in the future.

Consider, for example, the binomial model in which there are two states of the world at the next time step, and there are also two securities, cash and the stock. That is a complete market. Now, after two time steps there will be three possible states of the world, assuming the binomial model recombines so that an up–down move gets you to the same place as down–up. You might think that you therefore need three securities for a complete market. This is not the case because after the first time step you get to change the quantity of stock you are holding; this is where the dynamic part of the replication comes in.

In the equity world the two most popular models for equity prices are the lognormal, with a constant volatility, and the binomial. Both of these result in complete markets, you can replicate other contracts in these worlds.

In a complete market you can replicate derivatives with the simpler instruments. But you can also turn this on its head so that you can hedge the derivative with the underlying instruments to make a risk-free instrument. In the binomial model you can replicate an option from stock and cash, or you can hedge the option with the stock to make cash. Same idea, same equations, just move terms to be on different sides of the 'equals' sign.

As well as resulting in replication of derivatives, or the ability to hedge them, complete markets also have a nice mathematical property. Think of the binomial model. In this model you specify the probability of the stock rising (and hence falling because the probabilities must add to 1). It turns out that this probability does not affect the price of the option. This is a simple consequence of complete markets, since you can hedge the option with the stock you don't care whether the stock rises or falls, and so you don't care what the probabilities are. People can therefore disagree on the probability of a stock rising or falling but still agree on the value of an option, as long as they share the same view on the stock's volatility.

In probabilistic terms we say that in a complete market there exists a unique martingale measure, but for an incomplete market there is no unique martingale measure. The interpretation of this is that even though options are risky instruments in complete markets we don't have to specify our own degree of risk aversion in order to price them.

Enough of complete markets: where can we find incomplete markets? The answer is 'everywhere.' In practice, all markets are incomplete because of real-world effects that violate the assumptions of the simple models.

Take volatility as an example. As long as we have a lognormal equity random walk, no transaction costs, continuous hedging, perfectly divisible assets,..., and constant volatility then we have a complete market. If that volatility is a known time-dependent function then the market is still complete. It is even still complete if the volatility is a known function of stock price and time. But as soon as that volatility becomes random then the market is no longer complete. This is because there are now more states of the world than there are linearly independent securities. In reality, we don't know what volatility will be in the future so markets are incomplete.

We also get incomplete markets if the underlying follows a jump-diffusion process. Again more possible states than there are underlying securities.

Another common reason for getting incompleteness is if the underlying or one of the variables governing the behaviour of the underlying is random. Options on terrorist acts cannot be hedged since terrorist acts aren't traded (to my knowledge at least).

We still have to price contracts even in incomplete markets, so what can we do? There are two main ideas here. One is to price the actuarial way, the other is to try to make all option prices consistent with each other.

The actuarial way is to look at pricing in some average sense. Even if you can't hedge the risk from each option it doesn't necessarily matter in the long run. Because in that long run you will have made many hundreds or thousands of option trades, so all that really matters is what the average price of each contract should be, even if it is risky. To some extent this relies on results from the **Central Limit Theorem**. This is called the actuarial approach because it is how the insurance business works. You can't hedge the lifespan of individual policyholders but you can figure out what will happen to hundreds of thousands of them *on average* using actuarial tables.

The other way of pricing is to make options consistent with each other. This is commonly used when we have stochastic volatility models, for example, and is also often seen in fixed-income derivatives pricing. Let's work with the stochastic volatility model to get inspiration. Suppose we have a lognormal random walk with stochastic volatility. This means we have two sources of randomness (stock and volatility) but only one quantity with which to hedge (stock). That's like saying that there are more states of the world than underlying securities, hence incompleteness. Well, we know we can hedge the stock price risk with the stock, leaving us with only one source of risk that we can't get rid of. That's like saying there is one extra degree of freedom in states of the world than there are securities. Whenever you have risk that you can't get rid of you have to ask how that risk should be valued. The more risk the more return you expect to make in excess of the risk-free rate. This introduces the idea of the market price of risk. Technically in this case it introduces the market price of *volatility* risk. This measures the excess expected return in relation to unhedgeable risk. Now all options on this stock with the random volatility have the same sort of unhedgeable risk, some may have more or less risk than others but they are all exposed to volatility risk.

The end result is a pricing model which explicitly contains this market price of risk parameter. This ensures that the prices of all options are consistent with each other via this 'universal' parameter. Another interpretation is that you price options in terms of the prices of other options.

References and Further Reading

Joshi, M 2003 *The Concepts and Practice of Mathematical Finance.* Cambridge University Press

Merton, RC 1976 Option pricing when underlying stock returns are discontinuous. *Journal of Financial Economics* **3** 125–144

Wilmott, P 2006 *Paul Wilmott on Quantitative Finance*, second edition. John Wiley & Sons Ltd

Can I use Real Probabilities to Price Derivatives?

Short answer

Yes. But you may need to move away from classical quantitative finance.

Example

Some modern derivatives models use ideas from utility theory to price derivatives. Such models may find a use in pricing derivatives that cannot be dynamically hedged.

Long answer

Yes and no. There are lots of reasons why risk-neutral pricing doesn't work perfectly in practice, because markets are **incomplete** and dynamic hedging is impossible. If you can't continuously dynamically hedge then you cannot eliminate risk and so risk neutrality is not so relevant. You might be tempted to try to price using real probabilities instead. This is fine, and there are plenty of theories on this topic, usually with some element of utility theory about them. For example, some theories use ideas from **Modern Portfolio Theory** and look at real averages and real standard deviations.

For example you could value options as the **certainty equivalent** value under the real random walk, or maybe as the *real* expectation of the present value of the option's payoff plus or minus some multiple of the standard deviation. (Plus if you are selling, minus if buying.) The 'multiple' represents a measure of your risk aversion.

But there are two main problems with this.

1. You need to be able to measure real probabilities. In classical stochastic differential equation models this means knowing the real drift rate, often denoted by μ for

equities. This can be very hard, much harder than measuring volatility. Is it even possible to say whether we are in a bull or bear market? Often not! And you need to project forward, again even harder, and harder than forecasting volatility.

2. You need to decide on a utility function or a measure of risk aversion. This is not impossible, a bank could tell all its employees 'From this day forward the bank's utility function is ...' Or tests can be used to estimate an individual's utility function by asking questions about his attitude to various trades, this can all be quantified. But at the moment this subject is still seen as too academic.

Although the assumptions that lead to risk neutrality are clearly invalid the results that follow, and the avoidance of the above two problems, means that more people than not are swayed by its advantages.

References and Further Reading

Ahn, H & Wilmott, P 2003 Stochastic volatility and mean-variance analysis. *Wilmott* magazine No. 03 84–90

Ahn, H & Wilmott, P 2007 Jump diffusion, mean and variance: how to dynamically hedge, statically hedge and to price. *Wilmott* magazine May 96–109

Ahn, H & Wilmott, P 2008 Dynamic hedging is dead! Long live static hedging! *Wilmott* magazine January 80–87

What is Volatility?

Short answer
Volatility is annualized standard deviation of returns. Or is it? Because that is a statistical measure, necessarily backward looking, and because volatility seems to vary, and we want to know what it will be in the future, and because people have different views on what volatility will be in the future, things are not that simple.

Example
Actual volatility is the σ that goes into the Black–Scholes partial differential equation. Implied volatility is the number in the Black–Scholes formula that makes a theoretical price match a market price.

Long answer
Actual volatility is a measure of the amount of randomness in a financial quantity at any point in time. It's what Desmond Fitzgerald calls the 'bouncy, bouncy.' It's difficult to measure, and even harder to forecast but it's one of the main inputs into option-pricing models.

It's difficult to measure since it is defined mathematically via standard deviations, which requires historical data to calculate. Yet actual volatility is not a historical quantity but an instantaneous one.

Realized/historical volatilities are associated with a period of time, actually two periods of time. We might say that the daily volatility over the last sixty days has been 27%. This means that we take the last sixty days' worth of daily asset prices and calculate the volatility. Let me stress that this has two associated timescales, whereas actual volatility has none. This tends to be the default estimate of future volatility in the absence of any more sophisticated model. For example, we might assume that the volatility of the next sixty days is the same as over the previous sixty days. This will give us an idea of what a sixty-day option might be worth.

Implied volatility is the number you have to put into the Black–Scholes option-pricing equation to get the theoretical price to match the market price. Often said to be the market's estimate of volatility.

Let's recap. We have **actual volatility**, which is the instantaneous amount of noise in a stock price return. It is sometimes modelled as a simple constant, sometimes as time dependent, sometimes as stock and time dependent, sometimes as stochastic, sometimes as a jump process, and sometimes as uncertain, that is, lying within a range. It is impossible to measure exactly; the best you can do is to get a statistical estimate based on past data. But this is the parameter we would dearly love to know because of its importance in pricing derivatives. Some hedge funds believe that their edge is in forecasting this parameter better than other people, and so profit from options that are mispriced in the market.

Since you can't see actual volatility people often rely on measuring **historical** or **realized volatility**. This is a backward looking statistical measure of what volatility has been. And then one assumes that there is some information in this data that will tell us what volatility will be in the future. There are several models for measuring and forecasting volatility and we will come back to them shortly.

Implied volatility is the number you have to put into the Black–Scholes option-pricing *formula* to get the theoretical price to match the market price. This is often said to be the market's estimate of volatility. More correctly, option prices are governed by supply and demand. Is that the same as the market taking a view on future volatility? Not necessarily because most people buying options are taking a directional view on the market and so supply and demand reflects direction rather than volatility. But because people who hedge options are not exposed to direction only volatility it looks to them as if people are taking a view on volatility when they are more probably taking a view on direction, or simply buying out-of-the-money puts as insurance against a crash. For example, the market falls, people panic, they buy puts, the price of puts and hence implied volatility goes up. Where the price stops depends on supply and demand, not on anyone's estimate of future volatility, within reason.

Implied volatility levels the playing field so you can compare and contrast option prices across strikes and expirations.

There is also **forward volatility**. The adjective 'forward' is added to anything financial to mean values in the future. So forward volatility would usually mean volatility, either actual or implied, over some time period in the future. Finally **hedging volatility** means the parameter that you plug into a delta calculation to tell you how many of the underlying to sell short for hedging purposes.

Since volatility is so difficult to pin down it is a natural quantity for some interesting modelling. Here are some of the approaches used to model or forecast volatility.

Econometric models These models use various forms of time series analysis to estimate current and future expected actual volatility. They are typically based on some regression of volatility against past returns and they may involve autoregressive or moving-average components. In this category are the **GARCH** type of models. Sometimes one models the square of volatility, the variance, sometimes one uses high-low-open-close data and not just closing prices, and sometimes one models the logarithm of volatility. The latter seems to be quite promising because there is evidence that actual volatility is lognormally distributed. Other work in this area decomposes the volatility of a stock into components, market volatility, industry volatility and firm-specific volatility. This is similar to **CAPM** for returns.

Deterministic models   The simple Black–Scholes formulæ assume that volatility is constant or time dependent. But market data suggests that implied volatility varies with strike price. Such market behaviour cannot be consistent with a volatility that is a deterministic function of time. One way in which the Black–Scholes world can be modified to accommodate strike-dependent implied volatility is to assume that actual volatility is a function of both time and the price of the underlying. This is the **deterministic volatility (surface)** model. This is the simplest extension to the Black–Scholes world that can be made to be consistent with market prices. All it requires is that we have $\sigma(S, t)$, and the Black–Scholes partial differential equation is still valid. The interpretation of an option's value as the present value of the expected payoff under a risk-neutral random walk also carries over. Unfortunately the Black–Scholes closed-form formulæ are no longer correct. This is a simple and popular model, but it does not capture the dynamics of implied volatility very well.

Stochastic volatility   Since volatility is difficult to measure, and seems to be forever changing, it is natural to model it as stochastic. The most popular model of this type is due to Heston. Such models often have several parameters which can either be chosen to fit historical data or, more commonly, chosen so that theoretical prices calibrate to the market. Stochastic volatility models are better at capturing the dynamics of traded option prices better than deterministic models. However, different markets behave differently. Part of this is because of the way traders look at option prices. Equity traders look at implied volatility versus strike, FX traders look at implied volatility versus delta. It is therefore natural for implied volatility curves to behave differently in these two markets. Because of this there have grown up the sticky strike, sticky delta, etc., models, which model how the implied volatility curve changes as the underlying moves.

Poisson processes There are times of low volatility and times of high volatility. This can be modelled by volatility that jumps according to a Poisson process.

Uncertain volatility An elegant solution to the problem of modelling the unseen volatility is to treat it as uncertain, meaning that it is allowed to lie in a specified range but whereabouts in that range it actually is, or indeed the probability of being at any value, are left unspecified. With this type of model we no longer get a single option price, but a range of prices, representing worst-case scenario and best-case scenario.

References and Further Reading

Avellaneda, M, Levy, A & Parás, A 1995 Pricing and hedging derivative securities in markets with uncertain volatilities. *Applied Mathematical Finance* **2** 73–88

Derman, E & Kani, I 1994 Riding on a smile. *Risk* magazine **7** (2) 32–39 (February)

Dupire, B 1994 Pricing with a smile. *Risk* magazine **7** (1) 18–20 (January)

Heston, S 1993 A closed-form solution for options with stochastic volatility with application to bond and currency options. *Review of Financial Studies* **6** 327–343

Javaheri, A 2005 *Inside Volatility Arbitrage*. John Wiley & Sons Ltd

Lewis, A 2000 *Option Valuation under Stochastic Volatility*. Finance Press

Lyons, TJ 1995 Uncertain volatility and the risk-free synthesis of derivatives. *Applied Mathematical Finance* **2** 117–133

Rubinstein, M 1994 Implied binomial trees. *Journal of Finance* **69** 771–818

Wilmott, P 2006 *Paul Wilmott on Quantitative Finance*, second edition. John Wiley & Sons Ltd

What is the Volatility Smile?

Short answer

Volatility smile is the phrase used to describe how the implied volatilities of options vary with their strikes. A **smile** means that out-of-the-money puts and out-of-the-money calls both have higher implied volatilities than at-the-money options. Other shapes are possible as well. A slope in the curve is called a **skew**. So a negative skew would be a download-sloping graph of implied volatility versus strike.

Example

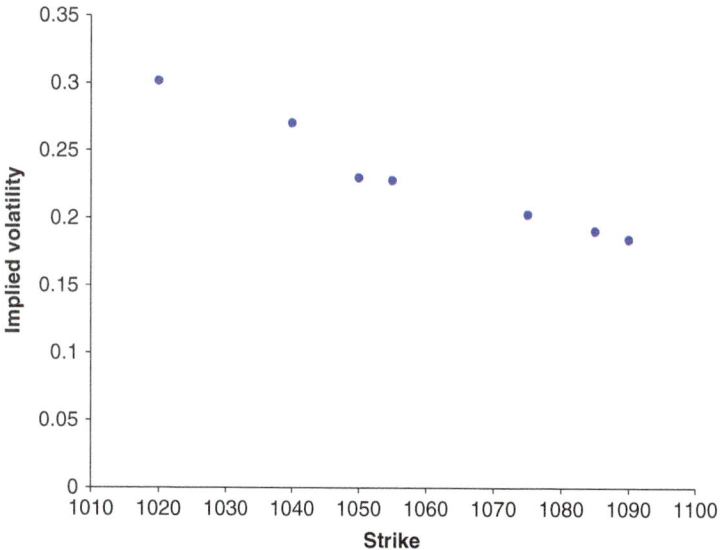

Figure 2.10: The volatility 'smile' for one-month SP500 options, February 2004.

Long answer

Let us begin with how to calculate the implied volatilities. Start with the prices of traded vanilla options, usually the mid price between bid and offer, and all other parameters needed in the Black–Scholes formulæ, such as strikes, expirations, interest rates, dividends, *except* for volatilities. Now ask the question: What volatility must be used for each option series so that the theoretical Black–Scholes price and the market price are the same?

Although we have the Black–Scholes formula for option values as a function of volatility, there is no formula for the implied volatility as a function of option value, it must be calculated using some bisection, Newton–Raphson, or other numerical technique for finding zeros of a function. Now plot these implied volatilities against strike, one curve per expiration. That is the implied volatility smile. If you plot implied volatility against both strike and expiration as a three-dimensional plot, then that is the implied volatility surface. Often you will find that the smile is quite flat for long-dated options, but getting steeper for short-dated options.

Since the Black–Scholes formulæ assume constant volatility (or with a minor change, time-dependent volatility) you might expect a flat implied volatility plot. This does not appear to be the case from real option-price data. How can we explain this? Here are some questions to ask.

- Is volatility constant?
- Are the Black–Scholes formulæ correct?
- Do option traders use the Black–Scholes formulæ?

Volatility does not appear to be constant. By this we mean that actual volatility is not constant, actual volatility being the amount of randomness in a stock's return. Actual volatility is something you can try to measure from a stock price time series, and would exist even if options didn't exist. Although it is easy to say with confidence that actual volatility is not constant, it is altogether much harder to estimate the future behaviour of volatility. So that might explain why implied volatility is not constant, and people believe that volatility is not constant.

If volatility is not constant then the Black–Scholes formulæ are not correct. (Again, there is the small caveat that the Black–Scholes formulæ can work if volatility is a known *deterministic* function of time. But I think we can also confidently dismiss this idea as well.)

Despite this, option traders do still use the Black–Scholes formulæ for vanilla options. Of all the models that have been invented, the Black–Scholes model is still the most popular for vanilla contracts. It is simple and easy to use, it has very few parameters, it is very robust. Its drawbacks are quite well understood. But very often, instead of using models without some of the Black–Scholes' drawbacks, people 'adapt' Black–Scholes to accommodate those problems. For example, when a stock falls dramatically we often see a temporary increase in its volatility. How can that be squeezed into the Black–Scholes framework? Easy, just bump up the implied volatilities for option with lower strikes. A low strike put option will be out of the money until the stock falls, at which point it may be at the money, and at the same time volatility might rise. So, bump up the volatility of all of the out-of-the-money puts. This deviation from the flat-volatility Black–Scholes world tends to get more pronounced closer to expiration.

A more general explanation for the volatility smile is that it incorporates the kurtosis seen in stock returns. Stock returns are not normal, stock prices are not lognormal. Both have fatter tails than you would expect from normally distributed returns. We know that, theoretically, the value of an option is the present value of the expected payoff under a risk-neutral random walk. If that risk-neutral probability density function has fat tails then you would expect option prices to be higher than Black–Scholes for very low and high strikes. Hence higher implied volatilities, and the smile.

Another school of thought is that the volatility smile and skew exist because of supply and demand. Option prices come less from an analysis of probability of tail events than from simple agreement between a buyer and a seller. Out-of-the-money puts are a cheap way of buying protection against a crash. But any form of insurance is expensive; after all, those selling the insurance also want to make a profit. Thus out-of-the-money puts are relatively over-priced. This explains high implied volatility for low strikes. At the other end, many people owning stock will write out-of-the-money call options (so-called covered call writing) to take in some premium, perhaps when markets are moving sideways. There will therefore be an over-supply of out-of-the-money calls, pushing the prices down. Net result, a negative skew. Although the simple supply/demand explanation is popular among traders it does not sit comfortably with quants because it does suggest that options are not correctly priced and that there may be arbitrage opportunities.

While on the topic of arbitrage, it is worth mentioning that there are constraints on the skew and the smile that come from examining simple option portfolios. For example, rather obviously, the higher the strike of a call option, the lower its price. Otherwise you could make money rather easily by buying the low strike call and selling the higher strike call. This imposes a constraint on the skew. Similarly, a butter-fly spread has to have a positive value since the payoff can never be negative. This imposes a constraint on the curvature of the smile. Both of these constraints are model independent.

There are many ways to build the volatility-smile effect into an option-pricing model, and still have no arbitrage. The most popular are, in order of complexity, as follows

- Deterministic volatility surface
- Stochastic volatility
- Jump diffusion.

The deterministic volatility surface is the idea that volatility is not constant, or even only a function of time, but a known function of stock price and time, $\sigma(S,t)$. Here the word 'known' is a bit misleading. What we really know are the market prices of vanilla options, a snapshot at one instant in time. We must now figure out the correct function $\sigma(S,t)$ such that the theoretical value of our options matches the market prices. This is mathematically an inverse problem, essentially find the parameter, volatility, knowing some solutions, market prices. This model may capture the volatility surface exactly at an instant in time, but it does a very poor job of capturing the dynamics, that is, how the data change with time.

Stochastic volatility models have two sources of randomness, the stock return and the volatility. One of the parameters in these models is the correlation between the two sources of randomness. This correlation is typically negative so that a fall in the stock price is often accompanied by a rise in volatility. This results in a negative skew for implied volatility. Unfortunately, this negative skew is not usually as pronounced as the real market skew. These models can also explain the smile. As a rule one pays for convexity. We see this in the simple Black–Scholes world where we pay for gamma. In the stochastic volatility world we can look at the second derivative of option value with respect to volatility, and if it is positive we would expect to have to pay for this convexity – that is, option values will be relatively higher wherever this quantity is largest. For a call or put in the world of constant volatility we have

$$\frac{\partial^2 V}{\partial \sigma^2} = S\sqrt{T-t}\,\frac{d_1 d_2 e^{-D(T-t)}e^{-d_1^2/2}}{\sqrt{2\pi}\,\sigma}.$$

This function is plotted in Figure 2.11 for $S = 100$, $T - t = 1$, $\sigma = 0.2$, $r = 0.05$ and $D = 0$. Observe how it is positive away from the money, and small at the money. (Of course, this is a bit of a cheat because on one hand I am talking about random volatility and yet using a formula that is only correct for constant volatility.)

Stochastic volatility models have greater potential for capturing dynamics, but the problem, as always, is knowing which stochastic volatility model to choose and how to find its parameters. When calibrated to market prices you will still usually find that supposed constant parameters in your model keep changing. This is often the case with calibrated

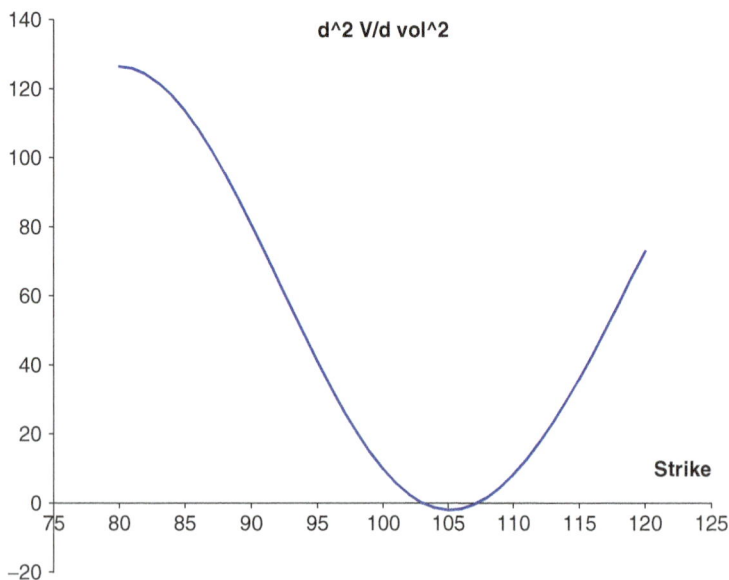

Figure 2.11: $\partial^2 V / \partial \sigma^2$ versus strike.

models and suggests that the model is still not correct, even though its complexity seems to be very promising.

Jump-diffusion models allow the stock (and even the volatility) to be discontinuous. Such models contain so many parameters that calibration can be instantaneously more accurate (if not necessarily stable through time).

References and Further Reading

Gatheral, J 2006 *The Volatility Surface*. John Wiley & Sons Ltd

Javaheri, A 2005 *Inside Volatility Arbitrage*. John Wiley & Sons Ltd

Taylor, SJ & Xu, X 1994 The magnitude of implied volatility smiles: theory and empirical evidence for exchange rates. *The Review of Futures Markets* **13**

Wilmott, P 2006 *Paul Wilmott on Quantitative Finance*, second edition. John Wiley & Sons Ltd

What is GARCH?

Short answer
GARCH stands for Generalized Auto Regressive Conditional Heteroscedasticity. This is an econometric model used for modelling and forecasting time-dependent variance, and hence volatility, of stock price returns. It represents current variance in terms of past variance(s).

Example
The simplest member of the GARCH family is GARCH(1,1) in which the variance, v_n, of stock returns at time step n is modelled by

$$v_n = (1 - \alpha - \beta)w_0 + \beta v_{n-1} + \alpha v_{n-1}B_{n-1}^2,$$

where w_0 is the long-term variance, α and β are positive parameters, with $\alpha + \beta < 1$, and B_n are independent Brownian motions, that is, random numbers drawn from a normal distribution. The latest variance, v_n, can therefore be thought of as a weighted average of the most recent variance, the latest square of returns, and the long-term average.

Long answer

What? GARCH is one member of a large family of econometric models used to model time-varying variance. They are popular in quantitative finance because they can be used for measuring and forecasting volatility.

It is clear from simple equity or index data that volatility is not constant. If it were then estimating it would be very simple. After all, in finance we have what sometimes seems like limitless quantities of data. Since volatility varies with time we would like at the very least to know what it is *right now*. And, more ambitiously, we would like to know what it is going to be in the future, if not precisely then perhaps know its future expected value. This requires a model.

The simplest popular model assumes that we can get an estimate for volatility over the next N days (the future) by looking at volatility over the previous N days (the past). This **moving window** volatility is initially appealing but suffers from the problem that if there was a one-off jump in the stock price it will remain in the data with the same weight for the next N days and then suddenly drop out. This leads to artificially inflated volatility estimates for a while. One way around this is to use the second most popular volatility model, the **exponentially weighted moving average** (EWMA). This takes the form

$$v_n = \beta v_{n-1} + (1 - \beta)R_{n-1}^2,$$

where β is a parameter between 0 and 1, and the R's are the returns, suitably normalized with the time step. This models the latest variance as a weighted average between the previous variance and the latest square of returns. The larger β the more weight is attached to the distant past and the less to the recent past. This model is also simple and appealing, but it has one drawback. It results in no term structure going into the future. The expected variance tomorrow, the day after, and every day in the future is just today's variance. This is counterintuitive, especially at times when volatility is at historical highs or lows.

And so we consider the third simplest model,

$$v_n = (1 - \alpha - \beta)w_0 + \beta v_{n-1} + \alpha R_{n-1}^2,$$

the GARCH(1,1) model. This adds a constant, long-term variance, to the EWMA model. The expected variance, k time steps in the future, then behaves like

$$E[v_{n+k}] = w_0 + (v_n - w_0)(\alpha + \beta)^n.$$

Since $\alpha + \beta < 1$ this is exponentially decay of the average to its mean. A much nicer, more realistic, time dependence than we get from the EWMA model.

In GARCH(p, q) the (p, q) refers to there being p past variances and q past returns in the estimate:

$$v_n = \left(1 - \sum_{i=1}^{q} \alpha_i - \sum_{i=1}^{p} \beta_i\right) w_0 + \sum_{i=1}^{p} \beta_i v_{n-i} + \sum_{i=1}^{q} \alpha_i R_{n-i}^2.$$

Why? Volatility is a required input for all classical option-pricing models, it is also an input for many asset-allocation problems and risk estimation, such as **Value at Risk**. Therefore it is very important to have a method for forecasting future volatility.

There is one slight problem with these econometric models, however. The econometrician develops his volatility models in discrete time, whereas the option-pricing quant would ideally like a continuous-time stochastic differential equation model. Fortunately, in many cases the discrete-time model can be reinterpreted as a continuous-time model (there is *weak convergence* as the time step gets smaller), and so both the econometrician and the quant are happy. Still, of course, the econometric models, being based on real stock price data, result in a model for the *real* and not the *risk-neutral* volatility process. To go from one to the other requires knowledge of the market price of volatility risk.

How? The parameters in these models are usually determined by **Maximum Likelihood Estimation** applied to the (log)likelihood function. Although this technique is usually quite straightforward to apply there can be difficulties in practice. These difficulties can be associated with

- having insufficient data
- the (log)likelihood function being very 'flat' with respect to the parameters, so that the maximum is insensitive to the parameter values
- estimating the wrong model, including having too many parameters (the best model may be simpler than you think).

Family members

Here are *some* of the other members of the GARCH family. New ones are being added all the time, they are breeding like rabbits. In these models the 'shocks' can typically either have a normal distribution, a Student's t-distribution or a Generalized Error distribution, the latter two having the fatter tails.

NGARCH

$$v_n = (1 - \alpha - \beta)w_0 + \beta v_{n-1} + \alpha \left(R_{n-1} - \gamma \sqrt{v_{n-1}}\right)^2.$$

This is similar to GARCH(1,1) but the parameter γ permits correlation between the stock and volatility processes.

AGARCH Absolute value GARCH. Similar to GARCH but with the volatility (not the variance) being linear in the absolute value of returns (instead of square of returns).

EGARCH Exponential GARCH. This models the logarithm of the variance. The model also accommodates asymmetry in that negative shocks can have a bigger impact on volatility than positive shocks.

REGARCH Range-based Exponential GARCH. This models the low to high range of asset prices over a 'day.'

IGARCH Integrated GARCH. This is a type of GARCH model with further constraints on the parameters.

FIGARCH Fractionally Integrated GARCH. This model uses the fractional differencing lag operator applied to the variance. This adds an extra parameter to the GARCH model, and is such that it includes GARCH and IGARCH as extremes. This model has the long memory, slow decay of volatility as seen in practice.

FIEGARCH Fractionally Integrated Exponential GARCH. This models the logarithm of variance and again has the long memory, slow decay of volatility as seen in practice.

TGARCH Threshold GARCH. This is similar to GARCH but includes an extra term that kicks in when the shock is negative. This gives a realistic asymmetry to the volatility model.

PGARCH Power GARCH. In this model the variance is raised to a power other than zero (logarithm), one (AGARCH) or two. This model can have the long memory, slow decay of volatility seen in practice.

CGARCH Component GARCH. This models variance as the sum of two or more 'components.' In a two-component model, for example, one component is used to capture short-term and another the long-term effects of shocks. This model therefore has the long memory, slow decay of volatility seen in practice.

References and Further Reading

Bollerslev, T 1986 Generalised Autoregressive Conditional Heteroskedasticity. *Journal of Econometrics* **31** 307–327

Engle, R 1982 Autoregressive Conditional Heteroskedasticity with estimates of the variance of United Kingdom inflation. *Econometrica* **5** 987–1008

How Do I Dynamically Hedge?

Short answer

Dynamic hedging, or delta hedging, means the continuous buying or selling of the underlying asset according to some formula or algorithm so that risk is eliminated from an option position. The key point in this is what formula do you use, and, given that in practice you can't hedge continuously, how should you hedge discretely? First, get your delta correct, and this means use the correct formula and estimates for parameters, such as volatility. Second, decide when to hedge based on the conflicting desires of wanting to hedge as often as possible to reduce risk, but as little as possible to reduce any costs associated with hedging.

Example

The implied volatility of a call option is 20% but you think that is cheap and volatility is nearer 40%. Do you put 20% or 40% into the delta calculation? The stock then moves, should you rebalance, incurring some inevitable transactions costs, or wait a bit longer while taking the risks of being unhedged?

Long answer

There are three issues, at least, here. First, what is the correct delta? Second, if I don't hedge very often how big is my risk? Third, when I do rehedge, how big are my transaction costs?

What is the correct delta? Let's continue with the above example, implied volatility 20% but you believe volatility will be 40%. Does 0.2 or 0.4 go into the Black–Scholes delta calculation, or perhaps something else? First let me reassure you that you won't theoretically lose money in either case (or even if you hedge using a volatility somewhere in the 20 to 40 range) as long as you are right about the 40% and you hedge continuously. There will however be a big impact on your P&L depending on which volatility you input.

If you use the actual volatility of 40% then you are guaranteed to make a profit that is the difference between the Black–Scholes formula using 40% and the Black–Scholes formula using 20%.

$$V(S, t; \sigma) - V(S, t; \tilde{\sigma}),$$

where $V(S, t; \sigma)$ is the Black–Scholes formula for the call option and σ denotes actual volatility and $\tilde{\sigma}$ is implied volatility.

That profit is realized in a stochastic manner, so that on a marked-to-market basis your profit will be random each day. This is not immediately obvious, nevertheless it is the case that each day you make a random profit or loss, both equally likely, but by expiration your total profit is a guaranteed number that was known at the outset. Most traders dislike the potentially large P&L swings that you get by hedging, using the forecast volatility that they hedge using implied volatility.

When you hedge with implied volatility, even though it is wrong compared with your forecast, you will still make money. But in this case the profit each day is non-negative and smooth, so much nicer than when you hedge using forecast volatility. The downside is that the final profit depends on the path taken by the underlying. If the stock stays close to the strike then you will make a lot of money. If the stocks goes quickly far into or out of the money then your profit will be small. Hedging using implied volatility gives you a nice, smooth, monotonically increasing P&L but at the cost of not knowing how much money you will make.

The profit each time step is

$$\frac{1}{2}(\sigma^2 - \tilde{\sigma}^2)S^2\Gamma^i \, dt,$$

where Γ^i is the Black–Scholes gamma using implied volatility. You can see from this expression that as long as actual volatility is greater than implied, you will make money from this hedging strategy. This means that you do not have to be all that accurate in your forecast of future actual volatility to make a profit.

How big is my hedging error? In practice you cannot hedge continuously. The Black–Scholes model, and the above analysis, requires continuous rebalancing of your position in the underlying. The impact of hedging discretely is quite easy to quantify.

When you hedge you eliminate a linear exposure to the movement in the underlying. Your exposure becomes quadratic and depends on the gamma of your position. If we use ϕ to denote a normally distributed random variable with mean of zero and variance one, then the profit you make over a time step δt due to the gamma is simply

$$\frac{1}{2}\sigma^2 S^2 \Gamma \, \delta t \, \phi^2.$$

This is in an otherwise perfect Black–Scholes world. The only reason why this is not exactly a Black–Scholes world is because we are hedging at discrete time intervals.

The Black–Scholes model prices in the *expected* value of this expression. You will recognize the $\frac{1}{2}\sigma^2 S^2 \Gamma$ from the Black–Scholes equation. So the **hedging error** is simply

$$\frac{1}{2}\sigma^2 S^2 \Gamma \, \delta t \, (\phi^2 - 1).$$

This is how much you make or lose between each rebalancing.

We can make several important observations about hedging error.

- It is large: it is $O(\delta t)$, which is the same order of magnitude as all other terms in the Black–Scholes model. It is usually much bigger than interest received on the hedged option portfolio.

- On average it is zero: hedging errors balance out.
- It is path dependent: the larger gamma, the larger the hedging errors.
- The total hedging error has standard deviation of $\sqrt{\delta t}$: total hedging error is your final error when you get to expiration. If you want to halve the error you will have to hedge four times as often.
- Hedging error is drawn from a chi-square distribution: that's what ϕ^2 is
- If you are long gamma you will lose money approximately 68% of the time: this is chi-square distribution in action. But when you make money it will be from the tails, and big enough to give a mean of zero. Short gamma you lose only 32% of the time, but they will be large losses
- In practice ϕ is not normally distributed: the fat tails, high peaks we see in practice, will make the above observation even more extreme, perhaps a long gamma position will lose 80% of the time and win only 20%. Still the mean will be zero

Can I optimize my hedge? Suppose I am allowed to rehedge 100 times in a year, should I rehedge at equal time intervals or is there something better? Yes, there is something better. Unfortunately the mathematics is a bit tricky. Take a look at page 343 for some further information on this important topic.

How much will transaction costs reduce my profit? To reduce hedging error we must hedge more frequently, but the downside of this is that any costs associated with trading the underlying will increase. Can we quantify transaction costs? Of course we can.

If we hold a short position in delta of the underlying and then rebalance to the new delta at a time δt later, then we will have had to have bought or sold whatever the change in delta was. As the stock price changes by δS then the delta changes by $\delta S \, \Gamma$. If we assume that costs are proportional to the absolute value of the amount of the underlying bought or sold, such that we pay in costs an amount κ times the value traded then the expected cost each δt will be

$$\kappa \sigma S^2 \sqrt{\delta t} \sqrt{\frac{2}{\pi}} |\Gamma|,$$

where the $\sqrt{\frac{2}{\pi}}$ appears because we have to take the expected value of the absolute value of a normal variable. Since this happens every time step, we can adjust the Black–Scholes equation by subtracting from it the above divided by δt to arrive at

$$\frac{\partial V}{\partial t} + \frac{1}{2}\sigma^2 S^2 \frac{\partial^V}{\partial S^2} + rS\frac{\partial V}{\partial S} - rV - \kappa \sigma S^2 \sqrt{\frac{2}{\pi \, \delta t}}|\Gamma| = 0.$$

This equation is interesting for being nonlinear, so that the value of a long call and a short call will be different. The long call will be less than the Black–Scholes value and a short call higher. The long position is worth less because we have to allow for the cost of hedging. The short position is even more of a liability because of costs.

Crucially we also see that the effect of costs grows like the inverse of the square root of the time between rehedges. As explained above, if we want to halve hedging error we must hedge four times as often. But this would double the effects of transaction costs.

Can I optimize my hedging when there are transaction costs? In practice, people do not rehedge at fixed intervals, except perhaps just before market close. There are many other possible strategies involving hedging when the underlying or delta moves a specified amount, or even strategies involving **utility theory**. Again, the mathematics is usually not easy, and is certainly too much for a FAQs book! If you are interested in this topic, and are feeling brave, take at look at some of the Whalley & Wilmott papers listed below.

References and Further Reading

Ahmad, R & Wilmott, P 2005 Which free lunch would you like today, Sir? *Wilmott* magazine, November

Ahn, H & Wilmott, P 2009 A note on hedging: restricted but optimal delta hedging; mean, variance, jumps, stochastic volatility, and costs. *Wilmott* magazine, in press

Whalley, AE & Wilmott, P 1993a Counting the costs. *Risk* magazine **6** (10) 59–66 (October)

Whalley, AE & Wilmott, P 1993b Option pricing with transaction costs. MFG Working Paper, Oxford

Whalley, AE & Wilmott, P 1994a Hedge with an edge. *Risk* magazine **7** (10) 82–85 (October)

Whalley, AE & Wilmott, P 1994b A comparison of hedging strategies. *Proceedings of the 7th European Conference on Mathematics in Industry* 427–434

Whalley, AE & Wilmott, P 1996 Key results in discrete hedging and transaction costs. In *Frontiers in Derivatives* (eds Konishi, A & Dattatreya, R) 183–196

Whalley, AE & Wilmott, P 1997 An asymptotic analysis of an optimal hedging model for option pricing with transaction costs. *Mathematical Finance* **7** 307–324

Wilmott, P 1994 Discrete charms. *Risk* magazine **7** (3) 48–51 (March)

Wilmott, P 2006 *Paul Wilmott on Quantitative Finance*, second edition. John Wiley & Sons Ltd

What is Serial Autocorrelation and Does it Have a Role in Derivatives?

Short answer
Serial autocorrelation (SAC) is a temporal correlation between a time series and itself, meaning that a move in, say, a stock price one day is not independent of the stock move on a previous day. Usually in quantitative finance we assume that there is no such memory, that's what Markov means. We can measure, and model, such serial autocorrelation with different 'lags.' We can look at the SAC with a one-day lag, this would be the correlation between moves one day and the day before, or with a two-day lag, that would be the correlation between moves and moves two days previously, etc.

Example
Figure 2.12 shows the 252-day rolling SAC, with a lag of one day, for the Dow Jones Industrial index. It is clear from this that there has been a longstanding trend since the late 1970s going from extremely positive SAC to the current extremely negative SAC. (I imagine that many people instinctively felt this!)

Long answer
Very, very few people have published on the subject of serial autocorrelation and derivatives pricing and hedging. Being a specialist in doing things that are important rather than doing what everyone else does, I am obviously one of those few!

Positive SAC is rather like trend following, negative SAC is rather like profit taking. (I use 'rather like' because technically speaking trending is, in stochastic differential equation terms, the function of the growth or *dt* term, whereas SAC is in the random term.) The current level has been seen before, in the early thirties, mid 1960s and late 1980s. (Note that what I have plotted here is a very simplistic

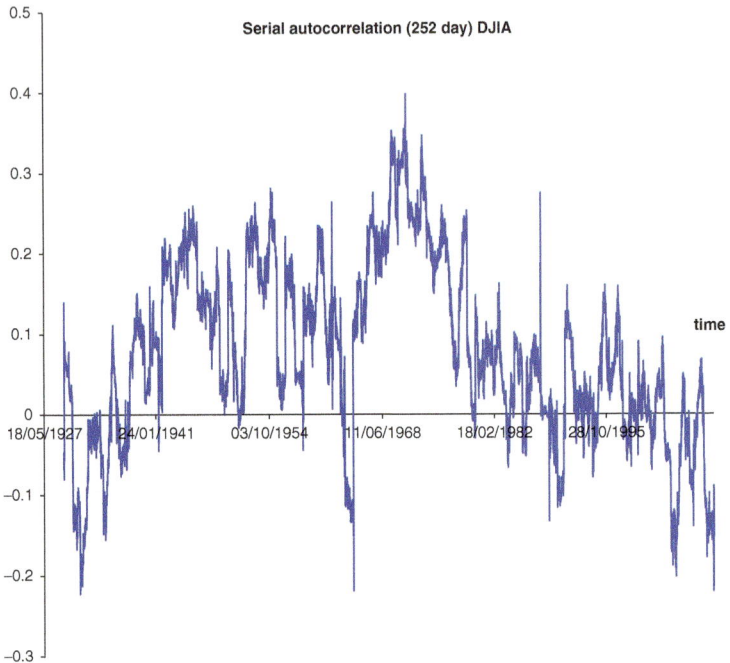

Figure 2.12: The 252-day rolling SAC, with a lag of one day, for the Dow Jones Industrial index.

SAC measure, being just a moving window and therefore with all the well-known faults. The analysis could be improved upon dramatically, but the consequences would not change.)

As far as pricing and hedging of derivatives is concerned there are three main points of interest (as I say, mentioned in very, very few quant books!).

1. The definition of 'volatility' is subtly different when there is SAC. The sequence $+1, -1, +1, -1, +1$, has perfect negative SAC and a volatility of zero! (The difference between volatility with and without SAC is a factor of $\sqrt{1 - \rho^2}$, where ρ is the SAC coefficient.

2. If we can hedge continuously then we don't care about the probability of the stock rising or falling and so we don't really care about SAC. (A fun consequence of this is that options paying off SAC always have zero value theoretically.)

3. In practice, however, hedging must be done discretely. And this is where non-zero SAC becomes important. If you expect that a stock will oscillate up and down wildly from one day to the next, like the above $+1, -1, +1, -1$, example, then what you should do depends on whether you are long or short gamma. If gamma is positive then you trade to capture the extremes if you can. Whereas if you are short gamma then you can wait, because the stock will return to its current level and you will have gained time value. Of course this is very simplistic, and for short gamma positions requires nerves of steel!

References and Further Reading

Bouchaud, J-P, Potters, M & Cornalba, L 2002 Option pricing and hedging with temporal correlations. *International Journal of Theoretical and Applied Finance* **5** 1–14

Wilmott, P 2006 *Paul Wilmott on Quantitative Finance*, second edition. John Wiley & Sons Ltd

What is Dispersion Trading?

Short answer

Dispersion trading is a strategy involving the selling of options on an index against buying a basket of options on individual stocks. Such a strategy is a play on the behaviour of correlations during normal markets and during large market moves. If the individual assets returns are widely dispersed then there may be little movement in the index, but a large movement in the individual assets. This would result in a large payoff on the individual asset options but little to payback on the short index option.

Example

You have bought straddles on constituents of the SP500 index, and you have sold a straddle on the index itself. On most days you don't make much of a profit or loss on this position, gains/losses on the equities balance losses/gains on the index. But one day half of your equities rise dramatically, and one half fall, with there being little resulting move in the index. On this day you make money on the equity options from the gammas, and also make money on the short index option because of time decay. That was a day on which the individual stocks were nicely dispersed.

Long answer

The volatility on an index, σ_I, can be approximated by

$$\sigma_I^2 = \sqrt{\sum_{i=1}^{N}\sum_{j=1}^{N} w_i w_j \rho_{ij} \sigma_i \sigma_j},$$

where there are N constituent stocks, with volatilities σ_i, weight w_i by value and correlations ρ_{ij}. (I say 'approximate' because technically we are dealing with a sum of lognormals which is not lognormal, but this approximation is fine.)

If you know the implied volatilities for the individual stocks and for the index option then you can back out an implied correlation, amounting to an 'average' across all stocks:

$$\frac{\sigma_I^2 - \sum_{i=1}^{N} w_i^2 \sigma_i^2}{\sum_{i=1}^{N} \sum_{i\neq j=1}^{N} w_i w_j \rho_{ij} \sigma_i \sigma_j}.$$

Dispersion trading can be interpreted as a view on this implied correlation versus one's own forecast of where this correlation ought to be, perhaps based on historical analysis.

The competing effects in a dispersion trade are

- gamma profits versus time decay on each of the long equity options
- gamma losses versus time decay (the latter a source of profit) on the short index options
- the amount of correlation across the individual equities.

In the example above we had half of the equities increasing in value, and half decreasing. If they each moved more than their respective implied volatilities would suggest then each would make a profit. For each stock this profit would depend on the option's gamma and the implied volatility, and would be parabolic in the stock move. The index would hardly move and the profit there would also be related to the index option's gamma. Such a scenario would amount to there being an average correlation of zero and the index volatility being very small.

But if all stocks were to move in the same direction the profit from the individual stock options would be the same but this profit would be swamped by the gamma loss on the index options. This corresponds to a correlation of one across all stocks and a large index volatility.

Why might dispersion trading be successful?

- Dynamics of markets are more complex than can be captured by the simplistic concept of correlation.

- Index options might be expensive because of large demand, therefore good to sell.
- You can choose to buy options on equities that are predisposed to a high degree of dispersion. For example, focus on stocks which move dramatically in different directions during times of stress. This may be because they are in different sectors, or because they compete with one another, or because there may be merger possibilities.
- Not all of the index constituents need to be bought. You can choose to buy the cheaper equity options in terms of volatility.

Why might dispersion trading be unsuccessful?

- It is too detailed a strategy to cope with large numbers of contracts with bid–offer spreads.
- You should delta hedge the positions which could be costly.
- You must be careful of downside during market crashes.

References and Further Reading

Grace, D & Van der Klink, R 2005 Dispersion Trading Project. Technical Report, École Polytechnique Fédérale de Lausanne

What is Bootstrapping using Discount Factors?

Short answer
Bootstrapping means building up a forward interest-rate curve that is consistent with the market prices of common fixed-income instruments such as bonds and swaps. The resulting curve can then be used to value other instruments, such as bonds that are not traded.

Example
You know the market prices of bonds with one, two three, five years to maturity. You are asked to value a four-year bond. How can you use the traded prices so that your four-year bond price is consistent?

Long answer
Imagine that you live in a world where interest rates change in a completely deterministic way, no randomness at all. Interest rates may be low now, but rising in the future, for example. The spot interest rate is the interest you receive from one instant to the next. In this deterministic interest-rate world this spot rate can be written as a function of time, $r(t)$. If you knew what this function was you would be able to value fixed-coupon bonds of all maturities by using the discount factor

$$\exp\left(-\int_t^T r(\tau)d\tau\right),$$

to present value a payment at time T to today, t.

Unfortunately you are not told what this r function is. Instead you only know, by looking at market prices of various fixed-income instruments, some constraints on this r function.

As a simple example, suppose you know that a zero-coupon bond, principal \$100, maturing in one year, is worth \$95 today. This tells us that

$$\exp\left(-\int_{t}^{t+1} r(\tau)d\tau\right) = 0.95.$$

Suppose a similar two-year zero-coupon bond is worth \$92, then we also know that

$$\exp\left(-\int_{t}^{t+2} r(\tau)d\tau\right) = 0.92.$$

This is hardly enough information to calculate the entire $r(t)$ function, but it is similar to what we have to deal with in practice. In reality, we have many bonds of different maturity, some without any coupons but most with, and also very liquid swaps of various maturities. Each such instrument is a constraint on the $r(t)$ function.

Bootstrapping is backing out a deterministic spot rate function, $r(t)$, also called the (**instantaneous**) **forward rate curve** that is consistent with all of these liquid instruments.

Note that usually only the simple 'linear' instruments are used for bootstrapping. Essentially this means bonds, but also includes swaps since they can be decomposed into a portfolio of bonds. Other contracts such as caps and floors contain an element of optionality and therefore require a stochastic model for interest rates. It would not make financial sense to assume a deterministic world for these instruments, just as you wouldn't assume a deterministic stock price path for an equity option.

Because the forward rate curve is not uniquely determined by the finite set of constraints that we encounter in practice, we have to impose some conditions on the function $r(t)$.

- Forward rates should be positive, or there will be arbitrage opportunities.

- Forward rates should be continuous (although this is commonsense rather than because of any financial argument).
- Perhaps the curve should also be smooth.

Even with these desirable characteristics the forward curve is not uniquely defined.

Finding the forward curve with these properties amounts to deciding on a way of interpolating 'between the points,' the 'points' meaning the constraints on the integrals of the r function. There have been many proposed interpolation techniques such as

- linear in discount factors
- linear in spot rates
- linear in the logarithm of rates
- piecewise linear continuous forwards
- cubic splines
- Bessel cubic spline
- monotone-preserving cubic spline
- quartic splines

and others.

Finally, the method should result in a forward rate function that is not too sensitive to the input data, the bond prices and swap rates, it must be fast to compute and must not be too local in the sense that if one input is changed it should only impact on the function nearby. And, of course, it should be emphasized that there is no 'correct' way to join the dots.

Because of the relative liquidity of the instruments it is common to use deposit rates in the very short term, bonds and FRAs for the medium term and swaps for the longer end of the forward curve.

Because the bootstrapped forward curve is assumed to come from deterministic rates it is dangerous to use it to price instruments with convexity since such instruments require a model for randomness, as explained by **Jensen's Inequality**.

Two other interpolation techniques are worth mentioning: first, that proposed by Jesse Jones and, second, the Epstein–Wilmott yield envelope.

The method proposed by Jesse Jones involves choosing the forward curve that satisfies all the constraints imposed by

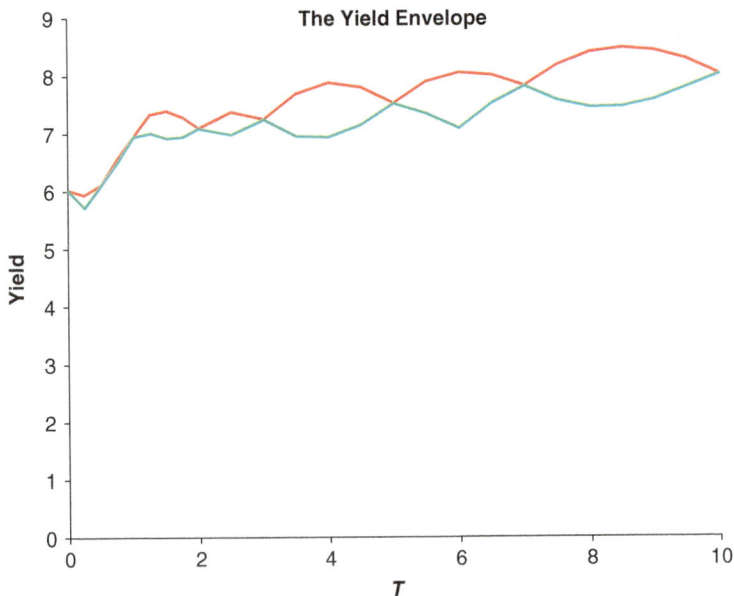

Figure 2.13: The Yield Envelope showing ranges of possible yields. The points at which the range is zero is where there are traded contracts.

traded instruments but is, crically, also not too far from the forward curve as found previously, the day before, say. The idea being simply that this will minimize changes in valuation for fixed-income instruments.

The Epstein–Wilmott model is nonlinear, posing constraints on the dynamics of the short rate. One of the outputs of this model is the **Yield Envelope** (Figure 2.13) which gives no-arbitrage bounds on the forward curve.

References and Further Reading

Epstein, D & Wilmott, P 1997 Yield envelopes. Net Exposure **2** August www.netexposure.co.uk

Epstein, D & Wilmott, P 1998 A new model for interest rates. *International Journal of Theoretical and Applied Finance* **1** 195–226

Epstein, D & Wilmott, P 1999 A nonlinear non-probabilistic spot interest rate model. *Philosophical Transactions A* **357** 2109–2117

Hagan, P & West, G 2008 Methods for constructing a yield curve. *Wilmott* magazine May 70–81

Jones, J 1995 Private communication

Ron, U 2000 A practical guide to swap curve construction. Technical Report 17, Bank of Canada

Walsh, O 2003 The art and science of curve building. *Wilmott* magazine November 8–10

What is the LIBOR Market Model and its Principal Applications in Finance?

Short answer
The LIBOR Market Model (LMM), also known as the BGM or BGM/J model, is a model for the stochastic evolution of forward interest rates. Its main strength over other interest rate models is that it describes the evolution of forward rates that exist, at market-traded maturities, as opposed to theoretical constructs such as the spot interest rate.

Example
In the LMM the variables are a set of forward rates for traded, simple fixed-income instruments. The parameters are volatilities of these and correlations between them. From no arbitrage we can find the risk-neutral drift rates for these variables. The model is then used to price other instruments.

Long answer
The history of interest-rate modelling begins with deterministic rates, and the ideas of yield to maturity, duration etc. The assumption of determinism is not at all satisfactory for pricing derivatives however, because of **Jensen's Inequality**.

In 1976 Fischer Black introduced the idea of treating bonds as underlying assets so as to use the Black–Scholes equity option formulæ for fixed-income instruments. This is also not entirely satisfactory since there can be contradictions in this approach. On the one hand bond prices are random, yet on the other hand interest rates used for discounting from expiration to the present are deterministic. An internally consistent stochastic rates approach was needed.

The first step on the stochastic interest rate path used a very short-term interest rate, the spot rate, as the random factor driving the entire yield curve. The mathematics of these spot-rate models was identical to that for equity models, and the fixed-income derivatives satisfied similar equations as equity derivatives. Diffusion equations governed the prices of derivatives, and derivatives prices could be interpreted as the risk-neutral expected value of the present value of all cash-flows as well. And so the solution methods of finite-difference methods for solving partial differential equations, trees and Monte Carlo simulation carried over. Models of this type are: Vasicek; Cox, Ingersoll & Ross; Hull & White. The advantage of these models is that they are easy to solve numerically by many different methods. But there are several aspects to the downside. First, the spot rate does not exist, it has to be approximated in some way. Second, with only one source of randomness the yield curve is very constrained in how it can evolve, essentially parallel shifts. Third, the yield curve that is output by the model will not match the market yield curve. To some extent the market thinks of each maturity as being semi-independent from the others, so a model should match all maturities otherwise there will be arbitrage opportunities.

Models were then designed to get around the second and third of these problems. A second random factor was introduced, sometimes representing the long-term interest rate (Brennan & Schwartz), and sometimes the volatility of the spot rate (Fong & Vasicek). This allowed for a richer structure for yield curves. And an arbitrary time-dependent parameter (or sometimes two or three such) was allowed in place of what had hitherto been constant(s). The time dependence allowed for the yield curve (and other desired quantities) to be instantaneously matched. Thus was born the idea of calibration, the first example being the Ho & Lee model.

The business of calibration in such models was rarely straightforward. The next step in the development of models was by **Heath, Jarrow & Morton** (HJM) who modelled the evolution of the *entire* yield curve directly so that calibration simply became a matter of specifying an initial curve. The model was designed to be easy to implement via simulation.

Because of the non-Markov nature of the general HJM model it is not possible to solve these via finite-difference solution of partial differential equations, the governing partial differential equation would generally be in an infinite number of variables, representing the infinite memory of the general HJM model. Since the model is usually solved by simulation it is straightforward having any number of random factors and so a very, very rich structure for the behaviour of the yield curve. The only downside with this model, as far as implementation is concerned, is that it assumes a continuous distribution of maturities and the existence of a spot rate.

The LIBOR Market Model (LMM) as proposed by Miltersen, Sandmann, Sondermann, Brace, Gatarek, Musiela and Jamshidian in various combinations and at various times, models *traded* forward rates of different maturities as correlated random walks. The key advantage over HJM is that only prices which exist in the market are modelled, the LIBOR rates. Each traded forward rate is represented by a stochastic differential equation model with a drift rate and a volatility, as well as a correlation with each of the other forward rate models. For the purposes of pricing derivatives we work as usual in a risk-neutral world. In this world the drifts cannot be specified independently of the volatilities and correlations. If there are N forward rates being modelled then there will be N volatility functions to specify and $N(N-1)/2$ correlation functions, the risk-neutral drifts are then a function of these parameters.

Again, the LMM is solved by simulation with the yield curve 'today' being the initial data. Calibration to the yield curve is therefore automatic. The LMM can also be made to be consistent with the standard approach for pricing caps, floors and swaptions using Black 1976. Thus calibration to volatility- and correlation-dependent liquid instruments can also be achieved.

Such a wide variety of interest-rate models have been suggested because there has not been a universally accepted model. This is in contrast to the equity world in which the lognormal random walk is a starting point for almost all models. Whether the LMM is a good model in terms of scientific accuracy is another matter, but its ease of use and calibration and its relationship with standard models make it very appealing to practitioners.

References and Further Reading

Brace, A, Gatarek, D & Musiela, M 1997 The market model of interest rate dynamics. *Mathematical Finance* **7** 127–154

Brennan, M & Schwartz, E 1982 An equilibrium model of bond pricing and a test of market efficiency. *Journal of Financial and Quantitative Analysis* **17** 301–329

Cox, J, Ingersoll, J & Ross, S 1985 A theory of the term structure of interest rates. *Econometrica* **53** 385–467

Fong, G & Vasicek, O 1991, Interest rate volatility as a stochastic factor. Working Paper

Heath, D, Jarrow, R & Morton, A 1992 Bond pricing and the term structure of interest rates: a new methodology. *Econometrica* **60** 77–105

Ho, T & Lee, S 1986 Term structure movements and pricing interest rate contingent claims. *Journal of Finance* **42** 1129–1142

Hull, JC & White, A 1990 Pricing interest rate derivative securities. *Review of Financial Studies* **3** 573–592

Rebonato, R 1996 *Interest-rate Option Models*. John Wiley & Sons Ltd

Vasicek, OA 1977 An equilibrium characterization of the term structure. *Journal of Financial Economics* **5** 177–188

What is Meant by the 'Value' of a Contract?

Short answer
Value usually means the theoretical cost of building up a new contract from simpler products, such as replicating an option by dynamically buying and selling stock.

Example
Wheels cost $10 each. A soapbox is $20. How much is a go-cart? The *value* is $60.

Long answer
To many people the value of a contract is what they see on a screen or comes out of their pricing software. Matters are actually somewhat more subtle than this. Let's work with the above go-cart example.

To the quant the **value** of the go-cart is simply $60, the cost of the soapbox and four wheels, ignoring nails and such-like, and certainly ignoring the cost of manpower involved in building it.

Are you going to sell the go-cart for $60? I don't think so. You'd like to make a profit, so you sell it for $80. That is the **price** of the go-cart.

Why did someone buy it from you for $80? Clearly the $80 must be seen by them as being a reasonable amount to pay. Perhaps they are going to enter a go-carting competition with a first prize of $200. Without the go-cart they can't enter, and they can't win the $200. The possibility of winning the prize money means that the go-cart is **worth** more to them than the $80. Maybe they would have gone as high as $100.

This simple example illustrates the subtlety of the whole valuation/pricing process. In many ways options are like go-carts and valuable insight can be gained by thinking on this more basic level.

The quant rarely thinks like the above. To him value and price are the same, the two words often used interchangeably. And the concept of worth does not crop up.

When a quant has to value an exotic contract he looks to the exchange-traded vanillas to give him some insight into what volatility to use. This is **calibration**. A vanilla trades at $10, say. That is the price. The quant then backs out from a Black–Scholes *valuation* formula the market's implied volatility. By so doing he is assuming that price and value are identical.

Related to this topic is the question of whether a mathematical model *explains* or *describes* a phenomenon. The equations of fluid mechanics, for example, do both. They are based on conservation of mass and momentum, two very sound physical principles. Contrast this with the models for derivatives.

Prices are dictated in practice by supply and demand. Contracts that are in demand, such as out-of-the-money puts for downside protection, are relatively expensive. This is the *explanation* for prices. Yet the mathematical models we use for pricing have no mention of supply or demand. They are based on random walks for the underlying with an unobservable volatility parameter, and the assumption of no arbitrage. The models try to *describe* how the prices ought to behave given a volatility. But as we know from data, if we plug in our own forecast of future volatility into the option-pricing formulæ we will get values that disagree with the market prices. Either our forecast is wrong and the market knows better, or the model is incorrect, or the market is incorrect. Commonsense says all three are to blame. Whenever you calibrate your model by backing out volatility from supply-demand driven prices using a valuation formula you are mixing apples and oranges.

To some extent what the quant is trying to do is the same as the go-cart builder. The big difference is that the go-cart builder does not need a dynamic model for the prices of wheels and soapboxes, his is a static calculation. One go-cart equals one soapbox plus four wheels. It is rarely so simple for the quant. His calculations are inevitably dynamic, his hedge changes as the stock price and time change. It would be like a go-cart for which you had to keep buying extra wheels during the race, not knowing what the price of wheels would be before you bought them. This is where the mathematical models come in, and errors, confusion, and opportunities appear.

And worth? That is a more subjective concept. Quantifying it might require a **utility** approach. As Oscar Wilde said "A cynic is a man who knows the price of everything but the value of nothing."

References and Further Reading

Wilde, O 2003 *The Complete Works of Oscar Wilde*. Harper Perennial

What is Calibration?

Short Answer
Calibration means choosing parameters in your model so that the theoretical prices for exchange-traded contracts output from your model match exactly, or as closely as possible, the market prices at an instant in time. In a sense it is the opposite of fitting parameters to historical time series. If you match prices exactly then you are eliminating arbitrage opportunities, and this is why it is popular.

Example
You have your favourite interest rate model, but you don't know how to decide what the parameters in the model should be. You realize that the bonds, swaps and swaptions markets are very liquid, and presumably very efficient. So you choose your parameters in the model so that your model's theoretical output for these simple instruments is the same as their market prices.

Long answer
Almost all financial models have some parameter(s) that can't be measured accurately. In the simplest non-trivial case, the Black–Scholes model, that parameter is volatility. If we can't measure that parameter how can we decide on its value? For if we don't have an idea of its value then the model is useless.

Two ways spring to mind. One is to use historical data, the other is to use today's price data.

Let's see the first method in action. Examine, perhaps, equity data to try to estimate what volatility is. The problem with that is that it is necessarily backward looking, using data from the past. This might not be relevant to the future. Another problem with this is that it might give prices that are inconsistent with the market. For example, you are interested in buying a certain option. You think volatility is 27%, so you use that number to price the option, and the price you get is $15. However, the market price of that option is $19. Are you still interested in buying it? You can either decide that the option is incorrectly priced or that your volatility estimate is wrong.

The other method is to assume, effectively, that there is information in the market prices of traded instruments. In the above example we ask what volatility must we put into a formula to get the 'correct' price of $19. We then use that number to price other instruments. In this case we have calibrated our model to an instantaneous snapshot of the market at one moment in time, rather than to any information from the past.

Calibration is common in all markets, but is usually more complicated than in the simple example above. Interest rate models may have dozens of parameters or even entire functions to be chosen by matching with the market.

Calibration can therefore often be time consuming. Calibration is an example of an inverse problem, in which we know the answer (the prices of simple contracts) and want to find the problem (the parameters). Inverse problems are notoriously difficult, for example being very sensitive to initial conditions.

Calibration can be misleading, since it suggests that your prices are correct. For example, if you calibrate a model to a set of vanilla contracts, and then calibrate a different model to the same set of vanillas, how do you know which model is better? Both correctly price vanillas today. But how will they perform tomorrow? Will you have to recalibrate? If you use the two different models to price an exotic contract how do you know which price to use? How do you know which gives the better hedge ratios? How will you even know whether you have made money or lost it?

References and Further Reading

Schoutens, W, Simons, E & Tistaert, J 2004 A perfect calibration! Now what? *Wilmott* magazine, March 66–78

What is Option Adjusted Spread?

Short answer

The Option Adjusted Spread (OAS) is the constant spread added to a forward or a yield curve to match the market price of some complex instrument and the present value of all its cash flows.

Example

Analyses using Option Adjusted Spreads are common in Mortgage-Backed Securities (MBS).

Long answer

We know from **Jensen's Inequality** that if there is any convexity (or optionality) together with randomness in a product and model then we have to be careful about not treating random quantities as deterministic, we may miss inherent value. In the case of the Mortgage-Backed Security we have two main sources of randomness, interest rates and prepayment. If we treat these two quantities as deterministic, saying that forward rates and prepayment rates are both fixed, then we will incorrectly value the contract, there will be additional value in the combination of randomness in these two quantities and convexity within the instrument. Treating them as deterministic will give the wrong value. Assuming that MBSs are valued better in the market than in this naive fashion, then there is bound to be a difference between the naive (deterministic) value and the market value. To allow for this one makes a parallel shift in rates and revalues the contract until the theoretical deterministic value and the market price match. The shift in the curve that ensured this is then the OAS. So Option Adjusted Spread just means the spread by which you have to adjust rates to allow for optionality (convexity).

There are problems with this analysis, however. It can be problematic when the instrument is not monotonic in the quantity that has been assumed deterministic. See **bastard greeks**.

References and Further Reading

Hull, JC 2006 *Options, Futures and Other Derivatives*, Pearson

What is the Market Price of Risk?

Short answer
The market price of risk is the return in excess of the risk-free rate that the market wants as compensation for taking risk.

Example
Historically a stock has grown by an average of 20% per annum when the risk-free rate of interest was 5%. The volatility over this period was 30%. Therefore, for each unit of risk this stock returns on average an extra 0.5 return above the risk-free rate. This is the market price of risk.

Long answer
In classical economic theory no rational person would invest in a risky asset unless they expect to beat the return from holding a risk-free asset. Typically risk is measured by standard deviation of returns, or volatility. The market price of risk for a stock is measured by the ratio of expected return in excess of the risk-free interest rate to the standard deviation of returns. Interestingly, this quantity is not affected by leverage. If you borrow at the risk-free rate to invest in a risky asset both the expected return and the risk increase, such that the market price of risk is unchanged. This ratio, when suitably annualized, is also the **Sharpe ratio**.

If a stock has a certain value for its market price of risk then an obvious question to ask is what is the market price of risk for an option on that stock? In the famous Black–Scholes world in which volatility is deterministic and you can hedge continuously and costlessly, then the market price of risk for the option is the same as that for the underlying equity. This is related to the concept of a **complete market** in which options are redundant because they can be replicated by stock and cash.

In derivatives theory we often try to model quantities as stochastic, that is, random. Randomness leads to risk, and risk makes us ask how to value risk, that is, how much return should we expect for taking risk. By far the most important determinant of the role of this market price of risk is the answer to the question, is the quantity you are modelling traded directly in the market?

If the quantity *is* traded directly, the obvious example being a stock, then the market price of risk does not appear in the Black–Scholes option-pricing model. This is because you can hedge away the risk in an option position by dynamically buying and selling the underlying asset. This is the basis of **risk-neutral valuation**. Hedging eliminates exposure to the direction that the asset is going and also to its market price of risk. You will see this if you look at the Black–Scholes equation. There the only parameter taken from the stock random walk is its volatility, there is no appearance of either its growth rate or its price of risk.

On the other hand, if the modelled quantity is not directly traded then there will be an explicit reference in the option-pricing model to the market price of risk. This is because you cannot hedge away associated risk. And because you cannot hedge the risk you must know how much extra return is needed to compensate for taking this unhedgeable risk. Indeed, the market price of risk will typically appear in classical option-pricing models any time you cannot hedge perfectly. So expect it to appear in the following situations:

- When you have a stochastic model for a quantity that is not traded. Examples: stochastic volatility; interest rates (this is a subtle one, the spot rate is *not* traded); risk of default.
- When you cannot hedge. Examples: jump models; default models; transaction costs.

When you model stochastically a quantity that is not traded, then the equation governing the pricing of derivatives is usually of diffusion form, with the market price of risk appearing in the 'drift' term with respect to the non-traded quantity. To make this clear, here is a general example.

Suppose that the price of an option depends on the value of a quantity of a substance called phlogiston. Phlogiston is not traded but either the option's payoff depends on the value of phlogiston, or the value of phlogiston plays a role in the dynamics of the underlying asset. We model the value of phlogiston as

$$d\Phi = \mu_\Phi dt + \sigma_\Phi dX_\Phi.$$

The market price of phlogiston risk is λ_Φ. In the classical option-pricing models we will end up with an equation for an option with the following term

$$\ldots + (\mu_\Phi - \lambda_\Phi \sigma_\Phi) \frac{\partial V}{\partial \Phi} + \ldots = 0.$$

The dots represent all the other terms that one usually gets in a Black–Scholes type of equation. Observe that the expected change in the value of phlogiston, μ_Φ, has been adjusted to allow for the market price of phlogiston risk. We call this the **risk-adjusted** or **risk-neutral drift**. Conveniently, because the governing equation is still of diffusive type, we can continue to use Monte Carlo simulation methods for pricing. Just remember to simulate the risk-neutral random walk

$$d\Phi = (\mu_\Phi - \lambda_\Phi \sigma_\Phi) \, dt + \sigma_\Phi dX_\Phi.$$

and not the real one.

You can imagine estimating the real drift and volatility for any observable financial quantity simply by looking at a time series of the value of that quantity. But how can you estimate its market price of risk? Market price of risk is only observable through option prices. This is the point at which practice and elegant theory start to part company. Market price of risk sounds like a way of calmly assessing required extra value to allow for risk. Unfortunately there is nothing calm about the way that markets react to risk. For example, it is quite simple to relate the slope of the yield curve to the market price of interest rate risk. But evidence from this suggests that market price of risk is itself random, and should perhaps also be modelled stochastically.

Note that when you calibrate a model to market prices of options you are often effectively calibrating the market price of risk. But that will typically be just a snapshot at one point in time. If the market price of risk is random, reflecting people's shifting attitudes from fear to greed and back again, then you are assuming fixed something which is very mobile, and calibration will not work.

There are some models in which the *market* price of risk does not appear because they typically involve using some form of **utility theory** approach to find a person's own price for an instrument rather than the market's.

References and Further Reading

Ahn, H & Wilmott, P 2003 Stochastic volatility and mean-variance analysis. *Wilmott* magazine November 84–90

Markowitz, H 1959 *Portfolio Selection: Efficient Diversification of Investment*. John Wiley & Sons Ltd

Wilmott, P 2006 *Paul Wilmott on Quantitative Finance*, second edition. John Wiley & Sons Ltd

Can I Reverse Engineer a Partial Differential Equation to get at the Model and Contract?

Short answer

Very often you can. You just need to understand what all the terms in a financial partial differential equation represent, all those $\frac{\partial \text{this}}{\partial \text{that}}$ terms and their coefficients. And the final condition for the PDE defines the contract's payoff.

Example

In a typical equation you will see a V, representing 'value.' What is the coefficient in front of it? If it's $r + p$ where r is a risk-free interest rate then the p probably represents a risk of default, so you are dealing with some contract that has the possibility of default.

Long answer

The first thing to look out for is how many independent variables and how many dimensions are there? And what are those variables?

There'll usually be a variable t representing time. The other variables can represent financial quantities that are either traded or not. Usually the symbol will give a clue. If one variable is S that might mean stock price, so you've got an equity option, or it might be an r, so you've got a fixed-income contract, or you might have both, so you've got a hybrid. (I could imagine an interviewer giving an interviewee a differential equation for deconstruction, but one in which the symbols are thoroughly mixed up to cause confusion. Don't worry, the tricks below will help you spot this!)

There are several different types of terms that you see in the financial partial differential equations used for valuing derivatives. There'll usually be a V for value, there'll be first derivatives of V with respect to various variables and there'll be second derivatives of V. There may be a term independent of V. Let's deal with each one of these.

Term independent of V Also called the 'source term' or the 'right-hand side.' This represents a cashflow. The contract will be earning, or paying, money throughout its life. If the term is a function of S then the cashflow is S dependent, if it's a function of t then it's time dependent. Or, if the contract has default risk, see next example, the term may represent a recovery amount.

The V term This is the present-valuing term, so its coefficient is usually r, the risk-free interest rate. If it's $r+p$ then the p is the probability of default, i.e. in a time step dt there is a probability $p\,dt$ of default.

First-derivative terms These can represent all sorts of things. There's always a $\frac{\partial V}{\partial t}$ (unless the contract is perpetual and time homogeneous, so no expiration).

Suppose there's a term like $\frac{\partial V}{\partial H}$ but there's no $\frac{\partial^2 V}{\partial H^2}$ term. In this case the H quantity is not random, it may represent a history-dependent term in a path-dependent option. Its coefficient will represent the quantity that is being sampled over the option's life and the payoff will probably be a function of H.

Suppose there's a term like $\frac{\partial V}{\partial S}$ and also a $\frac{\partial^2 V}{\partial S^2}$ term (although not necessarily using the symbol 'S,' of course). That means that the quantity S is stochastic. The question then becomes is this stochastic quantity traded, like an equity, or not, like volatility. We can tell this by looking at the coefficient of the first derivative. If it's rS (or $(r+p)S$ for a contract with credit risk) then the 'S' is traded. If it's zero then the S may be a futures contract. If it's neither of these then it's not traded, it's just some other financial quantity that is being modelled, such as volatility or an interest rate. (Note that there's a subtlety here, technically the interest rate r is not traded, fixed-income products are *functions* of r, and it's those functions that are traded.) Take a look at the FAQ on the **Market Price of Risk** (page 208) to see how the coefficient of the first derivative change depending on the nature of the independent variable.

Second-derivative terms These terms are associated with randomness, variables that are random. If you see a $\frac{\partial^2 V}{\partial S^2}$ term then you can figure out the amount of randomness (i.e. the coefficient of the dX in its stochastic differential equation) by taking what's in front of the second derivative, multiplying it by two and then taking the square root. That's why if it's an equity option you'll see $\frac{1}{2}\sigma^2 S^2$.

If there is more than one stochastic variable then you should see a cross-derivative term, for example $\frac{\partial^2 V}{\partial S \, \partial r}$. This is because there will typically be a correlation between two random variables. The correlation is backed out by taking the coefficient of this cross-derivative term and dividing by both the amounts of randomness (the coefficients of the two Wiener process terms) in the stochastic differential equations that you've calculated just above.

Other terms? If you see any non-linear terms (e.g. something depending on the value V that is squared, or its absolute value) then you are dealing with a very sophisticated model! (And if you are in a bank then it's a cutting-edge bank!)

Now you've seen how easy it is to reverse engineer the partial differential equation you'll realize that it is equally easy to write down a partial differential for many contracts without having to go through all the hoops of a 'proper derivation.'

Remember, approached correctly quantitative finance is the easiest real-world application of mathematics!

References and Further Reading

Wilmott, P 2006 *Paul Wilmott on Quantitative Finance*, second edition. John Wiley & Sons Ltd

What is the Difference Between the Equilibrium Approach and the No-Arbitrage Approach to Modelling?

Short answer

Equilibrium models balance supply and demand, they require knowledge of investor preferences and probabilities. No-arbitrage models price one instrument by relating it to the prices of other instruments.

Example

The Vasicek interest rate model can be calibrated to historical data. It can therefore be thought of as a representation of an equilibrium model. But it will rarely match traded prices. Perhaps it would therefore be a good trading model. The BGM model matches market prices each day and therefore suggests that there are never any profitable trading opportunities.

Long answer

Equilibrium models represent a balance of supply and demand. As with models of equilibria in other, non-financial, contexts there may be a single equilibrium point, or multiple, or perhaps no equilibrium possible at all. And equilibrium points may be stable such that any small perturbation away from equilibrium will be corrected (a ball in a valley), or unstable such that a small perturbation will grow (a ball on the top of a hill). The price output by an equilibrium model is supposedly correct in an absolute sense.

Genuine equilibrium models in economics usually require probabilities for future outcomes, and a representation of the preferences of investors. The latter perhaps quantified by utility functions. In practice neither of these is usually available, and so the equilibrium models tend to be of more academic than practical interest.

No-arbitrage, or arbitrage-free, models represent the point at which there aren't any arbitrage profits to be made. If the same future payoffs and probabilities can be made with two different portfolios then the two portfolios must both have the same value today, otherwise there would be an arbitrage. In quantitative finance the obvious example of the two port-folios is that of an option on the one hand and a cash and dynamically rebalanced stock position on the other. The end result being the pricing of the option relative to the price of the underlying asset. The probabilities associated with future stock prices falls out of the calculation and preferences are never needed. When no-arbitrage pricing is possible it tends to be used in practice. The price output by a no-arbitrage model is supposedly correct in a relative sense.

For no-arbitrage pricing to work we need to have markets that are **complete**, so that we can price one contract in terms of others. If markets are not complete and we have sources of risk that are unhedgeable then we need to be able to quantify the relevant **market price of risk**. This is a way of consis-tently relating prices of derivatives with the same source of unhedgeable risk, a stochastic volatility for example.

Both the equilibrium and no-arbitrage models suffer from problems concerning parameter stability.

In the fixed-income world, examples of equilibrium models are Vasicek, CIR, Fong & Vasicek. These have parameters which are constant, and which can be estimated from time series data. The problem with these is that they permit very simple arbitrage because the prices that they output for bonds will rarely match traded prices. Now the prices may be correct based on the statistics of the past but are they correct going forward? The models of Ho & Lee and Hull & White are a cross between the equilibrium models and no-arbitrage models. Superficially they look very similar to the former but by making one or more of the parameters time dependent they can be calibrated to market prices and so supposedly remove arbitrage opportunities. But still, if the parameters, be they constant or functions, are not stable then we will have arbitrage. But the question is whether that arbitrage is foreseeable. The interest rate models of HJM and BGM match market prices each day and are therefore even more in the no-arbitrage camp.

References and Further Reading

Brace, A, Gatarek, D & Musiela, M 1997 The market model of interest rate dynamics. *Mathematical Finance* **7** 127–154

Cox, J, Ingersoll, J & Ross, S 1985 A theory of the term structure of interest rates. *Econometrica* **53** 385–467

Fong, G & Vasicek, O 1991, Interest rate volatility as a stochastic factor. Working Paper

Heath, D, Jarrow, R & Morton, A 1992 bond pricing and the term structure of interest rates: a new methodology. *Econometrica* **60** 77–105

Ho, T & Lee, S 1986 Term structure movements and pricing interest rate contingent claims. *Journal of Finance* **42** 1129–1142

Hull, JC & White, A 1990 pricing interest rate derivative securities. *Review of Financial Studies* **3** 573–592

Vasicek, OA 1977 An equilibrium characterization of the term structure. *Journal of Financial Economics* **5** 177–188

How Good is the Assumption of Normal Distributions for Financial Returns?

Short answer

The answer has to be 'it depends.' It depends on the timescale over which returns are measured. For stocks over very short timescales, intraday to several days, the distributions are not normal, they have fatter tails and higher peaks than normal. Over longer periods they start to look more normal, but then over years or decades they look lognormal.

It also depends on what is meant by 'good.' They are very good in the sense that they are simple distributions to work with, and also, thanks to the **Central Limit Theorem**, sensible distributions to work with since there are sound reasons why they might appear. They are also good in that basic stochastic calculus and Itô's lemma assume normal distributions and those concepts are bricks and mortar to the quant.

Example

In Figure 2.14 is the probability density function for the daily returns on the S&P index since 1980, scaled to have zero mean and standard deviation of 1, and also the standardized normal distribution. The empirical peak is higher than the normal distribution and the tails are both fatter.

On 19 October 1987 the SP500 fell 20.5%. What is the probability of a 20% one-day fall in the SP500? Since we are working with over 20 years of daily data, we could argue that empirically there will be a 20% one-day fall in the SPX index every 20 years or so. To get a theoretical estimate, based on normal distributions, we must first estimate the daily standard deviation for SPX returns. Over that period it was 0.0106, equivalent to an average volatility of 16.9%. What is the probability of a 20% or more fall when the standard deviation is

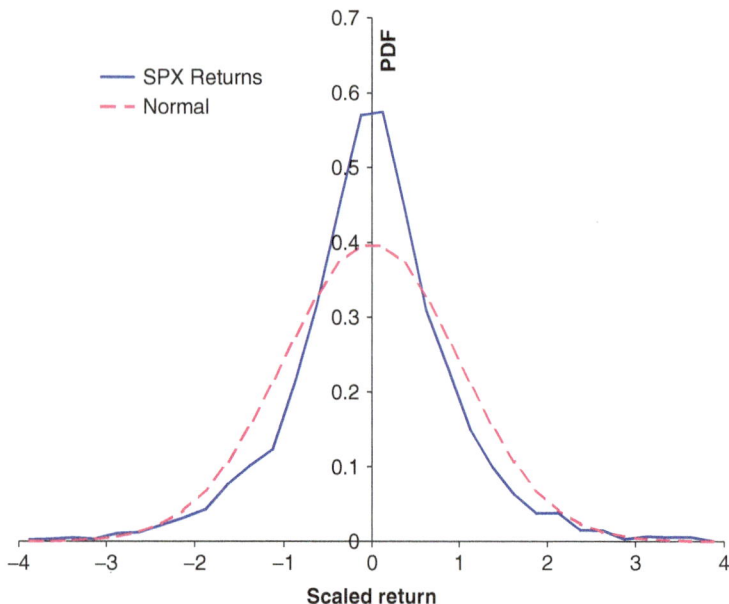

Figure 2.14: The standardized probability density functions for SPX returns and the normal distribution.

0.0106? This is a staggeringly small $1.8 \cdot 10^{-79}$. That is just once every $2 \cdot 10^{76}$ years. Empirical answer: Once every 20 years. Theoretical answer: Once every $2 \cdot 10^{76}$ years. That's how bad the normal-distribution assumption is in the tails.

Long answer
Asset returns are not normally distributed according to empirical evidence. Statistical studies show that there is significant kurtosis (fat tails) and some skewness (asymmetry). Whether this matters or not depends on several factors:

- Are you holding stock for speculation or are you hedging derivatives?
- Are the returns independent and identically distributed (i.i.d.), albeit non normally?
- Is the variance of the distribution finite?
- Can you hedge with other options?

Most basic theory concerning asset allocation, such as **Modern Portfolio Theory**, assumes that returns are normally distributed. This allows a great deal of analytical progress to be made since adding random numbers from normal distributions gives you another normal distribution. But speculating in stocks, without hedging, exposes you to asset direction; you buy the stock since you expect it to rise. Assuming that this stock isn't your only investment then your main concern is for the expected stock price in the future, and not so much its distribution. On the other hand, if you are hedging options then you largely eliminate exposure to asset direction. That's as long as you aren't hedging too infrequently.

If you are hedging derivatives then your exposure is to the range of returns, not the direction. That means you are exposed to variance, if the asset moves are small, or to the sizes and probabilities of discontinuous jumps. Asset models can be divided roughly speaking into those for which the variance of returns is finite, and those for which it is not.

If the variance is finite then it doesn't matter too much whether or not the returns are normal. No, more important is whether they are i.i.d. The 'independent' part is also not that important since if there is any relationship between returns from one period to the next it tends to be very small in practice. The real question is about variance, is it constant? If it is constant, and we are hedging frequently, then we may as well work with normal distributions and the Black–Scholes constant volatility model. However, if it is not constant then we may want to model this more accurately. Typical approaches include the deterministic or local volatility models, in which volatility is a function of asset and time, $\sigma(S, t)$, and stochastic volatility models, in which we represent volatility by another stochastic process. The latter models require a knowledge or specification of risk preferences since volatility risk cannot be hedged just with the underlying asset.

If the variance of returns is infinite, or there are jumps in the asset, then normal distributions and Black–Scholes are less relevant. Models capturing these effects also require a knowledge or specification of risk preferences. It is theoretically even harder to hedge options in these worlds than in the stochastic volatility world.

To some extent the existence of other traded options with which one can statically hedge a portfolio of derivatives can reduce exposure to assumptions about distributions or parameters. This is called hedging **model risk**. This is particularly important for market makers. Indeed, it is instructive to consider the way market makers reduce risk.

- The market maker hedges one derivative with another one, one sufficiently similar as to have similar model exposure.
- As long as the market maker has a positive expectation for each trade, although with some model risk, having a large number of positions he will reduce exposure overall by diversification. This is more like an actuarial approach to model risk.
- If neither of the above is possible then he could widen his bid–ask spreads. He will then only trade with those people who have significantly different market views from him.

References and Further Reading

Mandelbrot, B & Hudson, R 2004 *The (Mis)Behaviour of Markets: A Fractal View of Risk, Ruin and Reward*. Profile Books

How Robust is the Black–Scholes Model?

Short answer
Very robust. You can drop quite a few of the assumptions underpinning Black–Scholes and it won't fall over.

Example
Transaction costs? Simply adjust volatility. Time-dependent volatility? Use root-mean-square-average volatility instead. Interest rate derivatives? Black '76 explains how to use the Black–Scholes formulæ in situations where it wasn't originally intended.

Long answer
Here are some assumptions that seems crucial to the whole Black–Scholes model, and what happens when you drop those assumptions.

Hedging is continuous If you hedge discretely it turns out that Black–Scholes is right *on average*. In other words sometimes you lose because of discrete hedging, sometimes you win, but on average you break even. And Black–Scholes still applies.

There are no transaction costs If there is a cost associated with buying and selling the underlying for hedging this can be modelled by a new term in the Black–Scholes equation that depends on gamma. And that term is usually quite small. If you rehedge at fixed time intervals then the correction is proportional to the absolute value of the gamma, and can be interpreted as a simple correction to volatility in the standard Black–Scholes formulæ. So instead of pricing with a volatility of 20%, say, you might use 17% and 23% to represent the bid–offer spread dues to transaction costs. This little trick only works if the contract has a gamma that is everywhere the same sign, i.e. always and everywhere positive or always and everywhere negative.

Volatility is constant If volatility is time dependent then the Black–Scholes formulæ are still valid as long as you plug in the 'average' volatility over the remaining life of the option. Here average means the root-mean-square average since volatilities can't be added but variances can. Even if volatility is stochastic we can still use basic Black–Scholes formulæ provided the volatility process is independent of, and uncorrelated with, the stock price. Just plug the average variance over the option's lifetime, conditional upon its current value, into the formulæ.

There are no arbitrage opportunities Even if there are arbitrage opportunities because implied volatility is different from actual volatility you can still use the Black–Scholes formulæ to tell you how much profit you can expect to make, and use the delta formulæ to tell you how to hedge. Moreover, if there is an arbitrage opportunity and you don't hedge properly, it probably won't have that much impact on the profit you expect to make.

The underlying is lognormally distributed The Black–Scholes model is often used for interest-rate products which are clearly not lognormal. But this approximation is often quite good, and has the advantage of being easy to understand. This is the model commonly referred to as Black '76.

There are no costs associated with borrowing stock for going short Easily accommodated within a Black–Scholes model, all you need to do is make an adjustment to the risk-neutral drift rate, rather like when you have a dividend.

Returns are normally distributed Thanks to near-continuous hedging and the **Central Limit Theorem** all you really need is for the returns distribution to have a finite variance, the precise shape of that distribution, its skew and kurtosis, don't much matter.

Black–Scholes is a remarkably robust model.

References and Further Reading

Wilmott, P 2006 *Paul Wilmott on Quantitative Finance*, second edition. John Wiley & Sons Ltd

Why is the Lognormal Distribution Important?

Short answer
The lognormal distribution is often used as a model for the distribution of equity or commodity prices, exchange rates and indices. The *normal* distribution is often used to model *returns*.

Example
The stochastic differential equation commonly used to represent stocks,

$$dS = \mu S\, dt + \sigma S\, dX$$

results in a lognormal distribution for S, provided μ and σ are not dependent on stock price.

Long answer
A quantity is lognormally distributed if its logarithm is normally distributed, that is the definition of lognormal. The probability density function is

$$\frac{1}{\sqrt{2\pi}\,bx}\exp\left(-\frac{1}{2b^2}\left(\ln(x)-a\right)^2\right)\quad x\geq 0,$$

where the parameters a and $b > 0$ represent location and scale. The distribution is skewed to the right, extending to infinity and bounded below by zero. (The left limit can be shifted to give an extra parameter, and it can be reflected in the vertical axis so as to extend to minus infinity instead.)

If we have the stochastic differential equation above then the probability density function Figure 2.15 for S in terms of time and the parameters is

$$\frac{1}{\sigma S\sqrt{2\pi t}}e^{-\left(\ln(S/S_0)-(\mu-\frac{1}{2}\sigma^2)t\right)^2/2\sigma^2 t},$$

where S_0 is the value of S at time $t = 0$.

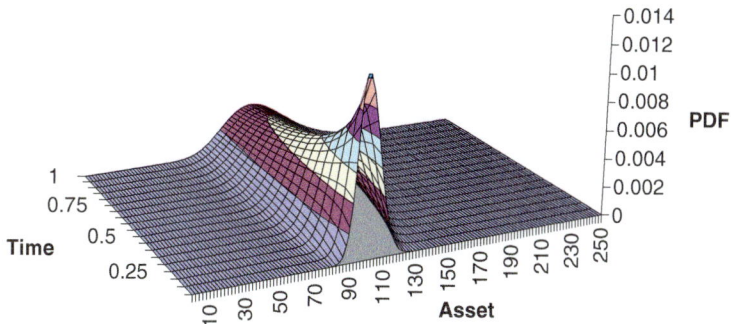

Figure 2.15: The probability density function for the lognormal random walk evolving through time.

You would expect equity prices to follow a random walk around an exponentially growing average. So take the logarithm of the stock price and you might expect that to be normal about some mean. That is the non-mathematical explanation for the appearance of the lognormal distribution.

More mathematically we could argue for lognormality via the **Central Limit Theorem**. Using R_i to represent the random return on a stock price from day $i-1$ to day i we have

$$S_1 = S_0(1 + R_1),$$

the stock price grows by the return from day zero, its starting value, to day 1. After the second day we also have

$$S_2 = S_1(1 + R_2) = S_0(1 + R_1)(1 + R_2).$$

After n days we have

$$S_n = S_0 \prod_{i=1}^{n}(1 + R_i),$$

the stock price is the initial value multiplied by n factors, the factors being one plus the random returns. Taking logarithms of this we get

$$\ln(S_n) = \ln(S_0) + \sum_{i=1}^{n} \ln(1 + R_i),$$

the logarithm of a product being the sum of the logarithms.

Now think **Central Limit Theorem**. If each R_i is random, then so is $\ln(1 + R_i)$. So the expression for $\ln(S_n)$ is just the sum of a large number of random numbers. As long as the R_i are independent and identically distributed and the mean and standard deviation of $\ln(1 + R_i)$ are finite then we can apply the CLT and conclude that $\ln(S_n)$ must be normally distributed. Thus S_n is normally distributed. Since here n is number of 'days' (or any fixed time period) the mean of $\ln(S_n)$ is going to be linear in n, i.e. will grow linearly with time, and the standard deviation will be proportional to the square root of n, i.e. will grow like the square root of time.

References and Further Reading

Wilmott, P 2006 *Paul Wilmott on Quantitative Finance*, second edition. John Wiley & Sons Ltd

What are Copulas and How are they Used in Quantitative Finance?

Short answer

Copulas are used to model joint distribution of multiple underlyings. They permit a rich 'correlation' structure between underlyings. They are used for pricing, for risk management, for pairs trading, etc., and are especially popular in credit derivatives.

Example

You have a basket of stocks which, during normal days, exhibit little relationship with each other. We might say that they are uncorrelated. But on days when the market moves dramatically they all move together. Such behaviour can be modelled by copulas.

Long answer

The technique now most often used for pricing credit derivatives when there are many underlyings is that of the **copula**. The copula[4] function is a way of simplifying the default dependence structure between many underlyings in a relatively transparent manner. The clever trick is to separate the distribution for default for each individual name from the dependence structure between those names. So you can rather easily analyse names one at a time, for calibration purposes, for example, and then bring them all together in a multivariate distribution. Mathematically, the copula way of representing the dependence (one marginal distribution per underlying, and a dependence structure) is no different from specifying a multivariate density function. But it can simplify the analysis.

---

[4]From the Latin for 'join.'

The copula approach in effect allows us to readily go from a single-default world to a multiple-default world almost seamlessly. And by choosing the nature of the dependence, the copula function, we can explore models with rich 'correlation' structure. For example, having a higher degree of dependence during big market moves is quite straightforward.

Take N uniformly distributed random variables $U_1, U_2, \ldots, U_N$, each defined on [0,1]. The copula function is defined as

$$C(u_1, u_2, \ldots, u_N) = \text{Prob}(U_1 \leq u_1, U_2 \leq u_2, \ldots, U_N \leq u_N).$$

Clearly we have

$$C(u_1, u_2, \ldots, 0, \ldots, u_N) = 0,$$

and

$$C(1, 1, \ldots, u_i, \ldots, 1) = u_i.$$

That is the copula function. The way it links many univariate distributions with a single multivariate distribution is as follows.

Let $x_1, x_2, \ldots, x_N$ be random variables with cumulative distribution functions (so-called **marginal** distributions) of $F_1(x_1), F_2(x_2), \ldots, F_N(x_N)$. Combine the Fs with the copula function,

$$C(F_1(x_1), F_2(x_2), \ldots, F_N(x_N)) = F(x_1, x_2, \ldots, x_N)$$

and it's easy to show that this function $F(x_1, x_2, \ldots, x_N)$ is the same as

$$\text{Prob}(X_1 \leq x_1, X_2 \leq x_2, \ldots, X_N \leq x_N).$$

In pricing basket credit derivatives we would use the copula approach by simulating default times of each of the constituent names in the basket. And then perform many such simulations in order to be able to analyse the statistics, the mean, standard deviation, distribution, etc., of the present value of resulting cashflows.

Here are some examples of bivariate copula functions. They are readily extended to the multivariate case.

Bivariate normal

$$C(u,v) = N_2\left(N_1^{-1}(u), N_1^{-1}(v), \rho\right), \quad -1 \leq \rho \leq 1,$$

where N_2 is the bivariate Normal cumulative distribution function, and N_1^{-1} is the inverse of the univariate Normal cumulative distribution function.

Frank

$$C(u,v) = \frac{1}{\alpha}\ln\left(1 + \frac{(e^{\alpha u} - 1)(e^{\alpha v} - 1)}{e^{\alpha} - 1}\right), \quad -\infty < \alpha < \infty.$$

Fréchet–Hoeffding upper bound

$$C(u,v) = \min(u,v).$$

Gumbel–Hougaard

$$C(u,v) = \exp\left(-\left((-\ln u)^{\theta} + (-\ln v)^{\theta}\right)^{1/\theta}\right), \quad 1 \leq \theta < \infty.$$

This copula is good for representing extreme value distributions.

Product

$$C(u,v) = uv$$

One of the simple properties to examine with each of these copulas, and which may help you decide which is best for your purposes, is the **tail index**. Examine

$$\lambda(u) = \frac{C(u,u)}{u}.$$

This is the probability that an event with probability less than u occurs in the first variable given that at the same time an event with probability less than u occurs in the second variable. Now look at the limit of this as $u \to 0$,

$$\lambda_L = \lim_{u \to 0} \frac{C(u, u)}{u}.$$

This tail index tells us about the probability of both extreme events happening together.

References and Further Reading

Li, D 2000 On Default Correlation: A Copula Function Approach. RiskMetrics Working Paper

Nelsen, RB 1999 *An Introduction to Copulas*. Springer Verlag

What is Asymptotic Analysis and How is it Used in Financial Modelling?

Short answer
Asymptotic analysis is about exploiting a large or small parameter in a problem to find simple(r) equations or even solutions. You may have a complicated integral that is much nicer if you approximate it. Or a partial differential equation that can be solved if you can throw away some of the less important terms. Sometimes these are called approximate solutions. But the word 'approximate' does not carry the same technical requirements as 'asymptotic.'

Example
The SABR model is a famous model for a forward rate and its volatility that exploits low volatility of volatility in order for closed-form solutions for option prices to be found. Without that parameter being small we would have to solve the problem numerically.

Long answer
Asymptotic analysis is about exploiting a large or small parameter to find simple(r) solutions/expressions. Outside finance asymptotic analysis is extremely common, and useful. For example, almost all problems in fluid mechanics use it to make problems more tractable. In fluid mechanics there is a very important non-dimensional parameter called the Reynolds number. This quantity is given by

$$Re = \frac{\rho UL}{\mu},$$

where ρ is the density of the fluid, U is a typical velocity in the flow, L is a typical lengthscale, and μ is the fluid's viscosity. This parameter appears in the Navier–Stokes equation which, together with the Euler equation for conservation of mass, governs the flow of fluids. And this means the flow of air around an aircraft, and the flow of glass. These equations are generally difficult to solve. In university lectures they are solved in special cases, perhaps special geometries. In real life during the design of aircraft they are solved numerically. But these equations can often be simplified, essentially approximated, and therefore made easier to solve, in special 'regimes.' The two distinct regimes are those of high Reynolds number and low Reynolds number. When Re is large we have fast flows, which are essentially inviscid to leading order. Assuming that $Re \gg 1$ means that the Navier–Stokes equation dramatically simplifies, and can often be solved analytically. On the other hand if we have a problem where $Re \ll 1$ then we have slow viscous flow. Now the Navier–Stokes equation simplifies again, but in a completely different way. Terms that were retained in the high Reynolds number case are thrown away as being unimportant, and previously ignored terms become crucial.

Remember we are looking at what happens when a parameter gets small, well, let's denote it by ϵ. (Equivalently we also do asymptotic analysis for large parameters, but then we can just define the large parameter to be $1/\epsilon$.) In asymptotic analysis we use the following symbols a lot: $O(\cdot)$, $o(\cdot)$ and $\sim$. These are defined as follows:

We say that $\quad f(\epsilon) = O\big(g(\epsilon)\big) \quad$ as $\epsilon \to 0$ if $\displaystyle\lim_{\epsilon \to 0} \frac{f(\epsilon)}{g(\epsilon)}$ is finite.

We say that $\quad f(\epsilon) = o\big(g(\epsilon)\big) \quad$ as $\epsilon \to 0$ if $\displaystyle\lim_{\epsilon \to 0} \frac{f(\epsilon)}{g(\epsilon)} \to 0$.

We say that $\quad f(\epsilon) \sim g(\epsilon) \quad$ as $\epsilon \to 0$ if $\displaystyle\lim_{\epsilon \to 0} \frac{f(\epsilon)}{g(\epsilon)} = 1$.

In finance there have been several examples of asymptotic analysis.

Transactions costs Transaction costs are usually a small percentage of a trade. There are several models for the impact that these costs have on option prices and in some cases these problems can be simplified by performing an asymptotic analysis as this cost parameter tends to zero. These costs models are invariably non linear.

SABR This model for forward rates and their volatility is a two-factor model. It would normally have to be solved numerically but as long as the volatility of volatility parameter is small then closed-form asymptotic solutions can be found. Since the model requires small volatility of volatility it is best for interest rate derivatives.

Fast drift and high volatility in stochastic volatility models These are a bit more complicated, singular perturbation problems. Now the parameter is large, representing both fast reversion of volatility to its mean and large volatility of volatility. This model is more suited to the more dramatic equity markets which exhibit this behaviour.

References and Further Reading

Hagan, P, Kumar, D, Lesniewski, A & Woodward, D 2002 Managing smile risk. *Wilmott* magazine, September

Rasmussen, H & Wilmott, P 2002 Asymptotic analysis of stochastic volatility models. In *New Directions in Mathematical Finance* (eds Wilmott, P & Rasmussen, H). John Wiley & Sons Ltd

Whalley, AE & Wilmott, P 1997 An asymptotic analysis of an optimal hedging model for option pricing with transaction costs. *Mathematical Finance* **7** 307–324

What is a Free-Boundary Problem and What is the Optimal-Stopping Time for an American Option?

Short answer

A boundary-value problem is typically a differential equation with specified solution on some domain. A free-boundary problem is one for which that boundary is also to be found as part of the solution. When to exercise an American option is an example of a free-boundary problem, the boundary representing the time and place at which to exercise. This is also called an optimal-stopping problem, the 'stopping' here referring to exercise.

Example

Allow a box of ice cubes to melt. As they do there will appear a boundary between the water and the ice, the free boundary. As the ice continues to melt so the amount of water increases and the amount of ice decreases.

Waves on a pond is another example of a free boundary.

Long answer

In a boundary-value problem the specification of the behaviour of the solution on some domain is to pin down the problem so that is has a unique solution. Depending on the type of equation being solved we must specify just the right type of conditions. Too few conditions and the solution won't be unique. Too many and there may not be any solution. In the diffusion equations found in derivatives valuation we must specify a boundary condition in time. This would be the final payoff, and it is an example of a **final condition**. We must also specify two conditions in the asset space. For example, a put option has zero value at infinite stock price and is the discounted strike at zero stock price. These are examples of **boundary conditions**. These three are just the right number and type of conditions for there to exist a unique solution of the Black–Scholes parabolic partial differential equation.

In the American put problem it is meaningless to specify the put's value when the stock price is zero because the option would have been exercised before the stock ever got so low. This is easy to see because the European put value falls below the payoff for sufficiently small stock. If the American option price were to satisfy the same equation and boundary conditions as the European then it would have the same solution, and this solution would permit arbitrage.

The American put should be exercised when the stock falls sufficiently low. But what is 'sufficient' here?

To determine when it is better to exercise than to hold we must abide by two principles:

- The option value must never fall below the payoff, otherwise there will be an arbitrage opportunity.
- We must exercise so as to give the option its highest value.

The second principle is not immediately obvious. The explanation is that we are valuing the option from the point of view of the writer. He must sell the option for the most it could possibly be worth, for if he undervalues the contract he may make a loss if the holder exercises at a better time. Having said that, we must also be aware that we value from the viewpoint of a delta-hedging writer. He is not exposed to direction of the stock. However the holder is probably not hedging and is therefore very exposed to stock direction. The exercise strategy that is best for the holder will probably not be what the writer thinks is best. More of this anon.

The mathematics behind finding the optimal time to exercise, the optimal-stopping problem, is rather technical. But its conclusion can be stated quite succinctly. At the stock price at which it is optimal to exercise we must have

- the option value and the payoff function must be continuous as functions of the underlying
- the delta, the sensitivity of the option value with respect to the underlying, must also be continuous as functions of the underlying.

This is called the **smooth-pasting condition** since it represents the smooth joining of the option value function to its payoff function. (Smooth meaning function and its first derivative are continuous.)

This is now a free-boundary problem. On a fixed, prescribed boundary we would normally impose one condition. (For example, the above case of the put's value at zero stock price.) But now we don't know where the boundary actually is. To pin it down uniquely we impose *two* conditions, continuity of function and continuity of gradient. Now we have enough conditions to find the unknown solution.

Free-boundary problems such as these are nonlinear. You cannot add two together to get another solution. For example, the problem for an American straddle is *not* the same as the sum of the American call and the American put.

Although the fascinating mathematics of free-boundary problems can be complicated, and difficult or impossible to solve analytically, they can be easy to solve by finite-difference methods. For example, if in a finite-difference solution we find that the option value falls below the payoff then we can just replace it with the payoff. As long as we do this each time step before moving on to the next time step, we should get convergence to the correct solution.

As mentioned above, the option is valued by maximizing the value from the point of view of the delta-hedging writer. If the holder is not delta hedging but speculating on direction, he may well find that he wants to exit his position at a time that the writer thinks is suboptimal. In this situation there are three ways to exit:

- sell the option
- delta hedge to expiration
- exercise the option.

The first of these is to be preferred because the option may still have market value in excess of the payoff. The second choice is only possible if the holder can hedge at low cost. If all else fails, he can always close his position by exercising. This is of most relevance in situations where the option is an exotic, over the counter, contract with an early-exercise feature when selling or delta hedging may not be possible.

There are many other contracts with decision features that can be treated in a way similar to early exercise as free-boundary problems. Obvious examples are conversion of a convertible bond, callability, shout options, choosers.

References and Further Reading

Ahn, H & Wilmott, P 2003 On exercising American options: the risk of making more money than you expected. *Wilmott* magazine March 52–63

Crank, JC 1984 *Free and Moving Boundary Value Problems*. Oxford

What are Low-Discrepancy Numbers?

Short answer

Low-discrepancy sequences are sequences of numbers that cover a space without clustering and without gaps, in such a way that adding another number to the sequence also avoids clustering and gaps. They give the appearance of randomness yet are deterministic. They are used for numerically estimating integrals, often in high dimensions. The best-known sequences are due to Faure, Halton, Hammersley, Niederreiter and Sobol'.

Example

You have an option that pays off the maximum of 20 exchange rates on a specified date. You know all the volatilities and correlations. How can you find the value of this contract? If we assume that each exchange rate follows a lognormal random walk, then this problem can be solved as a 20-dimensional integral. Such a high-dimensional integral must be evaluated by numerical quadrature, and an efficient way to do this is to use low-discrepancy sequences.

Long answer

Some financial problems can be recast as integrations, sometimes in a large number of dimensions. For example, the value of a European option on lognormal random variables can be written as the present value of the risk-neutral expected payoff. The expected payoff is an integral of the product of the payoff function and the probability density function for the underlying(s) at expiration. If there are n underlyings then there is typically an n-dimensional integral to be calculated. If the number of dimensions is small then there are simple efficient algorithms for performing this calculation. In one dimension, for example, divide the domain of integration up into uniform intervals and use the trapezium rule. This means evaluating the integrand at a number of points, and as the number of function evaluations increases so the accuracy of the method improves.

Unfortunately, in higher dimensions evaluating the function at uniformly spaced points becomes computationally inefficient.

If the domain of integration is a unit hypercube (and, of course, it can always be transformed into one) then the value of the integral is the same as the average of the function over that domain:

$$\int_0^1 \ldots \int_0^1 f(\mathbf{x}) \, d\mathbf{x} \approx \frac{1}{N} \sum_{i=1}^{N} f(\mathbf{x}_i).$$

where the $\mathbf{x}_i$ are uniformly distributed. This suggests that an alternative method of numerical evaluation of the integral is to select the points in the hypercube from a uniform random distribution and then compute their average. If N function evaluations are performed then the method converges like $O(N^{-1/2})$. This is the Monte Carlo method of numerical integration. Although very simple to perform it suffers from problems associated with the inevitable clustering and gapping that will happen with randomly chosen numbers.

Clearly we would like to use a sequence of numbers that do not suffer from the gapping/clustering problem. This is where low-discrepancy sequences come in.

Low-discrepancy numbers exploit the **Koksma–Hlawka inequality** which puts a bound on the error in the above averaging method for an arbitrary sets of sampling points $\mathbf{x}_i$. The Koksma–Hlawka inequality says that if $f(\mathbf{x})$ is of bounded variation $V(f)$ then

$$| \int_0^1 \ldots \int_0^1 f(\mathbf{x}) \, d\mathbf{x} - \frac{1}{N} \sum_{i=1}^{N} f(\mathbf{x}_i) | \le V(f) D_N^*(\mathbf{x}_1, \ldots, (\mathbf{x})_N)$$

where $D_N^*(\mathbf{x}_1, \ldots, (\mathbf{x})_N)$ is the discrepancy of the sequence. (This discrepancy measures the deviation from a uniform distribution. It is calculated by looking at how many of the sampling points can be found in sub intervals compared with how many there would be for a uniform distribution and then taking the worst case.)

Rather than the details, the important point concerning this result is that the bound is a product of one term specific to the function (its variation, which is independent of the set of sampling points) and a term specific to the set of sampling points (and independent of the function being sampled). So once you have found a set of points that is good, of low discrepancy, then it will work for all integrands of bounded variation.

The popular low-discrepancy sequences mentioned above have

$$D_N^* < C\frac{(\ln N)^n}{N}$$

where C is a constant. Therefore convergence of this **quasi-Monte Carlo** numerical quadrature method is faster than genuinely random Monte Carlo.

Another advantage of these low-discrepancy sequences is that if you collapse the points onto a lower dimension (for example, let all of the points in a two-dimensional plot fall down onto the horizontal axis) they will not be repeated, they will not fall on top of one another. This means that if there is any particularly strong dependence on one of the variables over the others then the method will still give an accurate answer because it will distribute points nicely over lower dimensions.

Unfortunately, achieving a good implementation of some low-discrepancy sequences remains tricky. Some practitioners prefer to buy off-the-shelf software for generating quasi-random numbers.

Intuition Suppose you want to attach a poster to the wall, just along its upper edge, and I am going to give you some pieces of blu-tack or poster putty you can use. Where would you attach the putty? The first piece I give you, you would probably put in the middle. If I gave you another piece you might add it near the end of the top edge. If I give you another piece you might add it near the other edge. The fourth piece would be used to start filling gaps between the other pieces. As I give you more and more pieces you put them in spaces and the poster is then held firmer and firmer. The position of the bits of blu-tack is rather like a low-discrepancy sequence. Note that I don't tell you how much blu-tack you can use, and nor can you remove old bits and place them in new places. If you were allowed to put the putty anywhere on the poster, not just along the top edge, then that would be like a two-dimensional low-discrepancy sequence. (There's also another analogy involving a row of urinals in a gentlemen's convenience.)

References and Further Reading

Barrett, JW, Moore, G & Wilmott, P 1992 Inelegant efficiency. *Risk* magazine **5** (9) 82–84

Cheyette, O 1990 Pricing options on multiple assets. *Adv. Fut. Opt. Res.* **4** 68–91

Faure, H 1969 Résultat voisin d'un théreme de Landau sur le nombre de points d'un réseau dans une hypersphere. *C. R. Acad. Sci. Paris Sér. A* **269** 383–386

Halton, JH 1960 On the efficiency of certain quasi-random sequences of points in evaluating multi-dimensional integrals. *Num. Maths.* **2** 84–90

Hammersley, JM & Handscomb, DC 1964 *Monte Carlo Methods*. Methuen, London

Haselgrove, CB 1961 A method for numerical integration. *Mathematics of Computation* **15** 323–337

Jäckel, P 2002 *Monte Carlo Methods in Finance*. John Wiley & Sons Ltd

Niederreiter, H 1992 *Random Number Generation and Quasi-Monte Carlo Methods.* SIAM

Ninomiya, S & Tezuka, S 1996 Toward real-time pricing of complex financial derivatives. *Applied Mathematical Finance* **3** 1–20

Paskov, SH 1996 New methodologies for valuing derivatives. In *Mathematics of Derivative Securities* (eds Pliska, SR & Dempster, M)

Paskov, SH & Traub, JF 1995 Faster valuation of financial derivatives. *Journal of Portfolio Managament* Fall 113–120

Press, WH, Flannery, BP, Teukolsky, SA & Vetterling, WT 1992 *Numerical Recipes in C.* Cambridge University Press

Sloan, IH & Walsh, L 1990 A computer search of rank two lattice rules for multidimensional quadrature. *Mathematics of Computation* **54** 281–302

Sobol', IM 1967 On the distribution of points in cube and the approximate evaluation of integrals. *USSR Comp. Maths and Math. Phys.* **7** 86–112

Traub, JF & Wozniakowski, H 1994 Breaking intractability. *Scientific American* January 102–107

Wilmott, P 2006 *Paul Wilmott on Quantitative Finance*, second edition. John Wiley & Sons Ltd

What are the Bastard Greeks?

Short answer
The greeks are sensitivities of values, such as option prices, to other financial quantities, such as price. Bastard means 'illegitimate,' here in the sense that sometimes such a concept is not mathematically justified and can give misleading information.

Example
Suppose you value a barrier option assuming constant volatility, σ, of 20% but are then worried whether that volatility is correct. You might measure $\frac{\partial V}{\partial \sigma}$ so that you know how sensitive the option's value is to volatility and whether or not it matters that you have used 20%. Because you are assuming volatility to be constant and then are effectively varying that constant you are measuring a strange sort of hybrid sensitivity which is not the true sensitivity. This could be very dangerous.

Long answer
Bastard greeks are sensitivities to parameters that have been assumed constant. The classic example is the measurement of vega, $\frac{\partial V}{\partial \sigma}$. Let's work with the above example in a bit more detail, and draw some graphs.

Suppose we had an up-and-out call option and we naively priced it using first a 17% volatility and then a 23% volatility, just to get a feel for the possible range of option values. We would get two curves looking like those in Figure 2.16.

This figure suggests that there is a point at which the value is insensitive to the volatility. Vega is zero. So you might think that at this point the option value is insensitive to your choice of volatility. Not so.

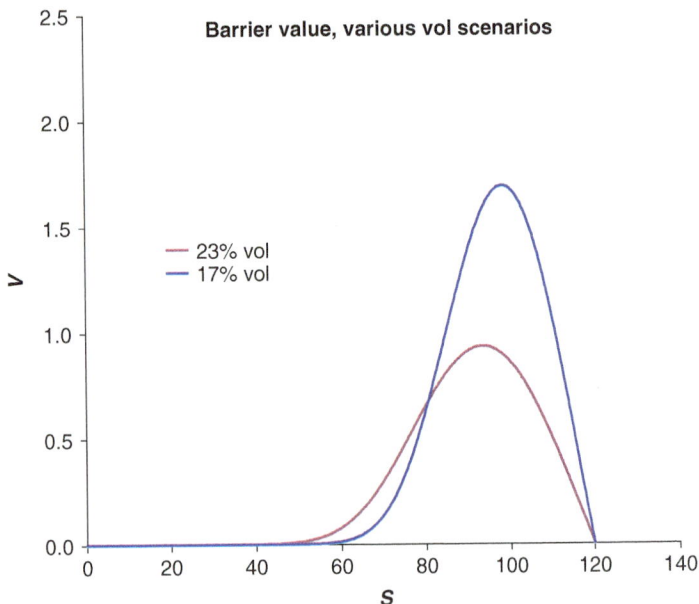

Figure 2.16: Barrier option valued using two different constant volatilities.

Actually, the value is very sensitive to volatility as we shall now see (and in the process also see why vega can be a poor measure of sensitivity).

Figure 2.17 shows the values for the same option, but using best- and worst-case volatilities. The volatility is still in the range 17–23% but, crucially, it is not a constant. Observe the very wide range of values at the point where the vega is zero. The wide range of values is a genuine measure of the sensitivity of the option value to a range of, non-constant, volatilities. Vega is not.

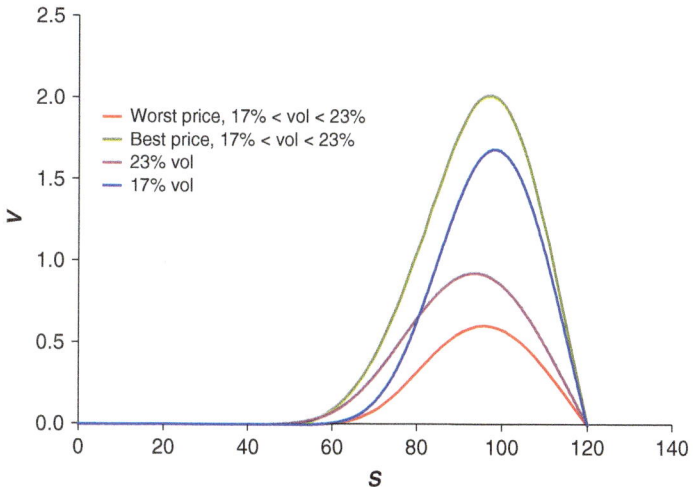

Figure 2.17: Barrier option valued using best and worst cases.

It is illegitimate to measure sensitivity to a parameter that has been assumed constant. (Of course, one way around this is to treat volatility as another variable in a stochastic volatility model for example.)

References and Further Reading

Wilmott, P 2006 *Paul Wilmott on Quantitative Finance*, second edition. John Wiley & Sons Ltd

What are the Stupidest Things People have Said about Risk Neutrality?

Short answer

Where do I start? Probably the stupidest and most dangerous thing is to implicitly (or sometimes even explicitly) assume that one can use ideas and results from risk neutrality in situations where it is not valid.

Example

Naming no names, I have seen the following written in research papers: 'Using risk-neutral pricing we replace μ with the risk-free rate r.' Naughty! As explained below you can only do this under certain very restrictive assumptions.

Long answer

Risk-neutral pricing means that you price as if traded contracts grow at the risk-free interest rate, and that non-traded financial quantities have a growth that is the real growth adjusted for risk. Sticking with the case of traded underlyings, it means that instead of using the 15.9% (or whatever) growth rate we have estimated from data we 'pretend' that the growth rate is actually the 4.5% (or whatever) risk-free rate.

For risk-neutral pricing to work you need **complete markets**. And that means enough traded quantities with which to hedge risk. Also you need to be able to hedge that risk continuously (and usually costlessly). And you need to be sure of parameters. And you usually can't have jumps. And so on. All highly unlikely.

Here are some things people say that are wrong because of the confusion of real and risk neutral:

- The forward price of some traded quantity is the market's expected value of it in the future. Wrong. Under various assumptions there is a simple arbitrage between spot price and forward price that links them via the interest rate. So there is no information in the forward price about anyone's expectations.

- The forward curve (of interest rates) is the market's expected value of the spot interest rate at future times. Wrong. If any expectation is involved then it is a risk-neutral expectation. The forward curve contains information about the expected future spot interest rate, yes, but it also contains information about the market's risk aversion. There are different risks in rolling over your money in an instant-access bank account and tying it up for years in a bond. That's why a risk premium is built into the forward curve.

- Using risk-neutral pricing we replace μ with the risk-free rate r. Only if your assumptions allow you to do this. (And, of course, reality never does!) Otherwise it's an assumption in its own right.

- The delta of an option is the probability of it ending up in the money. Wrong for two reasons. One is that the probability of ending up in the money depends on the real probabilities, and the real growth rate, and that's disappeared from the option value so it can't be true. The second reason is that there's a sign wrong! (If we have a call option then the probability you want is $N(d_2')$, where the prime (') means use μ instead of r, and not $N(d_1)$.)

References and Further Reading

Wilmott, P 2006 *Paul Wilmott on Quantitative Finance*, second edition. John Wiley & Sons Ltd

What is the Best-Kept Secret in Quantitative Finance?

Short answer
That inventors/discoverers/creators of models usually don't use them. They often use simpler models instead.

Example
Yeah, right, as if I'm going to give names!

Long answer
Named models are not necessarily used by their authors. Ok, perhaps not the best-kept secret but it is something that newbies ought to be aware of, so that they don't have unwarranted respect for models just because they've got a famous name attached to them.

In the early 1990s I was chatting to a famous quant who'd generously given his name to a fixed-income model. Let's call this person Dr X, and his model the X model. I asked him what fixed-income model his bank used. I was expecting an answer along the lines of 'We use the three-factor X model, of course.' No, his answer was 'We use the Vasicek model.' Dr X's model was at that time pretty sophisticated and so it was rather surprising to hear him admit to using what is essentially the 'starter' model.

A decade later I asked another inventor of a then state-of-the-art fixed-income model, let's call him Dr Y and his model the Y model, whether he used the Y model himself. Dr Y had just moved from a bank, and his reply was the very illuminating 'No! I work for a hedge fund now, and I need to make money!' You can figure out the implications.

I then asked another inventor of a popular ... Dr Z ... His answer: 'No, we don't use our model. Have you ever tried to calibrate it? It's terrible! We only published it to mislead other banks!' and he then named the model that he used in practice. Again, it was a much simpler model than his own.

The moral of this story is the same moral that we get from many quantitative finance experiences: Do not believe what it says on the tin, do your own modelling and think for yourself.

References and Further Reading

None, obviously!

Chapter 3

The Financial Modellers' Manifesto

Emanuel Derman and Paul Wilmott[1]

[1]This was published in a shortened version in *Business Week* in December 2008 and then in its full and final version, as here, online on 7 January 2009.

Preface

A spectre is haunting Markets – the spectre of illiquidity, frozen credit, and the failure of financial models.

Beginning with the 2007 collapse in subprime mortgages, financial markets have shifted to new regimes characterized by violent movements, epidemics of contagion from market to market, and almost unimaginable anomalies (who would have ever thought that swap spreads to Treasuries could go negative?). Familiar valuation models have become increasingly unreliable. Where is the risk manager that has not ascribed his losses to a once-in-a-century tsunami?

To this end, we have assembled in New York City and written the following manifesto.

Manifesto

In finance we study how to manage funds – from simple securities like dollars and yen, stocks and bonds to complex ones like futures and options, subprime CDOs and credit default swaps. We build financial models to estimate the fair value of securities, to estimate their risks and to show how those risks can be controlled. How can a model tell you the value of a security? And how did these models fail so badly in the case of the subprime CDO market?

Physics, because of its astonishing success at predicting the future behaviour of material objects from their present state, has inspired most financial modelling. Physicists study the world by repeating the same experiments over and over again to discover forces and their almost magical mathematical laws. Galileo dropped balls off the leaning tower, giant teams in Geneva collide protons on protons, over and over again. If a law is proposed and its predictions contradict experiments, it's back to the drawing board. The method works. The laws of atomic physics are accurate to more than ten decimal places.

It's a different story with finance and economics, which are concerned with the mental world of monetary value. Financial theory has tried hard to emulate the style and elegance of physics in order to discover its own laws. But markets are made of people, who are influenced by events, by their ephemeral feelings about events and by their expectations of other people's feelings. The truth is that there are no fundamental laws in finance. And even if there were, there is no way to run repeatable experiments to verify them.

You can hardly find a better example of confusedly elegant modelling than models of CDOs. The CDO research papers apply abstract probability theory to the price co-movements of thousands of mortgages. The relationships between so many mortgages can be vastly complex. The modellers, having built up their fantastical theory, need to make it useable; they resort to sweeping under the model's rug all unknown dynamics; with the dirt ignored, all that's left is a single number, called the default correlation. From the sublime to the elegantly ridiculous: all uncertainty is reduced to a single parameter that, when entered into the model by a trader, produces a CDO value. This over-reliance on probability and statistics is a severe limitation. Statistics is shallow description, quite unlike the deeper cause and effect of physics, and can't easily capture the complex dynamics of default.

Models are at bottom tools for approximate thinking; they serve to transform your intuition about the future into a price for a security today. It's easier to think intuitively about future housing prices, default rates and default correlations than it is about CDO prices. CDO models turn your guess about future housing prices, mortgage default rates and a simplistic default correlation into the model's output: a current CDO price.

Our experience in the financial arena has taught us to be very humble in applying mathematics to markets, and to be extremely wary of ambitious theories, which are in the end trying to model human behaviour. We like simplicity, but we like to remember that it is our models that are simple, not the world.

Unfortunately, the teachers of finance haven't learned these lessons. You have only to glance at business school textbooks on finance to discover stilts of mathematical axioms supporting a house of numbered theorems, lemmas and results. Who would think that the textbook is at bottom dealing with people and money? It should be obvious to anyone with commonsense that every financial axiom is wrong, and that finance can never in its wildest dreams be Euclid. Different endeavours, as Aristotle wrote, require different degrees of precision. Finance is not one of the natural sciences, and its invisible worm is its dark secret love of mathematical elegance and too much exactitude.

We do need models and mathematics – you cannot think about finance and economics without them – but one must never forget that models are not the world. Whenever we make a model of something involving human beings, we are trying to force the ugly stepsister's foot into Cinderella's pretty glass slipper. It doesn't fit without cutting off some essential parts. And in cutting off parts for the sake of beauty and precision, models inevitably mask the true risk rather than exposing it. The most important question about any financial model is how wrong it is likely to be, and how useful it is despite its assumptions. You must start with models and then overlay them with commonsense and experience.

Many academics imagine that one beautiful day we will find the 'right' model. But there is no right model, because the world changes in response to the ones we use. Progress in financial modelling is fleeting and temporary. Markets change and newer models become necessary. Simple clear models with explicit assumptions about small numbers of variables are therefore the best way to leverage your intuition without deluding yourself.

All models sweep dirt under the rug. A good model makes the absence of the dirt visible. In this regard, we believe that the Black–Scholes model of options valuation, now often unjustly maligned, is a model for models; it is clear and robust. Clear, because it is based on true engineering; it tells you how to manufacture an option out of stocks and bonds and what that will cost you, under ideal dirt-free circumstances that it defines. Its method of valuation is analogous to figuring out the price of a can of fruit salad from the cost of fruit, sugar, labor and transportation. The world of markets doesn't exactly match the ideal circumstances Black–Scholes requires, but the model is robust because it allows an intelligent trader to qualitatively adjust for those mismatches. You know what you are assuming when you use the model, and you know exactly what has been swept out of view.

Building financial models is challenging and worthwhile: you need to combine the qualitative and the quantitative, imagination and observation, art and science, all in the service of finding approximate patterns in the behaviour of markets and securities. The greatest danger is the age-old sin of idolatry. Financial markets are alive but a model, however beautiful, is an artifice. No matter how hard you try, you will not be able to breathe life into it. To confuse the model with the world is to embrace a future disaster driven by the belief that humans obey mathematical rules.

MODELLERS OF ALL MARKETS, UNITE!
You have nothing to lose but your illusions.

The modellers' hippocratic oath

- I will remember that I didn't make the world, and it doesn't satisfy my equations.
- Though I will use models boldly to estimate value, I will not be overly impressed by mathematics.
- I will never sacrifice reality for elegance without explaining why I have done so.
- Nor will I give the people who use my model false comfort about its accuracy. Instead, I will make explicit its assumptions and oversights.
- I understand that my work may have enormous effects on society and the economy, many of them beyond my comprehension.

Emanuel Derman and Paul Wilmott, 7 January 2009

Chapter 4

Essays

*I*f you've got this far you will have read me complaining about some theories and practices of quantitative finance. This continues in this section. But if you've managed to resist throwing this book at the cat so far then you should make it through ok!

Most of these essays have been previously published in blog form, some of them as part of a 'Science In Finance' series. You will notice, because they are numbered, that some of these appear to be missing. That's to avoid repetition because those essays have been expanded upon and formed the basis for the *FAQQF2* chapter on the commonest quant mistakes.

Science in Finance: Introduction

Having for most of my quant career attacked the majority of mathematical modelling in finance for being 'unscientific' (in the sense that the theories are rarely tested before being used, and when tested usually fail miserably) I feel somewhat heartened by the recent anti-Black–Scholes movement. Unfortunately this countermovement, although healthy in provoking debate, also does not quite match my (presumably rather high!) standards of rigour. With the aim of putting some science back into the quant debate I'm going to spend a few essays highlighting what I think are the weaknesses of financial modelling, and its strengths. I will even be defending Black–Scholes at times! Being scientific does not mean being without emotion, so although my reasoning will be logical my language will almost certainly, and as always, get quite demonstrative.

Topics to look out for, in no particular order: supply and demand; accuracy in different markets; distributions and fat tails; volatility and robustness; hedging errors; diversification; correlation; etc.

Science in Finance I Revisited: Supply and Demand, and Spoon Bending

I attended some of the recent Savoy auction by Bonhams and I couldn't resist observing the events from a quant perspective! In particular, I was drawn back again to the question of valuation versus supply and demand. We are taught that value comes from some complicated mathematical analysis involving lognormal random walks and stochastic calculus. However, we all ought to know that value comes about by a more obscure and more interesting and usually *ad hoc* procedure, often involving little logic and certainly no maths, and sometimes quite a lot of emotion. (Think women and shoes.) All of this was seen at the Savoy auction. Yes, there were people tut-tutting at the amount some were willing to pay for an ashtray, but they weren't those doing the buying. Those who bought the ashtrays probably had some doubts at the time, and also shortly afterwards, even this morning and maybe when they collect the ashtrays, but in the long run they'll at least have a funny story about themselves. (The latter not so easy to assign a value to, and certainly not risk neutral!)

Near the end of the three days there was a boring patch with 50 Savoy double beds going under the hammer, one after another. To amuse myself and in the spirit of scientific curiosity, I wrote down the 'time series' of prices for these identical items, see Figure 4.1. Now here was a room full of the same people, bidding for identical items with a known and limited supply, but even in this rather dull scenario the results were interesting, the plot of the times series is shown. Observations: the price did settle down to a value around £50, but that wasn't exactly stable; absentee bids mostly caused dramatic increases in the price (I'm sure economists will get excited about 'information' at this point, but this was the least interesting observation); later absentee bids were very low, people perhaps hoping for drying up of demand(?); a few lucky or clever people even got the price down below the £50; individual bidders did not seem to show consistency in their bidding; losing bidders often took a break for a few lots before coming back in. None of this is other than perfectly obvious (and much already covered in auction theory, I hope) but in my experience you really have to keep reminding quants that they are human beings as well, and that they should draw inspiration from the mundane.

I bumped into Uri Geller at the auction. He had just successfully bid for ... you guessed it, spoons! He's a very nice gentleman, and very kindly gave a few of us a private display of spoon bending!

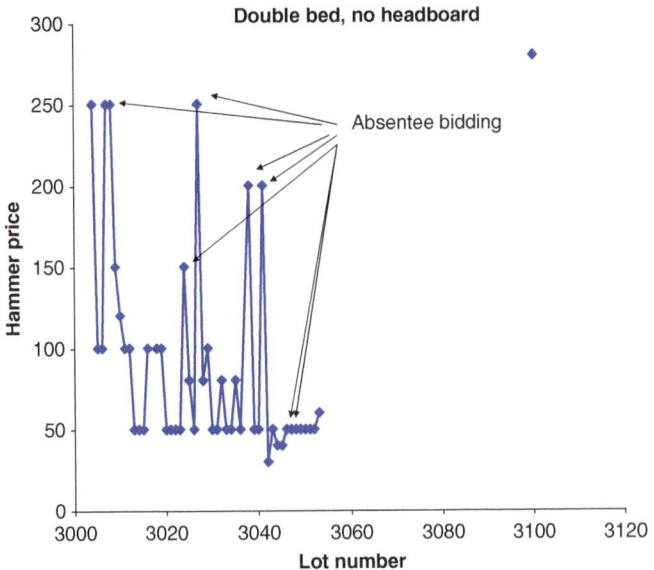

Figure 4.1: Bed price versus lot number at the Savoy auction.

Science in Finance II: ' . . . ists'

A century or two ago, finance was the career for the less talented members of the family. Sons of the aristocracy would eventually go to sit in the House of Lords, while overseeing their property. One son would join the military, Catholic families would send a son off to the church. Perhaps if they were of an enquiring mind one son might become a scientist. But if a son turned out to be intellectually challenged he would be sent off to be 'something in the City.' This didn't require any more brains than that required for an arts degree. This was the finance-is-for-artists (and long lunches) period, now long gone.

More often one now finds proper scientists working in finance. They have the analytical skills needed by investment banks and hedge funds. I imagine some must start out being frustrated by the lack of an established rigorous foundation for the subject. Where are the conservation laws? Where are the experimental results and the hypotheses? Quantitative finance has a well-used set of tools, but the popular models are essentially *ad hoc*.

Those in trading are undoubtedly pragmatists who really don't care for the port-and-cheese side of finance, nor for compact theories. Can it be put in a spreadsheet and does it make money? That's all that matters.

Unfortunately, most of the theory is built by axiomatists who really seem to believe in their models. These are the ones to be really frightened of. Speaking to them is like speaking to a god botherer, 'there is but one stochastic volatility model and its name is Heston.' (*News flash:* God and complete markets are simplifying assumptions that make life easier for the unimaginative, you aren't meant to believe in them once you've grown up!)

My feeling is that the best type of 'ist' working in finance is a pragmatic scientist, combining the curiosity and the scepticism of the scientist with the get-the-job-done attitude of the pragmatist.

Science in Finance IV: The Feedback Effect

For every buyer there is a seller and vice versa. So at a first glance derivatives is a zero-sum game, someone wins and someone loses, and the amounts are identical. Therefore there can be no impact on the rest of us or on the economy if two adults want to bet large sums of money on the outcome of what may just be the roll of a dice. Well, it isn't that simple for at least two reasons.

First, many of those trading derivatives are hedging with the underlying and this can affect the behaviour of the underlying: hedging positive gamma can decrease volatility and hedging negative gamma can increase volatility. When hedging positive gamma (i.e. replicating negative gamma) as the price rises you have to sell more of the underlying, and when the price falls you buy back, thus reducing volatility if your trades are in sufficient size to impact on the market. But hedging negative gamma is not so nice, you buy when the price rises and sell when it falls, exacerbating the moves and increasing volatility. The behaviour of stocks on which there are convertible bonds is often cited as a benign example, with the rather more dramatic '87 crash, replicating a put i.e. hedging negative gamma, as the evil version. (See Schönbucher, P and Wilmott, P 2000 The feedback effect of hedging in illiquid markets. *SIAM J. Appl. Math.* **61** 232–272, also PS's dissertation.) You will probably find some reluctance for people to sell certain derivatives if they are not permitted to dynamically hedge. (Not that it works particularly well anyway, but that is what people do, and that is what most pricing theory is based on. Static hedging with other derivatives is better, and does not cause such (in)stability problems.)

(We've had newspaper headlines about damage done by excessive risk taking, whether by single, roguish, individuals or by larger institutions such as hedge funds, or banks and corporates investing in products they don't fully understand. I expect it won't be long before the attempt to reduce risk is the cause of similar headlines!)

Second, with the leverage available with derivatives it is possible, and actually rather simple, for people to trade so much as to get themselves into a pickle when things go wrong. This has many consequences. For example a trader loses his bank so much money that the bank collapses or is taken over, job losses ensue and possibly the man in the street loses his savings. Is wealth conserved during this process, as would be the case in a zero-sum game? I think not.

Of course, we don't know what proportion of derivatives trades are being used for hedging, speculation with leverage, etc. and how many are being dynamically hedged. But while derivatives trading is such a large business and while pricing theory is underpinned by dynamic hedging then we can say that the game of derivatives is not zero sum. Of course, this should spur on the implementation of mathematical models for feedback...which may in turn help banks and regulators to ensure that the press that derivatives are currently getting is not as bad as it could be.

Science in Finance VI: True Sensitivities, CDOs and Correlations

One of the more quantie aspects of recent financial crises has been the valuation of CDOs, the highly complex credit instruments depending upon the behaviour of many, many underlyings. Now your typical quant favours just one tool to capture the interaction of two assets, and that tool is correlation. Of course, this is a very unsubtle tool which is being used to capture the extremely subtle interactions between companies. And when you have 100 underlyings the number of correlations will be $100 \times 99/2 = 4,950$. All of them unstable, all of them meaningless. Yet you will often find complex derivatives being priced using such wildly nonsensical data. Sometimes, in the interests of simplicity, some instruments are priced assuming all correlations are the same. The rationale behind this might be to return some robustness, in the sense that you might be more sure of one parameter than of 4,950 of them. If only it were that simple!

Returning to the subject of CDOs. I conducted a simple experiment on a CDO with just three underlyings. Really just a toy model to illustrate some important issues. I started by assuming a single correlation (instead of three) to capture the relationship between the underlyings, and a 'structural model.' I then looked at the pricing of three CDO tranches, and in particular their dependence on the correlation. Look at Figure 4.2, but ignore the exact numbers. First observe that the Senior Tranche decreases monotonically with correlation, the Equity Tranche is monotonically increasing, with the Mezzanine Tranche apparently being very insensitive to correlation.

Traditionally one would conduct such sensitivity experiments to test the robustness of ones prices or to assist in some form of parameter hedging. Here, for example, one might

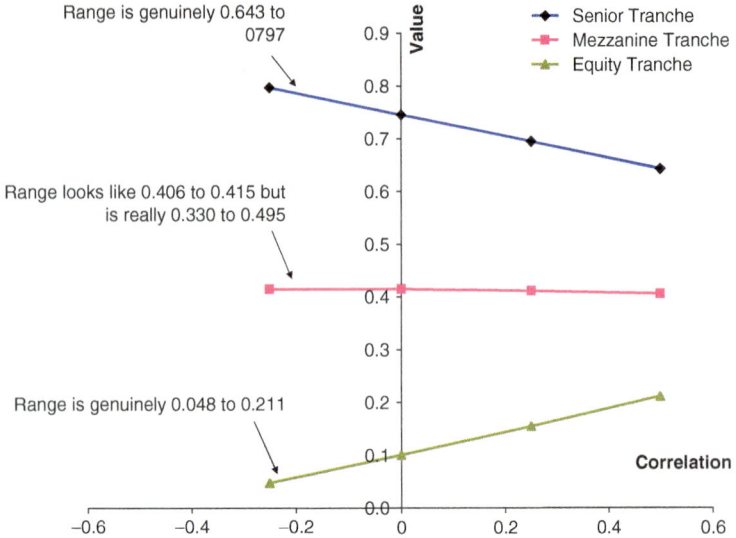

Figure 4.2: Constant correlation model.

conclude that the value of the Mezzanine Tranche was very accurate since it is insensitive to the correlation parameter. For a single correlation ranging from −0.25 to +0.5 the Senior Tranche value ranges from 0.643 to 0.797, the Equity Tranche from 0.048 to 0.211, and the Mezzanine Tranche from 0.406 to just 0.415. (Remember, don't worry about the numbers in this toy model, just look at the structure.) If you are confident in your valuation of the Mezzanine Tranche, then so will the next bank, and with competition being what it is, bid–offer prices will converge.

Such an analysis could not possibly be more misleading, such a conclusion could not possibly be more incorrect and such a response could not possibly be more financially dangerous.

Consider a more interesting, and more realistic, world in which correlation is state-dependent. Now allowing correlation to vary from -0.25 to $+0.5$, but not constant, and depending on 'state,' you will find that the Senior Tranche still varies from 0.643 to 0.797, the Equity Tranche still varies from 0.0408 to 0.211, but now the Mezzanine Tranche varies from 0.330 to 0.495, a factor of 18 in the sensitivity compared with the traditional naive analysis. The reason is simple, inside the Mezzanine Tranche structure there is a non-monotonic sensitivity to correlation which is masked when calculating the value; sometimes more correlation is good, sometimes more correlation is bad. (For the Senior Tranche correlation is always bad, for the Equity Tranche correlation is always good.)

Why on earth people thought it a good idea to measure sensitivity to a parameter that has been assumed to be constant escapes me still.

The moral of this example is simple, there is far more risk inside some of these instruments than you could ever hope to find with classical analyses. Stop using such convoluted models, use more straightforward models and start thinking about where your models' sensitivities really lie. Your models can fool some of the people all of the time, and all of the people some of the time, but your models cannot fool all of the people all of the time.

Science in Finance VII: Risk Management — What is the Point?

Another day, another financial institution collapses.[1] Bear Stearns, fifth largest US investment bank, has gone. I've worked closely with Bear brokerage in the past and quite enjoyed the experience. It's the prime brokerage that JP Morgan is presumably after. I'm a quant not an accountant so was surprised to see that Bear's assets were just 2–3% higher than their liabilities. If this is standard practice in this sector then crikey, we really are doomed! Who in their right mind would run a business that way? Sorry if I seem awfully naive, but as someone who has himself run a few businesses in his time, albeit on a somewhat smaller scale, to me this does seem highly irresponsible.

Investments (although that hardly feels like the right word) in mortgage-backed products and over-zealous lending combined with one particular scenario are at the bottom of this. This scenario is that of falling house prices. But isn't scenario analysis supposed to spot this sort of exposure? It's not as if falling property prices are totally unheard of. As those of you who have heard me lecture will know, I always like to boil things down to everyday experiences. And according to my experience there is a one in three chance of losing money in property! (Like most people with similar experiences it was the early 90s to 'blame' in my case.) And a one in three chance is not exactly the 10 standard deviation excuse *du jour*! It has been suggested that many bank employees are too young to have experienced negative equity and therefore it is off their radar, but if that is the case then what is the point of risk management at all? What is the point of all those risk management qualifications that are springing up like mushrooms? It has also been suggested that senior

---

[1]This essay was first written on 18 March 2008.

people don't have a clue about the instruments that their bank is trading. So I really would like to know how they fill their days, whatever they are doing it is clearly not productive.

Are those in positions of responsibility at Bear Stearns blameless? Did senior management really think that their downside was tolerable, that Value at Risk and stress testing were giving an accurate picture of potential losses and their probabilities? Again we come back to that old problem, if there's no downside then irresponsible people will prosper at the expense of the rest of us. And it seems that only the irresponsible rise to positions of responsibility in this business. Ironic.

Or maybe they are so lawyered up as to feel invincible. I am sure there will be civil suits in some of these cases because you can guarantee that the lawyers will, as always, be the big winners. They are paid to ensure that your back is covered no matter how unethical your behaviour, and then they are paid again when you are inevitably sued.

On the subject of ethical behaviour, don't some of these risk management courses teach about ethics? Or does understanding ethics these days amount to knowing who are the best lawyers? Personally, if I know someone had to go on a course to learn business ethics then I would ask myself whether that's a person I can trust. A risk management qualification is just another preventative measure against being sued, just like the 'Mind the Step' signs in restaurants? What, you broke your leg? Not our fault, mate, didn't you see the sign? (I was disappointed to discover recently, but not surprised, that they've taken peanuts out of Revels chocolates. Some people suffer from allergies, and presumably can't read, so we all have to do without.)

Risk management must be consistent with protecting the wider interests of the institution rather than being easy to manipulate towards the narrow interests of some employees. At present the concept of risk management only exists to make it easier for people to take risks that common sense would suggest are stupid, but risks that people still want to take because of the huge upside for these same people in terms of bonus. Let's face it, that's what rules and regulations are for. As Madness said in *Baggy Trousers*, 'All I learnt at school was how to bend not break the rules.'

I'd now like to explain how I think risk management should work. It's a simple combination of standard practices that I have used very successfully in the past. It's not exactly earth shattering, but it shows how to focus your attention on what matters. I will also finish with a small proposal for how to approach scenario analysis.

Roughly speaking, I tend to think in terms of three different levels or classes of risk management. These are

Level 1: Probabilities and VaR
Level 2: Worst-case scenarios
Level 3: Invasion by aliens, 'It's the end of the world as we know it, and I feel fine' (REM this time!)

Level 1: Typical day-to-day markets for which it is acceptable to work with probabilities and even possibly normal distributions. Correlations, while never exactly trustworthy, will not be a deciding factor in survival or collapse. Use probabilities and talk about Value at Risk by all means. This is really just classical mid 1990's risk management, with not too much worrying about fat tails. To some extent trust in a decent amount of diversification. The rationale behind this is simply that you never know what your parameters or distributions really are and so you are better off with simple calculations, more instruments and plenty of diversification. You may not make a profit but at least you won't be killed during a quiet day in the market.

Level 2: Situations which will cause your bank or hedge fund to collapse. Test your portfolio against a wide range of scenarios and see the results. But since these are situations resulting in the collapse of your institution you must never, ever talk about probabilities, except in terms of how many centuries before such events may happen. I would much prefer you work with worst-case scenarios (as in the very simple concept of CrashMetrics). I sometimes use the example of crossing the road. Imagine it's late, it's dark, and it's raining. If you cross the road there is a 5% chance of being hit by a bus and killed. That does not mean that tomorrow 95% of you goes to work! No, you assume the worst, because it is so bad, and cross the road elsewhere.

Certainly there is little role for Extreme Value Theory (EVT) in its fiddly, detailed sense. Consider these two statements about the same portfolio: 'According to Gaussian distributions the expected time to bank collapse is 10^{25} years' and 'According to EVT the expected time to bank collapse is 50 years.' The difference between these statements should only be of academic interest. Such a portfolio must be protected asap. Of course, many people would be happy with such a portfolio because 50 years is still longer than a trading career. Such people should not be in positions of responsibility. As I said above, 'risk management must be consistent with protecting the wider interests of the institution rather than being easy to manipulate towards the narrow interests of some employees.' To recap, if it's bad enough to cause bank/fund collapse you don't look at probabilities. Handle extreme events with worst-case scenario analysis.

Level 3: Scenarios which are so dire as to affect the world directly. I always use the example of invasion by aliens as an example, since there are whole bodies of literature and movies that have explored the effects of such an event, but we have little idea of the probability! If your hedge fund will collapse in the event of invasion by aliens, or drying up of oil supplies, or decimation of the world's population by bird flu, then I wouldn't necessarily change your portfolio! You'll have other things to worry about!

Finally, a small proposal. I would like to see risk management forced to engage in the following task, the reverse engineering of a bank collapse. Start with your current portfolio and imagine being called into the big boss's office to be told that the bank has lost $50 billion. Having put yourself in the frame of mind of having already lost this amount, now ask yourself what could have caused this to happen. As Einstein said: 'Imagination is more important than knowledge.' This should be the mantra for those in risk management. There is always going to be something that will come as a surprise at the time but with hindsight you realize could have been expected (if not necessarily predicted). Once you have figured out what could have caused this loss then you ask about the likelihood of this happening. The result of that analysis then determines what you should do with the portfolio. If, for example, the answer is simply that a fall in property prices caused the loss then you must get out this very instant, before it actually happens. You see the idea, work backwards from the result, the loss, rather than pick (possibly convenient) scenarios and look at the effects. Then estimate the likelihood of the chain of events happening, and act accordingly. Going the other way is more open to abuse. Scenario testing is a beautiful concept, if one gets to choose the scenarios to test. And those of weak character will not, of course, test any scenario that might jeopardize a juicy trade.

Science in Finance IX: In Defence of Black, Scholes and Merton

There's been a lot of criticism of the Black–Scholes model of late, on our Forum, in our blogs, in the magazine (see Haug & Taleb, *Wilmott* magazine, January 2008) and in other media. Most is warranted, but perhaps not all. I would now like to speak in its defence! This may seem perverse since I have been highly critical of this model for the last 15 years. But as I will explain, Black–Scholes is a remarkably robust model that copes very well even when its underlying assumptions are violated, as they inevitably are in practice. Before detailing my views on this matter, I'd like to explain how my personal relationship with the Black–Scholes model has evolved.

I was introduced to options in around 1987, well before the October crash, while I was a postdoc researching in various problems of industrial/applicable maths. For a while I researched in several areas of finance simultaneously: technical analysis; chaos theory; stochastic calculus. (Thanks to the technical analysis I was short the market coming into the crash of '87 but sadly only on paper!). I quickly dropped the TA and chaos theory, the latter seemed like a dead end, it was too easy to construct 'toy models' that looked plausible but were useless in practice. And so I began to focus on classical quant finance. Being in a maths department before most maths departments had heard of quant finance I had to rely on reading the literature in order to learn the subject. There were no courses for me to attend and no one more experienced to speak to. In those days whenever I read a paper I tended to believe everything in it. If the paper referred to volatility as a constant then I would believe that it was a constant. Black–Scholes was to me a good model, which just needed a minor bit of tweaking. My research from that era was on making small improvements to Black–Scholes to allow for transaction costs, and on the pricing of exotic derivatives in a constant-volatility world. This was the first phase in my relationship with Black and Scholes.

The second phase was as a consultant working for various investment banks, hedge funds and software companies. I was still in academia but moonlighting on the side. In this new capacity I finally got access to real data and was now speaking to practitioners rather than academics. (Fischer Black himself contacted me about the possibility of working for Goldman Sachs, and at this time I got to know Emanuel Derman. For a while I was sorely tempted to join them, but ultimately such a position would not have suited my personality.) It didn't take long for me to realize how unrealistic were the assumptions in the Black–Scholes model. For example, volatility was certainly not constant, and the errors due to discrete hedging were enormous. My research during the mid and late '90s was on making more dramatic improvements to the models for the underlyings and this was also the era when my interest in worst-case scenarios began. I worked with some very talented students and postdocs. Some great ideas and new models came out of this period. This was the height of my anti-Black–Scholes views.

A couple of years after leaving academia I became a partner in a volatility arbitrage hedge fund, and this was the start of phase three. In this fund we had to price and risk manage many hundreds of options series in real time. As much as I would have liked to, we just weren't able to use the 'better' models that I'd been working on in phase two. There just wasn't the time. So we ended up streamlining the complex models, reducing them to their simplest and most practical form. And this meant using good ol' constant volatility Black–Scholes, but with a few innovations since we were actively looking for arbitrage opportunities. From a pragmatic point of view I developed an approach that used Gaussian models for pricing but worst-case scenarios for risk management of tail risk. And guess what? It worked. Sometimes you really need to work with something that, while not perfect, is just good enough and is understandable enough that you don't do more harm than good. And that's Black–Scholes.

I had gone from a naive belief in Black–Scholes with all its simplifying assumptions at the start of my quant career, via some very sophisticated modelling, full circle back to basic Black–Scholes. But by making that journey I learned a lot about the robustness of Black–Scholes, when it works and when it doesn't, and have learned to appreciate the model despite its flaws. This is a journey that to me seems, in retrospect, an obvious one to take. However, most people I know working as quants rarely get even half way along. (As discussed elsewhere, I believe this to be because most people rather like being blinded by science.)

My research now continues to be aimed at questioning commonly held beliefs, about the nature of 'value,' about how to use stochastic calculus to make money rather than in a no-arbitrage world, about the validity of calibration (it's not valid!), and how people price risk (inconsistently is how!). All the time I strive to keep things understandable and meaningful, in the maths sweet spot that I've mentioned before.

That's my journey. But what about the criticisms of Black–Scholes? There are several main ones: Black–Scholes was known well before Black, Scholes and Merton; traders don't actually use Black–Scholes; Black–Scholes doesn't work.

I will happily accept that the Black–Scholes formulæ were around well before 1973. Espen Haug ('Collector') has done an excellent job hunting down the real history of derivatives theory (see his *Models on Models*). Ed Thorp plays a large role in that history. In the first issue of our magazine (*Wilmott* magazine, September 2002) the cover story was about Ed Thorp and his discovery of the formulae and their use for making money (rather than for publication and a Nobel Prize!). Ed wrote a series of articles 'What I Knew and When

I Knew It' to clarify his role in the discovery, including his argument for what is now called risk-neutral pricing. I particularly like the story of how Fischer Black asked Ed out to dinner to ask him how to value American options. By the side of his chair Ed had his briefcase in which there was an algorithm for valuation and optimal exercise but he decided not to share the information with Black since it was not in the interests of Ed's investors! Incorrect accreditation of discoveries is nothing new in mathematics, but usually there's a *quid pro quo* that if you don't get your name attached to your discovery then at some stage you'll get your name attached to someone else's!

They say traders don't use Black–Scholes because traders use an implied volatility skew and smile that is inconsistent with the model. (Do these same people complain about the illegitimate use of the 'bastard greek' vega? This is a far worse sin.) I think this is a red herring. Yes, sometimes traders use the model in ways not originally intended but they are still using a model that is far simpler than modern-day 'improvements.' One of the most fascinating things about the Black–Scholes model is how well it performs compared with many of these improvements. For example, the deterministic volatility model is an attempt by quants to make Black–Scholes consistent with the volatility smile. But the complexity of the calibration of this model, its sensitivity to initial data and ultimately its lack of stability make this far more dangerous in practice than the inconsistent 'trader approach' it tries to 'correct'!

The Black–Scholes assumptions are famously poor. Nevertheless my practical experience of seeking arbitrage opportunities, and my research on costs, hedging errors, volatility modelling and fat tails, for example, suggest that you won't go far wrong using basic Black–Scholes, perhaps with the smallest of adjustments, either for pricing new instruments or for exploiting mispriced options. Let's look at some of these model errors.

Transaction costs may be large or small, depending on which market you are in and who you are, but Black–Scholes doesn't need much modification to accommodate them. The Black–Scholes equation can often be treated as the foundation to which you add new terms to incorporate corrections to allow for dropped assumptions. (See anything by Whalley & Wilmott from the 1990s.)

Discrete hedging is a good example of robustness. It's easy to show that hedging errors can be very large. But even with hedging errors Black–Scholes is correct on average. (See *PWOQF2*.) If you only trade one option per year then, yes, worry about this. But if you are trading thousands then don't. It also turns out that you can get many of the benefits of (impossible) continuous dynamic hedging by using static hedging with other options. (See Ahn & Wilmott, *Wilmott* magazine, May 2007 and January 2008.) Even continuous hedging is not as necessary as people think.

As for volatility modelling, the average profit you make from an option is very insensitive to what volatility you actually use for hedging (see Ahmad & Wilmott, *Wilmott* magazine, November 2005). That alone is enough of a reason to stick with the uncomplicated Black–Scholes model, it shows just how robust the model is to changes in volatility! You cannot say that a calibrated stochastic volatility model is similarly robust.

And when it comes to fat tails, sure it would be nice to have a theory to accommodate them but why use a far more complicated model that is harder to understand and that takes much longer to compute just to accommodate an event that probably won't happen during the life of the option, or even during your trading career? No, keep it simple and price quickly and often, use a simpler model and focus more on diversification and risk management. I personally like worst-case scenarios for analysing hedge-fund-destroying risks. (See anything from the 1990s by Hua & Wilmott.)

The many improvements on Black–Scholes are rarely improvements, the best that can be said for many of them is that they are just better at hiding their faults. Black–Scholes also has its faults, but at least you can see them.

As a financial model Black–Scholes is perfect in having just the right number of 'free' parameters. Had the model had many unobservable parameters it would have been useless, totally impractical. Had all its parameters been observable then it would have been equally useless since there would be no room for disagreement over value. No, having one unobservable parameter that sort of has meaning makes this model ideal for traders. I speak as a scientist who still seeks to improve Black–Scholes, yes it can be done and there are better models out there. It's simply that more complexity is not the same as better, and the majority of models that people use in preference to Black–Scholes are not the great leaps forward that they claim, more often than not they are giant leaps backward.

Magicians and Mathematicians

Quantitative finance and risk management are not just about the numbers. Numbers play a part, but so does the human side of the business. When analysing risk it is important to be able to think creatively about scenarios. Unfortunately the training that most quants get seems to actively discourage creativity.

Some of the following appeared on the BBC website in December 2008.

We've learned the hard way how important it is to measure and manage risk. Despite the thousands of mathematics and science PhDs working in risk management nowadays we seem to be at greater financial and economic risk than ever before. To show you one important side of banking I'd like you to follow me in an exercise with parallels in risk management.

You are in the audience at a small, intimate theatre, watching a magic show. The magician hands a pack of cards to a random member of the audience, asks him to check that it's an ordinary pack, and would he please give it a shuffle. The magician turns to another member of the audience and asks her to name a card at random. 'Ace of Spades,' she says. The magician covers his eyes, reaches out to the pack of cards, and after some fumbling around he pulls out a card. The question to you is what is the probability of the card being the Ace of Spades?

Think about this question while I talk a bit about risk management. Feel free to interrupt me as soon as you have an answer. Oh, you already have an answer? What is that, 1 in 52, you say? On the grounds that there are 52 cards in an ordinary pack. It certainly is one answer. But aren't you missing something, possibly crucial, in the question? Ponder a bit more.

One aspect of risk management is that of 'scenario analysis.' Risk managers in banks have to consider possible future scenarios and the effects they will have on their bank's portfolio. Assign probabilities to each event and you can estimate the distribution of future profit and loss. Not unlike our exercise with the cards. Of course, this is only as useful as the number of scenarios you can think of.

You have another answer for me already? You'd forgotten that it was a magician pulling out the card. Well, yes, I can see that might make a difference. So your answer is now that it will be almost 100% that the card will be the Ace of Spades, the magician is hardly going to get this trick wrong. Are you right? Well, think just a while longer while I tell you more about risk and its management.

Sometimes the impact of a scenario is quite easy to estimate. For example, if interest rates rise by 1% then the bank's portfolio will fall in value by so many hundreds of millions. But estimating the probability of that interest rate rise in the first case might be quite tricky. And more complex scenarios might not even be considered. What about the effects of combining rising interest rates, rising mortgage defaults and falling house prices in America? Hmm, it's rather looking like that scenario didn't get the appreciation it deserved.

Back to our magician friend. Are those the only two possible answers? Either 1 in 52 or 100%? Suppose that you had billions of dollars of hedge-fund money riding on the outcome of this magic trick, would you feel so confident in your answers? (A hedge fund betting on the outcome of a magic show, how unrealistic! But did you know that there's at least one hedge fund that 'invests' in poker players, funding their play and taking a cut of their winnings? So who knows what they'll think of next?) When I ask this question of finance people I usually get either the 1 in 52 answer or the 100%. Some will completely ignore the word 'magician,' hence the first answer. Some will say 'I'm supposed to give the maths

answer, aren't I? But because he's a magician he will certainly
pick the Ace of Spades.' This is usually accompanied by an
aren't-I-clever smile! Rather frighteningly, some people trained
in the higher mathematics of risk management still don't see
the second answer even after being told.

This is really a question about whether modern risk managers are capable of thinking beyond maths and formulæ.
Do they appreciate the human side of finance, the herding
behaviour of people, the unintended consequences, what
I think of as all the fun stuff. And this is a nice question
because it very quickly sorts out different types of thinkers.

There is no correct answer to our magician problem. The
exercise is to think of as many possibilities as you can. For
example, when I first heard this question an obvious answer
to me was zero. There is no chance that the card is the Ace
of Spades. This trick is too simple for any professional magician. Maybe the trick is a small part of a larger effect, getting this part 'wrong' is designed to make a later feat more
impressive...the Ace of Spades is later found inside someone's pocket. Or maybe on the card are written the winning
lottery numbers that are drawn randomly 15 minutes later
on live TV. Or maybe the magician was Tommy Cooper. Or it
was all the magician's performance-anxiety dream the night
before. When I ask non-mathematicians this is the sort of
answer I get.

The answer 1 in 52 is almost the answer least likely to be
correct! (Unless the magician was using an ordinary deck of
cards, was aiming to pull out a different card but accidentally
pulled out the Ace of Spades instead! Accidentally not making
the intended 'mistake.')

A member of wilmott.com didn't believe me when I said how
many people get stuck on the 1 in 52 answer, and can't see
the 100% answer, never mind the more interesting answers.
He wrote 'I can't believe anyone (who has a masters/PhD

anyway) would actually say 1/52, and not consider that this is not ... a random pick?' So he asked some of his colleagues, and his experience was the same as mine. He wrote 'Ok I tried this question in the office (a maths postgraduate dept), the first guy took a fair bit of convincing that it wasn't 1/52!, then the next person (a hardcore pure mathematician) declared it an un-interesting problem, once he realized that there was essentially a human element to the problem!' Does that not send shivers down your spine, it does mine.

Once you start thinking outside the box of mathematical theories the possibilities are endless. And although a knowledge of advanced mathematics is important in modern finance I do rather miss the days when banking was populated by managers with degrees in History and who'd been leaders of the school debating team. A lot of mathematics is no substitute for a little bit of commonsense and an open mind.

How can we get quants and risk managers to think beyond the mathematics? I'm afraid I don't think we can the way they are currently educated.

Volatility Arbitrage

I continue to be staggered by the depth and detail of some people's understanding of complicated quant models while these same people have absolutely no appreciation of the bigger picture. A case in point is that of volatility modelling.

If you really get into the Heston stochastic volatility model you will find yourself having to do some numerical integration in the complex plane (thanks to the transform methods used to solve the governing equation). This can be quite tricky to do in practice. Is all that effort worth it? Well, in part this depends on how good the model is. So you might think people would test the accuracy of the model against the data. Do they do this? Rarely. It is deemed sufficient to calibrate to a static dataset of option values regardless of the dynamics of that dataset. Yes, I know you then hedge with vanillas to reduce model risk, but this is a fudge that is completely inconsistent with the initial modelling. The cynic in me says that the benefit of modelling in such oblivion is truly tested by the state of your bank balance at the end of the year. If you get a bonus, does it matter? I don't have too much of a problem with that, depending on where you are in the management structure. However, I suspect that this is not most people's justification for their inaccurate modelling. I suspect that people really do believe that they are doing good work, and the more complicated the mathematics the better.

So, many know all the ins and outs of the most advanced volatility models based in the classical no-arbitrage world. Well, what if your job is to find volatility arbitrage opportunities? 'There's no such thing as a free lunch' is drummed into most quants, thanks to academics and authors who take an almost axiomatic approach to our subject (see Derman's blog). Those who know the details of volatility arbitrage are few and far between. Take the example of how to hedge when you think that options are mispriced.

You forecast volatility to be much higher or lower than current implied volatility. Clearly this is an arbitrage opportunity. But to get at that profit you must hedge stock risk. Now, working within an otherwise very simple Black–Scholes world but with two volatilities, implied and forecast, how should you hedge and how much profit will you make?

The Same Old Same Old

Events of the last year seem to have passed a lot of researchers by. I find it both amusing and disturbing that the same people are still giving the same lectures about the same models at the same conferences without any sign of embarrassment whatsoever.[2] It's like a parallel universe! You can fool some of the people all of the time.

Sadly the easy ones to fool are people doing Finance PhDs and MFEs. On the forum there's always plenty of discussion about which qualifications people should go for, and how many. I find that the people who pick up new ideas fastest are those with a mathematics or science background, those actually with little hard-core quant education. They still have an open mind, something which is surely needed now more than ever before. The more time spent in academia learning the 'received wisdom' of quant finance the more one's brain atrophies it seems. As has been said on the forum many times, a finance PhD is for someone who wants to be a finance professor. You are better off getting a job, any job, in a bank or fund asap, start earning asap, move up the food chain as quickly as possible and leave your degree-collecting friends behind. This business will not be this lucrative forever.

I worry that people just can't distinguish between good and bad quant finance. There's plenty of evidence for this in journals, at conferences and in textbooks. People will certainly spot a mathematical error in a paper, but can they make the more subjective distinction between a good paper that advances the subject and a bad paper that sets it back?

There is nothing new in this, journals have almost always preferred to publish the 'reliable,' the 'brilliant new research

---

[2]This essay was first published on 1 September 2008.

by Professor X' that is really 'the same old stuff by a has-been plodder.' At this point a plug for our magazine is in order. *Portfolio magazine* was very flattering in its recent article about our magazine, saying 'Paul Wilmott, publisher and editor in chief of *Wilmott*, is looking pretty smart these days. Wilmott and his magazine, which is aimed at the quantitative-finance community, the math geeks at banks and hedge funds, foresaw many of the problems that dominate the headlines today. He and the contributors to the magazine, whose influence far outstrips its small circulation, were railing about the limits of math and financial models far in advance of the meltdown.'

It's not hard to find good research; our magazine seems to be particularly talented at this. The difficult part is knowing the difference between the good and the bad. This skill can be learned, but an open mind is needed. And they are increasingly hard to find.

Results and Ideas: Two Classical Putdowns

I spoke recently at a very academic conference.[3] I usually prefer trader and fund events because of their focus on practical matters. But this was in a place that I'd never visited and so I accepted. My lecture began in the traditional way of academic events with the audience being a bit hostile in their questioning. Being an old hand at this, I told myself not to rise to their baiting, but to see if I could win them over. It was clear that they knew little of the markets and practical finance, and so my 'winning them over' took the form of gently pointing out certain realities, certain constraints, and how interesting this subject is precisely because it is not a science. Getting them on my side turned out to be rather easier than usual, the hostility of most of them evaporated once they became intrigued. However, one person in the audience was not impressed with my efforts. He used two very famous putdowns on me, one of them is common only in academic circles and the other common in all circles.

The academic putdown was used in response to me talking about possibilities of arbitrage and whether the exploitation of arbitrage would make it go away. The putdown is to simply say 'There is a result about that.' Now I'm perfectly happy with people talking about 'results' in mathematics, in statistics, in particle physics, or in a hard science generally, but the use of the word 'result' in the context of a discussion about quantitative finance says more about the person using the word than anything about the subject matter. Human beings have this annoying habit of stubbornly not obeying theoretical 'results' (or indeed laws). As I keep saying, this subject is not a hard science and is somewhat more ephemeral than can be captured in a set of results.

---

[3]This essay was first published on 10 June 2008.

So although saying 'There's a result about that' can be aggressive and arrogant it can also be very naive, suggesting that whoever says it believes that finance is equivalent to a set of axioms. It is not, and to believe that it is can be very dangerous. This putdown is best just laughed off.

The other putdown came while I was explaining strategies that may be exploited for profit. The putdown is the simple 'If this works then why are you telling us about it and not doing it yourself?' There are many responses to this including:

1. I don't have the ability to do it myself, this is my marketing pitch, want to back me?
2. Ideas are cheap, I know which ones are good or bad but not everyone can tell the difference.
3. Do you know all the barriers to entry? $1 million in lawyers fees to set up a fund, months of software writing, years of knocking on doors trying to raise money. Forget it!
4. This is a great idea, but I've got better.
5. I don't want to spend the rest of my life doing this, even if it is profitable, variety is the spice of life.
6. I did, and now I've retired or, more simply, I've got enough money already.
7. My lawyer/doctor/wife says I mustn't.

And many more...

I was expecting this putdown from the well-known academic (he of the 'results') because of what happened in his lecture, which was earlier in the day than mine. He was talking about his model for something or other and right at the end he made the throw-away remark, 'Of course, if this worked in practice I wouldn't be telling you about it.' I confess to being shocked. (My turn to be naive!) This is a man who lectures on finance at a respected university, to students paying a lot of money, and here he was admitting that he lectures on things that do not work, that he keeps some of the good stuff to himself. Let me tell you that when I lecture, for example on the CQF, I keep nothing back (for at least one of the reasons listed above!). And unless I've signed some NDA, I will tell you everything.

It Is and It Isn't

I couldn't resist this rather trivial note, just a comment really on happenings at a recent quantie dinner. In attendance, going clockwise around the table at Union Square Cafe, PW, Bruno Dupire, Salih Neftci, Peter Carr, Jim Gatheral and Emanuel Derman.

Discussing the validity of all this Black–Scholes stuff that has got so much bad press recently, JG says 'I have a nice apartment in **** thanks to Black–Scholes being correct' to which yours truly responded 'Well, I have a nice flat in **** thanks to it being wrong!' Now, you can sort of see how that can be! It depends upon (a) to what use you put BS and, crucially, (b) how much profit margin you can add to any deal!

Not naming any more names, it was clear from the rest of the conversation (which concerned numerical integration in infinite-dimensional spaces!) that, if this sample is to be trusted and extrapolated, (a) half of all quants actually believe all this math finance modelling nonsense, (b) one third of all quants don't, and are rather concerned for the mental health of the first half, and (c) one sixth of all quants either don't care or have maybe been enjoying the excellent wine list at Union Square Cafe too much!

This is No Longer Funny

I've been critical of much of quant modelling for many years.[4] I don't like the assumptions, the models, the implementations. I've backed this up with sound reasons and wherever possible tried to find alternative approaches that I think are better. I don't honestly expect to change the world, much, but, hey, I do what I can. Human nature is such that very often things have to go from bad to worse to bloody awful before the necessary paradigm shift happens. I hope we are close to that point now.

Who am I kidding? As another hedge fund disappears thanks to mishandling of complex derivatives, I predict that things are going to get even worse.

When it was just a few hundred million dollars here and there that banks were losing we could all have a good laugh at those who had forgotten about convexity or whatever. But now the man in the street has been affected by these fancy financial instruments. It's no longer a laughing matter.

Part of the problem is that many of the people who produce mathematical models and write books know nothing about finance. You can see this in the abstractness of their writing, you can hear it in their voices when they lecture. Sometimes they are incapable of understanding the markets, mathematicians are not exactly famous for their interpersonal skills. And understanding human nature is very important in this business. It's not enough to say "all these interacting humans lead to Brownian Motion and efficient markets." Baloney. Sometimes they don't want to

---

[4]This essay was first published 10 March 2008.

understand the markets; somehow they believe that pure mathematics for its own sake is better than mathematics that can actually be used. Sometimes they don't know they don't understand.

Banks and hedge funds employ mathematicians with no financial-market experience to build models that no one is testing scientifically for use in situations where they were not intended by traders who don't understand them. And people are surprised by the losses!

I realized recently that I've been making a big mistake. I've been too subtle. Whenever I lecture I will talk calmly about where models go wrong and where they can be dangerous. I've said CDO models are bad because of assumptions about correlation. I've pointed out what you can do to improve the models. I've talked about hidden risks in all sorts of instruments and how sensible use of mathematics will unveil them. I've explained why some numerical methods are bad, and what the good methods are. But, yes, I've been too subtle. I now realize that one has to shout to be heard above the noise of finance professors and their theorems. Pointing people in the right direction is not enough. Screaming and shouting is needed.

So here, big and bold, gloves off, in capital letters (for this seems to help), are some fears and predictions for the future.

THERE WILL BE MORE ROGUE TRADERS While people are compensated as they are, while management look the other way to let the 'talent' do whatever they like, while people mistake luck for ability, there will be people of weak character who take advantage of the system. The bar is currently at £3 billion. There will be many happy to stay under that bar, it gives them some degree of anonymity when things go wrong. But that record will be broken.

GOOD SALESMEN WILL HOODWINK SMART PEOPLE   No matter what you or regulatory bodies or governments do we are all a pushover for the slick salesman.

CONVEXITY WILL BE MISSED   One of the more common reasons for losing money is assuming something to be known when it isn't. Option theory tells us that convexity plus randomness equals value.

CORRELATION PRODUCTS WILL BLOW UP DRAMATICALLY   This means anything with more than one underlying, including CDOs. Stop trading these contracts in quantity this very minute. These contracts are lethal. If you must trade correlation then do it small and with a big margin for error. If you ignore this then I hope you don't hurt anyone but yourself. (I am sometimes asked to do expert-witness work. If you blow up and hurt others, I am very happy to be against you in court.)

RISK MANAGEMENT WILL FAIL   Risk managers have no incentive to limit risk. If the traders don't take risks and make money, the risk managers won't make money.

VOLATILITY WILL INCREASE ENORMOUSLY AT TIMES FOR NO ECONOMIC REASON   Banks and hedge funds are in control of a ridiculous amount of the world's wealth. They also trade irresponsibly large quantities of complex derivatives. They slavishly and unimaginatively copy each other, all holding similar positions. These contracts are then dynamically hedged by buying and selling shares according to mathematical formulae. This can and does exacerbate the volatility of the underlying. So from time to time expect to see wild market fluctuations for no economic reason other than people are blindly obeying some formula.

TOO MUCH MONEY WILL GO INTO TOO FEW PRODUCTS   If you want the biggest house in the neighbourhood, and today not tomorrow, you can only do it by betting OPM (other people's money) big and undiversified. There are no incentives for spreading the money around responsibly.

MORE HEDGE FUNDS WILL COLLAPSE You can always start a new one. Hell, start two at the same time, one buys, the other sells!

POLITICIANS AND GOVERNMENTS WILL REMAIN COMPLETELY IN THE DARK Do you want to earn £50k p.a. working for the public sector, or £500k p.a. working for Goldman Sachs? Governments, who are supposed to set the rules, do not even know what the game is. They do not have the slightest clue about what happens in banks and hedge funds. Possibly, for the same reason. London will lose out to New York as a world financial centre.

Frustration

As you will no doubt know, I have been frustrated by quants for a long, long time. Their modelling of markets is a strange combination of the childishly naive and the absurdly abstract. On a one-to-one basis many people working in banks will complain to me about the models they have to implement. They will complain about instability of the Heston volatility model, for example. I will explain to them why it is unstable, why they shouldn't be using it, what they can do that's better and they will respond along the lines of 'I agree, but I don't have any choice in the matter.' Senior quants are clearly insisting on implementations that those on the front line know are unworkable.

And a large number of people complain to me in private about what I have started calling the 'Measure Theory Police.' These 'Police' write papers filled with jargon, taking 30 pages to do what proper mathematicians could do in four pages. They won't listen to commonsense unless it starts with 'Theorem,' contains a 'Proof,' and ends with a 'QED.' I'll write in detail about the Measure Theory Police at a later date, but in the meantime will all those people complaining to me about them please speak up ... you are preaching to the converted, go spread the word!

For several years I tried to argue scientifically, in papers, book, seminars, etc. about all the abysmal modelling I saw. Of all the conferences that I speak at, you would think that quant events would be the ones at which the audience would have the best appreciation of good versus bad modelling. Frustratingly, quant conferences have audiences with great technical skills but the least imagination. If you're not lecturing about the wonders of correlation, but about the stupidity of correlation, then expect a hostile ride. But I battled on, I have a very tough skin!

Then I thought I'd try a different tack. If data, scientific explanations and commonsense won't get the truth across then something else was required. (It turns out that the 'something else' was losses of trillions of dollars and a global recession!)

So I started introducing audiences to relevant aspects of human psychology. I explained about the famous experiments in peer pressure to highlight why people were adopting the same models as everyone else. I explained about the famous experiments in diffusion of responsibility, mentioned recently in an article by Taleb and Triana, so that people would understand why they were sitting around not doing anything about the terrible state of affairs. Perhaps a little bit of cognitive behavioural therapy might help them to understand their own motives and this would bring about a change of practice in finance. Of course, I was overambitious. Audiences were entertained and amused, a good time was had by all. And then they went back to their day jobs and the implementation of the same old copula nonsense.

Combine peer pressure with diffusion of responsibility and fear for their jobs and most people will keep quiet. Sad, but expected and, reluctantly I will admit, understandable.

What is not understandable is the role in recent events played by regulators and rating agencies. Their jobs are not to toe the party line. The job of the regulator is to hold up the yellow card to banks with bad practices and the job of the rating agencies is to give an honest assessment of creditworthiness. In neither case should they have been effectively colluding with banks in increasing the amount of risk taken.

I have an analogy for you.

A rating agency or a regulator visits a bank. They are being shown around the premises, looking at all the products they have and how they are managed. They come to one desk on which there is a pile of nuclear material. 'That's a large pile of nuclear material. How much does it weigh?' they ask. 'Oh, nothing to worry about, only half the critical mass,' comes the reply. They go on to the next desk and see a similar pile. 'Nothing to worry about, only half the critical mass.' They go next door to another bank, and they see the same story. It doesn't take a genius to see the potential risks. The regulators and the credit rating agencies saw something similar, with CDOs and the like being the explosive material.

In the early days of the current crisis the talk was of blame. That was precisely the wrong thing to consider at that time. Shore up the financial system asap, that was the most important thing to do. A quick response was what mattered, the details didn't. Now is the time to start considering blame and punishment. And yes, there has to be punishment. You cannot have obscene rewards for those working in banking, salaries tens or hundreds of times the national averages without expecting and demanding corresponding responsible behaviour. It is both morally objectionable and financially dangerous to not have the huge upside balanced by a matching downside for irresponsible actions. And so I point the finger at rating agencies and regulators as those near the top of those who must take the blame.

Realistically I expect further frustration and a return to business as usual.

Ponzi Schemes, Auditors, Regulators, Credit Ratings, and Other Scams

There are honest people, and there are dishonest people – a whole spectrum. I like to think I'm near the honest end; I would have worn a white hat in the old cowboy movies. And I've had the misfortune to have met a few from right up close to the other extreme, with the black hats. Most people wear hats of various shades of grey. High finance is a business which encourages people to shift towards the dishonest end of the spectrum by putting temptation in their way, and the dishonest are drawn to this field by its quick and easy rewards. Nothing that I have ever seen in investment banking and fund management has impressed me as a disincentive to crooked behaviour, absolutely nothing.

As a keen observer of human behaviour I have been fascinated watching people's attitude towards money. In academia they struggle with their mixed feelings, on the one hand hating the filthy stuff since they are supposed to be above such worldly matters, but on the other hand rather liking what they can do with it. The really rich see it as nothing more than a measure of their success in life, a score. Some balanced people, few and far between, realize they need it, and that more is better than less, but it's not the main focus in their lives. Then there is the common greed that we see in our business, nasty and unpleasant. And nasty, unpleasant greed is so easy to feed, it is encouraged in banking, but it has some unpleasant side effects.

The Madoff affair has highlighted several things, brought some corrupt practices to light, but we haven't really learned anything new from all of this. The old lessons, the ones that should have been learned years ago, are just as valid. As I keep saying, there is little reason for regulators to do anything: people have short memories; people are easily distracted; The legal system is now much better at protecting the guilty than protecting the innocent.

Just like the Social Services in the UK, regulators do such a useless job that they are now permanently on the defensive. I bet you that few people working for regulators are doing their jobs right now, I bet most of their day is spent figuring out how to protect themselves against the growing backlash.

Quite frankly I don't see much difference between Madoff's Ponzi scheme and naive auditors, self-serving regulators and morally corrupt ratings agencies. They are all part of a financial system that encourages scams, scams that may then take years to sort out and years before the culprits are punished, meanwhile out on comfortable bail. The US legal system is particularly easy to 'play' so as to drag proceedings out so long that the accused dies of natural causes before justice is done.

There is no disincentive for dishonest behaviour in investment banking at the moment, in fact the opposite. If someone wants to invest with a manager they think might be dishonest but successful then they will ignore the dishonesty. If the investor loses their shirt then tough, serves them right. (Of course, it won't be their money, so anyone found not having done their full due diligence ought to be arrested.) I know of several people who manage money who have broken serious laws, lawbreaking that would prevent them managing money. And I know of some investors who know that I know, but who, when considering investing with these people, deliberately do not ask for my opinion as part of their due diligence. Why not? Because once they hear what I have to say then they would no longer be able to invest with the crooked, but oh-so-smooth and convincing manager. If you've ever bought a dodgy DVD at the market, or a hi-fi from a man in the pub, then you are just as culpable. And you therefore might find some sympathy for a lot of people being blamed at the moment. I haven't, and I don't.

When I first realized, several years ago, that due diligence is deliberately not being done I proposed that formal psychometric testing be part of the process of setting up a hedge fund or managing money. I know this is easy to criticize or trivialize, especially by all the 'left-brainers' working in finance. But in this business trust is so important. In a world where we never get to know the people looking after our life savings, as we might have done in the old days, I can think of no other simple indicator of testing trustworthiness. Some people are dishonest, some can't be trusted. Do you care? I do, and always have. Maybe other people don't, that's greed at work, but they will eventually, perhaps only after they've lost lots and lots of money.

Economics Makes My Brain Hurt

A friend of mine, you may know him, you certainly know 'of' him, has called for the return of a couple of economics Nobel Prizes. It's Nassim Nicholas Taleb, in case you didn't know. I'm not fussed one way or the other whether or not they get to keep their prizes, I don't really see much difference between their work and that of many of the others awarded the economics Nobel. (Yes, I know, it's not a proper Nobel, blah, blah, blah, Bank of Sweden, blah, blah, we can take that much as read!) Or even those awarded the prize in other fields. The Nobel Prize for Literature seems to be political (political meaning either greasy pole, or as in politically correct), the Peace Prize is downright perverse, so the Economics Prize is no different for being pointless. In contrast, we probably all respect laureates in medicine, chemistry and physics for mostly decent work that has stood the test of time.

Economics is a queer subject. I like to boil things down to the very basics whenever I am trying to learn something new, doing research or teaching, as the students on the CQF can attest – think of some of my stranger analogies, guys! But this doesn't work with economics. Starting with a couple of blokes in a cave, one of whom has just invented the wheel, try to imagine the exchanges that take place and how that turns into General Motors. No, it makes my brain hurt. No matter how much red wine I've drunk it doesn't seem to work.

And I'm supposed to be clever. Why am I incapable of understanding economics, a straightforward enough subject that it's even taught in schools?

My failure led me to think about economists, as opposed to economics, and they're much easier to figure out. This is how it works. An economist starts with a few axioms, ones that bear a vague similarity to a small part of the human condition under restricted situations and in an idealized world. (You get my drift here?) From those axioms follows a theorem. More often than not this will be a theorem based upon rational behaviour. That theorem gets a name. And that's the point I identify as being the problem: The jargonizing of complex ideas based upon irrelevant assumptions into an easily used and abused building block on which to build the edifice of nonsense that is modern economics.

Small assumption by small assumption, the economist builds up his theories into useless gibberish. By acceptance of each step he is able to kid himself he is making progress. And that's why I struggle with economics. It is not mathematics where, barring mistakes, each step is true and indisputable and therefore you can accept it, even forget it, and move on. And others can do the same, using everyone else's results without question. This you cannot do in a soft science. I've mentioned this in another article, beware of anyone talking about 'results' in finance or economics, it says more about them and their perception of the world than it does about the subject.

Not so long ago Alan Greenspan famously said he had found a flaw in the 'critical functioning structure that defines how the world works.' 'I don't know how significant or permanent it is but I have been very distressed by that fact.' Ohmigod! His naivety and lack of self-knowledge is staggering. He has fallen into the same trap as other economists. By believing the theories he has believed the axioms on which they are based. The edifice of nonsense has collapsed on top of one of its builders.

You beautiful, complex, irrational people! Please, promise me that you will continue to violate every axiom and assumption of economics, maybe not all the time, that would be too predictable, but now and then, just so as to keep those pesky economists on their toes!

Greenspan also said that risk models and econometric models are still too simple. Lord, help us!

Let me tell you a story.

A decade or so ago I was browsing through the library of Imperial College, London, when I happened upon a book called something like 'The Treasury's Model of the UK Economy.' It was about one inch thick and full of difference equations. Seven hundred and seventy of them, one for each of 770 incredibly important economic variables. There was an equation for the rate of inflation, one for the dollar–sterling exchange rate, others for each of the short-term and long-term interest rates, there was the price of fish, etc. etc. (The last one I made up. I hope.) Could that be a good model with reliable forecasts? Consider how many parameters must be needed, every one impossible to measure accurately, every one unstable. I can't remember whether these were linear or non-linear difference equations, but every undergrad mathematician knows that you can get chaos with a single non-linear difference equation so think of the output you might get from 770. Putting myself in the mind of the Treasury economists I think 'Hmm, maybe the results of the model are so bad that we need an extra variable. Yes, that's it, if we can find the 771st equation then the model will finally be perfect.' No, gentlemen of the Treasury, that is not right. What you want to do is throw away all but the half dozen most important equations and then accept the inevitable, that the results won't be perfect.

A short distance away on the same shelf was the model of the Venezuelan economy. This was a much thinner book with a mere 160 equations. Again I can imagine the Venezuelan economists saying to each other, 'Amigos, one day we too will have as many equations as those British cabrones, no?' No, what you want to do is strip down the 160 equations you've got to the most important. In Venezuela maybe it's just one equation, for the price of oil.

We don't need more complex economics models. Nor do we need that fourteenth stochastic variable in finance. We need simplicity and robustness. We need to accept that the models of human behaviour will never be perfect. We need to accept all that, and then build in a nice safety margin in our forecasts, prices and measures of risk.

Name and Shame in Our New Blame Game!

(In late 2008 we ran a survey asking members of wilmott.com who or what they thought was to blame for the 'crisis.' Here are some of their responses together with comments from me.)

We now have the results for which are the worst quant models according to the contributing members of wilmott.com! Here I reveal these worst models and concepts (etc.), and other interesting bits and pieces mentioned by members. I will also give you a few words, condensing my thoughts on each culprit.

In alphabetical order, the guilty parties and ideas are below. The * means that I disagree.

Auditors: They are generally considered clueless. And that's also true of governments and regulators generally speaking. How can they hope to stop the determined big brains at most investment banks? (Even if those big brains did cause their own banks to collapse they did so while taking home enormous bonuses, this doesn't demean the size of those brains in any way! *Au contraire*.)

Basel: Committees! Effectively a little bit of public sector mentality infiltrating the private sector. Except that such committees are actually deceptively self serving and destructive.

Complete markets: See below for risk neutrality.

Collateralized Debt Obligations, etc. ABS, MBS: Probably among the stupidest, most naïve, and yet most complicated quantitative finance modelling can be found behind these instruments. I warned you they were dangerous, the two main reasons being they are credit instruments, see below, and because of correlation. All correlation instruments are dangerous because correlation is such a simplistic tool for modelling the subtle relationships between financial assets. At least they are dangerous unless there is a large inbuilt profit margin (margin for error) and unless they are traded in small quantities. Large quantities and small profit margins lead to disaster, but you know that now.

Credit modelling: Burn all credit books, except those that say that the modelling is rubbish. (Which I do in my books, so don't burn those!) Default is not a probabilistic event, a coin toss, it is a business decision.

Copulas: An abomination. Such abstract models that only a few people, mostly with severe emotional intelligence problems, really understand. (One often gets the impression when speaking to certain types of mathematician that 'they are not all there.' I think you know what I mean! And if you don't … oh, dear, you are one of them!) Quote from the section on copulas in *PWOQF2* written in 2005: "I have to say that some of these instruments and models fill me with nervousness and concern for the future of the global financial markets."

Efficient Market Hypothesis: Hypocrisy of the first magnitude. "You can't make money from the markets, but give me a million-dollar bonus." Either hypocrisy, or material for a psychiatric journal's article about lack of communication between left and right sides of the brain.

French Polytechniques: I interpret this entry as meaning generally education that is too abstract and lacking in practicality, i.e. those who think that 'maths is both necessary and sufficient for finance' when clearly it is only necessary! As someone who has devoted the better part of two decades trying to educate people to be responsible quants it has always annoyed and frightened me that universities have churned out so many 'quants' who are both over educated and under experienced. That universities often prey on young people just out of a first degree is therefore not surprising. It is pleasing to see at last a wider recognition that such people are better suited to academia than to banks.

Gaussian distribution*: (Note, this does not mean Gauss is to blame!) – I disagree about Gaussian distributions. See standard deviation.

Insurance methods: Presumably this means using the Central Limit Theorem in conditions where the CLT doesn't hold. An example of a great theory being misused. Actuaries have long felt a bit jealous of quants, since they start out with similar skills but actuaries aren't quite as glamorous (am I really talking about mathematicians being glamorous?!) and certainly don't earn as much. It goes back to quants' relationship with hedging, a trick that actuaries feel they ought to have spotted. Quants could learn a lot from actuaries, including the proper use of insurance methods. But I expect the 'education' will go the other way, actuaries will learn quant methods ... does this mean a collapse of the insurance industry next? Oh, how could I forget AIG?!

Mathematics: Well, you know my strong views on this! Dumbing down is bad because then you can't price sophisticated instruments and you don't know all the risk. Making things too complicated may be even worse, people fool themselves into believing the models, they are blinded by the maths (see Copulas and CDOs, and especially French Polytechniques, above). All is not lost ... from my blog: "Ok, the big secret ... Quantitative finance is one of the easiest branches of mathematics. Sure you can make it as complicated as you like, and plenty of authors and universities have a vested interest in so doing. But, approached correctly and responsibly, quant finance is easy." In a *Phil. Trans.* article published in 2000 (*The use, misuse and abuse of mathematics in finance*) I warned that "a major rethink [of financial modelling] is desperately required if the world is to avoid a mathematician-led market meltdown." Good, huh? We may have just about avoided this, at possible medium- or long-term cost to the taxpayer (but who could still profit if the accountants and the government get their acts together) and to the economy (which is definitely screwed for a while). If banks, funds, regulators, governments don't see the light now then lord help us!

Media*: Shoot the messenger! I disagree. When short selling was banned people said it's necessary for price discovery. In that case we need the media as well. (I'm in favour of short selling but I thought the argument about price discovery was silly. Go to a supermarket you'll see the price of products falling if no one wants them, and you can't short baked beans. Or maybe that's too slow a mechanism, perhaps we need short selling to speed up price discovery. What, are the markets too slow for you? Yee-ha!)

Off-balance Sheet Vehicles: Quants + Lawyers + Accountants = Chaos + Disaster + More money for Lawyers and Accountants. Hey, quants, you're getting a bum deal here!

Quants: Unwitting stooges or guilty accomplices? Perhaps even Mister Bigs, the masterminds. Did they get a bonus? Yes. Did they blow the whistle? No. Then guilty as charged, M'Lud.

Ratings agencies: As mentioned in my *NYT* Op-Ed piece, "moral hazard so strong you can almost taste it." Also my favourite contender for defendants in lawsuits, any day now! And I'm available for prosecution expert-witness work, very reasonable rates in a good cause.

Risk neutrality: I estimate that about 2% of people working in derivatives and risk management really understand this fundamental concept. Yet probably the vast majority of them use it on a daily basis, knowingly or not. Of course, the validity of this concept depends on certain assumptions, no frictions, perfect hedging, known parameters, i.e. it's not valid. But maybe it still works even if not technically valid, perhaps the idea is somehow robust? Well, sometimes it is, sometimes it isn't, but probably only 0.02% of people in this business know why and when.

RiskMetrics: Making VaR, see below, accessible to the masses. Why not give away handguns while you're at it?

Standard deviation*: I disagree. I see the point that standard deviations may not exist for many/most financial distributions. Thin tails versus fat tails. But the extreme events still only happen relatively infrequently, and throwing away standard deviations would be throwing away the baby with the bathwater! It might add complexity that would actually be worse than the simplicity and transparency that it replaces. For normal (in both sense of the word) markets standard deviations are fine. I advocate using worst-case scenarios for extremes that might cause banks, or economies, to collapse.

Value at Risk: As one of the cartoons in my books says "I've got a bad feeling about this." VaR is used to justify taking risks. Classic unintended consequences territory this. Yeah, right! Funny how "unintended consequences" are always rather obvious, even before the fact, but they are always brushed under the (expensive silk) rug. "Don't rock the boat, dear boy," cigar in one hand, Napoleon brandy in the other. Risk managers say there's no risk according to naïve VaR models, so management is free to trade in bigger, and bigger, and bigger, amounts. Oops ... it seems that VaR didn't quite capture all the risks ... who'd have considered rising interest rates and increasing mortgage defaults? Answer: Everyone, except those who had a vested interest in hiding the risks.

Chapter 5

The Commonest Mistakes in Quantitative Finance: A Dozen Basic Lessons in Commonsense for Quants and Risk Managers and the Traders Who Rely on Them

Introduction

Judging by research papers and books on quantitative finance, and from conversations with thousands of practitioners, not to mention well-publicized modelling mistakes, I believe that quants have totally lost the plot. They focus on making models increasingly complex when they should be making them more robust. They use the most abstract of mathematics and then make obscenely simplifying assumptions. They fine tune irrelevant detail and ignore fundamental issues of risk management. They obfuscate when they ought to educate.

Much of quantitative finance is dumbed down for the masses, partly, I am sure, to sell lots of books on the subject – there are sadly more non-mathematicians in the world than there are mathematicians. This is not too dangerous because you can't do much quant finance without mathematics, and therefore you can't really invent too many toxic contracts. But there are also at least as many people making quantitative finance too complicated. Overly abstract mathematics is being used by people who have never traded, yet whose models are respected precisely because of their complexity. These models (and people) are dangerous. Lack of transparency in financial models is not good. Given that the models can never be perfect in this 'soft' science, why is there so much focus on detail at the expense of the big picture? Some are easily blinded by science, unable to see the wood for the trees.

For the above reasons, and after many years experience in research, training and practice, I have come to believe in a mathematics sweet spot, using the right kind of mathematics for each job, not dumbing down and not making too sophisticated; a level of mathematics such that people can see what the assumptions are and where lie the weaknesses. Ideally spend more time seeking robustness of a model rather than trying to make it 'better.' Sadly, 'better' these days seems to mean simply adding more and more factors. It is easy to impress people with difficult mathematics, but a quant's job is not to impress, it is to allow banks and funds to trade products, perhaps new products, and to trade profitably and with well-understood and controlled risk.

In this chapter I outline 12 of the most common causes of errors in quant finance. These 12 lessons are most definitely not about inverting your transform, or about convergence of Monte Carlo simulations, or how to speed up your calibration of Hull & White. Those are precisely the sort of questions that should only be asked after the more fundamental issues have been successfully addressed. This chapter is about the fundamental issues.

All of these lessons are basic, all of them are easily quantified, all of them have cost banks and funds huge sums of money, and all of them are still under-appreciated. In 2000 I wrote, 'It is clear that a major rethink is desperately required if the world is to avoid a mathematician-led market meltdown' (Wilmott, 2000). In 2006 I wrote about credit 'some of these instruments and models being used for these instruments fill me with some nervousness and concern for the future of the global financial markets. Not to mention mankind, as well. Never mind, it's probably just me' (Wilmott, 2006a). The first draft of the chapter you are reading was written in mid 2007. I am putting the finishing touches to it in late 2008 when it has become apparent that the man in the street has also been dramatically affected by our 'high finance.'

If you think quantitative finance is only about the likes of Radon–Nikodym derivatives, squared Bessel processes and numerical quadrature in the complex plane, then this chapter is not for you. If you think quantitative finance is more interesting than that, read on!

The subjects are:

- Lack of diversification
- Supply and demand
- Jensen's Inequality arbitrage
- Sensitivity to parameters
- Correlation
- Reliance on continuous hedging (arguments)
- Feedback
- Reliance on closed-form solutions
- Valuation is not linear
- Calibration
- Too much precision
- Too much complexity

But first a simple test-yourself quiz, to encourage reader participation!

Quiz

(Answers on page 378)

Question 1: What are the advantages of diversification among products, or even among mathematical models?

Question 2: If you add risk and curvature what do you get?

Question 3: If you increase volatility what happens to the value of an option?

Question 4: If you use ten different volatility models to value an option and they all give you very similar values, what can you say about volatility risk?

Question 5: One apple costs 50p, how much will 100 apples cost you?

Lesson 1: Lack of Diversification

One of the first lessons in any course on quantitative finance will be about portfolio construction and the benefits of diversification, how to maximize expected return for a given level of risk. If assets are not correlated then as you add more and more of them to your portfolio you can maintain a decent expected return and reduce your risk asymptotically to zero. (Risk falls off like the inverse square root of the number of different uncorrelated assets.) Colloquially, we say don't put all your eggs into one basket.

Of course, that's only theory. In practice there are many reasons why things don't work out so nicely. Correlations never behave as they should, the relationship between two assets can never be captured by a single scalar quantity. We'll save detailed discussion of correlation for later in the chapter! For the moment I'm more worried about people or banks not even *attempting* to diversify.

Part of the problem with current mechanisms for compensation is that people are encouraged to not diversify. I don't mean 'not encouraged to,' I do mean 'encouraged to not.'

Example It's your first day as a trader in a bank. You're fresh out of an Ivy League Masters programme. You're keen and eager, you want to do the best you can in your new job, you want to impress your employer and make your family proud. So, what do you trade? What strategies should you adopt? Having been well educated in theoretical finance you know that it's important to diversify, that by diversifying you can increase expected return and decrease your risk. Let's put that into practice.

Let's suppose that you have the freedom to trade whatever you like. Would you make the same trades as others around you? You look around and see that a certain trade is popular, should you copy this or do something 'uncorrelated'? Suppose that you choose the uncorrelated trade. Several things can happen, let's look at a couple of possibilities. First, you lose while all around are raking it in. Not necessarily your fault, maybe just a stat-arb strategy that was unlucky, next month will probably be better. Tough, you don't have a month, you are taking up valuable desk space, space better given to those people making the money. You're fired. But what if the opposite happens? You make money while all the others with their popular trade are losing it. Couldn't be better, right? Sadly, the others have lost so much money that there isn't going to be a bonus this year. Your relatively tiny profit hardly begins to fill in the hole made by the others. You certainly won't be getting any bonus, no one will. If you are lucky you get to keep your job this time. As Keynes said, 'It is better to fail conventionally than to succeed unconventionally.'

There is no incentive to diversify while you are playing with OPM (Other People's Money).

Example   Exactly the same as above but replace 'trades' with 'models.' There is also no incentive to use different models from everyone else, even if yours are better.

The problem is in the way that bank employees are rewarded by gambling with OPM, the compensation system that rewards excessive risk taking and punishes diversification. Diversification is *not* rewarded.

Now, I'm all in favour of using the 'best' possible models, but I can see that there is an argument for different people to use different models, again on the grounds of diversification because ultimately there is no 'perfect' model and perhaps even seeking the 'best' model is asking too much. Model error wouldn't matter so much if there was more diversification. But sadly how good the models are is of secondary or even tertiary consideration within banks. How can one take as much risk as possible while appeasing risk management? That's number one (and two).

If everyone else is doing similar trades then, yes, you should do the same. Let's do some very simple mathematical modelling of the current system of compensation, nothing complicated, and very easily understood by non-mathematicians. To do a thorough job of modelling compensation we ought to look at:

- Probabilities of each trader making money, distributions, etc.
- How skilful you think you are versus how skilful you think other traders are. (Note that reality may be irrelevant!)
- Number of traders
- Details of the compensation scheme

But we are just going to take a very simple example. Suppose you think you are clever, but you think all your colleagues are fools. And these fools are all stupidly doing pretty much the same trades as each other. To get any bonus two criteria must be satisfied, first that you make a profit and second that between you all you make a profit. Now if your colleagues are idiots you might reckon that it's 50–50 whether they make a profit between them, think of tossing a coin. And they are all betting on the same toss of the same coin. You, on the other hand, are much cleverer, the probability of you making money is 75%, say. Now there are far more of them than you so the probability of it being a profitable year for the group is about 50%. For you to get a bonus first the group as a whole must make a profit, that's 50%, and then you must also make a profit, that's 75%. If you and they are independent then there is a 37.5% chance of you getting a bonus. Now who's stupid? If you copy their trades the probability of you getting a bonus is a significantly bigger 50%!

So what is the logical reaction? All do the same! This is just classical game theory.

Add to this the natural (for most people) response to seeing a person making a profit (even on a coin toss) and you can easily see how everyone gravitates towards following a trading strategy that perhaps made money once upon a time.

And that is the logical thing to do given the nature of the compensation.

Even if everyone starts off by following independent strategies, if you or anyone thinks that one of your colleagues is really clever, with a great strategy, then the logical thing to do is drop your strategy and copy his.

It is easy to see that the tendency is for everyone to converge to the same strategy, perhaps the one that has performed well initially, but this does not guarantee 'evolution' to the best strategy or even one that works.

The same happens between banks as well. They copy each other with little thought to whether that is the right thing to do. But this has other consequences as well. The banks compete with each other and if they trade the same contracts then this inevitably reduces profit margins. But profit margins are also margins for error. Reduction of profit margin increases the chance of large losses, and such losses will then happen simultaneously across all banks doing the same trade.

Finally, there's a timescale issue here as well. Anyone can sell deep OTM puts for far less than any 'theoretical' value, not hedge them, and make a fortune for a bank, which then turns into a big bonus for the individual trader. You just need to be able to justify this using some convincing model. Eventually things will go pear shaped and you'll blow up. However, in the meantime everyone jumps onto the same (temporarily) profitable bandwagon, and everyone is getting a tidy bonus. The moving away from unprofitable trades and models seems to be happening slower than the speed at which people are accumulating bonuses from said trades and models!

Unless the compensation system changes then as long as you want a bonus you must do the same trade as everyone else and use the same models. It doesn't matter whether the trade or the models are good. No wonder the man in the street thinks that bankers are crooks. And this does rather make the remaining 11 lessons rather a waste of time!

My scientist within would prefer each bank/hedge fund to have 'one' model, with each bank/hedge fund having a different model from its neighbour. Gives Darwin a fighting chance! I see so many banks using the same model as each other, and rarely are they properly tested, the models are just taken on trust. (And as we know from everyone's problems with calibration, when they are tested they are usually shown not to work but the banks still keep using them. Again, to be discussed later.)

There are fashions within investing. New contracts become popular, profits margins are big, everyone piles in. Not wanting to miss out when all around are reaping huge rewards, it is human nature to jump onto any passing bandwagon. Again this is the exact opposite of diversification, often made even worse because many of those jumping on the bandwagon (especially after it's been rolling along for a while) don't really have a clue what they are doing. To mix metaphors, many of those on the bandwagon are in over their heads.

The key point to remember is something that every successful gambler knows (a phrase I use often, but shouldn't have to), no single trade should be allowed to make or break you. If you trade like it is then you are doomed.

We all know of behavioural finance experiments such as the following two questions.

First question, people are asked to choose which world they would like to be in, all other things being equal, World A or World B where

A. You have 2 weeks' vacation, everyone else has 1 week
B. You have 4 weeks' vacation, everyone else has 8 weeks

The large majority of people choose to inhabit World B. They prefer more holiday to less in an absolute sense, they do not suffer from vacation envy. But then the second question is to choose between World A and World B in which

A. You earn $50,000 per year, others earn $25,000 on average
B. You earn $100,000 per year, others earn $200,000 on average

Goods have the same values in the two worlds. Now most people choose World A, even though you won't be able to buy as much 'stuff' as in World B. But at least you'll have more 'stuff' than your neighbours. People suffer a great deal from financial envy.

In banking the consequences are that people feel the need to do the same as everyone else, for fear of being left behind. Again, diversification is just not in human nature.

Now none of this matters as long as there is no impact on the man in the street or the economy. (Although the meaning of 'growth' and its 'benefits' are long due a critical analysis.) And this has to be a high priority for the regulators, banks clearly need more regulatory encouragement to diversify. Meanwhile, some final quick lessons. Trade small and trade often. Don't try to make your retirement money from one deal. And work on that envy!

Lesson 2: Supply and Demand

Supply and demand is what ultimately drives everything! But where is the supply and demand parameter or variable in Black–Scholes?

In a nutshell, the problem lies with people being so fond of complete markets. Complete markets are essentially markets in which you can hedge away risk. You can see why people like to work with such models. It makes them believe that they are safe![1] Hence the popularity of the deterministic volatility model. And even those models which are clearly not in complete markets, such as stochastic volatility or jump diffusion, people try to make complete by calibration! Of which more later.

A trivial observation: The world is net long equities after you add up all positions and options. So, net, people worry about falling markets. Therefore people will happily pay a premium for out-of-the-money puts for downside protection. The result is that put prices rise and you get a negative skew. That skew contains information about demand and supply and *not* about the only 'free' parameter in Black–Scholes, the volatility.

The complete-market assumption is obviously unrealistic, and importantly it leads to models in which a small number of parameters are used to capture a large number of effects.

Whenever a quant calibrates a model to the prices of options in the market he is saying something about the information content of those prices, often interpreted as a volatility, implied volatility. But really just like the price of a pint of milk is about far more than the cost of production, the price of an option is about much more than simple replication.

The price of milk is a scalar quantity that has to capture in a single number all the behind-the-scenes effects of, yes, production, but also supply and demand, salesmanship, etc. Perhaps the pint of milk is even a 'loss leader.' A vector of inputs produces a scalar price. So, no, you cannot back out the cost of production from a single price. Similarly you cannot back out a precise volatility from the price of an option when that price is also governed by supply and demand, fear

---

[1]How many trillions must be lost before people realize that hedging is not perfect?

and greed, not to mention all the imperfections that mess up your nice model (hedging errors, transaction costs, feedback effects, etc.).

Supply and demand dictate everything. The role of assumptions (such as no arbitrage) and models (such as the continuous lognormal random walk) is to simply put bounds on the relative prices among all the instruments. For example, you cannot have an equity price being 10 and an at-the-money call option being 20 without violating a simple arbitrage. The more realistic the assumption/model and the harder it is to violate in practice, the more seriously you should treat it. The arbitrage in that example is trivial to exploit and so should be believed. However, in contrast, the theoretical profit you might think could be achieved via dynamic hedging is harder to realize in practice because delta hedging is not the exact science that one is usually taught. Therefore results based on delta hedging should be treated less seriously.

Supply and demand dictate prices, assumptions and models impose constraints on the relative prices among instruments. Those constraints can be strong or weak depending on the strength or weakness of the assumptions and models.

Lesson 3: Jensen's Inequality Arbitrage

Jensen's Inequality states that if $f(\cdot)$ is a convex function and x is a random variable then

$$E[f(x)] \geq f(E[x]).$$

This justifies why non-linear instruments, options, have inherent value.

Example   You roll a die, square the number of spots you get, and you win that many dollars. How much is this game worth? (Assuming you expect to break even.) We know that the average number of spots on a fair die is $3\frac{1}{2}$ but the fair 'price' for this bet is not $(3\frac{1}{2})^2$.

For this exercise $f(x)$ is x^2, it is a convex function. So

$$E[x] = 3\frac{1}{2}$$

and

$$f(E[x]) = \left(3\frac{1}{2}\right)^2 = 12\frac{1}{4}.$$

But

$$E[f(x)] = \frac{1 + 4 + 9 + 16 + 25 + 36}{6} = 15\frac{1}{6} > f(E[x]).$$

The fair price is $15\frac{1}{6}$.

Jensen's Inequality and convexity can be used to explain the relationship between randomness in stock prices and the value inherent in options, the latter typically having some convexity.

Suppose that a stock price S is random and we want to consider the value of an option with payoff $P(S)$. We could calculate the expected stock price at expiration as $E[S_T]$, and then the payoff at that expected price $P(E[S_T])$. That might make some sense; ask yourself what you think the stock price will be at expiration and then look at the corresponding payoff.

Alternatively we could look at the various option payoffs and then calculate the expected payoff as $E[P(S_T)]$. The latter actually makes more sense, and is indeed the correct way to value options (provided the expectation is with respect to the *risk-neutral* stock price, of course).

If the payoff is convex then

$$E[P(S_T)] \geq P(E[S_T]).$$

We can get an idea of how much greater the left-hand side is than the right-hand side by using a Taylor series approximation around the mean of S. Write

$$S = \overline{S} + \epsilon,$$

where $\overline{S} = E[S]$, so $E[\epsilon] = 0$. Then

$$E[f(S)] = E[f(\overline{S} + \epsilon)] = E\left[f(\overline{S}) + \epsilon f'(\overline{S}) + \frac{1}{2}\epsilon^2 f''(\overline{S}) + \cdots\right]$$

$$\approx f(\overline{S}) + \frac{1}{2}f''(\overline{S})E[\epsilon^2]$$

$$= f(E[S]) + \frac{1}{2}f''(E[S])E[\epsilon^2].$$

Therefore the left-hand side is greater than the right by approximately

$$\frac{1}{2}f''(E[S])\,E[\epsilon^2].$$

This shows the importance of two concepts

- $f''(E[S])$: This is the **convexity** of an option. As a rule this adds value to an option. It also means that any intuition we may get from linear contracts (forwards and futures) might not be helpful with non-linear instruments such as options.
- $E[\epsilon^2]$: This is the **variance** of the return on the random underlying. Modelling randomness is the key to valuing options.

The lesson to learn from this is that whenever a contract has convexity in a variable or parameter, and that variable or parameter is random, then allowance must be made for this in the pricing.

Example   Anything depending on forward rates. If you price a fixed-income instrument with the assumption that forward rates are fixed (the deterministic models of yield, duration, etc.) and there is some non-linearity in those rates, then you are missing value. How much value depends on the convexity with respect to the forward rates and forward rate volatility.[2]

Example   Some things are tricky to model and so one tends to assume they are deterministic. Mortgage-backed securities have payoffs, and therefore values, that depend on prepayment. Often one assumes prepayment to be a deterministic function of interest rates, but this can be dangerous. Try to quantify the convexity with respect to prepayment and the variance of prepayment.

Lesson 4: Sensitivity to Parameters

If volatility goes up, what happens to the value of an option? Did you say the value goes up? Oh dear, bottom of the class for you! I didn't ask what happens to the value of a vanilla option, I just said 'an' option, of unspecified terms.[3]

Your boss asks you to price an up-and-out call option. What could be easier? You get out your well-used copy of Espen Haug's *Complete Guide to Option Pricing Formulas* (Haug, 2007) and code up the relevant option price and greeks. You've got to plug in a number for volatility so you look at some vanilla options, and they all seem to be around

---

[2]By 'convexity with respect to forward rates' I do not mean the curvature in the forward rate curve, I mean the second derivative of the contract with respect to the rates.

[3]If Bill Clinton can ask what the meaning of 'is' is then I can ask how important is an 'an.'

20% implied volatility. So you put 20% into the formula and tell your boss the resulting option value. A small profit margin is added on top, the client is happy, the deal is done and the option sold. All down to Corney and Barrow to celebrate.

At three o'clock in the morning you wake up in a cold sweat, and not due to excessive alcohol intake for once. What if volatility turns out to be something other than 20%? You completely forgot to test the sensitivity of the price to your volatility assumption. What an idiot you've been! You get out of bed and take out your home copy of Espen Haug's book (everyone should own two copies). You code up the formula again and see how the price varies as you change volatility from 17% to 23%. The price seems to be insensitive to volatility, and is anyway within the profit margin (a.k.a. margin for error). You breathe a sigh of relief, Phew!, and go back to bed.

That morning you go into work, perhaps looking a bit more tired than usual after all the champagne and the early-morning panic. Your boss calls you into his office, tells you that a fortune has been lost on your barrier option and you are fired.

Apart from the short time between the pricing and the loss and some risk-management issues this scenario has happened in the past, and looks like it will continue to happen in the future. So what went wrong? How could money have been lost after all that stress testing?

What went wrong was that you assumed volatility to be constant in the option formula/model and then you changed that constant. This is only valid if you know that the parameter is constant but are not sure what that constant is. But that's not a realistic scenario in finance. In fact, I can only think of a couple of scenarios where this makes sense...

The first scenario is when every contract in your portfolio has gamma of the same sign, either all have positive gamma everywhere or all have negative gamma everywhere. We'll see the significance of the sign of gamma in a moment. But, anyway, who only buys options or only sells options? Most people buy some and sell some, even Nassim Taleb.

The other scenario is...

The telephone rings, you answer. At the other end of the line a deep, manly voice says 'This is God here. I've got a hot tip for you. The volatility of IBM will be constant for the next year with value...' And the line goes dead. Damn, a hot tip from the top man and my battery dies! Never mind, all is not lost. We may not know what volatility is going to be, but at least we know it is going to be constant, and that is useful information.

Ok, so that's not a realistic scenario, unless you are an ex President of the US or an ex Prime Minister of the UK.

By varying a constant parameter you are effectively measuring

$$\frac{\partial V}{\partial \text{ parameter}}.$$

This is what you are doing when you measure the 'greek' vega:

$$\text{vega} = \frac{\partial V}{\partial \sigma}.$$

But this greek is misleading. Those greeks which measure sensitivity to a 'variable' are fine, those which supposedly measure sensitivity to a 'parameter' are not. Plugging different constants for volatility over the range 17% to 23% is *not* the same as examining the sensitivity to volatility when it is allowed to roam freely between 17 and 23% *without the constraint of being constant*. I call such greeks 'bastard greeks' because they are illegitimate.

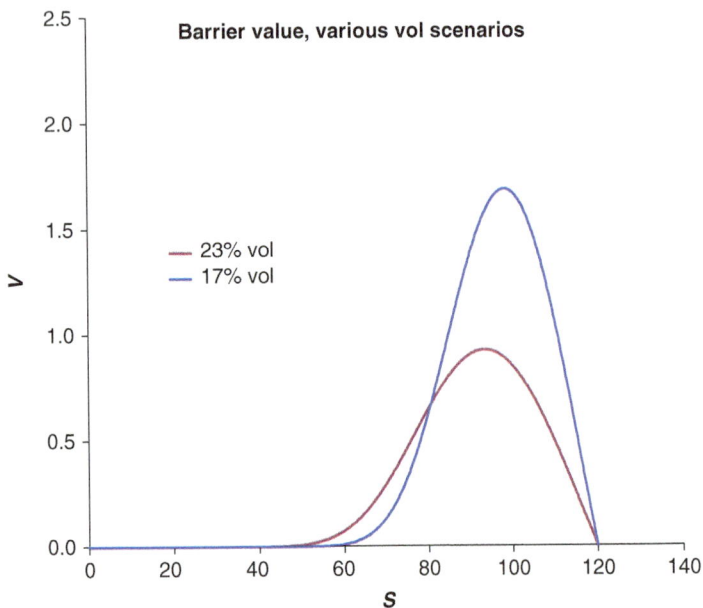

Figure 5.1: The value of some up-and-out call option using volatilities 17% and 23%.

The following example demonstrates this.

Example In Figure 5.1 is shown the value of some up-and-out call option using the two volatilities 17% and 23%. Notice that at an asset value of around 80 the two curves cross. This is because the higher volatility increases the option's value for lower asset prices but decreases the option's value above. If you are sitting around the 80 asset value you would conclude that the option value is insensitive to the volatility. Vega here is zero.

The problem arises because this option has a gamma that changes sign. For lower asset values it is positive and for higher it is negative. Generally speaking, if you increase volatility where the gamma is positive then the price will rise. If you increase it where gamma is negative the price will fall.[4]

The relationship between sensitivity to volatility and gamma is because they always go together. In the Black–Scholes equation we have a term of the form

$$\frac{1}{2}\sigma^2 S^2 \frac{\partial^2 V}{\partial S^2}.$$

The bigger this combined term, the more the option is worth. But if gamma is negative then large volatility makes this big in absolute value, but negative, so it decreases the option's value.

So what happens if there is a negative skew in our barrier-option problem? Increase volatility where gamma is positive and the price will rise. Decrease volatility where the gamma is negative and the price will...rise. The result is that with a negative skew the option value rises *everywhere*. You should have sold the option for significantly more than you did, hence your loss of money and job.

It is quite simple to measure the true sensitivity of an option value to a range of volatilities as above and that is to solve the Black–Scholes equation with volatility being 17% whenever gamma is positive and 23% whenever gamma is negative. This will give the lowest possible option value. And then price again using 23% when gamma is positive and 17% when gamma is negative. This will give the highest possible option value. This is easily done, but not by Monte Carlo, you'll have

---

[4]I say 'Generally speaking' because this is not exactly true. We are dealing with diffusion equations here and for them any change to a parameter in one place will affect the solution everywhere.

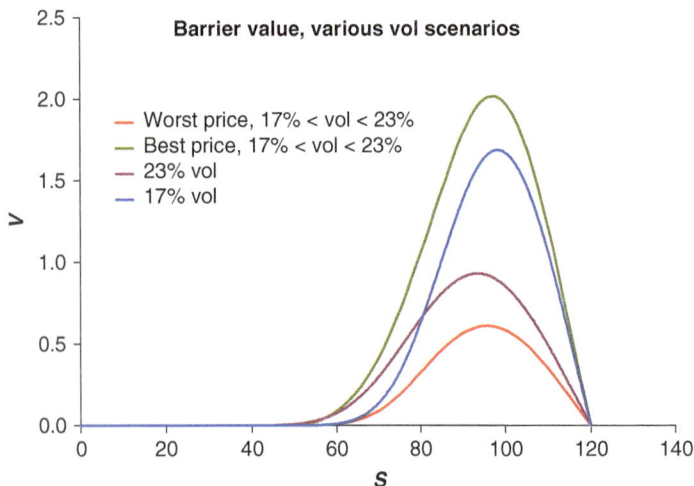

Figure 5.2: Uncertain volatility model, best and worst cases.

to solve by finite-difference methods.[5] This model is called the Uncertain Volatility Model (see Avellaneda, Levy & Parás, 1995).

In Figure 5.2 are shown the best and worst cases for this up-and-out call option. Note that at the point where vega is zero there is actually a factor of 3 difference between the worst and best cases. That is an enormous range considering volatility is only allowed between 17 and 23%. Yet it is far more realistic than what you get by 'varying a constant.'

---

[5]If you have a finite-difference code working for a constant volatility model then rewriting the code to price in this model should take less than a minute. To modify your Monte Carlo code to do the same things will takes weeks!

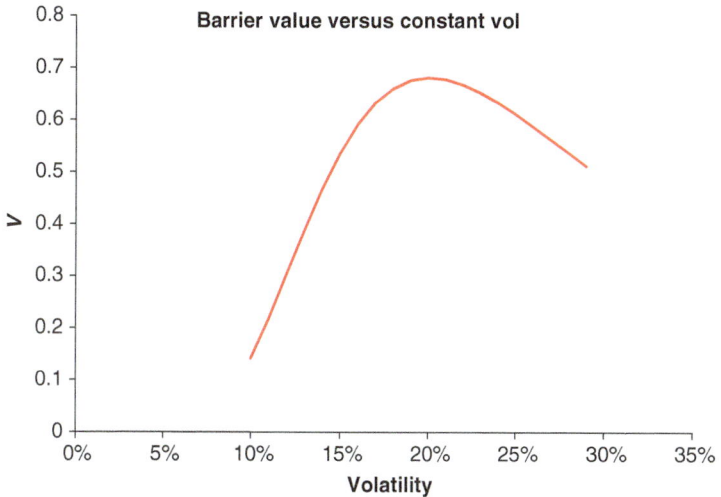

Figure 5.3: Value versus constant volatility.

As well as looking out for gamma changing sign you can spot potential hazards of the above form by plotting the value of an option versus a constant parameter. This is shown in Figure 5.3 for the up-and-out call option. If you ever see non-monotonicity then it should set alarm bells ringing. Non-monotonicity is telling you that sometimes the higher the parameter value the better, sometimes the lower the better. Beware.[6] And, by the way, you get the same thing happening in some CDO tranches.

---

[6]People also use plots like this to back out implied volatilities. This is meaningless when there is non-monotonicity. You can get multiple implied volatilities, or no implied volatility at all. The naive would say that the latter means arbitrage. It doesn't, unless you live in a world where the parameter is definitely constant. That's not my world.

Traditionally minded quants have fudges to try to address this problem.[7] These fudges involve measuring delta and seeing how delta changes as volatility changes. This is a very poor substitute for doing the job properly.

Example Another obvious example is the cliquet option. With some of these cliquet contracts you find that they are insensitive to volatility in classical models. Suppose that you price a cliquet using a volatility of 20%. You find that the price is $17.1. You then use a volatility of 15% and the price becomes $17.05. Continuing with the test for robustness you use a volatility of 25% and find a price of $17.07. Seems pretty insensitive to volatility. You now use a volatility of 10%, and then 30%, both times the theoretical price hardly changes. You then use the model that everyone else thinks of as 'cutting edge,' the Heston model (Heston, 1993), again $17 give or take a few cents. Finally, the ultimate test, you call up another bank, disguising your voice, and ask their price. Yet again, $17.

By now you are thinking that the cliquet is insensitive to volatility, that its price is close to $17. So you add on a tiny profit margin (after all, these contracts are so popular, lots of demand and therefore not much room for a profit margin), sell it to your client and relax after a job well done. Risk management will be proud of all the stress testing you've done.

Christ! A few weeks later you're fired, again, after huge losses on cliquet options. What went wrong?

There's a big clue that you found during your stress testing. It seems that the price was insensitive to simple volatility models. From this what can you conclude?

---

[7]It is common practice to fudge your way out of a hole in this business. Although the subject could be far more 'scientific' this tendency to apply fixes without addressing fundamental issues restricts the subject to being a branch of 'carpentry.'

The incorrect and naive, although common, conclusion is that indeed your volatility assumption does not matter. You could not be more wrong. There is a lot of volatility risk in this contract, it just happens to be cleverly hidden.

What contract is insensitive to volatility? Simply stock. Is the cliquet option the same as stock? No way, it is far more complicated than that!

Therefore the apparent insensitivity to volatility is masking the 'change of sign of gamma' that we've seen above. See Wilmott (2002) for details about these contracts, how sensitive they really are and why the traditional 'fudges' will not help you.

Lesson 5: Correlation

Many derivatives contracts depend on more than a single underlying, these are basket options. Many derivatives contracts have multiple sources of randomness, such as stochastic stock price *and* stochastic volatility. Many derivatives contracts require modelling of an entire forward curve. These situations have something in common; they all, under current theory frameworks, require the input of parameters representing the relationship between the multiple underlyings/factors/forward rates.

And so the quant searches around in his quant toolbox for some mathematical device that can be used to model the relationship between two or more assets or factors. Unfortunately the number of such tools is limited to correlation and, er,..., correlation. It's not that correlation is particularly brilliant, as I'll explain, but it is easy to understand. Unfortunately, it is also easy to misunderstand.

One problem concerning correlation is its relevance in different applications, we'll look at this next in the context of

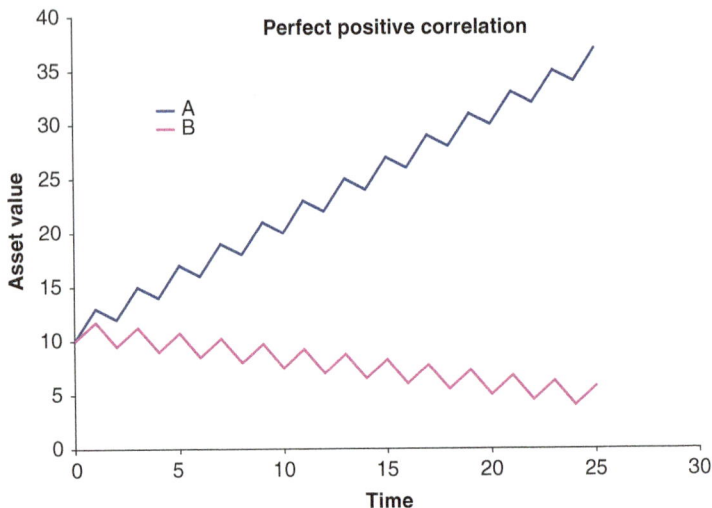

Figure 5.4: Two perfectly correlated assets.

timescales, and another is its simplicity, and inability to capture interesting dynamics.

When we think of two assets that are highly correlated then we are tempted to think of them both moving along side by side almost. Surely if one is growing rapidly then so must the other? This is not true. In Figure 5.4 we see two asset paths that are perfectly correlated but going in opposite directions.

And if two assets are highly negatively correlated then they go in opposite directions? No, again not true, as illustrated in Figure 5.5.

If we are modelling using stochastic differential equations then correlation is about what happens at the smallest,

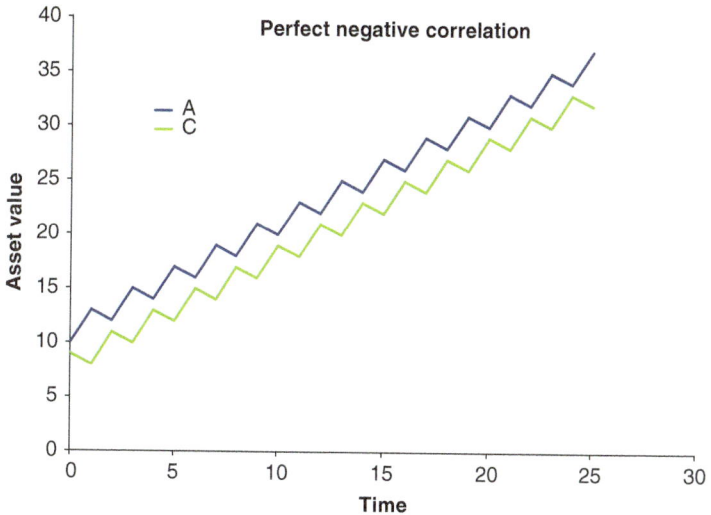

Figure 5.5: Two perfectly negatively correlated assets.

technically infinitesimal, timescale. It is not about the 'big picture' direction. This can be very important and confusing. For example, if we are interested in how assets behave over some finite time horizon then we still use correlation even though we typically don't care about short timescales, only our longer investment horizon (at least in theory). Really we ought to be modelling drift better, and any longer-term interaction between two assets might be represented by a clever drift term (in the stochastic differential equation sense).

However, if we are hedging an option that depends on two or more underlying assets then, conversely, we don't care about direction (because we are hedging), only about dynamics over the hedging timescale. The use of correlation may then be easier to justify. But then we have to ask how stable is this correlation.

So when wondering whether correlation is meaningful in any problem you must answer two questions (at least), one concerning timescales (investment horizons or hedging period) and another about stability.

It is difficult to model interesting and realistic dynamic using a simple concept like correlation. This is illustrated in Figure 5.6 and the following story. In the figure are plotted the share prices against time of two makers of running shoes.

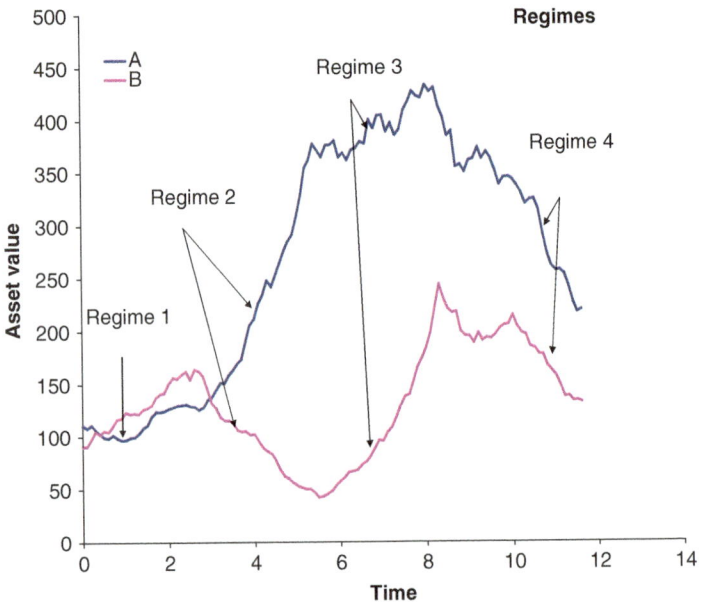

Figure 5.6: Two assets, four regimes.

In Regime 1 both shares are rising, the companies are seen as great investments, who doesn't want to go jogging and get healthy, or hang out in the 'hood wearing their gang's brand? See how both shares rise together (after all, they are in the same business). In Regime 2 company A has just employed a hotshot basketball player to advertise their wares; stock A grows even faster but the greater competition causes share B to fall (after all, they are in the same business). News Flash! Top basketball player in sex and drugs scandal! Parents stop buying brand A and switch to brand B. The competition is on the other foot so to speak. Stock A is not doing so well now and stock B recovers, they are taking away stock A's customers (after all, they are in the same business). Another News Flash! Top advocate of jogging drops dead...while jogging! Sales of both brands fall together (after all, they are in the same business).

Now that is what happens in real life.

In practice there will also be some delay between trading in one stock and trading in the other. If company A is much bigger and better known that company B then A's stocks will trade first and there may be a short delay until people 'join the dots' and think that stock B might be affected as well. This is causality, and not something that correlation models.

And, of course, all this stock movement is based on shifting sentiment. If one company defaults on a payment then there is a tendency for people to think that other companies in the same sector will do the same. This is contagion. Although this could actually decrease the real probability of default even as the perceived probability is increasing! This is because of decreasing competition. Correlation is a poor tool for representing the opposing forces of competition and contagion.

As you can see, the dynamics between just two companies can be fascinating. And can be modelled using all sorts of interesting mathematics. One thing is for sure, and that is such dynamics while fascinating are certainly not captured by a correlation of 0.6!

Is this good news or bad news? If you like modelling then it is great news, you have a blank canvas on which to express your ideas. But if you have to work with correlation on a day-to-day basis it is definitely bad news.

Example In South Korea they are very partial to options on two underlyings. Typically worst-of options, but also with a barrier. The value of such a contract will depend on the correlation between the two assets. But because of the barriers these contracts can have a cross gamma that changes sign. Remember what happens when this happens? It's straight from Lesson 4 above.

In theory there is a term of the form

$$\rho \sigma_1 \sigma_2 S_1 S_2 \frac{\partial^2 V}{\partial S_1 \, \partial S_2}$$

in the governing equation. If the cross gamma term changes sign, then sensitivity to correlation cannot be measured by choosing a constant ρ and then varying it.

In Figure 5.7 is a contour map of the cross gamma of one of these two-asset worst-of barrier options. Note the change of sign. There are risk-management troubles ahead for those naive enough to measure $\frac{\partial V}{\partial \rho}$!

Please remember to plot lots of pictures of values and greeks before ever trading a new contract!

Example Synthetic CDOs suffer from problems with correlation. People typically model these using a copula approach, and then argue about which copula to use. Finally because

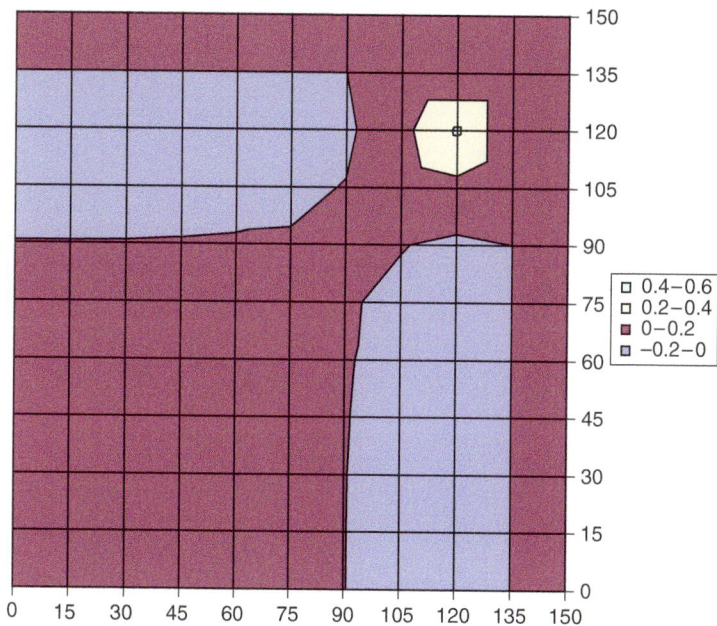

Figure 5.7: Contour plot of cross gamma of a two-asset, worst-of, knock-out option.

there are so many parameters in the problem they say 'Let's assume they are all the same!' Then they vary that single constant correlation to look for sensitivity (and to back out implied correlations). Where do I begin criticizing this model? Let's say that just about everything in this model is stupid and dangerous. The model does not capture the true nature of the interaction between underlyings, correlation never does, and then making such an enormously simplifying assumption about correlation is just bizarre. (I grant you not

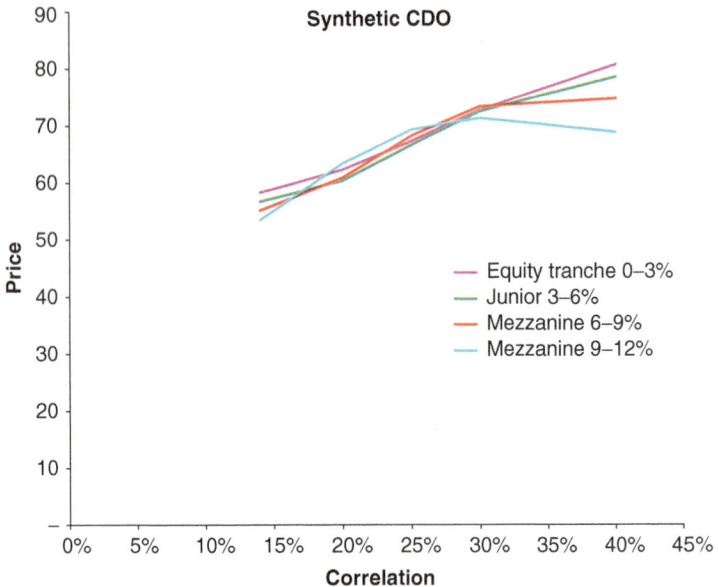

Figure 5.8: Various tranches versus correlation.

as bizarre as the people who lap this up without asking any questions.)[8]

Figure 5.8 is a plot of various CDO tranches versus constant correlation. Note how one of the lines is not monotonic. Can you hear the alarm bells? That tranche is dangerous.[9]

---

[8]We know why people do this though, don't we? It's because everyone else does. And people can't bear watching other people getting big bonuses when they're not.

[9]You know that now do you? And how much did that lesson cost you? The most important lesson in life is to make all your lessons cheap ones. There, I've got you started.

Lesson 6: Reliance on Continuous Hedging (Arguments)

One of the most important concepts in quantitative finance is that of delta or dynamic hedging. This is the idea that you can hedge risk in an option by buying and selling the underlying asset. This is called delta hedging since 'delta' is the Greek letter used to represent the amount of the asset you should sell. Classical theories require you to rebalance this hedge continuously. In some of these theories, and certainly in all the most popular, this hedging will perfectly eliminate all risk. Once you've got rid of risk from your portfolio it is easy to value since it should then get the same rate of return as putting money in the bank.

This is a beautiful, elegant, compact theory, with lots of important consequences. Two of the most important consequences (as well as the most important which is ... no risk!) are that, first, only volatility matters in option valuation, the direction of the asset doesn't, and, second, if two people agree on the level of volatility they will agree on the value of an option, personal preferences are not relevant.

The assumption of continuous hedging seems to be crucial to this theory. But is this assumption valid?

Continuous hedging is not one of those model assumptions that may or may not be correct, requiring further study. It is blatantly obvious that hedging more frequently than every nanosecond is impossible. And even if it were possible, people are clearly not doing it. Therefore of all the assumptions in classical Black–Scholes theory this is one of the easiest to dismiss.

So why are there so few papers on hedging discretely when there are tens of thousands of papers on volatility modelling?

Perhaps because of these nice 'results,' most quants simply adore working within this sort of framework, in which continuous hedging is possible. Only a very tiny number are asking whether the framework is valid, and if it's not (which it isn't) then what are the consequences? This is unfortunate since it turns out that Black–Scholes is very robust to assumptions about volatility (see Ahmad & Wilmott, 2005) whereas robustness to discrete hedging is less well understood.

I continue to find myself in the middle of the argument over validity of Black–Scholes. On one side are those who we might call 'the risk neutrals' – those heavily invested in the concepts of complete markets, continuous hedging, no arbitrage, etc.; those with a relatively small comfort zone. On the other side there are those who tell us to throw away Black–Scholes because there are so many fallacious assumptions in the model that it is worthless. Let's call them the 'dumpers.' And then there are a tiny number of us saying yes, we agree, that there are many, many reasons why Black–Scholes should not work, but nevertheless the model is still incredibly robust to the model assumptions and to some extent you can pretend to be a risk neutral in practice.

Discrete hedging is the perfect example of this. The theory says that to get the Black–Scholes model you need to hedge continuously. But this is impossible in practice. The risk neutrals bury their heads in the sand when this topic is discussed and carry on regardless, and the dumpers tell us to throw all the models away and start again. In the middle we say calm down, let's look at the maths.

Yes, discrete hedging is the cause of large errors in practice. I've discussed this in depth in Wilmott (2006a). Hedging error is large, of the order of the square root of the time between rehedges, it is path dependent, depending on the realized gamma. The distribution of errors on each rehedge is highly skewed (even worse in practice than in theory). But most analysis of hedging error assumes the simple model in which

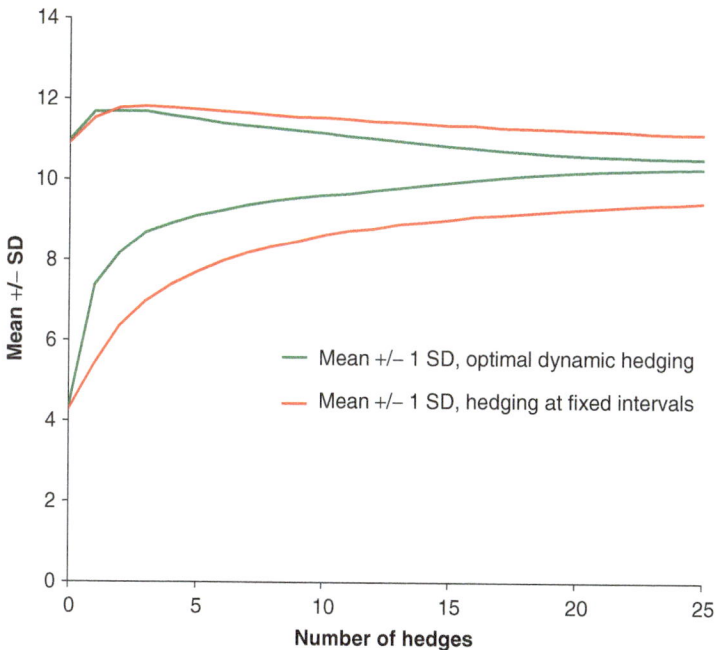

Figure 5.9: Risk reduction when hedging discretely.

you rehedge at fixed time intervals. This is a very restrictive assumption. Can we do better than this? The answer is yes. If we are allowed a certain number of rehedges during the life of an option then rehedging at fixed intervals is not at all optimal. We can do much better (Ahn & Wilmott, 2009).

Figure 5.9 shows a comparison between the values of an at-the-money call, strike 100, one year to expiration, 20% volatility, 5% interest rate, when hedged at fixed intervals (the red line) and hedged optimally (the green line). The lines are the mean value plus and minus one standard deviation.

All curves converge to the Black–Scholes complete-market, risk-neutral, price of 10.45, but hedging optimally gets you there much faster. If you hedge optimally you will get as much risk reduction from just 10 rehedges as if you use 25 equally spaced rehedges.

From this we can conclude that as long as people know the best way to dynamically hedge then we may be able to get away with using risk neutrality even though hedging is not continuous. But do they know this? Everyone is brought up on the results of continuous hedging, and they rely on them all the time, but they almost certainly do not have the necessary ability to make those results valid! The risk neutrals, even the cleverest and most well-read, almost certainly do not know the details of the mathematics of discrete hedging.

I think the risk neutrals need to focus their attention more on hedging than on making their volatility models even more complicated.

Lesson 7: Feedback

Are derivatives a good thing or a bad thing? Their origins are in hedging risk, allowing producers to hedge away financial risk so they can get on with growing pork bellies or whatever. Now derivatives are used for speculation, and the purchase/sale of derivatives for speculation outweighs their use for hedging.

Does this matter? We know that speculation with linear forwards and futures can affect the spot prices of commodities, especially in those that cannot easily be stored. But what about all the new-fangled derivatives that are out there?

A simplistic analysis would suggest that derivatives are harmless, since for every long position there is an equal and opposite short position, and they cancel each other out.

But this misses the important point that usually one side or the other is involved in some form of dynamic hedging used to reduce their risk. Often one side buys a contract so as to speculate on direction of the underlying. The seller is probably not going to have exactly the opposite view on the market and so they must hedge away risk by dynamically hedging with the underlying. And that dynamic hedging using the underlying can move the market. This is the tail wagging the dog! This was quantified in Schönbucher & Wilmott (1995), important results from this work concern the role of gamma, and in particular its sign. For the following you will need to remember that hedging a short (long) gamma position is essentially the same as replicating a long (short) position.

There are two famous examples of this feedback effect:

- Convertible bonds – volatility decrease
- 1987 crash and (dynamic) portfolio insurance – volatility increase

Example When a company issues convertible bonds it does so with a discount to encourage people to buy. It would be very embarrassing if they remained unsold. This obviously presents a profit opportunity, buy the cheap CB and make some money. This is not quite that simple because if you own a CB then you are exposed to risk caused by movement of the underlying. To hedge this risk you must sell the underlying asset according to the dynamic-hedging theory. If all goes well you will then realize the profit, being on average the difference between the correct price, based on the actual volatility, and the market/issue price, based on implied volatility. So far so good. The problem arises because these days the vast majority of CBs are in the hands of banks and hedge funds. And that means if one firm is delta hedging, then so are they all.

If the stock rises, then because gamma is positive you have to sell some stock to maintain a delta-neutral position. If there are a lot of you simultaneously selling stock then this will put some downward pressure on the stock. This may or may not be enough to change its direction, that will depend on the relative sizes of the delta hedgers and other traders. But the larger the gamma the greater the pressure.

Now if the stock does fall then you will all have to buy back stock, and the pressure is now upwards. The result is that volatility can be suppressed. And that is a bit of a nuisance if you have just bought the CB for the potential profit; your actions aimed at realizing that profit cause the profit to decrease!

A simple simulation is shown in Figure 5.10. Here a long put with expiration five years is being hedged dynamically. The volatility should be 20%, and after expiration that is what you see, but before expiration the volatility is much lower. The level of the stock matters because the effect is more pronounced if the asset is around the strike, where gamma is largest.

The opposite side of the coin was seen in 1987. Dynamic portfolio insurance was partly blamed for the dramatic stock market crash. Portfolio insurance was invented in the late 1970s by Leland, O'Brien and Rubinstein and was the neat idea that if you were worried about losing money during a falling market then you could limit this by replicating a put option. As the market falls you sell, according to some Black–Scholes-like formula. This is replicating a long gamma position, or equivalently hedging a short gamma position. The opposite of the CB example. Now as markets fall you have to sell, putting *downward* pressure on the stock, increasing the rate of fall. Again, whether this matters depends on the ratio of insurers to other traders. In 1987 this ratio turns out to be big enough to cause or at least exacerbate the crash.[10] Again

---

[10]This was not entirely Leland, O'Brien and Rubinstein's fault. Others in the market knew about this idea and were using it as well.

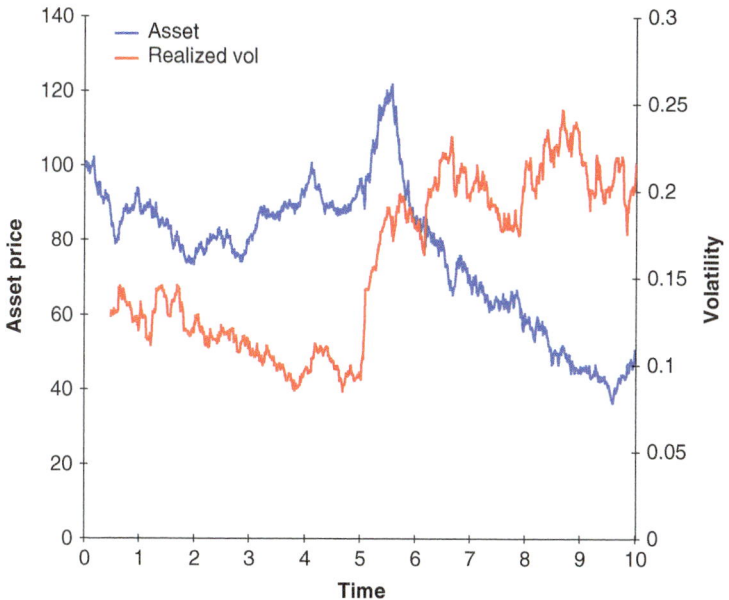

Figure 5.10: Simulation when hedging long gamma.

the result was to cause precisely that event against which it was supposed to insure! Figure 5.11 shows a simulation. This uses the same method as in the previous figure, just with a sign change because here it is a positive gamma that is being replicated.

The simple lesson here is that derivatives do not make a zero-sum game, they can be beneficial or harmful, affecting the underlying via dynamic hedging or replication. Maybe you care about your impact on the world's economy, maybe you don't, but you should definitely look deeper into the impact on your P&L.

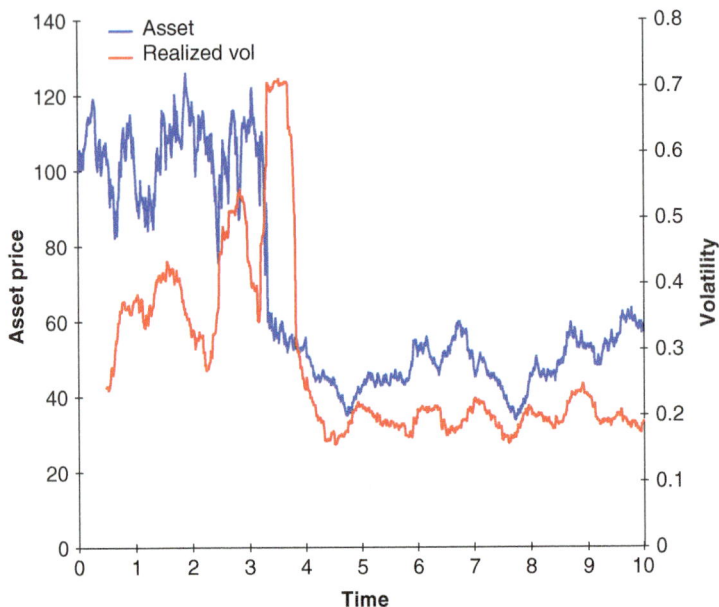

Figure 5.11: Simulation when hedging short gamma.

Lesson 8: Reliance on Closed-Form Solutions

Quants work long hours. Some work almost as hard as nurses. It is surely too much to ask that they also solve an equation numerically!

Example You need to value a fixed-income contract and so you have to choose a model. Do you (a) analyse historical fixed-income data in order to develop an accurate model, which is then solved numerically, and finally back-tested using a decade's worth of past trades to test for robustness, or (b) use Professor X's model because the formulæ are simple and, quite frankly, you don't know any numerical analysis, or (c) do whatever everyone else is doing? Typically people will go for (c), partly for reasons already discussed, which amounts to (b).

Example   You are an aeronautical engineer designing a new airplane. Boy, those Navier–Stokes equations are hard! How do you solve non-linear equations? Let's simplify things, after all you made a paper plane as a child, so let's just scale things up. The plane is built, a big engine is put on the front, it's filled with hundreds of passengers, and it starts its journey along the runway. You turn your back, without a thought for what happens next, and start on your next project.

One of those examples is fortunately not real. Unfortunately, the other is.

Quants love closed-form solutions. The reasons are

1. Pricing is faster
2. Calibration is easier
3. You don't have to solve numerically.

Popular examples of closed-form solutions/models are, in equity derivatives, the Heston stochastic volatility model (Heston, 1993), and in fixed income, Vasicek (1977),[11] Hull & White (1990), etc.

---

[11]To be fair to Vasicek I'm not sure he ever claimed he had a great model, his paper set out the general theory behind the spot-rate models, with what is now known as the Vasicek model just being an example.

Although the above reasons for choosing models with closed-form solutions may be true they are not important criteria *per se* in the scheme of things. Indeed, there are a couple of obvious downsides to restricting yourself to such models. Just because you want an easy life doesn't make the model work. By choosing ease of solution or calibration over accuracy of the model you may be making calibration less stable.

Models with closed-form solutions have several roles in applied mathematics and quantitative finance. Closed-form solutions are

- useful for preliminary insight
- good for testing your numerical scheme before going on to solve the real problem
- for examining second-year undergraduate mathematicians.

People who only know about the 'popular' models do not make good quants, good risk managers, or good traders. They don't even make good researchers.

Lesson 9: Valuation is Not Linear

You want to buy an apple, so you pop into Waitrose. An apple will cost you 50p. Then you remember you've got friends coming around that night and these friends really adore apples. Maybe you should buy some more? How much will 100 apples cost?

I've started asking this question when I lecture. And although it is clearly a trick question, the first answer I get is always £50.

Anyone who thinks that is the right answer will make a fantastic, classically trained, old-fashioned, and eventually loss-making, and finally unemployed, quant. As anyone who has ever shopped should know, the answer is 'less than £50.' Economies of scale.

Here's a quote from a well-known book (my emphasis): 'The change of numeraire technique probably seems mysterious. Even though one may agree that it works after following the steps in the chapter, there is probably a lingering question about why it works. Fundamentally it works *because valuation is linear*.... The linearity is manifested in the statement that the value of a cash flow is the sum across states of the world of the state prices multiplied by the size of the cash flow in each state.... After enough practice with it, it will seem as natural as other computational tricks one might have learned.'

Note it doesn't say that linearity is an assumption, it is casually taken as a fact. Valuation is apparently linear. Now there's someone who has never bought more than a single apple!

Example   The same author may be on a sliding royalty scale so that the more books he sells the bigger his percentage. How can nonlinearity be a feature of something as simple as buying apples or book royalties yet not be seen in supposedly more complex financial structured products? (Maybe he is selling so few books that the nonlinearity has not kicked in!)

Example   A bank makes a million dollars profit on CDOs. Fantastic! Let's trade 10 times as much! They make $10 million profit. The bank next door hears about this and decides it wants a piece of the action. They trade the same size. Between the two banks they make $18 million profit. Where'd the $2 million go? Competition between them brings the price and profit margin down. To make up the shortfall, and because of simple greed, they increase the size of the trades. Word spreads and more banks join in. Profit margins are squeezed. Total profit stops rising even though the positions are getting bigger and bigger. And then the inevitable happens, the errors in the models exceed the profit margin (margin for error), and between them the banks lose billions. 'Fundamentally it works because valuation is linear.' Oh dear!

This is not really the place for me to explain all the non-linear quantitative finance models in existence. There are many, and I will give some references below. But how many do *you* know? I suspect you'll struggle to name a single one. Researchers, modellers, banks, software companies, everyone has a lot invested in this highly unrealistic assumption of linearity, and yet many of the best models I've seen are non-linear.[12]

To appreciate the importance of nonlinearity you have to understand that there is a difference between the value of a portfolio of contracts and the sum of the values of the individual contracts.[13] In pseudomath, if the problem has been set up properly, you will get

$$\text{Value}(A + B) \geq \text{Value}(A) + \text{Value}(B).$$

Imagine we have just inherited a barrier option from someone who got fired earlier today. As with many barrier options it has a lot of volatility risk because of the way gamma changes sign. We value it at $10 using one of the non-linear models to be mentioned shortly. Not worth as much as I'd hoped. Because of all that volatility risk I'm being conservative in my valuation. The volatility risk is because the contract has gamma. If I could reduce gamma then I will reduce volatility

---

[12]I have to declare an interest here, I and colleagues have developed some of these.

[13]What I call, to help people remember it, the 'Beatles effect.' The Fab Four being immeasurably more valuable as a group than as the sum of individuals...Wings, Thomas the Tank Engine,...

risk and the value should increase, there'll be less risk and so less reason to be conservative. I look around and I see an exchange-traded, vanilla option selling for $5. This option has caught my eye because it has similar gamma to the barrier, around the same asset value, etc. *but of the opposite sign*. If I buy this option it will reduce my volatility risk! I buy the option, it costs $5. I now value the portfolio consisting of the barrier and the vanilla, valued as one unit, and I get the answer … $16. In other words, the benefit to my portfolio of buying the vanilla has outweighed its cost. I seem to have made $1. This is 'static hedging.' We could try buying two of these options, thinking that buying one vanilla makes us $1 'out of thin air' so we can conjure up $2 by buying two options. Sadly, we find that the portfolio of barrier option plus two vanillas is actually only $20.5, not the hoped-for $22. Again, this is because of nonlinearity and what this tells us is that somewhere between buying no vanillas and buying two is the optimal static hedge.

There are many papers on static hedging of exotics (often barriers) with vanillas, and they all have in common that there is no financial benefit whatsoever to such hedging. They are *ad hoc* fixes to poor models. However, when the model is non-linear the benefit is clearly seen in terms of extra value.

Here is a partial list of the advantages to be found in some non-linear models.

- **Perfect calibration**:   Actual and implied quantities are not confused. We don't have to believe that there is any useful information about parameters contained in the market prices of derivatives. Nonlinearity ensures that reasonable market prices of liquid instruments are matched by default. No more tying yourself in numerical knots to calibrate your unstable stochastic volatility model. Nonlinearity means that there are genuine model-based reasons for static hedging, a benefit of which is perfect calibration.

Calibration is automatic. And you can calibrate to both bid and ask prices, and to liquidity. How many of you calibrating Heston can make that claim?

- **Speed**: The models will be almost as fast to solve numerically as their equivalent linear models (sometimes faster because calibration happens by default).
- **Easy to add complexity to the model**: The modular form of the models means that it is easy to add complexity in terms of jumps, stochastic volatility, etc.
- **Optimal static hedging**: Hedging exotics with traded vanillas will increase 'value' because of the non-linearity. This can be optimized.
- **Can be used by buy and sell sides**: Traditionally the buy side uses one type of models and the sell side another. This is because the buy side is looking for arbitrage while the sell side are valuing exotics which their risk management insists are priced to be consistent with vanillas (i.e. the thought of accepting that there may be arbitrage is abhorrent!) By changing the 'target function' in certain optimization problems some of the models can be used by hedge funds looking for statistical arbitrage and by investment banks selling exotics that are calibrated to vanillas.

That list is just to whet your appetite. Even if you think everything else in this chapter is baloney, you must at least look up the following articles. That's assuming you are ready to move outside your comfort zone.

And now the reading list:

- Hoggard, Whalley & Wilmott (1994) is an early paper on a non-linear model, in this case a model for pricing in the presence of transaction costs. Also look at other papers on costs by Whalley *et al.*
- Avellaneda, Levy & Parás (1995) introduce the Uncertain Volatility Model (UVM). (See also Avellaneda & Parás, 1976

and Avellaneda & Buff, 1977.) This is a very simple and clever model, very compact in form compared with models such as Heston and considerably easier to solve and to calibrate (it's automatic). The trick is to price conservatively and look at worst-case scenarios. A follow-up paper showed just why nonlinearity is so important (optimal static hedging and value maximization).

- In Hua & Wilmott (1997, 1998, 1999, 2001) we look at modelling crashes in a worst-case scenario framework, and again a non-linear model results. This model and the UVM both permit perfect hedging and are complete-market models.[14] In later articles we show how to strip the model down to its bare essentials into a wonderfully simple (and very popular with investors!) risk management technique called CrashMetrics.

- In Ahn & Wilmott (2003, 2007, 2008) and several follow-up articles we introduce a model based on stochastic volatility, but with a twist. Instead of taking the common route of introducing a market price of volatility risk to derive an equation we work within a framework in which we calculate the mean option value and its standard deviation. Effectively we say that, let's be honest, you can't hedge volatility no matter what academics say, so let's just accept it as fact and get on with reducing risk as much as we can. As well as being no harder to implement than standard volatility models – actually it's easier because calibration is automatic – it can be used for both arbitrage and for valuation of exotics. It's about the nearest thing to an all-singing, all-dancing, model as you can find at the moment.

---

[14]'Complete market' is a common phrase and framework, but its meaning can be a bit ambiguous once you move outside classical, linear models. Here I say the models are complete in the same way that the Black–Scholes for pricing American options is complete.

Lesson 10: Calibration

Note: This Lesson has been censored to protect the innocent.

'A cynic is a man who knows the price of everything and the value of nothing,' said Oscar Wilde. At least a cynic may know that there is a difference between price and value. A typical quant thinks that these two are the same. To fully appreciate finance theory and practice you need to distinguish between these two and also to understand the concept of worth. Go back to page 200 and remind yourself (or maybe you remember the go-cart example?)

One of the most damaging effects of confusing price and value is the ubiquity of unthinking calibration. By assuming that there is perfect information about the future contained in option prices we are abdicating responsibility for performing any analysis, estimation or forecasting for that future. We are in effect saying that 'the market knows best,' which has to be one of the stupidest knee-jerk statements that people make in quantitative finance. I know that markets do not know best; I have two pieces of information for this. First, I have been involved in successful forecasting, making money because of the difference between forecasts of the future and the market's view of the future. Second, I speak to more people in this business than almost anyone else, and I know that the vast, vast majority of them are using models that make ridiculous assumptions about the market and its knowledge (and aren't even properly tested). If almost everyone is basing their models around the prices of some coked-up 23-year-old trader and not on any statistical analysis then there are going to be plenty of (statistical) arbitrage opportunities for a long time to come.

I hold three people responsible for the popularity of calibration. Three very nice, very intelligent people who all published similar work at about the same time. These three are
_____ _____,[15] _____ _____ and _____ _____.[16]

Professor _____ is a very experienced practitioner, now academic in the city of N__ Y____. He has a great enthusiasm for understanding and modelling the markets. I get the impression that whenever he finds (yet) another violation of a model's assumptions he is first disturbed, then intellectually stimulated, and finally turns his mind to improving and quantifying. Dr _____ is a practitioner. He takes a very European, laid-back, approach to this business, almost as if he knows he will never come up with perfection. But he keeps trying! I do not know Professor _____ very well, only having met him once and exchanged some emails. Clearly he is very talented, and seems quite charming, with the looks of a 1930's swashbuckling matinee idol! Had his book with _____ ___, published in 19_, been printed in paperback and cheaper[17] then I have no doubt that quantitative finance would be a completely different, and better, subject from what it is now.

All of these researchers are men I admire and respect, and they have all produced brilliant work over the years. But by some once-in-a-lifetime alignment of the heavenly stars they all in 19_/_ published independently the same idea of _____ _____, the model that _____ is a function of _____ price and ____. And this is the

---

[15] _____'s work was joint with _____. However, I don't know this latter gentleman so won't comment on his niceness or intelligence!
[16] I don't *really* blame them. Their research was interesting and clever, just in my view misguided. It's the sheep who implemented the ideas without testing that I blame.
[17] It is still one of the most expensive books I have ever bought!

idea I hate more than any other in quantitative finance![18]

The function in question is found by looking at the market prices of exchange-traded contracts. In other words, rather than estimating or forecasting _____ and then finding the prices of options, we work backwards from the prices to the _____ model. This is calibration.

To be fair to these three, this wasn't the invention of calibration. Ho & Lee (1986) published a fixed-income paper which did something similar. But in fixed income this is not so bad – interest rate volatility is lower than in equities and there are many contracts with which to hedge.

First of all how does calibration work? I'll explain everything using this _____ _____ model.

When you look at the market prices of exchange-traded options you see how there are strike and term structures for implied volatility. Implied volatility is not constant. The strike structure goes by the names of skews and smiles. _If_ volatility is constant _and_ the Black–Scholes model is correct, _then_ these prices cannot be correct otherwise there'd be arbitrage opportunities. The existence of arbitrage opportunities seems to make some people uncomfortable.[19] What is the simplest way to make our model output theoretical prices that exactly match market prices? In equities the simplest such model is the _____ _____ model.

---

[18]Heston (1993) is a very close second.

[19]As I've said elsewhere, life and everything in it is about arbitrage opportunities and their exploitation. I don't see this as a bit problem. It's an ... opportunity. Evolution is statistical arbitrage in action! Ok, now I see why maybe Americans don't like arbitrage, they don't believe in evolution!

Implied volatility is a function of two variables, strike and expiration, so let's make actual volatility a function of asset price and calendar time, two variables again. There is enough freedom here that if we choose this actual volatility function carefully enough then the solution of the Black–Scholes equation will match market prices of vanilla options of all strikes and expirations. That's calibration.

And why do people do it? Here's another story. Your task is to price some exotic equity option. It just so happens that you've been doing a part-time PhD in volatility forecasting, so naturally you'll want to use your new volatility model. So you price up the exotic and show the results to your boss. 'Fantastic,' he says, 'I'm sure you've done a great job. But there's one small problem.' Here it comes. 'I think your model is wonderful, I know how clever you are. But those @*&%$ in risk management are going to need some convincing before they'll let you use your new model. Tell you what, if you can value some vanillas using your model for comparison with market prices then I'm sure that'd go a long way to persuading them.' So you do as you are told. You value the vanillas using your model. However your model only happens to be a fantastic volatility-forecasting model, it is not a model that calibrates to market prices. Therefore your values and the market prices of the vanillas disagree. Your boss tells you to dump your model and use the _____ _____ model like everyone else. Your bank has just missed a fantastic opportunity to make a killing, and will probably now lose millions instead.

This model was adopted with little thought simply because of quants obsession with no arbitrage! Ask a quant for an estimate of volatility and he will look to option prices. Ask him to estimate volatility using only the stock price, or for an asset on which there are no traded options, and watch the look of confusion that comes over his face.

Advocates of calibrated models will defend it by saying two things. First, how do you know that your volatility model is so great? Second, in practice we hedge with vanillas to minimize risk that the model is wrong.

The first defence is silly. I know very few walks of life in which we know anything with any certainty. Or any walks of life in which we know the probabilities of events, outside of a few casino games. Does this stop people going about their day-to-day business? Getting drunk, chatting up women, starting families, having an affair, nothing has either a certain outcome or has known consequences with known probabilities. We are spoiled in quantitative finance that we seem, according to theories, to need little knowledge of asset price distributions to value derivatives. We don't need to know asset growth rates for example. And this seems to have caused our ability to attempt to forecast or to analyse historical data to have completely atrophied. And worse, not only have people become lazy in this respect, but they also seem to think that somehow it is a fundamental law of finance that we be given everything we need in order to correctly value an option. This is utter nonsense. Here's an arbitrage that some people believe exists: do a Masters in Financial Engineering, get a job in a bank, do a little bit of programming, take home a big pay packet, and retire at 35. If you are terrified of the thought of the existence of arbitrage, why is this one any different?[20] No, I'm afraid that sometimes a little bit of effort and originality of thought is required.

The second defence is really saying, well we know that calibrated models are wrong but we solve this by hedging with other options so as to reduce model risk. This is a big, fat fudge. At least these people accept that calibration isn't as good as they've been led to believe. My problem with this is that this fudge is completely *ad hoc* in nature, and no

---

[20]Note that I'm not saying I think this arbitrage exists, only that many people do.

one really tests whether the fudge actually works. And the reason for this is that risk management don't really know enough about the markets, the mathematics or the research literature.

The above strongly hints that the _____ _____ model and calibrated models generally are rubbish. They are. I will now tell you how to prove it for yourself, and then explain why.

Today you take price data for exchange-traded vanillas. You work backwards from these prices to find the actual volatility using the _____ _____ model (details in Wilmott, 2006a, even though I don't believe in it) or any other calibrated model. You have now found the local volatility surface or model parameters. Imagine making the local volatility surface out of modelling clay, which is then baked in the oven. Once found, this surface, or model parameters, are not allowed to change. It is set in stone. If there is a change then the model was wrong. You come back a week later when the data has changed. You recalculate (recalibrate) the model. Now look at the local volatility surface or parameters and compare with what you found last week. Are they the same? If they are then the model may be right. If they are not, *and they never, ever are* (just ask *anyone* who has ever calibrated a model) then that model is wrong. If our subject were a science (which it could be if people wanted it to be) then the model would be immediately thrown away. As it is, people continue to use the model (with the sort of *ad hoc* fudges mentioned above) and pretend all is well. See Schoutens *et al.* (2004) for nice examples of this.

A simple analogy is that one day you go to a fortune teller. She tells you that in August next year you will win the lottery. But then you go back a week later, she doesn't recognize you, and now she says that sadly you will be run over by a bus and killed...in June next year. These two pieces of information cannot both be right, so you conclude that fortune telling is nonsense. Similarly you should conclude that calibration is nonsense.

Mathematically we have here what is called an 'inverse problem,' meaning that we work backwards from answers/values to find parameters. Such problems are notoriously unstable in the sense that a small change to initial conditions (implied volatility) can have a huge effect on the results (actual volatility). Diffusion equations, such as the Black–Scholes equation, cannot be 'run backwards in time.' But you get inverse problems in many branches of applied mathematics. In an episode of CSI Miami there was a murder on a yacht. I think one of the big-breasted and bronzed babes was the vic and H. had to find the murderer. The clue as to the perp was a piece of fabric on which there was some writing. Unfortunately the fabric had got wet and the ink had diffused. H. takes the fabric back to the lab, runs it through one of their hi-tech gizmos and before our eyes the lettering appears. What they had done was to reverse time in a diffusion process, an inverse problem not unlike calibration. As every applied mathematician knows this is a no-no, and at this point I lost all respect for CSI! Actually it's not as bad as that, as long as the diffusion has not acted for too long and as long as we know that the image on the fabric was made up of letters then we can with a certain degree of confidence figure out what the writing might have been. With inverse problems in finance such as the _____ _____ model such reverse engineering would only make sense if the assumed model, that volatility is a function of asset price and time, were a good one. It just is not. And no amount of fancy mathematics or numerical analysis is going to make this bad model any good.

So that's how you prove that calibrated models are rubbish: Calibrate now and recalibrate a week later. Then take your results to the most senior risk managers you can find. Tell them that what they want you to do is dangerous and insist on implementing a decent model instead!

Here are a few problems with calibrated models.

- **Over fitting**:   You lose important predictive information if your model fits perfectly. The more instruments you calibrate to the less use that model is.
- **Fudging hides model errors**:   Perfect calibration makes you think you have no model risk, when in fact you probably have more than if you hadn't calibrated at all.
- **Always unstable**:   The parameters or surfaces always change when you recalibrate.
- **Confusion between actual parameter values and those seen via derivatives**:   For example there are two types of credit risk, the actual risk of default and the market's perceived risk of default. If you hold an instrument to maturity then you may not care about perceived risk of default, if you sell quickly then all you care about is market perception since there is little risk of actual default in that time.

Why is calibration unstable?

In a recent piece of research (Ahmad & Wilmott, 2007) we showed how in the fixed-income markets one can back out the 'market price of interest rate risk.' For every random quantity there is a market price of risk, measuring how much expected return in excess of the risk-free rate is needed for every unit of risk. Economists and believers that humans are rational will probably say that this quantity should be, oh I don't know, 3, say. It should be a nice stable parameter representing the nice stable behaviour of investors. Of course, sensible people know better and indeed when we look at this parameter, shown in Figure 5.12, we see exactly what you would expect, a lot of variation. (For technical reasons this parameter ought to be negative.) In some periods people need more return for taking risk, sometimes less, sometimes they'll even pay to take risk! And this is why calibration is

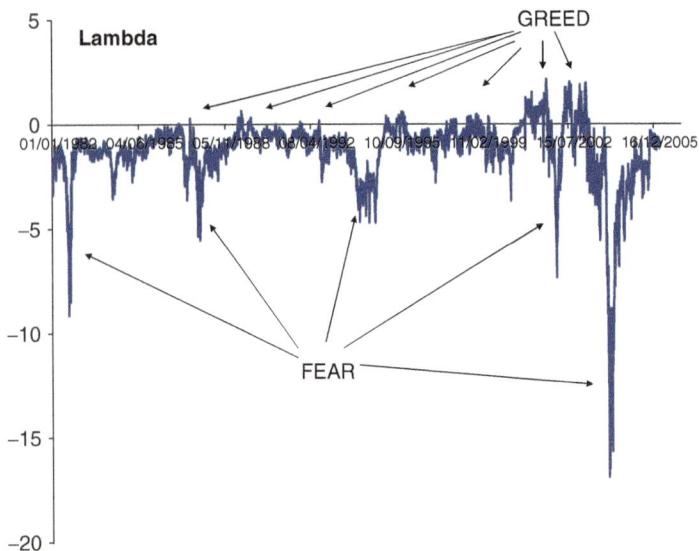

Figure 5.12: Market price of interest rate risk versus time.

doomed. When you calibrate you are saying that whatever
the market sentiment is today, as seen in option prices, is
going to pertain forever. So if the market is panicking today it
will always panic. But Figure 5.12 shows that such extremes
of emotion are shortlived. And so if you come back a week
later you will now be calibrating to a market that has ceased
panicking and is perhaps now greedy![21]

Calibration assumes a structure for the future that is inconsistent with experience, inconsistent with commonsense, and
that fails all tests.

---

[21]So I would advocate models with stochastic market price of risk,
as being sensible and not too far removed from classical models.

And finally, can we do better? Yes, much better! And to get you started go back to Lesson 9 and go through that reading list!

Note: If your goal is to fool risk managers into believing that you are taking little risk while actually taking enormous risks then, yes, use any of these calibrated models, the _____ _____ model, Heston, etc. I can even tell you which model is best for hiding risk. Not hedging risk, note, I mean *hiding* it from anyone who might want to restrict the size of your trades and hence your bonus. But, for obvious topical reasons, I think we've gone beyond that now!

Lesson 11: Too Much Precision

Given all the errors in the models, their unrealistic assumptions, and the frankly bizarre ways in which they are used, it is surprising that banks and funds make money at all!

Actually there is a sound reason why they make money and it has nothing to do with clever models. As mentioned above, if you take all equities and derivatives based on those equities, and sum them up across all banks, hedge funds, individuals, etc., then all the complicated derivatives will cancel themselves out since for every long there is a short, leaving just the equities, plain and simple. Now put most of those equities in the hands of banks and funds, rather than in the hands of the man in the street, and you'll see that as long as the stock market is rising those banks and funds will make money, bonuses all around. All derivatives do is to redistribute the profit, some banks/funds win, some lose, but net no impact.[22] This argument only works during growing markets. In bear

---

[22]Feedback being a caveat.

markets you need to look elsewhere for profit, ways of making money whether stocks are going up, down or sideways, and that means derivatives.

But derivatives come with a lot of risk, some well understood and some not. And as people get more 'sophisticated' they believe that they can increase their exposure to derivatives and so make money regardless of market conditions. Sometimes this is true, and the models seem to work, sometimes it is not and the models fall over. It's because of potential model error that one has to build in a decent margin, based on a decent understanding of possible risks. But once banks start competing between themselves for the same contracts then the margin for error will inevitably succumb to the powerful forces of supply and demand.

One part of the above paragraph glosses over something that is very important in practice. When I say 'Sometimes this is true, and the models seem to work,' you should ask how do we know? The truth of the matter is that we don't. Let's look at the story of a single trade in some exotic. There are several stages.

1. There is demand for some contract, real or perceived
2. The contract must be understood in terms of risk, valuation, potential market, profit, etc.
3. A deal gets done with an inbuilt profit margin.
4. The contract is then thrown into some big pot with lots of other contracts and they are risk managed together.
5. A profit is accrued, perhaps marking to model, or perhaps at expiration.

This is naturally a simplification but I wanted to list this procedure to highlight a disconnection between theory and practice. At Stage 2 here there is a valuation procedure that will probably involve some complicated model, maths, and numerics. The underlying model makes certain assumptions about the financial world and the contract is valued accordingly. But then at Stage 4 you throw this contract into the same pot as other contracts, and you don't actually implement the theory upon which the valuation was based. And finally, you never really know whether that particular contract made money because it gets hedged simultaneously with other contracts. You never follow the valuation, static and dynamic hedging, with all its cash flows and accrued interest, etc., that the theory is using. Instead you look at the pot containing many contracts and say that it has made a profit (or a loss). You have no idea whether each contract has 'washed its own face' as they say.

I have to ask why bother going to all this trouble of valuation and risk management when you lump everything together anyway? I'm not saying that it is wrong to lump everything together, on the contrary, in the above lesson on nonlinearity you can see sound financial reasons why you should do that. I am saying that such effort in valuation hardly seems worth it when ultimately you are probably going to be making money from the Central Limit Theorem! Errors in the models and the implementation of the models are probably large enough that on a contract-by-contract basis you may make or lose money, but so what? As long as on average you make money then you should be happy.

The point of this lesson is to suggest that more effort is spent on the benefits of portfolios than on fiddly niceties of modelling to an obsessive degree of accuracy. Accept right from the start that the modelling is going to be less than perfect. It is not true that one makes money from every instrument because of the accuracy of the model. Rather one makes money *on average* across *all* instruments *despite* the model. These observations suggest to me that less time should be spent on dodgy models, meaninglessly calibrated, but more time on models that are accurate *enough* and that build in the benefits of portfolios.

While we are on the topic of model accuracy, I just want to make a few comments about models in different markets.

Some models are better than others. Sometimes even working with not-so-good models is not too bad. To a large extent what determines the success of models is the type of market. Let me give some examples.

Equity, FX and commodity markets Here the models are only so-so. There has been a great deal of research on improving these models, although not necessarily productive work. Combine less-than-brilliant models with potentially very volatile markets and exotic, non-transparent, products and the result can be dangerous. On the positive side as long as you diversify across instruments and don't put all your money into one basket then you should be ok.

Fixed-income markets These models are pretty dire. So you might expect to lose (or make) lots of money. Well, it's not as simple as that. There are two features of these markets which make the dire modelling less important; these are (a) the underlying rates are not very volatile and (b) there are plenty of highly liquid vanilla instruments with which to try to hedge model risk. (I say 'try to' because most model-risk hedging is really a fudge, inconsistent with the framework in which it is being used.)

Correlation markets Oh, Lord! Instruments whose pricing requires input of correlation (FI excepted, see above) are accidents waiting to happen. The dynamic relationship between just two equities can be beautifully complex, and certainly never to be captured by a single number, correlation. Fortunately these instruments tend not to be bought or sold in non-diversified, bank-destroying quantities. (Except for CDOs, of course!)

Credit markets   Single-name instruments are not too bad *as long as the trades are kept small*. Except that often the models assume risk neutrality and an ability to hedge that is often not possible in practice. Again problems arise with any instrument that has multiple 'underlyings,' so the credit derivatives based on baskets...you know who you are. But as always, as long as the trades aren't too big then it's not the end of the world.[23]

Lesson 12: Too Much Complexity

'Four stochastic parameters good, two stochastic parameters bad.' (Thanks to George Orwell.)

Maths is fun. I've had many jobs and careers in the last three decades, and started various businesses, but the one thing that I keep coming back to is mathematics. There's something peaceful and relaxing about an interesting maths problem that means you can forget all your troubles, just get totally absorbed in either the detail of a formulation, calculation or solution, or lie back and think of deep concepts. I wonder if one of the reasons quantitative finance is in such a mess is that people treat the subject as if it's of academic interest only, to be made as abstract and complicated, and therefore as respectable, as possible.

I'm going to let you in on the big secret of quantitative finance, and you must keep this secret because if word got out then that would be the end of all masters in financial engineering programs. And universities make a lot of money from those.

---

[23]I'd like to have added another 'lesson' on credit derivatives and models, but that would require me to have a solution or better models. I don't. Yet. So the best I can do for the moment is to suggest that you avoid this market like the plague.

Ok, the big secret ... Quantitative finance is one of the easiest branches of mathematics.

Sure you can make it as complicated as you like, and plenty of authors and universities have a vested interest in so doing. But, approached correctly and responsibly, quant finance is easy.

Let's talk about the different levels of maths you see in quant finance.

As I said earlier, some people try to dumb the subject down. There are plenty of textbooks that kid you into thinking that there is almost no mathematics in the subject at all. These books may dabble in the binomial model but go no deeper. Now anyone with a second-year undergraduate knowledge of numerical methods will recognize the binomial model for the inadequate and cumbersome dinosaur that it is. I like the binomial method as a teaching tool to explain delta hedging, no arbitrage and risk neutrality. But as a way of pricing derivatives for real? No way! Watching the contortions people go through on the wilmott.com Forums in order to make their binomial code work is an illuminating experience. Dumbing the subject down is not good. You cannot price sophisticated contracts unless you have a decent mathematical toolbox, and the understanding of how to use those tools. Now let's look at the opposite extreme.

Some people try to make the subject as complicated as they can. It may be an academic author who, far from wanting to pass on knowledge to younger generations, instead wants to impress the professor down the corridor. He hopes that one day he will get to be the professor down the corridor who everyone is trying to impress. Or maybe it's a university seeing the lucrative QF bandwagon. Perhaps they don't have any faculty with knowledge of finance, certainly no practical knowledge, but they sure do have plenty of people with a deep knowledge of measure theory. Hey presto, they've just launched a masters in financial engineering! Making this subject too complicated is worse than dumbing it down. At least if you only work with the binomial method you can't do much harm, simply because you can't do much of anything. But with all those abstract math tools at your command you can kid yourself into believing you are a derivatives genius. Never mind that you don't understand the markets, never mind that the people using your models haven't a clue what they are doing. I believe that the obscenely over-complicated models and mathematics that some people use are a great danger. This sort of maths is wonderful, if you want to do it on your own time, fine. Or become a finance professor. Or move into a field where the maths is hard and the models are good, such as aeronautics. But please don't bring this nonsense into an important subject like finance where even the best models are rubbish. Every chain has its weakest link. In QF the weakest links are the models, not the maths, and not the numerical methods. So spend more time thinking about your models and their robustness and less on numerical inversion of a transform in the complex plane.

Here's a true story that illustrates my point quite nicely. Not long ago I was approached by someone wanting to show me a paper they hoped to get published. The paper was about 30 pages long, all maths, quite abstractly presented, no graphs. When I'd read the paper I said to the author that I thought this was a good piece of work. And I told him that the reason I thought it was good was because, unfortunately for him, I'd done exactly the same piece of research myself with Hyung-sok Ahn a few years earlier. What I didn't tell him was that Hyungsok and I only took four pages to do what he'd needed 30 for. The reason for the huge difference in derivations was simply that we'd used the right kind of maths for the job in hand, we didn't need to couch everything in the most complicated framework.[24] We used straightforward maths to present a straightforward problem. Actually, what he had done was worse than just unnecessarily obscure the workings of the model. There was a point in the paper where he trotted out the old replacement-of-drift-with-the-risk-free-rate business. He did this because he'd seen it done a thousand times before in similarly abstract papers. But, because the paper was about incomplete markets, the whole point of the model was that you were not allowed to make this substitution! He didn't understand the subtle arguments behind risk-neutral valuation. That was the place where his paper and ours diverged, ours started to get interesting, his then followed a well-worn, and in this case incorrect, path.

Rule 1 of quant finance seems to be 'Make this as difficult as we can.' It's going to be years before the tendency for people to make quantitative finance as difficult as they possibly can is eradicated. And that'll be years while money is lost because of lack of transparency and lack of robustness in pricing and risk-management models. (But on the other hand, there'll be lots of research papers. So not all bad news then!)

There've been a couple of recent Forum threads that perfectly illustrate this unnecessary complexity. One thread was a brainteaser and the other on numerical methods.

The brainteaser concerned a random walk and the probability of hitting a boundary. Several methods were proposed for solving this problem involving Girsanov, Doleans-Dade martingales, and optimal stopping. It must have been a really difficult problem to need all that heavyweight machinery, no? Well, no, actually. The problem they were trying to solve was a linear, homogeneous, second-order, constant-coefficient, ordinary differential equation! (Really only first order because

---

[24]And we weren't afraid of the measure-theory police, so we did things that mathematicians have been doing for a century and we did them without any fuss.

there weren't even any non-derivative terms!) The problem was utterly trivial. Talk about sledgehammers and nuts.

The other thread was on using non-recombining trees to price a simple vanilla option. People were really helpful to the person asking for advice on this topic. But no one, except for me, of course, asked the obvious question, 'Why on Earth are you doing such a silly thing?' I can hardly imagine a more cumbersome, slow, and generally insane way to solve a simple problem.

It disturbs me when people have been educated to such a level of complexity that they can throw about references to obscure theorems while at the same time being unable to think for themselves. To me, mathematics is about creativity in the use of tools not about being able to quote 'results.' Even knowledge of the names of mathematicians and what they are famous for is something I find a bit suspect. If you know the names of all the theorems but don't know when to use them then you are a historian not a mathematician. Perhaps maths is an art, and I'm not impressed with painting by numbers.

If you look through the various Forums on wilmott.com you will see that we have some areas for people to talk about mathematics, research papers, etc., and then there are areas to talk about trading, general finance, etc. You will notice that the majority of people are comfortable in only either the maths areas or the trading areas. Not many people are comfortable in both. That should tell you something, the overlap of skills is far less than one would expect or hope. Who would you trust your money to? A mathematician who doesn't know the markets or a trader who doesn't know maths? Ideally, find someone who is capable in both areas.

And so to the middle ground, not too dumb, not too clever for its own good. Let's start with the diffusion equation. As every mathematician knows there are three important classes of partial differential equation: elliptic, hyperbolic, parabolic. There are various standard techniques for solving these equations, some of them numerical. The diffusion equations that we see so often in QF are of parabolic type. Rather conveniently for us working in QF, parabolic equations are by far the simplest of these different types to solve numerically. By far the simplest. And our equations are almost always linear. Boy, are we spoiled! (I've thought of publishing the 'Wilmott Ratio' of salary to mathematical complexity for various industries. Finance would blow all others out of the water!)

Or take the example of some fancy exotic/OTC contract. You start with a set of model assumptions, then you do the maths, and then the numerics. Most of the time the maths can be 100% correct, i.e. no approximations, etc. Given the assumptions, the pricing model will follow as night follows day. Then you have to crunch the numbers. Now the numerics can be as accurate as you like. Let's say you want the value and greeks to be 99% accurate. That's easy! It may take a few seconds, but it can usually be done. So where's the problem? Not the maths, not the numerics. The problem is in the model, the assumptions. Maybe you get 70% accuracy if you are lucky. It seems odd therefore that so many people worry about the maths and the numerics, when it is very obvious where the main errors lie!

There is a maths sweet spot, not too dumb, not too smart, where quants should focus. In this sweet spot we have basic tools of probability theory, a decent grasp of calculus, and the important tools of numerical analysis. The models are advanced enough to be able to be creative with new instruments, and robust enough not to fall over all the time. They are transparent so that the quant and the trader and the salesperson can understand them, at least in their assumptions and use.

Because the models are necessarily far, far from perfect, one must be suspicious of any analytical technique or numerical method that is too fiddly or detailed. As I said above, the weakest link in the chain is not the maths or the numerics but the model assumptions. Being blinded by mathematical science and consequently believing your models is all too common in quantitative finance.

Bonus Lesson 13: The Binomial Method is Rubbish

Thanks for bearing with me through a dozen lessons. As a reward for your patience and tolerance I am going to give you a bonus lesson! And this bonus lesson is probably the easiest one for quants to implement immediately. The lesson is . . . dump the binomial method!

I really like the binomial method. But only as a teaching aid. It is the easiest way to explain

1. hedging to eliminate risk
2. no arbitrage
3. risk neutrality.

I use it in the CQF to explain these important, and sometimes difficult to grasp, concepts.[25] But once the CQFers have understood these concepts they are instructed never to use the binomial model again, on pain of having their CQFs withdrawn!

Ok, I exaggerate a little. The binomial model was the first of what are now known as finite-difference methods. It dates

---

[25]It's also instructive to also take a quick look at the trinomial version, because then you see immediately how difficult it is to hedge in practice.

back to 1911 and was the creation of Lewis Fry Richardson, all-round mathematician, sociologist, and poet.

A lot of great work has been done on the development of these numerical methods in the last century. The binomial model is finite differences with one hand tied behind its back, hopping on one leg, while blindfolded. So when I refer to the 'binomial method' here what I am really criticizing is people's tendency to stick with the simplest, most naive finite-difference method, without venturing into more sophisticated territory, and without reading up on the more recent numerical-methods literature.

Why is the binomial method so ubiquitous? Again, habit is partly to blame. But also all those finance professors who know bugger all about numerical methods but who can just about draw a tree structure, they are the ones responsible. Once an academic writes his lecture notes then he is never going to change them. It's too much effort. And so generations of students are led to believe that the binomial method is state of the art when it is actually prehistoric.

Summary

Question 1: What are the advantages of diversification among products, or even among mathematical models?

Answer 1: No advantage to your pay whatsoever!

Question 2: If you add risk and curvature what do you get?

Answer 2: Value!

Question 3: If you increase volatility what happens to the value of an option?

Answer 3: It depends on the option!

Question 4: If you use ten different volatility models to value an option and they all give you very similar values what can you say about volatility risk?

Answer 4: You may have a lot more than you think!

Question 5: One apple costs 50p, how much will 100 apples cost you?

Answer 5: Not £50!

How did you do in the quiz at the start? If you are new to quant finance you may have got some of the answers correct. If you have just come out of a Masters in Financial Engineering then you probably got most of them wrong. But if you're a quant or risk manager who likes to think for himself and is not happy with the classical 'results' of quantitative finance, then maybe you even got all of them right!

QF is interesting and challenging, not because the mathematics is complicated, it isn't, but because putting maths and trading and market imperfections and human nature together and trying to model all this, knowing all the while that it is probably futile, now that's fun!

References and Further Reading

Ahmad, R & Wilmott, P 2005 Which free lunch would you like today, Sir? Delta hedging, volatility arbitrage and optimal portfolios. *Wilmott* magazine November 64–79

Ahmad, R & Wilmott, P 2007 The market price of interest rate risk: Measuring and modelling fear and greed in the fixed-income markets. *Wilmott* magazine January

Ahn, H & Wilmott, P 2003 Stochastic volatility and mean-variance analysis. *Wilmott* magazine November 84–90

Ahn, H & Wilmott, P 2007 Jump diffusion, mean and variance: how to dynamically hedge, statically hedge and to price. *Wilmott* magazine May 96–109

Ahn, H & Wilmott, P 2008 Dynamic hedging is dead! Long live static hedging! *Wilmott* magazine January 80–87

Ahn, H & Wilmott, P 2009 A note on hedging: restricted but optimal delta hedging; mean, variance, jumps, stochastic volatility, and costs. In preparation

Avellaneda, M & Buff, R 1997 *Combinatorial implications of nonlinear uncertain volatility models: the case of barrier options.* Courant Institute, NYU

Avellaneda, M & Parás, A 1996 Managing the volatility risk of derivative securities: the Lagrangian volatility model. *Applied Mathematical Finance* **3** 21–53

Avellaneda, M, Levy, A & Parás, A 1995 Pricing and hedging derivative securities in markets with uncertain volatilities. *Applied Mathematical Finance* **2** 73–88

Derman, E & Kani, I 1994 Riding on a smile. *Risk* magazine **7** (2) 32–39 (February)

Dupire, B 1993 Pricing and hedging with smiles. Proc AFFI Conf, La Baule June 1993

Dupire, B 1994 Pricing with a smile. *Risk* magazine **7** (1) 18–20 (January)

Haug, EG 2007 *Complete Guide to Option Pricing Formulas.* McGraw–Hill

Heston, S 1993 A closed-form solution for options with stochastic volatility with application to bond and currency options. *Review of Financial Studies* **6** 327–343

Ho, T & Lee, S 1986 Term structure movements and pricing interest rate contingent claims. *Journal of Finance* **42** 1129–1142

Hoggard, T, Whalley, AE & Wilmott, P 1994 Hedging option portfolios in the presence of transaction costs. *Advances in Futures and Options Research* **7** 21–35

Hua, P & Wilmott, P 1997 Crash courses. *Risk* magazine **10** (6) 64–67 (June)

Hua, P & Wilmott, P 1998 Value at risk and market crashes. *Derivatives Week*

Hua, P & Wilmott, P 1999 Extreme scenarios, worst cases, Crash-Metrics and Platinum Hedging. *Risk Professional*

Hua, P & Wilmott, P 2001 CrashMetrics. In *New Directions in Mathematical Finance* (eds Wilmott, P & Rasmussen, H)

Hull, JC & White, A 1990 Pricing interest rate derivative securities. *Review of Financial Studies* **3** 573–592

Rubinstein, M 1994 Implied binomial trees. *Journal of Finance* **69** 771–818

Schönbucher, PJ & Wilmott, P 1995 Hedging in illiquid markets: nonlinear effects. *Proceedings of the 8th European Conference on Mathematics in Industry*

Schoutens, W, Simons, E & Tistaert, J 2004 A perfect calibration! Now what? *Wilmott* magazine March 66–78

Vasicek, OA 1977 An equilibrium characterization of the term structure. *Journal of Financial Economics* **5** 177–188

Whalley, AE & Wilmott, P 1993a Counting the costs. *Risk* magazine **6** (10) 59–66 (October)

Whalley, AE & Wilmott, P 1993b Option pricing with transaction costs. MFG Working Paper, Oxford

Whalley, AE & Wilmott, P 1994a Hedge with an edge. *Risk* magazine **7** (10) 82–85 (October)

Whalley, AE & Wilmott, P 1994b A comparison of hedging strategies. *Proceedings of the 7th European Conference on Mathematics in Industry* 427–434

Whalley, AE & Wilmott, P 1995 An asymptotic analysis of the Davis, Panas and Zariphopoulou model for option pricing with transaction costs. MFG Working Paper, Oxford University

Whalley, AE & Wilmott, P 1996 Key results in discrete hedging and transaction costs. In *Frontiers in Derivatives* (eds Konishi, A & Dattatreya, R) 183–196

Whalley, AE & Wilmott, P 1997 An asymptotic analysis of an optimal hedging model for option pricing with transaction costs. *Mathematical Finance* **7** 307–324

Wilmott, P 2000 The use, misuse and abuse of mathematics in finance. Royal Society Science into the Next Millennium: Young scientists give their visions of the future. *Philosophical Transactions* **358** 63–73

Wilmott, P 2002 Cliquet options and volatility models. *Wilmott* magazine December 2002

Wilmott, P 2006a *Paul Wilmott on Quantitative Finance*, second edition. John Wiley & Sons Ltd

Wilmott, P 2006b *Frequently Asked Questions in Quantitative Finance*. John Wiley & Sons Ltd

Chapter 6

The Most Popular Probability Distributions and Their Uses in Finance

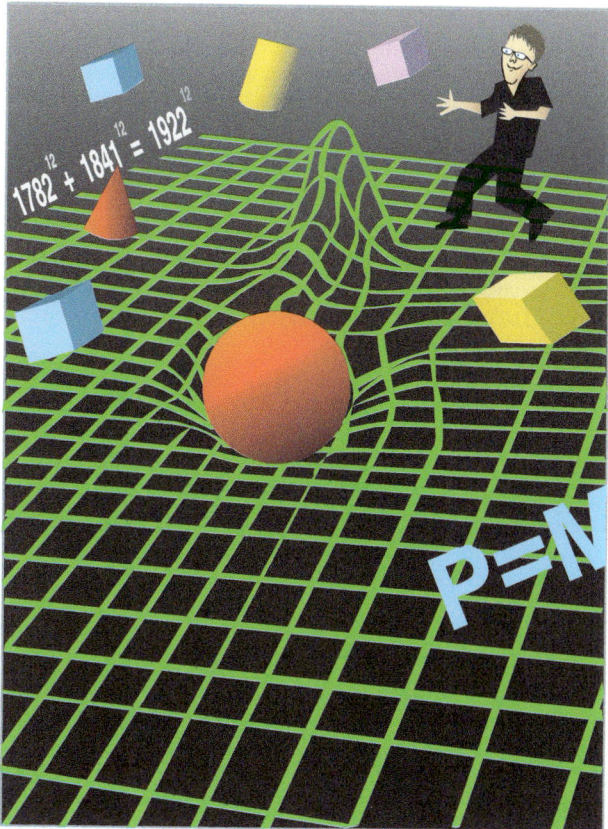

Random variables can be continuous or discrete (the latter denoted below by *). Or a combination. New distributions can also be made up using random variables from two or more distributions.

Here is a list of distributions seen in finance (mostly), and some words on each.

Normal or Gaussian This distribution is unbounded below and above, and is symmetrical about its mean. It has two parameters: a, location; $b > 0$ scale. Its probability density function is given by

$$\frac{1}{\sqrt{2\pi}\, b} e^{-\frac{(x-a)^2}{2b^2}}.$$

This distribution is commonly used to model equity returns, and, indeed, the changes in many financial quantities. Errors in observations of real phenomena are often normally distributed. The normal distribution is also common because of the **Central Limit Theorem**.

Mean a.

Variance b^2.

Lognormal Bounded below, unbounded above. It has two parameters: a, location; $b > 0$ scale. Its probability density function is given by

$$\frac{1}{\sqrt{2\pi}\, bx} \exp\left(-\frac{1}{2b^2}(\ln(x) - a)^2\right) \quad x \geq 0.$$

This distribution is commonly used to model equity prices. Lognormality of *prices* follows from the assumption of normally distributed *returns*.

Normal

a = 0
b = 1

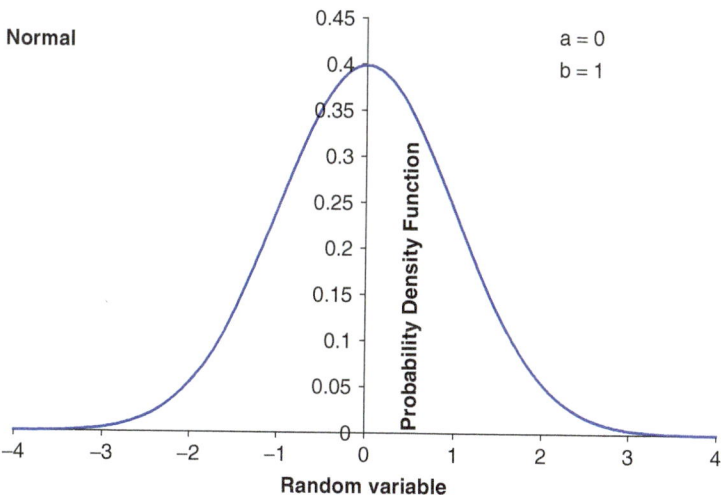

Probability Density Function

Random variable

Lognormal

a = 0.4
b = 0.3

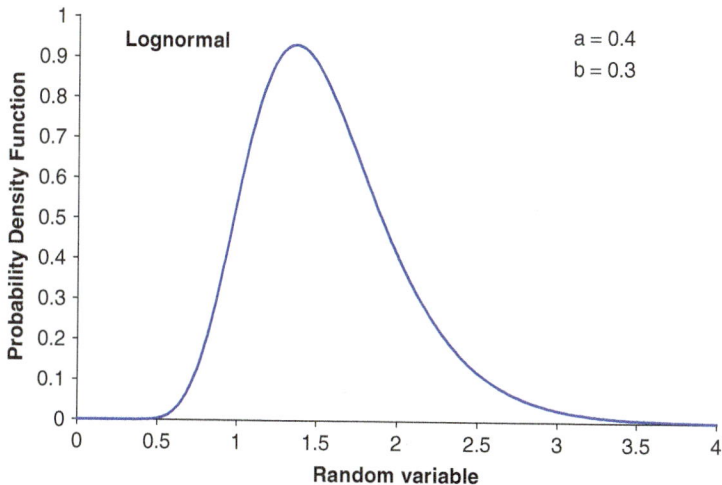

Probability Density Function

Random variable

Mean	$e^{a+\frac{1}{2}b^2}.$
Variance	$e^{2a+b^2}(e^{b^2}-1).$

Poisson* The random variables take non-negative integer values only. The distribution has one parameter: $a > 0$. Its probability density function is given by

$$\frac{e^{-a}a^x}{x!}, \quad x = 0, 1, 2, 3, \ldots.$$

This distribution is used in credit risk modelling, representing the number of credit events in a given time.

Mean	$a.$
Variance	$a.$

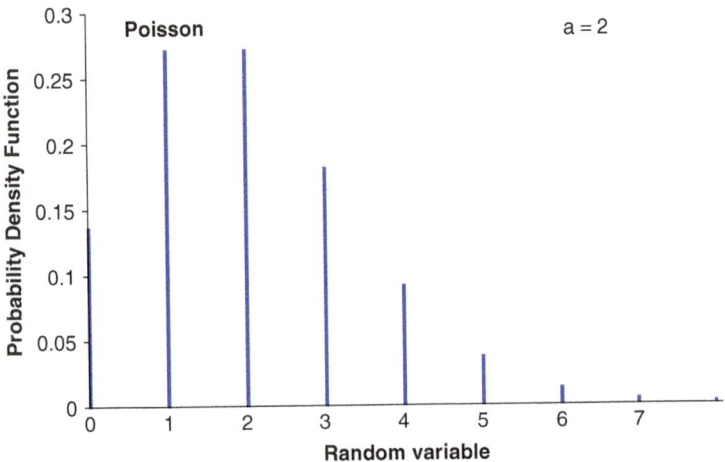

Chi square   Bounded below and unbounded above. It has two parameters $a \geq 0$, the location; ν, an integer, the degrees of freedom. Its probability density function is given by

$$\frac{e^{-(x+a)/2}}{2^{\nu/2}} \sum_{i=0}^{\infty} \frac{x^{i-1+\nu/2}a^i}{2^{2i}j!\Gamma(i+\nu/2)}, \quad x \geq 0,$$

where $\Gamma(\cdot)$ is the Gamma function. The chi-square distribution comes from adding up the squares of ν normally distributed random variables. The chi-square distribution with one degree of freedom is the distribution of the hedging error from an option that is hedged only discretely. It is therefore a very important distribution in option practice, if not option theory.

Mean $\nu + a$.

Variance $2(\nu + 2a)$.

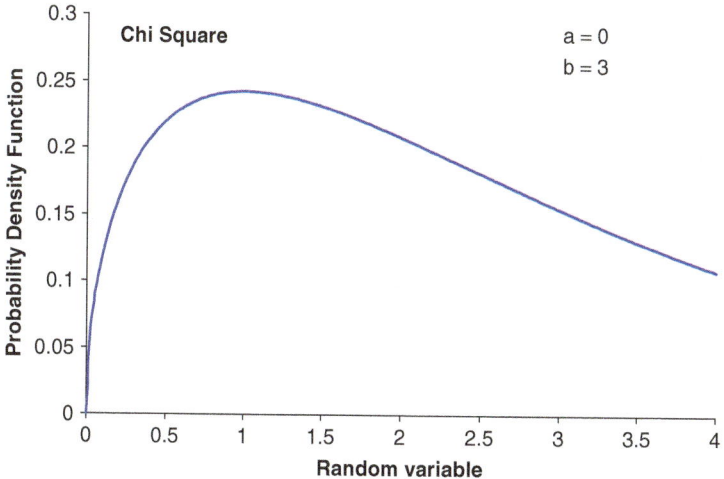

Gumbel Unbounded above and below. It has two parameters: a, location; $b > 0$ scale. Its probability density function is given by

$$\frac{1}{b} e^{\frac{a-x}{b}} e^{-e^{\frac{a-x}{b}}}.$$

The Gumbel distribution is useful for modelling extreme values, representing the distribution of the maximum value out of a large number of random variables drawn from an unbounded distribution.

Mean $\qquad\qquad\qquad a + \gamma b,$

where γ is Euler's constant, $0.577216\ldots$.

Variance $\qquad\qquad\qquad \frac{1}{6}\pi^2 b^2.$

Gumbel

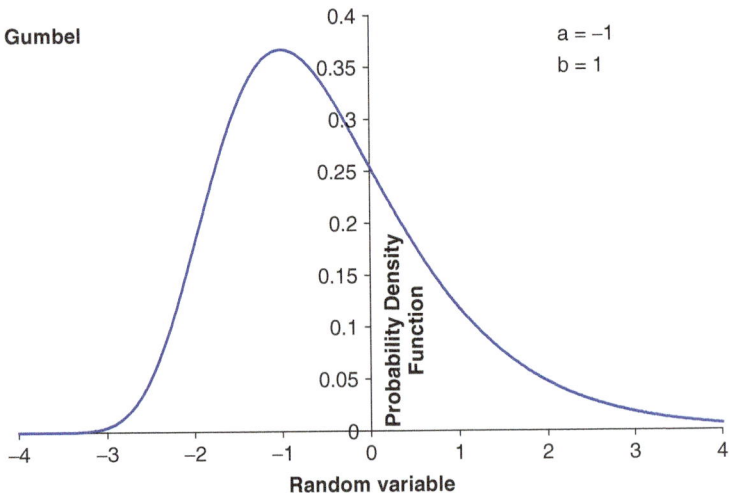

$a = -1$
$b = 1$

Weibull Bounded below and unbounded above. It has three parameters: a, location; $b > 0$, scale; $c > 0$, shape. Its probability density function is given by

$$\frac{c}{b} \left(\frac{x-a}{b} \right)^{c-1} \exp\left(-\left(\frac{x-a}{b} \right)^c \right), \quad x > a.$$

The Weibull distribution is also useful for modelling extreme values, representing the distribution of the maximum value out of a large number of random variables drawn from a bounded distribution. (The figure shows a 'humped' Weibull, but depending on parameter values the distribution can be monotonic.)

Mean $\qquad\qquad\qquad a + b\Gamma\left(\frac{c+1}{c}\right).$

Variance $\qquad\qquad b^2\left(\Gamma\left(\frac{c+2}{c}\right) - \Gamma\left(\frac{c+1}{c}\right)^2\right),$

where $\Gamma(\cdot)$ is the Gamma function.

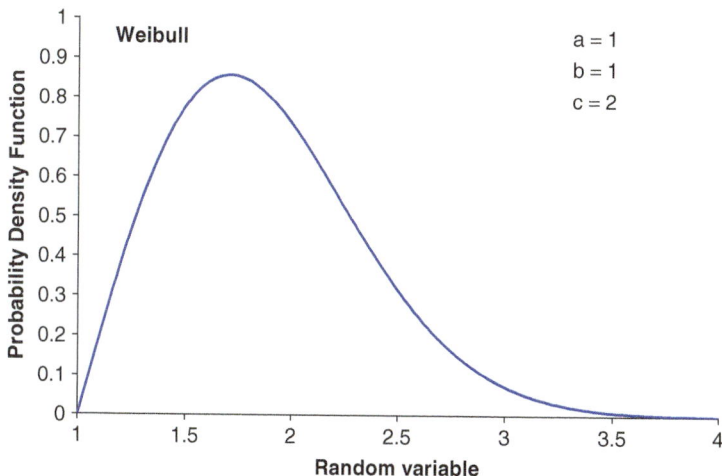

$a = 1$
$b = 1$
$c = 2$

Student's t Unbounded above and below. It has three parameters: a, location; $b > 0$, scale; $c > 0$, degrees of freedom. Its probability density function is given by

$$\frac{\Gamma\left(\frac{c+1}{2}\right)}{b\sqrt{\pi c}\,\Gamma\left(\frac{c}{2}\right)}\left(1 + \frac{\left(\frac{x-a}{b}\right)^2}{c}\right)^{-\frac{c+1}{2}},$$

where $\Gamma(\cdot)$ is the Gamma function. This distribution represents small-sample drawings from a normal distribution. It is also used for representing equity returns.

Mean a.

Variance $\left(\frac{c}{c-2}\right)b^2$.

Note that the nth moment only exists if $c > n$.

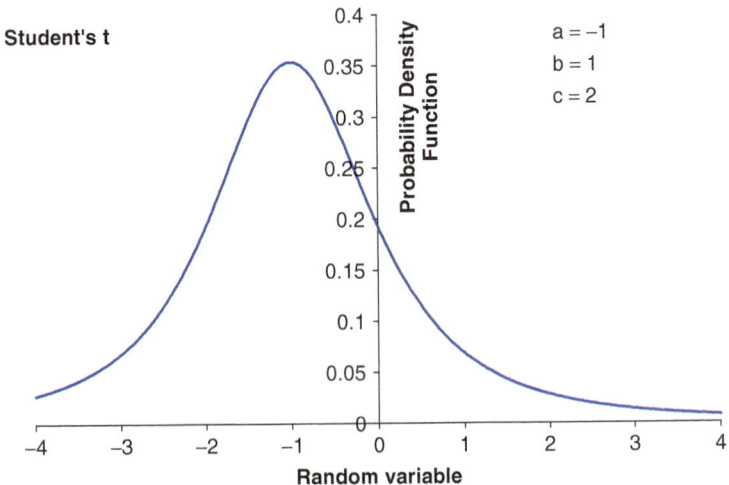

Pareto   Bounded below, unbounded above. It has two parameters: $a > 0$, scale; $b > 0$ shape. Its probability density function is given by

$$\frac{ba^b}{x^{b+1}}, \quad x \geq a.$$

Commonly used to describe the distribution of wealth, this is the classical power-law distribution.

Mean $\frac{ab}{b-1}.$

Variance $\frac{a^2 b}{(b-2)(b-1)^2}.$

Note that the nth moment only exists if $b > n$.

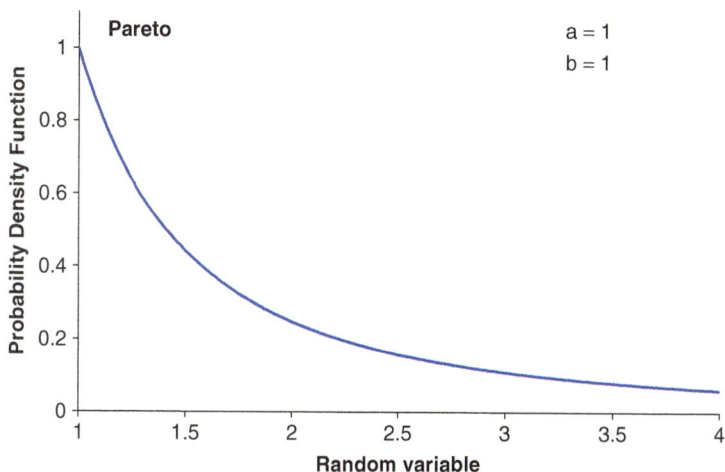

Uniform Bounded below and above. It has two location parameters, a and b. Its probability density function is given by

$$\frac{1}{b - a}, \quad a < x < b.$$

Mean $\frac{a+b}{2}$.

Variance $\frac{(b-a)^2}{12}$.

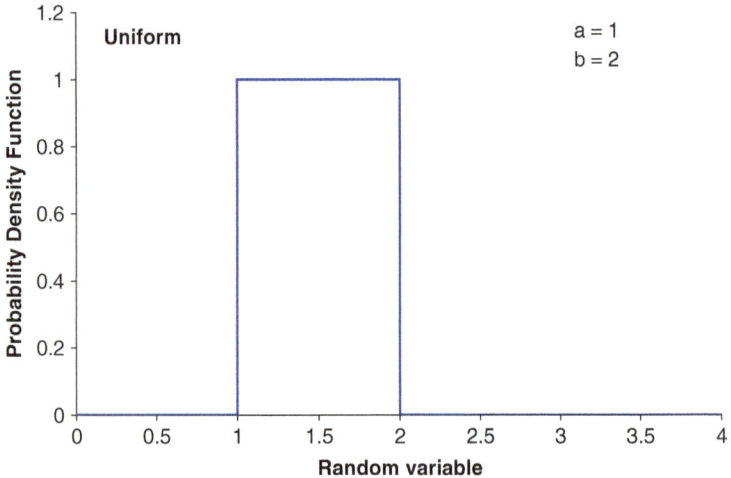

Inverse normal Bounded below, unbounded above. It has two parameters: $a > 0$, location; $b > 0$ scale. Its probability density function is given by

$$\sqrt{\frac{b}{2\pi x^3}} \; e^{-\frac{b}{2x}\left(\frac{x-a}{a}\right)^2}, \quad x \geq 0.$$

This distribution models the time taken by a Brownian motion to cover a certain distance.

Mean $a.$

Variance $\frac{a^3}{b}.$

Gamma   Bounded below, unbounded above. It has three parameters: a, location; $b > 0$ scale; $c > 0$ shape. Its probability density function is given by

$$\frac{1}{b\Gamma(c)} \left(\frac{x-a}{b} \right)^{c-1} e^{\frac{a-x}{b}}, \quad x \geq a,$$

where $\Gamma(\cdot)$ is the Gamma function. When $c = 1$ this is the exponential distribution and when $a = 0$ and $b = 2$ this is the chi-square distribution with $2c$ degrees of freedom.

Mean $a + bc.$

Variance $b^2 c.$

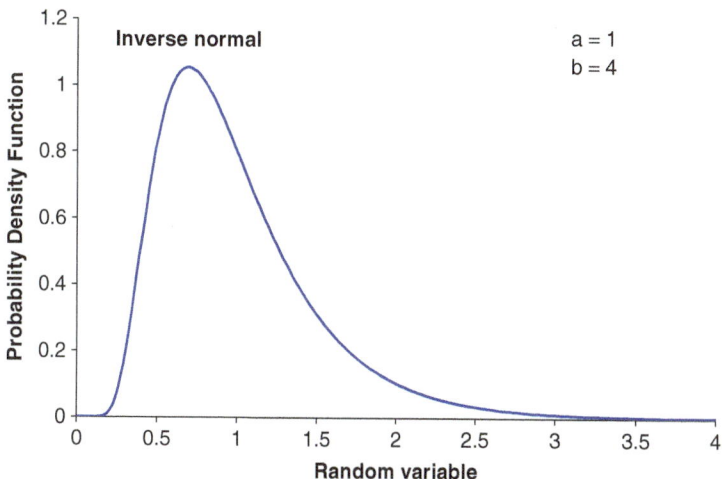

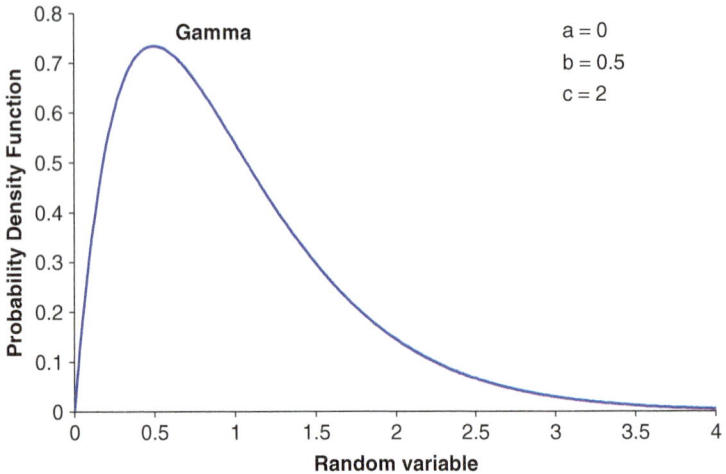

Logistic This distribution is unbounded below and above. It has two parameters: a, location; $b > 0$ scale. Its probability density function is given by

$$\frac{1}{b}\frac{e^{\frac{x-a}{b}}}{\left(1 + e^{\frac{x-a}{b}}\right)^2}.$$

The logistic distribution models the mid value of highs and lows of a collection of random variables, as the number of samples becomes large.

Mean $a.$

Variance $\frac{1}{3}\pi^2 b^2.$

Laplace This distribution is unbounded below and above. It has two parameters: a, location; $b > 0$ scale. Its probability

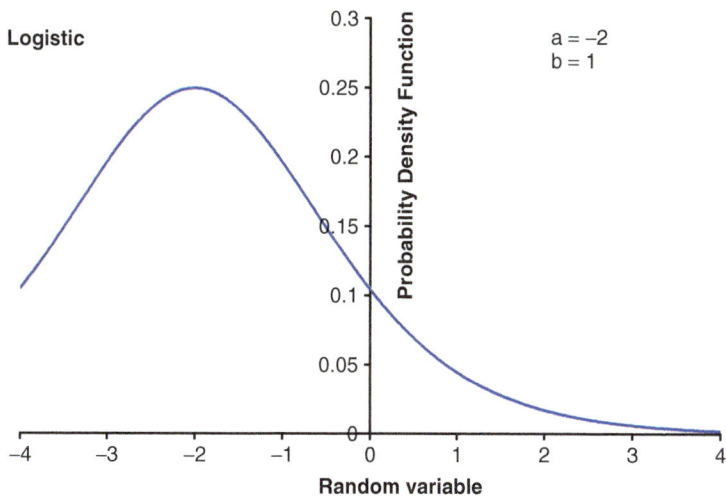

Logistic

a = −2
b = 1

Probability Density Function

Random variable

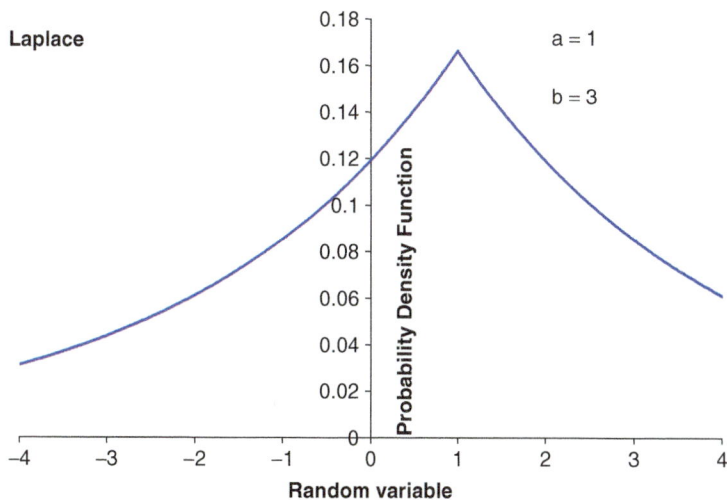

Laplace

a = 1

b = 3

Probability Density Function

Random variable

density function is given by

$$\frac{1}{2b}e^{-\frac{|x-a|}{b}}.$$

Errors in observations are usually either normal or Laplace.

Mean $a.$

Variance $2b^2.$

Cauchy This distribution is unbounded below and above. It has two parameters: a, location; $b > 0$ scale. Its probability density function is given by

$$\frac{1}{\pi b \left(1 + \left(\frac{x-a}{b}\right)^2\right)}.$$

This distribution is rarely used in finance. It does not have any finite moments, but its mode and median are both a.

Cauchy

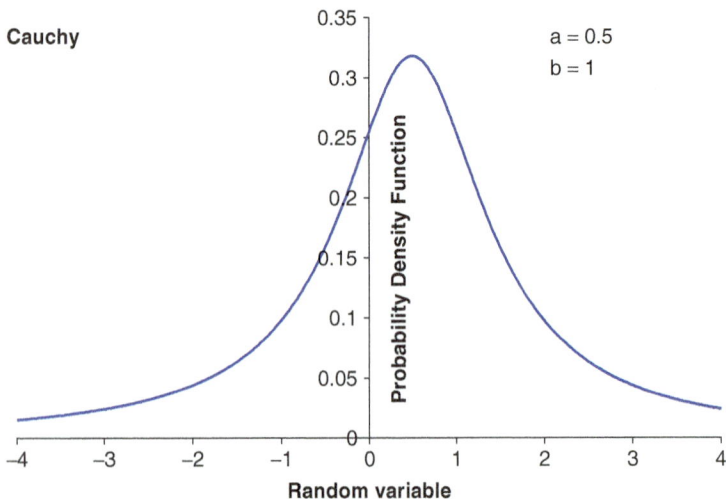

$a = 0.5$
$b = 1$

Probability Density Function

Random variable

Beta This distribution is bounded below and above. It has four parameters: a, location of lower limit; $b > a$ location of upper limit; $c > 0$ and $d > 0$ shape. Its probability density function is given by

$$\frac{\Gamma(c+d)}{\Gamma(c)\Gamma(d)(b-a)^{c+d-1}}\,(x-a)^{c-1}\,(b-x)^{d-1}, \quad a \leq x \leq b,$$

where $\Gamma(\cdot)$ is the Gamma function. This distribution is rarely used in finance.

Mean $\qquad\qquad\qquad\qquad\qquad \frac{ad+bc}{c+d}$.

Variance $\qquad\qquad\qquad\qquad\quad \frac{cd(b-a)^2}{(c+d+1)(c+d)^2}$.

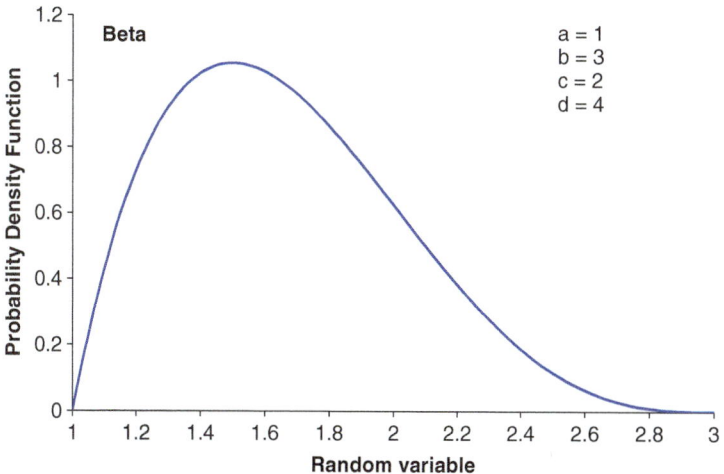

Exponential Bounded below, unbounded above. It has two parameters: a, location; $b > 0$ scale. Its probability density function is given by

$$\frac{1}{b}e^{\frac{a-x}{b}}, \quad x \geq a.$$

This distribution is rarely used in finance.

Mean $a + b.$

Variance $b^2.$

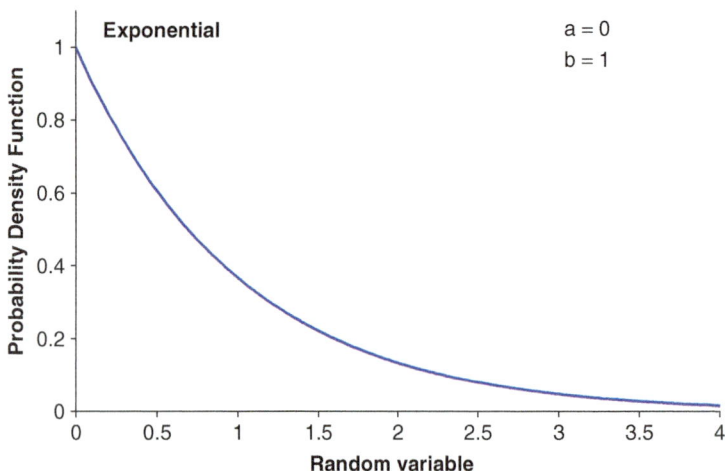

Lévy   Unbounded below and above. It has four parameters: μ, a location (mean); $0 < \alpha \leq 2$, the peakedness; $-1 < \beta < 1$, the skewness; $\nu > 0$, a spread. (Conventional notation is used here.) This distribution has been saved to last because its probability density function does not have a simple closed form. Instead it must be written in terms of its characteristic function. If $P(x)$ is the probability density function then the

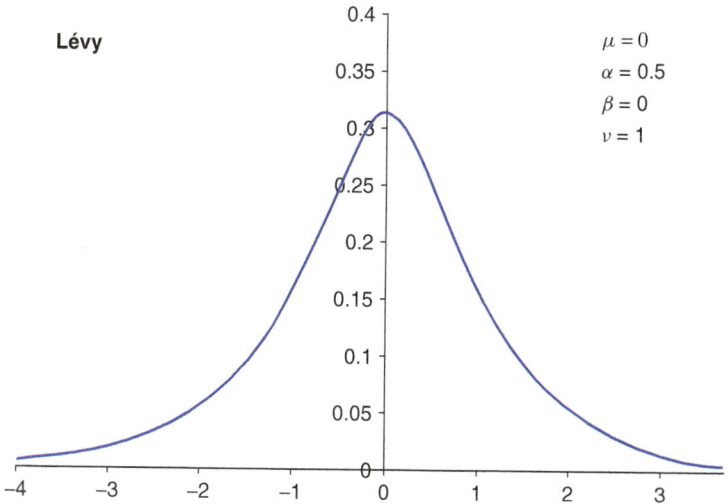

moment generating function is given by

$$M(z) = \int_{-\infty}^{\infty} e^{izx} P(x) \, dx,$$

where $i = \sqrt{-1}$. For the Lévy distribution

$$\ln(M(z)) = i\mu z - v^\alpha |z|^\alpha \left(1 - i\beta \, \mathrm{sgn}(z) \tan(\pi a/2)\right), \quad \text{for } \alpha \neq 1$$

or

$$\ln(M(z)) = i\mu z - v|z| \left(1 + \frac{2i\beta}{\pi} \mathrm{sgn}(z) \ln(|z|)\right), \quad \text{for } \alpha = 1.$$

The normal distribution is a special case of this with $\alpha = 2$ and $\beta = 0$, and with the parameter v being one half of the variance. The Lévy distribution, or Pareto Lévy distribution, is increasingly popular in finance because it matches data well, and has suitable fat tails. It also has the important theoretical property of being a stable distribution in that the sum of independent random numbers drawn from the Lévy distribution will itself be Lévy. This is a useful property for the distribution of returns. If you add up n independent numbers from the Lévy distribution with the above parameters then you will get a number from another Lévy distribution with the same α and β but with mean of $n^{1/\alpha}\mu$ and spread $n^{1/\alpha}v$. The tail of the distribution decays like $|x|^{-1-\alpha}$.

Mean $\qquad\qquad\qquad\qquad\qquad \mu.$

Variance $\qquad\qquad\qquad$ infinite, unless $\alpha = 2,$ when it is $2v.$

References and Further Reading

Spiegel, MR, Schiller & JJ Srinivasan, RA 2000 *Schaum's Outline of Probability and Statistics.* McGraw–Hill

Chapter 7

Twelve Different Ways to Derive Black–Scholes

*T*he twelve different ways of deriving the Black–Scholes equation or formulæ that follow use different types of mathematics, with different amounts of complexity and mathematical baggage. Some derivations are useful in that they can be generalized, and some are very specific to this one problem. Naturally we will spend more time on those derivations that are most useful or give the most insight. The first eight ways of deriving the Black–Scholes equation/formulæ are taken from the excellent paper by Jesper Andreason, Bjarke Jensen and Rolf Poulsen (1998).

Note that the title of this chapter doesn't explicitly refer to the Black–Scholes *equation* or the Black–Scholes *formulæ*. That's because some of the derivations result in the famous partial differential equation and some result in the famous formulæ for calls and puts.

In most cases we work within a framework in which the stock path is continuous, the returns are normally distributed, there aren't any dividends, or transaction costs, etc. To get the closed-form formulæ (the Black–Scholes *formulæ*) we need to assume that volatility is constant, or perhaps time dependent, but for the derivations of the equation relating the greeks (the Black–Scholes *equation*) the assumptions can be weaker, if we don't mind not finding a closed-form solution.

In many cases, some assumptions can be dropped. The final derivation, Black–Scholes for accountants, uses perhaps the least amount of formal mathematics and is easy to generalize. It also has the advantage that it highlights one of the main reasons why the Black–Scholes model is less than perfect in real life. I will spend more time on that derivation than on most of the others.

I am curious to know which derivation(s) readers prefer. Please mail your comments to paul@wilmott.com. Also if you are aware of other derivations please let me know.

Hedging and the Partial Differential Equation

The original derivation of the Black–Scholes partial differential equation was via stochastic calculus, Itô's lemma and a simple hedging argument (Black & Scholes, 1973).

Assume that the underlying follows a lognormal random walk

$$dS = \mu S \, dt + \sigma S \, dX.$$

Use Π to denote the value of a portfolio of one long option position and a short position in some quantity Δ of the underlying:

$$\Pi = V(S, t) - \Delta S. \tag{7.1}$$

The first term on the right is the option and the second term is the short asset position.

Ask how the value of the portfolio changes from time t to $t + dt$. The change in the portfolio value is due partly to the change in the option value and partly to the change in the underlying:

$$d\Pi = dV - \Delta \, dS.$$

From Itô's lemma we have

$$d\Pi = \frac{\partial V}{\partial t} dt + \frac{\partial V}{\partial S} dS + \frac{1}{2} \sigma^2 S^2 \frac{\partial^2 V}{\partial S^2} dt - \Delta \, dS.$$

The right-hand side of this contains two types of terms, the deterministic and the random. The deterministic terms are those with the dt, and the random terms are those with the dS. Pretending for the moment that we know V and its derivatives then we know everything about the right-hand side *except for the value of dS*, because this is random.

These random terms can be eliminated by choosing

$$\Delta = \frac{\partial V}{\partial S}.$$

After choosing the quantity Δ, we hold a portfolio whose value changes by the amount

$$d\Pi = \left(\frac{\partial V}{\partial t} + \frac{1}{2}\sigma^2 S^2 \frac{\partial^2 V}{\partial S^2} \right) dt.$$

This change is completely *riskless*. If we have a completely risk-free change $d\Pi$ in the portfolio value Π then it must be the same as the growth we would get if we put the equivalent amount of cash in a risk-free interest-bearing account:

$$d\Pi = r\Pi \, dt.$$

This is an example of the no-arbitrage principle.

Putting all of the above together to eliminate Π and Δ in favour of partial derivatives of V gives

$$\frac{\partial V}{\partial t} + \frac{1}{2}\sigma^2 S^2 \frac{\partial^2 V}{\partial S^2} + rS\frac{\partial V}{\partial S} - rV = 0,$$

the Black–Scholes equation.

Solve this quite simple linear diffusion equation with the final condition

$$V(S, T) = \max(S - K, 0)$$

and you will get the Black–Scholes call option formula.

This derivation of the Black–Scholes equation is perhaps the most useful since it is readily generalizable (if not necessarily still analytically tractable) to different underlyings, more complicated models, and exotic contracts.

Martingales

The martingale pricing methodology was formalized by Harrison & Kreps (1979) and Harrison & Pliska (1981).[1]

We start again with

$$dS_t = \mu S \, dt + \sigma S \, dW_t$$

The W_t is Brownian motion with measure $\mathbb{P}$. Now introduce a new equivalent martingale measure $\mathbb{Q}$ such that

$$\tilde{W}_t = W_t + \eta t,$$

where $\eta = (\mu - r)/\sigma$.

Under $\mathbb{Q}$ we have

$$dS_t = rS \, dt + \sigma S \, d\tilde{W}_t.$$

Introduce

$$G_t = e^{-r(T-t)} E_t^{\mathbb{Q}}[\max(S_T - K, 0)].$$

The quantity $e^{r(T-t)}G_t$ is a $\mathbb{Q}$-martingale and so

$$d\left(e^{r(T-t)}G_t\right) = \alpha_t e^{r(T-t)}G_t \, d\tilde{W}_t$$

for some process α_t. Applying Itô's lemma,

$$dG_t = (r + \alpha\eta)G_t dt + \alpha G_t \, dW_t.$$

This stochastic differential equation can be rewritten as one representing a strategy in which a quantity $\alpha G_t/\sigma S$ of the stock and a quantity $(G - \alpha G_t/\sigma)e^{r(T-t)}$ of a zero-coupon bond maturing at time T are bought:

$$dG_t = \frac{\alpha G_t}{\sigma S} dS + \frac{G - \dfrac{\alpha G_t}{\sigma S} S}{e^{-r(T-t)}} d(e^{-r(T-t)}).$$

---

[1]If my notation changes, it is because I am using the notation most common to a particular field. Even then the changes are minor, often just a matter of whether one puts a subscript t on a dW for example.

Such a strategy is self financing because the values of the stock and bond positions add up to G. Because of the existence of such a self-financing strategy and because at time $t = T$ we have that G_T is the call payoff we must have that G_t is the value of the call before expiration. The role of the self-financing strategy is to ensure that there are no arbitrage opportunities.

Thus the price of a call option is

$$e^{-r(T-t)}E_t^{\mathbb{Q}}[\max(S_T - K, 0)].$$

The interpretation is simply that the option value is the present value of the expected payoff under a risk-neutral random walk.

For other options simply put the payoff function inside the expectation.

This derivation is most useful for showing the link between option values and expectations, as it is the theoretical foundation for valuation by Monte Carlo simulation.

Now that we have a representation of the option value in terms of an expectation we can formally calculate this quantity and hence the Black–Scholes formulæ. Under $\mathbb{Q}$ the logarithm of the stock price at expiration is normally distributed with mean $m = \ln(S_t) + \left(r - \frac{1}{2}\sigma^2\right)(T - t)$ and variance $v^2 = \sigma^2(T - t)$. Therefore the call option value is

$$e^{-r(T-t)} \int_{\frac{\ln K - m}{v}}^{\infty} (e^{m+vx} - K)\frac{e^{-\frac{x^2}{2}}}{\sqrt{2\pi}}\, dx.$$

A simplification of this using the cumulative distribution function for the standardized normal distribution results in the well-known call option formula.

Change of Numeraire

The following is a derivation of the Black–Scholes call (or put) formula, not the equation, and is really just a trick for simplifying some of the integration.

It starts from the result that the option value is

$$e^{-r(T-t)}E_t^{\mathbb{Q}}[\max(S_T - K, 0)].$$

This can also be written as

$$e^{-r(T-t)}E_t^{\mathbb{Q}}[(S_T - K)\mathcal{H}(S - K)],$$

where $\mathcal{H}(S - K)$ is the Heaviside function, which is zero for $S < K$ and 1 for $S > K$.

Now define another equivalent martingale measure $\mathbb{Q}'$ such that

$$\tilde{W}_t' = W_t + \eta t - \sigma t.$$

The option value can then be written as

$$S_t E_t^{\mathbb{Q}'}\left[\frac{(S_T - K)\mathcal{H}(S - K)}{S_T}\right].$$

where

$$dS_t = (r + \sigma^2)S\, dt + \sigma S\, d\tilde{W}_t'.$$

It can also be written as a *combination* of the two expressions,

$$S_t E_t^{\mathbb{Q}'}\left[\frac{S_T \mathcal{H}(S - K)}{S_T}\right] - K e^{-r(T-t)}E_t^{\mathbb{Q}}[\mathcal{H}(S - K)].$$

Notice that the same calculation is to be performed, an expectation of $\mathcal{H}(S - K)$, but under two different measures. The end result is the Black–Scholes formula for a call option.

This method is most useful for simplifying valuation problems, perhaps even finding closed-form solutions, by using the most suitable traded contract to use for the numeraire.

The relationship between the change of numeraire result and the partial differential equation approach is very simple, and informative.

First let us make the comparison between the risk-neutral expectation and the Black–Scholes equation as transparent as possible. When we write

$$e^{-r(T-t)}E_t^{\mathbb{Q}}[\max(S_T - K, 0)]$$

we are saying that the option value is the present value of the expected payoff under the risk-neutral random walk

$$dS = rS\,dt + \sigma S\,d\tilde{W}_t.$$

The partial differential equation

$$\frac{\partial V}{\partial t} + \frac{1}{2}\sigma^2 S^2 \frac{\partial^2 V}{\partial S^2} + rS\frac{\partial V}{\partial S} - rV = 0$$

means exactly the same because of the relationship between it and the Fokker–Planck equation. In this equation the diffusion coefficient is always just one half of the square of the randomness in dS. The coefficient of $\partial V/\partial S$ is always the risk-neutral drift rS and the coefficient of V is always minus the interest rate, $-r$, and represents the present valuing from expiration to now.

If we write the option value as $V = S\overline{V}$ then we can think of $\overline{V}$ as the number of shares the option is equivalent to, in value terms. It is like using the stock as the unit of currency. But if we rewrite the Black–Scholes equation in terms of $\overline{V}$ using

$$\frac{\partial V}{\partial t} = S\frac{\partial \overline{V}}{\partial t}, \qquad \frac{\partial V}{\partial S} = S\frac{\partial \overline{V}}{\partial S} + \overline{V}, \quad \text{and} \quad \frac{\partial^2 V}{\partial S^2} = S\frac{\partial^2 \overline{V}}{\partial S^2} + 2S\frac{\partial \overline{V}}{\partial S},$$

then we have

$$\frac{\partial \overline{V}}{\partial t} + \frac{1}{2}\sigma^2 S^2 \frac{\partial^2 \overline{V}}{\partial S^2} + (r + \sigma^2)S\frac{\partial \overline{V}}{\partial S} = 0.$$

The function $\overline{V}$ can now be interpreted, using the same comparison with the Fokker–Planck equation, as an expectation, but this time with respect to the random walk

$$dS = (r + \sigma^2)S\,dt + \sigma S\,d\tilde{W}'_t.$$

And there is no present valuing to be done. Since at expiration we have for the call option

$$\frac{\max(S_T - K, 0)}{S_T}$$

we can write the option value as

$$S_t E_t^{\mathbb{Q}'}\left[\frac{(S_T - K)\mathcal{H}(S - K)}{S_T}\right].$$

where

$$dS_t = (r + \sigma^2)S\,dt + \sigma S\,d\tilde{W}'_t.$$

Change of numeraire is no more than a change of dependent variable.

Local Time

The most obscure of the derivations is the one involving the concept from stochastic calculus known as 'local time.' Local time is a very technical idea involving the time a random walk spends in the vicinity of a point.

The derivation is based on the analysis of a stop-loss strategy in which one attempts to hedge a call by selling one share short if the stock is above the present value of the strike, and holding nothing if the stock is below the present value of the strike. Although at expiration the call payoff and the stock position will cancel each other exactly, this is not a strategy that eliminates risk. Naively you might think that this strategy would work, after all when you sell short one of the stock as it passes through the present value of the strike you will neither make nor lose money (assuming there are no transaction costs). But if that were the case then an option initially with strike above the forward stock price should have zero value. So clearly something is wrong here.

To see what goes wrong you have to look more closely at what happens as the stock goes through the present value of the strike. In particular, look at discrete moves in the stock price.

As the forward stock price goes from K to $K + \epsilon$ sell one share and buy K bonds. And then every time the stock falls below the present value of the strike you reverse this. Even in the absence of transaction costs, there will be a slippage in this process. And the total slippage will depend on how often the stock crosses this point. Herein lies the rub. This happens an infinite number of times in continuous Brownian motion.

If $U(\epsilon)$ is the number of times the forward price moves from K to $K + \epsilon$, which will be finite since ϵ is finite, then the financing cost of this strategy is

$$\epsilon U(\epsilon).$$

Now take the limit as $\epsilon \to 0$ and this becomes the quantity known as local time. This local-time term is what explains the apparent paradox with the above example of the call with zero value.

Now we go over to the risk-neutral world to value the local-time term, ending up, eventually, with the Black–Scholes formula.

It is well worth simulating this strategy on a spreadsheet, using a finite time step and let this time step get smaller and smaller.

Parameters as Variables

The next derivation is rather novel in that it involves differentiating the option value with respect to the parameters strike, K, and expiration, T, instead of the more usual differentiation with respect to the variables S and t. This will lead to a partial differential equation that can be solved for the Black–Scholes formulæ. But more importantly, this technique can be used to deduce the dependence of volatility on stock price and time, given the market prices of options as functions of strike and expiration. This is an idea due to Dupire (1994) (also see Derman & Kani, 1994, and Rubinstein, 1994, for related work done in a discrete setting) and is the basis for deterministic volatility models and calibration.

We begin with the call option result from above

$$V = e^{-r(T-t)}E_t^{\mathbb{Q}}[\max(S_T - K, 0)],$$

that the option value is the present value of the risk-neutral expected payoff. This can be written as

$$V(K, T) = e^{-r(T-t^*)} \int_0^\infty \max(S - K, 0)p(S^*, t^*; S, T)\,dS$$

$$= e^{-r(T-t^*)} \int_K^\infty (S - K)p(S^*, t^*; S, T)\,dS,$$

where $p(S^*, t^*; S, T)$ is the transition probability density function for the risk-neutral random walk with S^* being today's asset price and t^* today's date. Note that here the arguments of V are the 'variables' strike, K, and expiration, T.

If we differentiate this with respect to K we get

$$\frac{\partial V}{\partial K} = -e^{-r(T-t^*)} \int_K^\infty p(S^*, t^*; S, T)\,dS.$$

After another differentiation, we arrive at this equation for the probability density function in terms of the option prices

$$p(S^*, t^*; K, T) = e^{r(T-t^*)}\frac{\partial^2 V}{\partial K^2}$$

We also know that the forward equation for the transition probability density function, the Fokker–Planck equation, is

$$\frac{\partial p}{\partial T} = \frac{1}{2}\frac{\partial^2}{\partial S^2}(\sigma^2 S^2 p) - \frac{\partial}{\partial S}(rSp).$$

Here $\sigma(S,t)$ is evaluated at $t = T$. We also have

$$\frac{\partial V}{\partial T} = -rV + e^{-r(T-t^*)} \int_K^\infty (S-K)\frac{\partial p}{\partial T}\, dS.$$

This can be written as

$$\frac{\partial V}{\partial T} = -rV + e^{-r(T-t^*)} \int_K^\infty \left(\frac{1}{2}\frac{\partial^2(\sigma^2 S^2 p)}{\partial S^2} - \frac{\partial(rSp)}{\partial S} \right)(S-K)\, dS.$$

using the forward equation. Integrating this by parts twice we get

$$\frac{\partial V}{\partial T} = -rV + \frac{1}{2}e^{-r(T-t^*)}\sigma^2 K^2 p + re^{-r(T-t^*)} \int_K^\infty Sp\, dS.$$

In this expression $\sigma(S,t)$ has $S = K$ and $t = T$. After some simple manipulations we get

$$\frac{\partial V}{\partial T} = \frac{1}{2}\sigma^2 K^2 \frac{\partial^2 V}{\partial K^2} - rK\frac{\partial V}{\partial K}.$$

This partial differential equation can now be solved for the Black–Scholes formulæ.

This method is not used in practice for finding these formulæ, but rather, knowing the traded prices of vanillas as a function of K and T we can turn this equation around to find σ, since the above analysis is still valid even if volatility is stock and time dependent.

Continuous-Time Limit of the Binomial Model

Some of our twelve derivations lead to the Black–Scholes partial differential equation, and some to the idea of the option value as the present value of the option payoff under a risk-neutral random walk. The following simple model (Figure 7.1) does both.

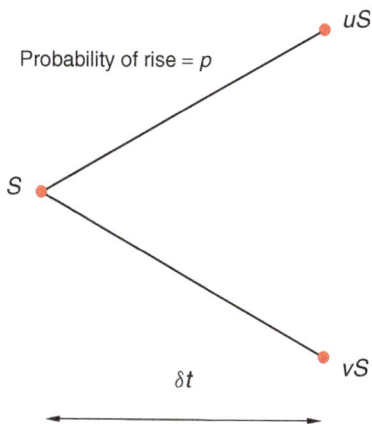

Figure 7.1: The model.

In the binomial model the asset starts at S and over a time step δt either rises to a value $u \times S$ or falls to a value $v \times S$, with $0 < v < 1 < u$. The probability of a rise is p and so the probability of a fall is $1 - p$.

We choose the three constants u, v and p to give the binomial walk the same drift, μ, and volatility, σ, as the asset we are modelling. This choice is far from unique and here we use the choices that result in the simplest formulæ:

$$u = 1 + \sigma\sqrt{\delta t},$$

$$v = 1 - \sigma\sqrt{\delta t}$$

and

$$p = \frac{1}{2} + \frac{\mu\sqrt{\delta t}}{2\sigma}.$$

Having defined the behaviour of the asset we are ready to price options.

Suppose that we know the value of the option at the time $t + \delta t$. For example, this time may be the expiration of the option. Now construct a portfolio at time t consisting of one option and a short position in a quantity Δ of the underlying. At time t this portfolio has value

$$\Pi = V - \Delta S,$$

where the option value V is for the moment unknown. At time $t + \delta t$ the option takes one of two values, depending on whether the asset rises or falls

$$V^+ \quad \text{or} \quad V^-.$$

At the same time the portfolio of option and stock becomes either

$$V^+ - \Delta u S \quad \text{or} \quad V^- - \Delta v S.$$

Having the freedom to choose Δ, we can make the value of this portfolio the same whether the asset rises or falls. This is ensured if we make

$$V^+ - \Delta u S = V^- - \Delta v S.$$

This means that we should choose

$$\Delta = \frac{V^+ - V^-}{(u - v)S}$$

for hedging. The portfolio value is then

$$V^+ - \Delta u S = V^+ - \frac{u(V^+ - V^-)}{(u - v)} = V^- - \Delta v S = V^- - \frac{v(V^+ - V^-)}{(u - v)}.$$

Let's denote this portfolio value by

$$\Pi + \delta \Pi.$$

This just means the original portfolio value plus the change in value. But we must also have $\delta \Pi = r \Pi \, \delta t$ to avoid arbitrage opportunities. Bringing all of these expressions together to eliminate Π, and after some rearranging, we get

$$V = \frac{1}{1 + r\,\delta t}\left(p'V^+ + (1-p')V^-\right),$$

where

$$p' = \frac{1}{2} + \frac{r\sqrt{\delta t}}{2\sigma}.$$

This is an equation for V given V^+ and V^-, the option values at the next time step, and the parameters r and σ.

The right-hand side of the equation for V can be interpreted, rather clearly, as the present value of the expected future option value using the probabilities p' for an up move and $1 - p'$ for a down.

Again this is the idea of the option value as the present value of the expected payoff under a risk-neutral random walk. The quantity p' is the risk-neutral probability, and it is this that determines the value of the option not the real probability. By comparing the expressions for p and p' we see that this is equivalent to replacing the real asset drift μ with the risk-free rate of return r.

We can examine the equation for V in the limit as $\delta t \to 0$. We write

$$V = V(S, t), \quad V^+ = V(uS, t + \delta t) \quad \text{and} \quad V^- = V(vS, t + \delta t).$$

Expanding these expressions in Taylor series for small δt we find that

$$\Delta \sim \frac{\partial V}{\partial S} \quad \text{as} \quad \delta t \to 0,$$

and the binomial pricing equation for V becomes

$$\frac{\partial V}{\partial t} + \frac{1}{2}\sigma^2 S^2 \frac{\partial^2 V}{\partial S^2} + rS\frac{\partial V}{\partial S} - rV = 0.$$

This is the Black–Scholes equation.

CAPM

This derivation, originally due to Cox & Rubinstein (1985) starts from the **Capital Asset Pricing Model** in continuous time. In particular it uses the result that there is a linear relationship between the expected return on a financial instrument and the covariance of the asset with the market. The latter term can be thought of as compensation for taking risk. But the asset and its option are perfectly correlated, so the compensation in excess of the risk-free rate for taking unit amount of risk must be the same for each.

For the stock, the expected return (dividing by dt) is μ. Its risk is σ.

From Itô we have

$$dV = \frac{\partial V}{\partial t}dt + \frac{1}{2}\sigma^2 S^2 \frac{\partial^2 V}{\partial S^2}dt + \frac{\partial V}{\partial S}dS.$$

Therefore the expected return on the option in excess of the risk-free rate is

$$\frac{1}{V}\left(\frac{\partial V}{\partial t} + \frac{1}{2}\sigma^2 S^2 \frac{\partial^2 V}{\partial S^2} + \mu S\frac{\partial V}{\partial S} - rV\right)$$

and the risk is

$$\frac{1}{V}\sigma S\frac{\partial V}{\partial S}.$$

Since both the underlying and the option must have the same compensation, in excess of the risk-free rate, for unit risk

$$\frac{\mu - r}{\sigma} = \frac{\dfrac{1}{V}\left(\dfrac{\partial V}{\partial t} + \dfrac{1}{2}\sigma^2 S^2 \dfrac{\partial^2 V}{\partial S^2} + \mu S\dfrac{\partial V}{\partial S} - rV\right)}{\dfrac{1}{V}\sigma S\dfrac{\partial V}{\partial S}}.$$

Now rearrange this. The μ drops out and we are left with the Black–Scholes equation.

Utility Theory

The utility theory approach is not exactly the most useful of the twelve derivation methods, requiring that we value from the perspective of a particularly unrepresentative investor, an investor with a utility function that is a power law. This idea was introduced by Rubinstein (1976). Even though not the best way to derive the famous formulæ utility theory is something which deserves better press than it has received so far.

The steps along the way to finding the Black–Scholes formulæ are as follows. We work within a single-period framework, so that the concept of continuous hedging, or indeed anything continuous at all, is not needed. We assume that the stock price at the terminal time (which will shortly also be an option's expiration) and the consumption are both log-normally distributed with some correlation. We choose a utility function that is a power of the consumption. A valuation expression results. For the market to be in equilibrium requires a relationship between the stock's and consumption's expected growths and volatilities, the above-mentioned correlation and the degree of risk aversion in the utility function. Finally, we use the valuation expression for an option, with the expiration being the terminal date. This valuation expression can be interpreted as an expectation, with the usual and oft-repeated interpretation.

Taylor Series

Taylor series is just a discrete-time version of Itô's lemma. So you should find this derivation of the Black–Scholes partial differential equation very simple.

$V(S,t)$ is the option value as a function of asset S and time t. Set up a portfolio long the option and short Δ

of the stock:
$$\Pi = V(S, t) - \Delta S.$$

Now look at the change in this portfolio from time t to $t + \delta t$, with δt being a small time step:
$$\delta \Pi = V(S + \delta S, t + \delta t) - V(S, t) - \Delta \delta S,$$

where
$$\delta S = \mu S \, \delta t + \sigma S \sqrt{\delta t} \, \phi$$

is a discrete-time model for the stock and ϕ is a random variable drawn from a normal distribution with zero mean and unit standard deviation. (*Aside:* Does it matter that ϕ is normally distributed? It's a nice little exercise to see what difference it makes if ϕ comes from another distribution.)

Now expand $\delta \Pi$ in Taylor series for small δt to get
$$\delta \Pi \approx \frac{\partial V}{\partial t} \delta t + \frac{\partial V}{\partial S} \left(\mu S \, \delta t + \sigma S \sqrt{\delta t} \, \phi \right) + \frac{1}{2} \sigma^2 S^2 \, \delta t \, \frac{\partial^2 V}{\partial S^2} \, \phi^2$$
$$- \Delta \left(\mu S \, \delta t + \sigma S \sqrt{\delta t} \, \phi \right) + O(\delta t^{3/2}).$$

where all terms are now evaluated at S and t.

The variance of this expression is
$$\sigma^2 S^2 \, \delta t \left(\frac{\partial V}{\partial S} - \Delta \right)^2 + O(\delta t^{3/2})$$

which is minimized by the choice
$$\Delta = \frac{\partial V}{\partial S}.$$

Now put this choice for Δ into the expression for $\delta \Pi$, and set
$$\delta \Pi = r \Pi \, \delta t.$$

This is a bit naughty, but I'll come back to it in a second.

Take the resulting equation, divide by δt so the leading terms are $O(1)$ and let $\delta t \to 0$. Bingo, you have the Black–Scholes partial differential equation, honest.

The naughty step in this was setting the return on the portfolio equal to the risk-free rate. This is fine as long as the portfolio is itself risk free. Here it is not, not exactly; there is still a little bit of risk. The variance, after choosing the best Δ, is $O(\delta t^{3/2})$. Since there are $O(T/\delta t)$ rehedges between the start of the option's life and expiration, where T is the time to expiration, the total variance does decay to zero as $\delta t \to 0$, thank goodness. And that's the *a posteriori* justification for ignoring risk.

(In Wilmott, 1994, this analysis goes to higher order in δt to find an even better hedge than the classic Black–Scholes – one that is relevant if δt is not so small, or if gamma is large, or if you are close to expiration. In that paper there is a small typo, corrected in Wilmott, 2006.)

In our final derivation you will see a less mathsy version of this same argument.

Mellin Transform

This derivation (see Yakovlev & Zhabin, 2003) is another one that I am only going to do in spirit rather than in detail. Again it is in discrete time but with continuous asset price. In that sense it's rather like the previous derivation and also our final derivation, Black–Scholes for accountants, only far, far more complicated.

$V_k(S)$ is the option value when the stock price is S at the kth time step. You set up a portfolio, Π, long one option and short a quantity, Δ, of the underlying asset. The delta is chosen to minimize the variance of this portfolio at the next time step; the resulting expression for Δ involves the covariance between the stock and the option.

The pricing equation is then

$$e^{r\,\delta t}\Pi_{k=1} = E\left[\Pi_k\right],$$

with the obvious notation. There is a slight problem with this, in that there is really no justification for equating value and expectation, at least not until you look at (or check *a posteriori*) the total variance at expiration and show that it is small enough to ignore (if the time steps are small enough). Anyway...

This equation can be rewritten just in terms of V as

$$V_{k+1}(S) = \int_{-\infty}^{\infty} f_k(x)\, V_k(S\,e^x)\, dx.$$

And since we know the option value at expiration, this is $V_0(S)$ then we can in principle find $V_k(S)$ for all k. Next you go over to the Mellin transform domain (this is not the place to explain transform theory!)

So far none of this has required the stock to be lognormally distributed, it is more general than that. But if it is lognormal then the above iteration will result in the class formulæ for calls and puts.

A Diffusion Equation

The penultimate derivation of the Black–Scholes partial differential equation is rather unusual in that it uses just pure thought about the nature of Brownian motion and a couple of trivial observations. It also has a very neat punchline that makes the derivation helpful in other modelling situations.

It goes something like this.

Stock prices can be modelled as Brownian motion, the stock price plays the role of the position of the 'pollen particle' and time is time. In mathematical terms Brownian motion is just an example of a diffusion equation. So let's write down a diffusion equation for the value of an option as a function of space and time, i.e. stock price and time, that's $V(S, t)$. What's the general linear diffusion equation? It is

$$\frac{\partial V}{\partial t} + a \frac{\partial^2 V}{\partial S^2} + b \frac{\partial V}{\partial S} + cV = 0.$$

Note the coefficients a, b and c. At the moment these could be anything.

Now for the two trivial observations.

First, cash in the bank must be a solution of this equation. Financial contracts don't come any simpler than this. So plug $V = e^{rt}$ into this diffusion equation to get

$$re^{rt} + 0 + 0 + ce^{rt} = 0.$$

So $c = -r$.

Second, surely the stock price itself must also be a solution? After all, you could think of it as being a call option with zero strike. So plug $V = S$ into the general diffusion equation. We find

$$0 + 0 + b + cS = 0.$$

So $b = -cS = rS$.

Putting b and c back into the general diffusion equation we find

$$\frac{\partial V}{\partial t} + a \frac{\partial^2 V}{\partial S^2} + rS \frac{\partial V}{\partial S} - rV = 0.$$

This is the risk-neutral Black–Scholes equation. Two of the coefficients (those of V and $\partial V / \partial S$) have been pinned down exactly without any modelling at all. Ok, so it doesn't tell us what the coefficient of the second derivative term is, but even that has a nice interpretation. It means at least a couple of interesting things.

First, if we do start to move outside the Black–Scholes world then chances are it will be the diffusion coefficient that we must change from its usual $\frac{1}{2}\sigma^2 S^2$ to accommodate new models.

Second, if we want to fudge our option prices, to massage them into line with traded prices for example, we can only do so by fiddling with this diffusion coefficient, i.e. what we now know to be the volatility. This derivation tells us that our only valid fudge factor is the volatility.

Black–Scholes for Accountants

The final derivation of the Black–Scholes equation requires very little complicated mathematics, and doesn't even need assumptions about Gaussian returns, all we need is for the variance of returns to be finite.

The Black–Scholes analysis requires *continuous* hedging, which is possible in theory but impossible, and even undesirable, in practice. Hence one hedges in some discrete way. Let's assume that we hedge at equal time periods, δt. And consider the value changes associated with a delta-hedged option.

- We start with zero cash
- We buy an option
- We sell some stock short
- Any cash left (positive or negative) is put into a risk-free account.

We start by borrowing some money to buy the option. This option has a delta, and so we sell delta of the underlying

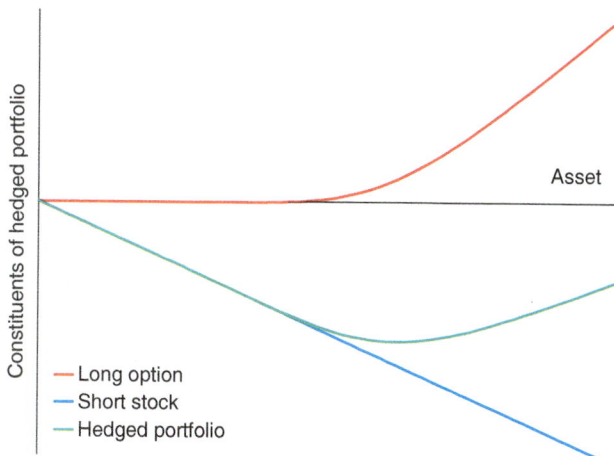

Figure 7.2: How our portfolio depends on S.

stock in order to hedge. This brings in some money. The cash from these transactions is put in the bank. At this point in time our net worth is zero.

Our portfolio has a dependence on S as shown in Figure 7.2.

We are only concerned with small movements in the stock over a small time period, so zoom in on the current stock position. Locally the curve is approximately a parabola, see Figure 7.3.

Now think about how our net worth will change from now to a time δt later. There are three reasons for our total wealth to change over that period.

1. The option price curve changes.
2. There is an interest payment on the money in the bank.
3. The stock moves

Figure 7.3: The curve is approximately quadratic.

The option curve falls by the time value, the theta multiplied by the time step:

$$\Theta \times \delta t.$$

To calculate how much interest we received we need to know how much money we put in the bank. This was

$$\Delta \times S$$

from the stock sale and

$$-V$$

from the option purchase. Therefore the interest we receive is

$$r(S\Delta - V)\,\delta t.$$

Finally, look at the money made from the stock move. Since gamma is positive, any stock price move is good for us. The larger the move the better.

The curve in Figure 7.3 is locally quadratic, a parabola with coefficient $\frac{1}{2}\Gamma$. The stock move over a time period δt is proportional to three things:

- the volatility σ
- the stock price S

• the square root of the time step

Multiply these three together, square the result because the curve is parabolic and multiply that by $\frac{1}{2}\Gamma$ and you get the profit made from the stock move as

$$\frac{1}{2}\sigma^2 S^2 \Gamma \, \delta t.$$

Put these three value changes together (ignoring the δt term which multiplies all of them) and set the resulting expression equal to zero, to represent no arbitrage, and you get

$$\Theta + \frac{1}{2}\sigma^2 S^2 \Gamma + r(S\Delta - V) = 0,$$

the Black–Scholes equation.

Now there was a bit of cheating here, since the stock price move is really random. What we should have said is that

$$\frac{1}{2}\sigma^2 S^2 \Gamma \, \delta t$$

is the profit made from the stock move *on average*. Crucially all we need to know is that the variance of returns is

$$\sigma^2 S^2 \delta t,$$

we don't even need the stock returns to be normally distributed. There is a difference between the square of the stock prices moves and its average value and this gives rise to hedging error, something that is always seen in practice. If you hedge discretely, as you must, then Black–Scholes only works on average. But as you hedge more and more frequently, going to the limit $\delta t = 0$, then the total hedging error tends to zero, so justifying the Black–Scholes model.

Other Derivations

There are other ways of deriving the Black–Scholes equation or formulæ but I am only going to give the references (see

Gerber & Shiu, 1994, and Hamada & Sherris, 2003). One of the reasons why I have drawn a line by not including them is summed up very nicely by a reader (who will remain anonymous for reasons which will be apparent) who submitted a couple of possible new derivations, in particular one using 'distortion risk theory.' In an email to me he wrote: 'Unfortunately distortion risk theory is completely unknown to quants ... maybe because this theory originated in insurance mathematics, but more probably because is useless, except research paper writing. I wrote master thesis on this topic, from time perspective, completely waste of time.'

References and Further Reading

Andreason, J, Jensen, B & Poulsen, R 1998 Eight valuation methods in financial mathematics: the Black–Scholes formula as an example. *Math. Scientist* **23** 18–40

Black, F & Scholes, M 1973 The pricing of options and corporate liabilities. *Journal of Political Economy* **81** 637–659

Cox, J & Rubinstein, M 1985 *Options Markets*. Prentice–Hall

Derman, E & Kani, I 1994 Riding on a smile. *Risk* magazine **7** (2) 32–39

Dupire, B 1994 Pricing with a smile. *Risk* magazine **7** (1) 18–20

Gerber, HU & Shiu, ESW 1994 Option pricing by Esscher transforms. *Transactions of the Society of Actuaries* **46** 99–191

Hamada, M & Sherris, M 2003 Contingent claim pricing using probability distortion operators: methods from insurance risk pricing and their relationship to financial theory. *Applied Mathematical Finance* **10** 1 19–47

Harrison, JM & Kreps, D 1979 Martingales and arbitrage in multi-period securities markets. *Journal of Economic Theory* **20** 381–408

Harrison, JM & Pliska, SR 1981 Martingales and stochastic integrals in the theory of continuous trading. *Stochastic Processes and their Applications* **11** 215–260

Joshi, M 2003 *The Concepts and Practice of Mathematical Finance*. Cambridge University Press.

Rubinstein, M 1976 The valuation of uncertain income streams and the pricing of options. *Bell Journal of Economics* **7** 407–425

Rubinstein, M 1994 Implied binomial trees. *Journal of Finance* **69** 771–818

Wilmott, P 1994 Discrete charms. *Risk* magazine **7** (3) 48–51 (March)

Wilmott, P 2006 *Paul Wilmott on Quantitative Finance*, second edition. John Wiley & Sons Ltd

Yakovlev, DE & Zhabin, DN 2003 About discrete hedging and option pricing

Chapter 8

Models and Equations

Equity, Foreign Exchange and Commodities

The lognormal random walk

The most common and simplest model is the lognormal random walk:

$$dS + \mu S \, dt + \sigma S \, dX.$$

The Black–Scholes hedging argument leads to the following equation for the value of non-path-dependent contracts,

$$\frac{\partial V}{\partial t} + \frac{1}{2}\sigma^2 S^2 \frac{\partial^2 V}{\partial S^2} + (r - D)S\frac{\partial V}{\partial S} - rV = 0.$$

The parameters are volatility σ, dividend yield D and risk-free interest rate r. All of these can be functions of S and/or t, although it wouldn't make much sense for the risk-free rate to be S dependent.

This equation can be interpreted probabilistically. The option value is

$$e^{-\int_t^T r(\tau)\,d\tau} E_t^{\mathbb{Q}}\left[\text{Payoff}(S_T)\right],$$

where S_T is the stock price at expiry, time T, and the expectation is with respect to the risk-neutral random walk

$$dS = r(t)S \, dt + \sigma(S,t)S \, dX.$$

When σ, D and r are only time dependent we can write down an explicit formula for the value of any non-path-dependent option without early exercise (and without any decision feature) as

$$\frac{e^{-\bar{r}(T-t)}}{\bar{\sigma}\sqrt{2\pi(T-t)}} \int_0^\infty$$
$$e^{-\left(\ln(S/S') + \left(\bar{r} - \bar{D} - \frac{1}{2}\bar{\sigma}^2\right)(T-t)\right)^2 / 2\bar{\sigma}^2(T-t)} \text{Payoff}(S') \frac{dS'}{S'},$$

where

$$\overline{\sigma} = \sqrt{\frac{1}{T-t} \int_t^T \sigma(\tau)^2 \, d\tau},$$

$$\overline{D} = \frac{1}{T-t} \int_t^T D(\tau) \, d\tau$$

and

$$\overline{r} = \frac{1}{T-t} \int_t^T r(\tau) \, d\tau.$$

The $\overline{\cdot}$ parameters represent the 'average' of the parameters from the current time to expiration. For the volatility parameter the relevant average is the root-mean-square average, since variances can be summed but standard deviations (volatilities) cannot.

The above is a very general formula which can be greatly simplified for European calls, puts and binaries.

Multi-dimensional lognormal random walks

There is a formula for the value of a European non-path-dependent option with payoff of Payoff$(S_1, \ldots, S_d)$ at time T:

$$V = e^{-r(T-t)} \left(2\pi(T-t)\right)^{-d/2} (\text{Det}\boldsymbol{\Sigma})^{-1/2} (\sigma_1 \cdots \sigma_d)^{-1}$$
$$\int_0^\infty \cdots \int_0^\infty \frac{\text{Payoff}(S_1' \cdots S_d')}{S_1' \cdots S_d'}$$
$$\times \exp\left(-\frac{1}{2}\boldsymbol{\alpha}^T \, \boldsymbol{\Sigma}^{-1}\boldsymbol{\alpha}\right) dS_1' \cdots dS_d'$$

where

$$\alpha_i = \frac{1}{\sigma_i(T-t)^{1/2}} \left(\ln\left(\frac{S_i}{S_i'}\right) + \left(r - D_i - \frac{\sigma_i^2}{2}\right)(T-t)\right),$$

Σ is the correlation matrix and there is a continuous dividend yield of D_i on each asset.

Stochastic volatility

If the risk-neutral volatility is modelled by

$$d\sigma = (p - \lambda q)\, dt + q\, dX_2,$$

where λ is the market price of volatility risk, with the stock model still being

$$dS = \mu S\, dt + \sigma S\, dX_1,$$

with correlation between them of ρ, then the option-pricing equation is

$$\frac{\partial V}{\partial t} + \frac{1}{2}\sigma^2 S^2 \frac{\partial^2 V}{\partial S^2} + \rho \sigma S q \frac{\partial^2 V}{\partial S\, \partial \sigma} + \frac{1}{2}q^2 \frac{\partial^2 V}{\partial \sigma^2}$$
$$+ rS\frac{\partial V}{\partial S} + (p - \lambda q)\frac{\partial V}{\partial \sigma} - rV = 0.$$

This pricing equation can be interpreted as representing the present value of the expected payoff under risk-neutral random walks for both S and σ. So for a call option, for example, we can price via the expected payoff

$$V(S, \sigma, t) = e^{-r(T-t)} E_t^{\mathbb{Q}}[\max(S_T - K, 0)].$$

For other contracts replace the maximum function with the relevant, even path-dependent, payoff function.

Hull & White (1987) Hull & White considered both general and specific volatility models. They showed that when the stock and the volatility are uncorrelated and the risk-neutral dynamics of the volatility are unaffected by the stock (i.e. $p - \lambda q$ and q are independent of S) then the fair value of an option is the average of the Black–Scholes values for the option, with the average taken over the distribution of σ^2.

Square-root model/Heston (1993)   In Heston's model

$$dv = (a - bv)dt + c\sqrt{v}\, dX_2,$$

where $v = \sigma^2$. This has arbitrary correlation between the underlying and its volatility. This is popular because there are closed-form solutions for European options.

3/2 model

$$dv = (av - bv^2)dt + cv^{3/2}\, dX_2,$$

where $v = \sigma^2$. Again, this has closed-form solutions.

GARCH-diffusion   In stochastic differential equation form the GARCH(1,1) model is

$$dv = (a - bv)dt + cv\, dX_2.$$

Here $v = \sigma^2$.

Ornstein–Uhlenbeck process   With $y = \ln v$, $v = \sigma^2$,

$$dy = (a - by)dt + c\, dX_2.$$

This model matches real, as opposed to risk-neutral, data well.

Asymptotic analysis   If the volatility of volatility is large and the speed of mean reversion is fast in a stochastic volatility model,

$$dS = rS\, dt + \sigma S\, dX_1 \quad \text{and} \quad d\sigma = \frac{p - \lambda q}{\epsilon}\, dt + \frac{q}{\sqrt{\epsilon}}\, dX_2$$

with a correlation ρ, then closed-form approximate solutions (asymptotic solutions) of the pricing equation can be found for simple options for arbitrary functions $p - \lambda q$ and q. In the above model the ϵ represents a small parameter. The asymptotic solution is then a power series in $\epsilon^{1/2}$.

Schönbucher's stochastic implied volatility Schönbucher begins with a stochastic model for implied volatility and then finds the actual volatility consistent, in a no-arbitrage sense, with these implied volatilities. This model calibrates to market prices by definition.

Jump diffusion

Given the jump-diffusion model

$$dS = \mu S \, dt + \sigma S \, dX + (J - 1)S \, dq,$$

the equation for an option is

$$\frac{\partial V}{\partial t} + \frac{1}{2}\sigma^2 S^2 \frac{\partial^2 V}{\partial S^2} + rS\frac{\partial V}{\partial S} - rV$$
$$+ \lambda E\left[V(JS, t) - V(S, t)\right] - \lambda \frac{\partial V}{\partial S} SE\left[J - 1\right] = 0.$$

$E[\cdot]$ is the expectation taken over the jump size. If the logarithm of J is Normally distributed with standard deviation σ' then the price of a European non-path-dependent option can be written as

$$\sum_{n=0}^{\infty} \frac{1}{n!} e^{-\lambda'(T-t)} (\lambda'(T - t))^n V_{BS}(S, t; \sigma_n, r_n),$$

where

$$k = E[J - 1], \quad \lambda' = \lambda(1 + k), \quad \sigma_n^2 = \sigma^2 + \frac{n\sigma'^2}{T - t}$$

and

$$r_n = r - \lambda k + \frac{n\ln(1 + k)}{T - t},$$

and V_{BS} is the Black–Scholes formula for the option value in the absence of jumps.

Fixed Income

In the following we use the continuously compounded interest convention. So that one dollar put in the bank at a constant rate of interest r would grow exponentially, e^{rt}. This is the convention used outside the fixed-income world. In the fixed-income world where interest is paid discretely, the convention is that money grows according to

$$\left(1 + r'\tau\right)^{n},$$

where n is the number of interest payments, τ is the time interval between payments (here assumed constant) and r' is the annualized interest rate.

To convert from discrete to continuous use

$$r = \frac{1}{\tau}\ln(1 + r'\tau).$$

The yield to maturity (YTM) or internal rate of return (IRR) Suppose that we have a zero-coupon bond maturing at time T when it pays one dollar. At time t it has a value $Z(t; T)$. Applying a constant rate of return of y between t and T, then one dollar received at time T has a present value of $Z(t; T)$ at time t, where

$$Z(t; T) = e^{-y(T-t)}.$$

It follows that

$$y = -\frac{\ln Z}{T - t}.$$

Suppose that we have a coupon-bearing bond. Discount all coupons and the principal to the present by using some interest rate y. The present value of the bond, at time t, is then

$$V = Pe^{-y(T-t)} + \sum_{i=1}^{N} C_i e^{-y(t_i - t)},$$

where P is the principal, N the number of coupons, C_i the coupon paid on date t_i. If the bond is a traded security then we know the price at which the bond can be bought. If this is the case then we can calculate the **yield to maturity** or **internal rate of return** as the value y that we must put into the above to make V equal to the traded price of the bond. This calculation must be performed by some trial and error/iterative procedure.

The plot of yield to maturity against time to maturity is called the **yield curve**.

Duration Since we are often interested in the sensitivity of instruments to the movement of certain underlying factors it is natural to ask how does the price of a bond vary with the yield, or vice versa. To a first approximation this variation can be quantified by a measure called the duration.

By differentiating the value function with respect to y we find that

$$\frac{dV}{dy} = -(T-t)Pe^{-y(T-t)} - \sum_{i=1}^{N} C_i(t_i-t)e^{-y(t_i-t)}.$$

This is the slope of the price/yield curve. The quantity

$$-\frac{1}{V}\frac{dV}{dy}$$

is called the **Macaulay duration**. (The **modified duration** is similar but uses the discretely compounded rate.) The Macaulay duration is a measure of the average life of the bond.

For small movements in the yield, the duration gives a good measure of the change in value with a change in the yield. For larger movements we need to look at higher order terms in the Taylor series expansion of $V(y)$.

Convexity   The Taylor series expansion of V gives

$$\frac{dV}{V} = \frac{1}{V}\frac{dV}{dy}\delta y + \frac{1}{2V}\frac{d^2V}{dy^2}(\delta y)^2 + \cdots,$$

where δy is a change in yield. For very small movements in the yield, the change in the price of a bond can be measured by the duration. For larger movements we must take account of the curvature in the price/yield relationship.

The **dollar convexity** is defined as

$$\frac{d^2V}{dy^2} = (T-t)^2 Pe^{-y(T-t)} + \sum_{i=1}^{N} C_i(t_i-t)^2 e^{-y(t_i-t)}.$$

and the **convexity** is

$$\frac{1}{V}\frac{d^2V}{dy^2}.$$

Yields are associated with individual bonds. Ideally we would like a consistent interest rate theory that can be used for all financial instruments simultaneously. The simplest of these assumes a deterministic evolution of a spot rate.

The spot rate and forward rates   The interest rate we consider will be what is known as a **short-term interest rate** or **spot interest rate** $r(t)$. This means that the rate $r(t)$ is to apply at time t. Interest is compounded at this rate at each moment in time but *this rate may change*, generally we assume it to be time dependent.

Forward rates are interest rates that are assumed to apply over given periods *in the future* for *all* instruments. This contrasts with yields which are assumed to apply from the present up to maturity, with a different yield for each bond.

Let us suppose that we are in a perfect world in which we have a continuous distribution of zero-coupon bonds with all maturities T. Call the prices of these at time t, $Z(t; T)$. Note the use of Z for zero-coupon.

The **implied forward rate** is the curve of a time-dependent spot interest rate that is consistent with the market price of instruments. If this rate is $r(\tau)$ at time τ then it satisfies

$$Z(t; T) = e^{-\int_t^T r(\tau)d\tau}.$$

On rearranging and differentiating this gives

$$r(T) = -\frac{\partial}{\partial T}(\ln Z(t; T)).$$

This is the forward rate for time T as it stands today, time t. Tomorrow the whole curve (the dependence of r on the future) may change. For that reason we usually denote the forward rate at time t applying at time T in the future as $F(t; T)$ where

$$F(t; T) = -\frac{\partial}{\partial T}(\ln Z(t; T)).$$

Writing this in terms of yields $y(t; T)$ we have

$$Z(t; T) = e^{-y(t;T)(T-t)}$$

and so

$$F(t; T) = y(t; T) + \frac{\partial y}{\partial T}.$$

This is the relationship between yields and forward rates when everything is differentiable with respect to maturity.

In the less-than-perfect real world we must do with only a discrete set of data points. We continue to assume that we have zero-coupon bonds but now we will only have a discrete set of them. We can still find an implied forward rate curve as follows. (In this I have made the simplifying assumption that rates are piecewise constant. In practice one uses other functional forms to achieve smoothness.)

Rank the bonds according to maturity, with the shortest maturity first. The market prices of the bonds will be denoted by Z_i^M where i is the position of the bond in the ranking.

Using only the first bond, ask the question 'What interest rate is implied by the market price of the bond?' The answer is given by y_1, the solution of

$$Z_1^M = e^{-r_1(T_1-t)},$$

i.e.

$$r_1 = -\frac{\ln(Z_1^M)}{T_1 - t}.$$

This rate will be the rate that we use for discounting between the present and the maturity date T_1 of the first bond. And it will be applied to *all* instruments whenever we want to discount over this period.

Now move on to the second bond having maturity date T_2. We know the rate to apply between now and time T_1, but at what interest rate must we discount between dates T_1 and T_2 to match the theoretical and market prices of the second bond? The answer is r_2, which solves the equation

$$Z_2^M = e^{-r_1(T_1-t)}e^{-r_2(T_2-T_1)},$$

i.e.

$$r_2 = -\frac{\ln\left(Z_2^M/Z_1^M\right)}{T_2 - T_1}.$$

By this method of **bootstrapping** we can build up the forward rate curve. Note how the forward rates are applied between two dates, for which period I have assumed they are constant.

This method can easily be extended to accommodate coupon-bearing bonds. Again rank the bonds by their maturities, but now we have the added complexity that we may only have one market value to represent the sum of several cash flows. Thus one often has to make some assumptions to get the right number of equations for the number of unknowns.

To price non-linear instruments, options, we need a model that captures the randomness in rates.

Black 1976

Market practice with fixed-income derivatives is often to treat them as if there is an underlying asset that is lognormal. This is the methodology proposed by Black (1976).

Bond options   A simple example of Black '76 would be a European option on a bond, as long as the maturity of the bond is significantly greater than the expiration of the option. The relevant formulæ are, for a call option

$$e^{-r(T-t)} \left(FN(d_1) - KN(d_2) \right),$$

and for a put

$$e^{-r(T-t)} \left(-FN(-d_1) + KN(-d_2) \right),$$

where

$$d_1 = \frac{\ln(F/K) + \frac{1}{2}\sigma^2(T_i - t)}{\sigma\sqrt{T_i - t}},$$

$$d_2 = \frac{\ln(F/K) - \frac{1}{2}\sigma^2(T_i - t)}{\sigma\sqrt{T_i - t}}.$$

Here F is the forward price of the underlying bond at the option maturity date T. The volatility of this forward price is σ. The interest rate r is the rate applicable to the option's expiration and K is the strike.

Caps and floors   A cap is made up of a string of caplets with a regular time interval between them. The payoff for the ith caplet is $\max(r_i - K, 0)$ at time T_{i+1} where r_i is the interest rate applicable from t_i to t_{i+1} and K is the strike.

Each caplet is valued under Black '76 as

$$e^{-r(T_{i+1}-t)} \left(FN(d_1) - KN(d_2) \right),$$

where r is the continuously compounded interest rate applicable from t to T_{i+1}, F is the forward rate from time T_i to time T_{i+1}, K the strike and

$$d_1 = \frac{\ln(F/K) + \frac{1}{2}\sigma^2(T_i - t)}{\sigma\sqrt{T_i - t}},$$

$$d_2 = \frac{\ln(F/K) - \frac{1}{2}\sigma^2(T_i - t)}{\sigma\sqrt{T_i - t}},$$

where σ is the volatility of the forward rate.

The floorlet can be thought of in a similar way in terms of a put on the forward rate and so its formula is

$$e^{-r(T_{i+1}-t)} \left(KN(-d_2) - FN(-d_1) \right).$$

Swaptions A payer swaption, which is the right to pay fixed and receive floating, can be modelled as a call on the forward rate of the underlying swap. Its formula is then

$$\frac{1 - [1/(1 + (F/m))^{\tau m}]}{F} \, e^{-r(T-t)} \left(FN(d_1) - KN(d_2) \right),$$

where r is the continuously compounded interest rate applicable from t to T, the expiration, F is the forward swap rate, K the strike and

$$d_1 = \frac{\ln(F/K) + \frac{1}{2}\sigma^2(T - t)}{\sigma\sqrt{T - t}},$$

$$d_2 = \frac{\ln(F/K) - \frac{1}{2}\sigma^2(T - t)}{\sigma\sqrt{T - t}},$$

where σ is the volatility of the forward swap rate. τ is the tenor of the swap and m the number of payments per year in the swap.

The receiver swaption is then

$$\frac{1 - [1/(1 + (F/m))^{\tau m}]}{F} \, e^{-r(T-t)} \left(KN(-d_2) - FN(-d_1)\right).$$

Spot rate models

The above method for pricing derivatives is not entirely internally consistent. For that reason there have been developed other interest rate models that are internally consistent.

In all of the spot rate models below we have

$$dr = u(r,t)dt + w(r,t)dX$$

as the real process for the spot interest rate. The risk-neutral process which governs the value of fixed-income instruments is

$$dr = (u - \lambda w)dt + w \, dX$$

where λ is the market price of interest rate risk. In each case the stochastic differential equation we describe is for the risk-neutral spot rate process, not the real.

The differential equation governing the value of non-path-dependent contracts is

$$\frac{\partial V}{\partial t} + \frac{1}{2}w^2\frac{\partial^2 V}{\partial r^2} + (u - \lambda w)\frac{\partial V}{\partial r} - rV = 0.$$

The value of fixed-income derivatives can also be interpreted as

$$E_t^{\mathbb{Q}}\left[\text{Present value of cash flows}\right],$$

where the expectation is with respect to the risk-neutral process.

Vasicek   In this model the risk-neutral process is

$$dr = (a - br)dt + c\,dX,$$

with a, b and c being constant. It is possible for r to go negative in this model.

There is a solution for bonds of the form $\exp(A(t; T) - B(t; T)r)$.

Cox, Ingersoll & Ross   In this model the risk-neutral process is

$$dr = (a - br)dt + cr^{1/2}dX,$$

with a, b and c being constant. As long as a is sufficiently large this process cannot go negative.

There is a solution for bonds of the form $\exp(A(t; T) - B(t; T)r)$.

Ho & Lee   In this model the risk-neutral process is

$$dr = a(t)dt + c\,dX,$$

with c being constant. It is possible for r to go negative in this model.

There is a solution for bonds of the form $\exp(A(t; T) - B(t; T)r)$.

The time-dependent parameter $a(t)$ is chosen so that the theoretical yield curve matches the market yield curve initially. This is calibration.

Hull & White   There are Hull & White versions of the above models. They take the form

$$dr = (a(t) - b(t)r)\,dt + c(t)dX,$$

or

$$dr = (a(t) - b(t)r) \, dt + c(t)r^{1/2}dX.$$

The functions of time allow various market data to be matched or calibrated.

There are solutions for bonds of the form $\exp(A(t; T) - B(t; T)r)$.

Black & Karasinski   In this model the risk-neutral spot-rate process is

$$d(\ln r) = (a(t) - b(t)\ln r) \, dt + c(t)dX.$$

There are no closed-form solutions for simple bonds.

Two-factor models

In the two-factor models there are two sources of randomness, allowing a much richer structure of theoretical yield curves than can be achieved by single-factor models. Often, but not always, one of the factors is still the spot rate.

Brennan & Schwartz   In the Brennan & Schwartz model the risk-neutral spot rate process is

$$dr = (a_1 + b_1(l - r))dt + \sigma_1 r \, dX_1$$

and the long rate satisfies

$$dl = l(a_2 - b_2 r + c_2 l)dt + \sigma_2 l \, dX_2.$$

Fong & Vasicek   Fong & Vasicek consider the following model for risk-neutral variables

$$dr = a(\bar{r} - r)dt + \sqrt{\xi} \, dX_1$$

and

$$d\xi = b(\bar{\xi} - \xi)dt + c\sqrt{\xi} \, dX_2.$$

Thus they model the spot rate, and ξ the square root of the volatility of the spot rate.

Longstaff & Schwartz   Longstaff & Schwartz consider the following model for risk-neutral variables

$$dx = a(\overline{x} - x)dt + \sqrt{x}\,dX_1$$

and

$$dy = b(\overline{y} - y)dt + \sqrt{y}\,dX_2,$$

where the spot interest rate is given by

$$r = cx + dy.$$

Hull & White   The risk-neutral model,

$$dr = (\eta(t) - u - \gamma r)dt + c\,dX_1$$

and

$$du = -au\,dt + b\,dX_2,$$

is a two-factor version of the one-factor Hull & White. The function $\eta(t)$ is used for fitting the initial yield curve.

All of the above, except for the Brennan & Schwartz model, have closed-form solutions for simple bonds in terms of the exponential of a linear function of the two variables.

The market price of risk as a random factor   Suppose that we have the two *real* random walks

$$dr = u\,dt + w\,dX_1$$

and

$$d\lambda = p\,dt + q\,dX_2,$$

where λ is the market price of r risk. The zero-coupon bond pricing equation is then

$$\frac{\partial Z}{\partial t} + \frac{1}{2}w^2\frac{\partial^2 Z}{\partial r^2} + \rho wq\frac{\partial^2 Z}{\partial r\,\partial \lambda} + \frac{1}{2}q^2\frac{\partial^2 Z}{\partial \lambda^2}$$
$$+ (u - \lambda w)\frac{\partial Z}{\partial r} + (p - \lambda_\lambda q)\frac{\partial Z}{\partial \lambda} - rZ = 0.$$

Since the market price of risk is related to the slope of the yield curve as the short end, there is only one unobservable in this equation, λ_λ.

SABR

The SABR (stochastic, α, β, ρ) model by Hagan, Kumar, Lesniewski & Woodward (2002) is a model for a forward rate, F, and its volatility, α, both of which are stochastic:

$$dF = \alpha F^\beta dX_1 \quad \text{and} \quad d\alpha = \nu \alpha \, dX_2.$$

There are three parameters, β, ν and a correlation ρ. The model is designed for the special case where the volatility α and volatility of volatility, ν, are both small. In this case there are relatively simple closed-form approximations (asymptotic solutions). The model is therefore most relevant for markets such as fixed income, rather than equity. Equity markets typically have large volatility making the model unsuitable.

The model calibrates well to simple fixed-income instruments of specified maturity, and if the parameters are allowed to be time dependent then a term structure can also be fitted.

Heath, Jarrow & Morton

In the Heath, Jarrow & Morton (HJM) model the evolution of the entire forward curve is modelled. The risk-neutral forward curve evolves according to

$$dF(t; T) = m(t, T) \, dt + \nu(t, T) \, dX.$$

Zero-coupon bonds then have value given by

$$Z(t; T) = e^{-\int_t^T F(t;s)ds},$$

the principal at maturity is here scaled to $1. A hedging argument shows that the drift of the risk-neutral process for F cannot be specified independently of its volatility and so

$$m(t, T) = v(t, T) \int_t^T v(t, s) \, ds.$$

This is equivalent to saying that the bonds, which are traded, grow at the risk-free spot rate on average in the risk-neutral world.

A multi-factor version of this results in the following risk-neutral process for the forward rate curve

$$dF(t, T) = \left(\sum_{i=1}^N v_i(t, T) \int_t^T v_i(t, s) \, ds \right) dt + \sum_{i=1}^N v_i(t, T) \, dX_i.$$

In this the dX_i are uncorrelated with each other.

Brace, Gatarek & Musiela

The Brace, Gatarek & Musiela (BGM) model is a discrete version of HJM where only traded bonds are modelled rather than the unrealistic entire continuous yield curve.

If $Z_i(t) = Z(t; T_i)$ is the value of a zero-coupon bond, maturing at T_i, at time t, then the forward rate applicable between T_i and T_{i+1} is given by

$$F_i = \frac{1}{\tau} \left(\frac{Z_i}{Z_{i+1}} - 1 \right),$$

where $\tau = T_{i+1} - T_i$. Assuming equal time periods between all maturities we have the risk-neutral process for the forward rates, given by

$$dF_i = \left(\sum_{j=1}^i \frac{\sigma_j F_j \tau \rho_{ij}}{1 + \tau F_j} \right) \sigma_i F_i \, dt + \sigma_i F_i \, dX_i.$$

Modelling interest rates is then a question of the functional forms for the volatilities of the forward rates σ_i and the correlations between them, ρ_{ij}.

Prices as expectations

For all of the above models the value of fixed-income derivatives can be interpreted as

$$E_t^{\mathbb{Q}}\left[\text{Present value of cash flows}\right],$$

where the expectation is with respect to the risk-neutral process(es). The 'present value' here is calculated pathwise. If performing a simulation for valuation purposes you must discount cash flows for each path using the relevant discount factor for that path.

Credit

Credit risk models come in two main varieties, the structural and the reduced form.

Structural models

Structural models try to model the behaviour of the firm so as to represent the default or bankruptcy of a company in as realistic a way as possible. The classical work in this area was by Robert Merton who showed how to think of a company's value as being a call option on its assets. The strike of the option being the outstanding debt.

Merton assumes that the assets of the company A follow a random walk

$$dA = \mu A\, dt + \sigma A\, dX.$$

If V is the current value of the outstanding debt, allowing for risk of default, then the value of the equity equals assets less liabilities:

$$S = A - V.$$

Here S is the value of the equity. At maturity of this debt

$$S(A, T) = \max(A - D, 0) \quad \text{and} \quad V(A, T) = \min(D, A),$$

where D is the amount of the debt to be paid back at time T.

If we can hedge the debt with a dynamically changing quantity of equity, then the Black–Scholes hedging argument applies and we find that the current value of the debt, V, satisfies

$$\frac{\partial V}{\partial t} + \frac{1}{2}\sigma^2 A^2 \frac{\partial^2 V}{\partial A^2} + rA \frac{\partial V}{\partial A} - rA = 0$$

subject to

$$V(A, T) = \min(D, A)$$

and exactly the same partial differential equation for the equity of the firm S but with

$$S(A, T) = \max(A - D, 0).$$

The problem for S is exactly that for a call option, but now we have S instead of the option value, the underlying variable is the asset value A and the strike is D, the debt. The formula for the equity value is the Black–Scholes value for a call option.

Reduced form

The more popular approach to the modelling of credit risk is to use an instantaneous risk of default or hazard rate, p. This means that if at time t the company has not defaulted then the probability of default between times t and $t + dt$ is $p \, dt$. This is just the same Poisson process seen in jump-diffusion models. If p is constant then this results in the probability of a company still being in existence at time T, assuming that it wasn't bankrupt at time t, being simply

$$e^{-p(T-t)}.$$

If the yield on a risk-free, i.e. government bond, with maturity T is r, then its value is

$$e^{-r(T-t)}.$$

If we say that an equivalent bond on the risky company will pay off 1 if the company is not bankrupt and zero otherwise, then the present value of the expected payoff comes from multiplying the value of a risk-free bond by the probability that the company is not in default to get

$$e^{-r(T-t)} \times e^{-p(T-t)} = e^{-(r+p)(T-t)}.$$

So to represent the value of a risky bond just add a credit spread of p to the yield on the equivalent risk-free bond. Or, conversely, knowing the yields on equivalent risk-free and risky bonds one can estimate p, the implied risk of default.

This is a popular way of modelling credit risk because it is so simple and the mathematics is identical to that for interest rate models.

References and Further Reading

Black F 1976 The pricing of commodity contracts. *Journal of Financial Economics* **3** 167–179

Black, F & Scholes, M 1973 The pricing of options and corporate liabilities. *Journal of Political Economy* **81** 637–659

Brace, A, Gatarek, D & Musiela, M 1997 The market model of interest rate dynamics. *Mathematical Finance* **7** 127–154

Cox, J, Ingersoll, J & Ross, S 1985 A theory of the term structure of interest rates. *Econometrica* **53** 385–467

Hagan, P, Kumar, D, Lesniewski, A & Woodward, D 2002 Managing smile risk. *Wilmott* magazine, September

Haug, EG 1997 *The Complete Guide to Option Pricing Formulas*. McGraw–Hill

Heath, D, Jarrow, R & Morton, A 1992 Bond pricing and the term structure of interest rates: a new methodology. *Econometrica* **60** 77–105

Heston, S 1993 A closed-form solution for options with stochastic volatility with application to bond and currency options. *Review of Financial Studies* **6** 327–343

Ho, T & Lee, S 1986 Term structure movements and pricing interest rate contingent claims. *Journal of Finance* **42** 1129–1142

Hull, JC & White, A 1987 The pricing of options on assets with stochastic volatilities. *Journal of Finance* **42** 281–300

Hull, JC & White, A 1990 Pricing interest rate derivative securities. *Review of Financial Studies* **3** 573–592

Lewis, A 2000 *Option Valuation under Stochastic Volatility*. Finance Press

Merton, RC 1973 Theory of rational option pricing. *Bell Journal of Economics and Management Science* **4** 141–183

Merton, RC 1974 On the pricing of corporate debt: the risk structure of interest rates. *Journal of Finance* **29** 449–470

Merton, RC 1976 Option pricing when underlying stock returns are discontinuous. *Journal of Financial Economics* **3** 125–144

Rasmussen, H & Wilmott, P 2002 Asymptotic analysis of stochastic volatility models. In *New Directions in Mathematical Finance* (eds Wilmott, P & Rasmussen, H). John Wiley & Sons Ltd

Schönbucher, PJ 1999 A market model for stochastic implied volatility. *Philosophical Transactions A* **357** 2071–2092

Schönbucher, PJ 2003 *Credit Derivatives Pricing Models*. John Wiley & Sons Ltd

Vasicek, OA 1977 An equilibrium characterization of the term structure. *Journal of Financial Economics* **5** 177–188

Wilmott, P 2006 *Paul Wilmott on Quantitative Finance*, second edition. John Wiley & Sons Ltd

Chapter 9

The Black–Scholes Formulæ and the Greeks

n the following formulæ

$$N(x) = \frac{1}{\sqrt{2\pi}} \int_{-\infty}^{x} e^{-\frac{1}{2}\phi^2} d\phi,$$

$$d_1 = \frac{\ln(S/K) + (r - D + \frac{1}{2}\sigma^2)(T - t)}{\sigma\sqrt{T - t}}$$

and

$$d_2 = \frac{\ln(S/K) + (r - D - \frac{1}{2}\sigma^2)(T - t)}{\sigma\sqrt{T - t}}.$$

The formulæ are also valid for time-dependent σ, D and r, just use the relevant 'average' as explained in the previous chapter.

Warning

The greeks which are 'greyed out' can sometimes be misleading. They are those greeks which are partial derivatives with respect to a parameter (σ, r or D) as opposed to a variable (S and t) *and* which are not single signed (i.e. always greater than zero or always less than zero). Differentiating with respect a parameter, *which has been assumed to be constant* so that we can find a closed-form solution, is internally inconsistent. For example, $\partial V/\partial \sigma$ is the sensitivity of the option price to volatility, but if volatility is constant, as assumed in the formula, why measure sensitivity to it? This may not matter if the partial derivative with respect to the parameter is of one sign, such as $\partial V/\partial \sigma$ for calls and puts. But if the partial derivative changes sign then there may be trouble. For example, the binary call has a positive vega for low stock prices and negative vega for high stock prices, in the middle vega is small, and even zero at a point. However, this does not mean that the binary call is insensitive to volatility in the middle. It is precisely in the middle that the binary call value is very sensitive to volatility, but not the level, rather the volatility skew.

Table 9.1: Formulæ for European call.

	Call
Payoff	$\max(S - K, 0)$
Value V Black–Scholes value	$Se^{-D(T-t)}N(d_1)$ $-Ke^{-r(T-t)}N(d_2)$
Delta $\frac{\partial V}{\partial S}$ Sensitivity to underlying	$e^{-D(T-t)}N(d_1)$
Gamma $\frac{\partial^2 V}{\partial S^2}$ Sensitivity of delta to underlying	$\frac{e^{-D(T-t)}N'(d_1)}{\sigma S\sqrt{T-t}}$
Theta $\frac{\partial V}{\partial t}$ Sensitivity to time	$-\frac{\sigma Se^{-D(T-t)}N'(d_1)}{2\sqrt{T-t}} + DSN(d_1)e^{-D(T-t)}$ $-rKe^{-r(T-t)}N(d_2)$
Speed $\frac{\partial^3 V}{\partial S^3}$ Sensitivity of gamma to underlying	$-\frac{e^{-D(T-t)}N'(d_1)}{\sigma^2 S^2(T-t)} \times \left(d_1 + \sigma\sqrt{T-t}\right)$
Charm $\frac{\partial^2 V}{\partial S\,\partial t}$ Sensitivity of delta to time	$De^{-D(T-t)}N(d_1) + e^{-D(T-t)}N'(d_1)$ $\times \left(\frac{d_2}{2(T-t)} - \frac{r-D}{\sigma\sqrt{T-t}}\right)$
Colour $\frac{\partial^3 V}{\partial S^2\,\partial t}$ Sensitivity of gamma to time	$\frac{e^{-D(T-t)}N'(d_1)}{\sigma S\sqrt{T-t}}$ $\times \left(D + \frac{1-d_1 d_2}{2(T-t)} - \frac{d_1(r-D)}{\sigma\sqrt{T-t}}\right)$
Vega $\frac{\partial V}{\partial \sigma}$ Sensitivity to volatility	$S\sqrt{T-t}\,e^{-D(T-t)}N'(d_1)$
Rho (r) $\frac{\partial V}{\partial r}$ Sensitivity to interest rate	$K(T-t)e^{-r(T-t)}N(d_2)$
Rho (D) $\frac{\partial V}{\partial D}$ Sensitivity to dividend yield	$-(T-t)Se^{-D(T-t)}N(d_1)$
Vanna $\frac{\partial^2 V}{\partial S\,\partial \sigma}$ Sensitivity of delta to volatility	$-e^{-D(T-t)}N'(d_1)\frac{d_2}{\sigma}$
Volga/Vomma $\frac{\partial^2 V}{\partial \sigma^2}$ Sensitivity of vega to volatility	$S\sqrt{T-t}\,e^{-D(T-t)}N'(d_1)\frac{d_1 d_2}{\sigma}$

Table 9.2: Formulæ for European put.

	Put
Payoff	$\max(K - S, 0)$
Value V Black–Scholes value	$-Se^{-D(T-t)}N(-d_1)$ $+Ke^{-r(T-t)}N(-d_2)$
Delta $\frac{\partial V}{\partial S}$ Sensitivity to underlying	$e^{-D(T-t)}(N(d_1) - 1)$
Gamma $\frac{\partial^2 V}{\partial S^2}$ Sensitivity of delta to underlying	$\frac{e^{-D(T-t)}N'(d_1)}{\sigma S\sqrt{T-t}}$
Theta $\frac{\partial V}{\partial t}$ Sensitivity to time	$-\frac{\sigma Se^{-D(T-t)}N'(-d_1)}{2\sqrt{T-t}}$ $-DSN(-d_1)e^{-D(T-t)}$ $+rKe^{-r(T-t)}N(-d_2)$
Speed $\frac{\partial^3 V}{\partial S^3}$ Sensitivity of gamma to underlying	$-\frac{e^{-D(T-t)}N'(d_1)}{\sigma^2 S^2(T-t)} \times$ $\left(d_1 + \sigma\sqrt{T-t}\right)$
Charm $\frac{\partial^2 V}{\partial S \partial t}$ Sensitivity of delta to time	$De^{-D(T-t)}(N(d_1) - 1)$ $+e^{-D(T-t)}N'(d_1)$ $\times \left(\frac{d_2}{2(T-t)} - \frac{r-D}{\sigma\sqrt{T-t}}\right)$
Colour $\frac{\partial^3 V}{\partial S^2 \partial t}$ Sensitivity of gamma to time	$\frac{e^{-D(T-t)}N'(d_1)}{\sigma S\sqrt{T-t}}$ $\times \left(D + \frac{1-d_1 d_2}{2(T-t)} - \frac{d_1(r-D)}{\sigma\sqrt{T-t}}\right)$
Vega $\frac{\partial V}{\partial \sigma}$ Sensitivity to volatility	$S\sqrt{T-t}e^{-D(T-t)}N'(d_1)$
Rho (r) $\frac{\partial V}{\partial r}$ Sensitivity to interest rate	$-K(T-t)e^{-r(T-t)}N(-d_2)$
Rho (D) $\frac{\partial V}{\partial D}$ Sensitivity to dividend yield	$(T-t)Se^{-D(T-t)}N(-d_1)$
Vanna $\frac{\partial^2 V}{\partial S \partial \sigma}$ Sensitivity of delta to volatility	$-e^{-D(T-t)}N'(d_1)\frac{d_2}{\sigma}$
Volga/Vomma $\frac{\partial^2 V}{\partial \sigma^2}$ Sensitivity of vega to volatility	$S\sqrt{T-t}e^{-D(T-t)}N'(d_1)\frac{d_1 d_2}{\sigma}$

Table 9.3: Formulæ for European binary call.

	Binary Call
Payoff	1 if $S > K$ otherwise 0
Value V Black–Scholes value	$e^{-r(T-t)}N(d_2)$
Delta $\frac{\partial V}{\partial S}$ Sensitivity to underlying	$\frac{e^{-r(T-t)}N'(d_2)}{\sigma S\sqrt{T-t}}$
Gamma $\frac{\partial^2 V}{\partial S^2}$ Sensitivity of delta to underlying	$-\frac{e^{-r(T-t)}d_1 N'(d_2)}{\sigma^2 S^2 (T-t)}$
Theta $\frac{\partial V}{\partial t}$ Sensitivity to time	$re^{-r(T-t)}N(d_2) + e^{-r(T-t)}N'(d_2)$ $\times \left(\frac{d_1}{2(T-t)} - \frac{r-D}{\sigma\sqrt{T-t}} \right)$
Speed $\frac{\partial^3 V}{\partial S^3}$ Sensitivity of gamma to underlying	$-\frac{e^{-r(T-t)}N'(d_2)}{\sigma^2 S^3 (T-t)} \times \left(-2d_1 + \frac{1-d_1 d_2}{\sigma\sqrt{T-t}} \right)$
Charm $\frac{\partial^2 V}{\partial S \partial t}$ Sensitivity of delta to time	$\frac{e^{-r(T-t)}N'(d_2)}{\sigma S\sqrt{T-t}}$ $\times \left(r + \frac{1-d_1 d_2}{2(T-t)} + \frac{d_2(r-D)}{\sigma\sqrt{T-t}} \right)$
Colour $\frac{\partial^3 V}{\partial S^2 \partial t}$ Sensitivity of gamma to time	$-\frac{e^{-r(T-t)}N'(d_2)}{\sigma^2 S^2 (T-t)} \times$ $\left(rd_1 + \frac{2d_1+d_2}{2(T-t)} - \frac{r-D}{\sigma\sqrt{T-t}} \right.$ $\left. -d_1 d_2 \left(\frac{d_1}{2(T-t)} - \frac{r-D}{\sigma\sqrt{T-t}} \right) \right)$
Vega $\frac{\partial V}{\partial \sigma}$ Sensitivity to volatility	$-e^{-r(T-t)}N'(d_2)\frac{d_1}{\sigma}$
Rho (r) $\frac{\partial V}{\partial r}$ Sensitivity to interest rate	$-(T-t)e^{-r(T-t)}N(d_2)$ $+\frac{\sqrt{T-t}}{\sigma}e^{-r(T-t)}N'(d_2)$
Rho (D) $\frac{\partial V}{\partial D}$ Sensitivity to dividend yield	$-\frac{\sqrt{T-t}}{\sigma}e^{-r(T-t)}N'(d_2)$
Vanna $\frac{\partial^2 V}{\partial S \partial \sigma}$ Sensitivity of delta to volatility	$-\frac{e^{-r(T-t)}}{\sigma^2 S\sqrt{T-t}}N'(d_2)(1-d_1 d_2)$
Volga/Vomma $\frac{\partial^2 V}{\partial \sigma^2}$ Sensitivity of vega to volatility	$\frac{e^{-r(T-t)}}{\sigma^2}N'(d_2)(d_1^2 d_2 - d_1 - d_2)$

Table 9.4: Formulæ for European binary put.

	Binary Put
Payoff	1 if $S < K$ otherwise 0
Value V Black–Scholes value	$e^{-r(T-t)}(1 - N(d_2))$
Delta $\frac{\partial V}{\partial S}$ Sensitivity to underlying	$-\dfrac{e^{-r(T-t)}N'(d_2)}{\sigma S\sqrt{T-t}}$
Gamma $\frac{\partial^2 V}{\partial S^2}$ Sensitivity of delta to underlying	$\dfrac{e^{-r(T-t)}d_1 N'(d_2)}{\sigma^2 S^2(T-t)}$
Theta $\frac{\partial V}{\partial t}$ Sensitivity to time	$re^{-r(T-t)}(1 - N(d_2))$ $-e^{-r(T-t)}N'(d_2)$ $\times\left(\dfrac{d_1}{2(T-t)} - \dfrac{r-D}{\sigma\sqrt{T-t}}\right)$
Speed $\frac{\partial^3 V}{\partial S^3}$ Sensitivity of gamma to underlying	$\dfrac{e^{-r(T-t)}N'(d_2)}{\sigma^2 S^3(T-t)}\times$ $\left(-2d_1 + \dfrac{1-d_1 d_2}{\sigma\sqrt{T-t}}\right)$
Charm $\frac{\partial^2 V}{\partial S\,\partial t}$ Sensitivity of delta to time	$-\dfrac{e^{-r(T-t)}N'(d_2)}{\sigma S\sqrt{T-t}}$ $\times\left(r + \dfrac{1-d_1 d_2}{2(T-t)} + \dfrac{d_2(r-D)}{\sigma\sqrt{T-t}}\right)$
Colour $\frac{\partial^3 V}{\partial S^2\,\partial t}$ Sensitivity of gamma to time	$\dfrac{e^{-r(T-t)}N'(d_2)}{\sigma^2 S^2(T-t)}$ $\times\left(rd_1 + \dfrac{2d_1+d_2}{2(T-t)} - \dfrac{r-D}{\sigma\sqrt{T-t}}\right.$ $\left.-d_1 d_2\left(\dfrac{d_1}{2(T-t)} - \dfrac{r-D}{\sigma\sqrt{T-t}}\right)\right)$
Vega $\frac{\partial V}{\partial \sigma}$ Sensitivity to volatility	$e^{-r(T-t)}N'(d_2)\dfrac{d_1}{\sigma}$
Rho (r) $\frac{\partial V}{\partial r}$ Sensitivity to interest rate	$-(T-t)e^{-r(T-t)}(1 - N(d_2))$ $-\dfrac{\sqrt{T-t}}{\sigma}e^{-r(T-t)}N'(d_2)$
Rho (D) $\frac{\partial V}{\partial D}$ Sensitivity to dividend yield	$\dfrac{\sqrt{T-t}}{\sigma}e^{-r(T-t)}N'(d_2)$
Vanna $\frac{\partial^2 V}{\partial S\,\partial \sigma}$ Sensitivity of delta to volatility	$-\dfrac{e^{-r(T-t)}}{\sigma^2 S\sqrt{T-t}}N'(d_2)\left(1 - d_1 d_2\right)$
Volga/Vomma $\frac{\partial^2 V}{\partial \sigma^2}$ Sensitivity of vega to volatility	$\dfrac{e^{-r(T-t)}}{\sigma^2}N'(d_2)\left(d_1^2 d_2 - d_1 - d_2\right)$

Chapter 10

Common Contracts

Things to Look Out For in Exotic Contracts

There are six important features to look out for in exotic contracts. Understanding these features will help you to price a contract. These features are as follows:

1. Time dependence
2. Cash flows
3. Path dependence
4. Dimensionality
5. Order
6. Embedded decisions

If you can classify an exotic contract according to these characteristics you will be able to determine the following:

- What kind of pricing method should best be used.
- Whether you can re-use some old code.
- How long it will take you to code it up.
- How fast it will eventually run.

Time dependence is when the terms of an exotic contract specify special dates or periods on or during which something happens, such as a cash flow, or early exercise, or an event is triggered. Time dependence is first on our list of features, since it is a very basic concept.

- Time dependence in an option contract means that our numerical discretization may have to be lined up to coincide with times at which, or periods during which, something happens.
- This means that our code will have to keep track of time, dates, etc. This is not difficult, just annoying.

Cash flows are when money changes hands during the life of the contract (as opposed to an initial premium or a final payoff). When there is a cash flow the value of the contract will instantaneously jump by the amount of the cash flow.

- When a contract has a discretely paid cash flow you should expect to have to apply jump conditions. This also means that the contract has time dependence, see above.
- Continuously paid cash flows mean a modification, although rather simple, to the governing equation.

Path dependence is when an option has a payoff that depends on the path taken by the underlying asset, and not just the asset's value at expiration. Path dependency comes in two varieties, strong and weak.

Strong path dependent contracts have payoffs that depend on some property of the asset price path in addition to the value of the underlying at the present moment in time; in the equity option language, we cannot write the value as $V(S, t)$. The contract value is a function of at least one more independent variable. Strong path dependency comes in two forms, **discretely sampled** and **continuously sampled**, depending on whether a discrete subset of asset prices is used or a continuous distribution of them.

- Strong path dependency means that we have to work in higher dimensions. A consequence of this is that our code may take longer to run.

Weak path dependence is when a contract does depend on the history of the underlying but an extra state variable is not required. The obvious example is a barrier option.

- Weak path dependency means that we *don't* have to work in higher dimensions, so our code should be pretty fast.

Dimensionality   refers to the number of underlying independent variables. The vanilla option has two independent variables, S and t, and is thus two dimensional. The weakly path-dependent contracts have the same number of dimensions as their non-path-dependent cousins.

We can have two types of three-dimensional problem. The first type of problem that is three dimensional is the strongly path-dependent contract. Typically, the new independent variable is a measure of the path-dependent quantity on which the option is contingent. In this case, derivatives of the option value with respect to this new variable are only of the first order. Thus the new variable acts more like another time-like variable.

The second type of three-dimensional problem occurs when we have a second source of randomness, such as a second underlying asset. In the governing equation we see a second derivative of the option value with respect to each asset. We say that there is diffusion in two dimensions.

- Higher dimensions means longer computing time.
- The number of dimensions we have also tells us what kind of numerical method to use. High dimensions mean that we probably want to use Monte Carlo; low means finite difference.

The order of an option   refers to options whose payoff, and hence value, is contingent on the value of *another* option. The obvious second-order options are compound options, for example, a call option giving the holder the right to buy a put option.

- When an option is second or higher order we have to solve for the first-order option, first. We thus have a layer cake, we must work on the lower levels and the results of those feed into the higher levels.

- This means that computationally we have to solve more than one problem to price our option.

Embedded decisions are when the holder or the writer has some control over the payoff. He may be able to exercise early, as in American options, or the issuer may be able to call the contract back for a specified price.

When a contract has embedded decisions you need an algorithm for deciding how that decision will be made. That algorithm amounts to assuming that the holder of the contract acts to *make the option value as high as possible for the delta-hedging writer*. The pricing algorithm then amounts to searching across all possible holder decision strategies for the one that maximizes the option value. That sounds hard, but approached correctly is actually remarkably straightforward, especially if you use the finite-difference method. The justification for seeking the strategy that maximizes the value is that the writer cannot afford to sell the option for anything less, otherwise he would be exposed to 'decision risk.' When the option writer or issuer is the one with the decision to make, then the value is based on seeking the strategy that minimizes the value.

- Decision features mean that we'd really like to price via finite differences.
- The code will contain a line in which we seek the best price, so watch out for $\geq$ or $\leq$ signs.

Examples

Accrual is a generic term applied to contracts in which an amount gradually builds up until it is paid off in a lump sum. An example would be an accrual range note in which for every day that some underlying is within a specified range a specified amount is accrued, to eventually be paid off in a lump sum on a specified day. As long as there are no decision features in the contract then the accrual is easily dealt with by Monte Carlo simulation. If one wants to take a partial differential approach to modelling then an extra state variable will often be required to keep track of how much money has been accrued.

American option is one where the holder has the right to exercise at any time before expiration and receive the payoff. Many contracts have such early exercise American features. Mathematically, early exercise is the same as conversion of a convertible bond. These contracts are priced assuming that the holder exercises so as to give the contract its highest value. Therefore a comparison must be made between the value of the option assuming you don't exercise and what you would get if you immediately exercised. This makes finite differences a much more natural numerical method for pricing such contracts than Monte Carlo.

Asian option is an option whose payoff depends on the average value of the underlying during some period of the option's life. The average can be defined in many ways, as an arithmetic or geometric mean, for example, and can use a large set of data points in a continuously sampled Asian or only a smaller set, in the discretely sampled Asian. In an Asian tail the averaging only occurs over a short period before option expiration. There are closed-form formulæ for some of the simpler Asian options based on geometric averages, and approximations for others. Otherwise they can be priced using Monte Carlo methods, or sometimes by finite differences. Because the average of an asset price path is less volatile than the asset path itself these options can be cheaper than their equivalent vanillas, but this will obviously depend on the nature of the payoff. These contracts are very common in the commodity markets because users of commodities tend to be exposed to prices over a long period of time, and hence their exposure is to the average price.

Asset swap is the exchange of one asset for interest payments for a specified period.

Balloon option is an option where the quantity of option bought will increase if certain conditions are met, such as barriers being triggered.

Barrier option has a payoff that depends on whether or not a specified level of the underlying is reached before expiration. In an 'out' option if the level is reached (triggered) then the option immediately becomes worthless. In an 'in' option the contract is worthless *unless* the level is triggered before expiration. An 'up' option is one where the trigger level is above the initial price of the underlying and a 'down' option is one where the trigger level is below the initial price of the underlying. Thus one talks about contracts such as the 'up-and-in call' which will have the same payoff as a call option but only if the barrier is hit from below. In these contracts one must specify the barrier level, whether it is in or out, and the payoff at expiration. A double barrier option has both an upper and a lower barrier. These contracts are bought by those with very specific views on the direction of the underlying, and its probability of triggering the barrier. These contracts are weakly path dependent. There are formulæ for many types of barrier option, assuming that volatility is constant. For more complicated barrier contracts or when volatility is not constant these contracts must be valued using numerical methods. Both Monte Carlo and finite differences can be used but the latter is often preferable.

Basis swap is an exchange of floating interest payments of one tenor for floating interest payments of another tenor, a six-month rate for a two-year rate for example. Since the two payments will generally move together if the yield curve experiences parallel shifts, the basis swap gives exposure to non-parallel movements in the yield curve such as flattening or steepening. More generally basis swap refers to any exchange in which the two floating rates are closely related, and therefore highly correlated.

Basket option has a payoff that depends on more than one underlying. A modest example would be an option that gives you at expiration the value of the higher performing out of two stocks. Another example would be a contract that pays the average of the values of 20 stocks at expiration provided that value is above a specified strike level. These contracts can be valued straightforwardly by Monte Carlo simulation as long as there is no early exercise feature. You would not use finite-difference methods because of the high dimensionality. If the contract is European, non-path dependent with all of the underlyings following lognormal random walks with constant parameters, then there is a closed-form formula for the value of the contract, and this can be calculated by numerical integration (quadrature). Basket options are popular in foreign exchange for those with exposure to multiple exchange rates. They can also be used as options on your own index. Although pricing these contracts can be theoretically straightforward they depend crucially on the correlation between the underlyings. These correlations can be very difficult to estimate since they can be quite unstable.

Bermudan option is one where the holder has the right to exercise on certain dates or periods rather than only at expiration (European exercise) or at any time (American exercise). Bermudan options cannot be worth less than their European equivalent and cannot be worth more than their American equivalent.

Binary option has a payoff that is discontinuous. For example a binary call pays off a specified amount if the underlying ends above the strike at expiration and is otherwise worthless. A one-touch pays off the specified amount as soon as the strike is reached; it can be thought of as an American version of the European binary. These contracts are also called digitals.

Break/Cancellable forward is a forward contract, usually FX, where the holder can terminate the contract at certain times if he so wishes.

Coupe option is a periodic option in which the strike gets reset to the worst of the underlying and the previous strike. Similar to a cliquet option, but cheaper.

Call option is an option to buy the underlying asset for a specified price, the strike or exercise price, at (European) or before (American) a specified data, the expiry or expiration. The underlying can be any security. They are bought to benefit from upward moves in the underlying, or if volatility is believed to be higher than implied. In the latter case the buyer would delta hedge the option to eliminate exposure to direction. Calls are written for the opposite reasons, of course. Also a holder of the underlying stock might write a call to gain some premium in a market where the stock is not moving much. This is called covered call writing. Simultaneous buying of the stock and writing a call is a buy–write strategy. For calls on lognormal underlyings in constant or time-dependent volatility worlds there are closed-form expressions for prices. With more complicated underlyings or volatility models these contracts can be priced by Monte Carlo or finite difference, the latter being more suitable if there is early exercise.

Other contracts may have call features or an embedded call. For example, a bond may have a call provision allowing the issuer to buy it back under certain conditions at specified times. If the issuer has this extra right then it may decrease the value of the contract, so it might be less than an equivalent contract without the call feature. Sometimes the addition of a call feature does not affect the value of a contract, this would happen when it is theoretically never optimal to exercise the call option. The simplest example of this is an

American versus a European call on a stock without any dividends. These both have the same theoretical value since it is never optimal to exercise early.

Cap is a fixed-income option in which the holder receives a payment when the underlying interest rate exceeds a specified level, the strike. This payment is the interest rate less the strike. These payments happen regularly, monthly, or quarterly, etc., as specified in the contract, and the underlying interest rate will usually be of the same tenor as this interval. The life of the cap will be several years. They are bought for protection against rises in interest rates. Market practice is to quote prices for caps using the Black '76 model. A contract with a single payment as above is called a caplet.

Chooser option is an option on an option, therefore a second-order option. The holder has the right to decide between getting a call or a put, for example, on a specified date. The expiration of these underlying options is further in the future. Other similar contracts can be readily imagined. The key to valuing such contracts is the realization that the two (or more) underlying options must first be valued, and then one values the option on the option. This means that finite-difference methods are the most natural solution method for this kind of contract. There are some closed-form formulæ for simple choosers when volatility is at most time dependent.

Cliquet option is a path-dependent contract in which amounts are locked in at intervals, usually linked to the return on some underlying. These amounts are then accumulated and paid off at expiration. There will be caps and/or floors on the locally locked-in amounts and on the global payoff. Such contracts might be referred to as locally capped, globally floored, for example. These contracts are popular with investors because they have the eternally appreciated upside participation and the downside protection, via the exposure to the returns and the locking in of returns and global floor. Because of the locking in of returns and the global cap/floor on the sum of returns, these contracts are strongly path dependent. Typically there will be four dimensions, which may in special cases be reduced to three via a similarity reduction. This puts the numerical solution on the Monte Carlo, finite difference border. Neither are ideal, but neither are really inefficient either. Because these contracts have a gamma that changes sign, the sensitivity is not easily represented by a simple vega calculation. Therefore, to be on the safe side, these contracts should be priced using a variety of volatility models so as to see the true sensitivity to the model.

Constant Maturity Swap (CMS)   is a fixed-income swap. In the vanilla swap the floating leg is a rate with the same maturity as the period between payments. However, in the CMS the floating leg is of longer maturity. This apparently trivial difference turns the swap from a simple instrument, one that can be valued in terms of bonds without resort to any model, into a model-dependent instrument.

Collateralized Debt Obligation (CDO)   is a pool of debt instruments securitized into one financial instrument. The pool may consist of hundreds of individual debt instruments. They are exposed to credit risk, as well as interest risk, of the underlying instruments. CDOs are issued in several tranches which divide up the pool of debt into instruments with varying degrees of exposure to credit risk. One can buy different tranches so as to gain exposure to different levels of loss. As with all correlation products they can be dangerous, so trade small.

The aggregate loss is the sum of all losses due to default. As more and more companies default so the aggregate loss will increase. The tranches are specified by levels, as percentages of notional. For example, there may be the 0–3% tranche, and the 3–7% tranche, etc. As the aggregate loss increases past each of the 3%, 7%, etc., hurdles so the owner of that tranche will begin to receive compensation, at the same rate as the losses are piling up. You will only be compensated once your attachment point has been reached, and until the detachment point. The pricing of these contracts requires a model for the relationship between the defaults in each of the underlying instruments. A common approach is to use copulas. However, because of the potentially large number of parameters needed to represent the relationship between underlyings, the correlations, it is also common to make simplifying assumptions. Such simplifications might be to assume a single common random factor representing default, and a single parameter representing all correlations.

Collateralized Debt Obligation squared (CDO^2) is a CDO-like contract in which the underlyings are other CDOs instead of being the simpler risky bonds.

Collateralized Mortgage Obligation (CMO) is a pool of mortgages securitized into one financial instrument. As with CDOs there are different tranches allowing investors to participate in different parts of the cash flows. The cash flows in a mortgage are interest and principal, and the CMOs may participate in either or both of these depending on the structure. The different tranches may correspond to different maturities of the underlying mortgages, for example. The risk associated with CMOs are interest rate risk and prepayment risk, therefore it is important to have a model representing prepayment.

Compound option is an option on an option, such as a call on a put which would allow the holder the right to buy a specified put at a later date for a specified amount. There is no element of choice in the sense of which underlying option to buy (or sell).

Contingent premium option is paid for at expiration only if the option expires in the money, not up front. If the option expires below the strike, for a call, then nothing is paid, but then nothing is lost. If the asset is just slightly in the money then the agreed premium is paid, resulting in a loss for the holder. If the underlying ends up significantly in the money then the agreed premium will be small relative to the payoff and so the holder makes a profit. This contract can be valued as a European vanilla option and a European digital with the same strike. This contract has negative gamma below the strike (for a call) and then positive gamma at the strike and above, so its dependence on volatility is subtle. The holder clearly wants the stock to end up either below the strike (for a call) or far in the money. A negative skew will lower the price of this contract.

Convertible bond is a bond issued by a company that can, at the choosing of the holder, be converted into a specified amount of equity. When so converted the company will issue new shares. These contracts are a hybrid instrument, being part way between equity and debt. They are appealing to the issuer since they can be issued with a lower coupon than straight debt, yet do not dilute earnings per share. If they are converted into stock that is because the company is doing well. They are appealing to the purchaser because of the upside potential with the downside protection. Of course, that downside protection may be limited because these instruments are exposed to credit risk. In the event of default the convertible bond ranks alongside debt, and above equity.

These instruments are best valued using finite-difference methods because that takes into account the optimal conversion time quite easily. One must have a model for volatility and also risk of default. It is common to make risk of default depend on the asset value, so the lower the stock price the greater the probability of default.

Credit Default Swap (CDS)   is a contract used as insurance against a credit event. One party pays interest to another for a prescribed time or until default of the underlying instrument. In the event of default the counterparty then pays the principal in return. The CDS is the dominant credit derivative in the structured credit market. The premium is usually paid periodically (quoted in basis points per notional). Premium can be an up-front payment, for short-term protection. On the credit event, settlement may be the delivery of the reference asset in exchange for the contingent payment or settlement may be in cash (that is, value of the instrument before default less value after, recovery value). The mark-to-market value of the CDS depends on changes in credit spreads. Therefore they can be used to get exposure to or hedge against changes in credit spreads. To price these contracts one needs a model for risk of default. However, commonly, one backs out an implied risk of default from the prices of traded CDSs.

Diff(erential) swap   is an interest rate swap of floating for fixed or floating, where one of the floating legs is a foreign interest rate. The exchange of payments are defined in terms of a domestic notional. Thus there is a quanto aspect to this instrument. One must model interest rates and the exchange rate, and as with quantos generally, the correlation is important.

Digital option   is the same as a binary option.

Exponential Collateralized Debt Obligation (ECDO)   You've heard of CDOs. You've heard of CDO squared. So why not CDO cubed? Hell, why not e^{CDO}? That's an ECDO. Or what about LCDO? The logarithm of a CDO, after all CDOs can only go to zero … now minus infinity is attainable! No, these contracts don't exist, I made them up. I made up the ECDO while listening, many years pre-global financial crisis, to what I thought were the stupidest models in the hope that a bit of satire might make people realize how dangerous these products could be. You've read the news, the message did not get across!

Extendible option/swap is a contract that can have its expiration date extended. The decision to extend may be at the control of the writer, the holder or both. If the holder has the right to extend the expiration then it may add value to the contract, but if the writer can extend the expiry it may decrease the value. There may or may not be an additional premium to pay when the expiration is extended. These contracts are best valued by finite-difference means because the contract contains a decision feature.

Floating Rate Note (FRN) is a bond with coupons linked to a variable interest rate issued by a company. The coupon will typically have a spread in excess of a government interest rate, and this spread allows for credit risk. The coupons may also have a cap and/or a floor. The most common measure of a floating interest rate is the London Interbank Offer Rate or LIBOR. LIBOR comes in various maturities, one-month, three-month, six-month, etc., and is the rate of interest offered between Eurocurrency banks for fixed-term deposits.

Floor is a fixed-income option in which the holder receives a payment when the underlying interest rate falls below a specified level, the strike. This payment is the strike less the interest rate. These payments happen regularly, monthly, or quarterly, etc., as specified in the contract, and the underlying interest rate will usually be of the same tenor as this interval. The life of the floor will be several years. They are bought for protection against falling interest rates. Market practice is to quote prices for floors using the Black '76 model. A contract with a single payment as above is called a floorlet.

Forward is an agreement to buy or sell an underlying, typically a commodity, at some specified time in the future.

The holder is obliged to trade at the future date. This is in contrast to an option where the holder has the right but not the obligation. Forwards are OTC contracts. They are linear in the underlying and so convexity is zero, meaning that the volatility of the commodity does not matter and a dynamic model is not required. The forward price comes from a simple, static, no-arbitrage argument.

Forward Rate Agreement (FRA) is an agreement between two parties that a specified interest rate will apply to a specified principal over some specified period in the future. The value of this exchange at the time the contract is entered into is generally not zero and so there will be a transfer of cash from one party to the other at the start date.

Forward-start option is an option that starts some time in the future. The strike of the option is then usually set to be the value of the underlying on the start date, so that it starts life as an at-the-money option. It is also possible to have contracts that begin in or out of the money by a specified amount. Although the option comes into being at a specified date in the future it is usually paid for as soon as the contract is entered into. In a Black–Scholes world, even with time-dependent volatility, these contracts have simple closed-form formulæ for their values. Provided the strike is set to be a certain fraction of the underlying at the start date then the value of a vanilla call or put at that start date is linear in the price of the underlying, and so prior to the start date there is no convexity. This means that forward-start options are a way of locking in an exposure to the volatility from the option's start date to the expiration.

Future is an agreement to buy or sell an underlying, typically a commodity, at some specified time in the future. The holder is obliged to trade at the future date. The difference between a forward and a future is that forwards are OTC and futures are exchange traded. Therefore futures have standardized contract terms and are also marked to market on a daily basis. Being exchange traded they also do not carry any credit risk exposure.

Hawai'ian option is a cross between Asian and American.

Himalayan option is a multi-asset option in which the best performing stock is thrown out of the basket at specified sampling dates, leaving just one asset in at the end on which the payoff is based. There are many other, similar, mountain range options.

HYPER option High Yielding Performance Enhancing Reversible options are like American options but which you can exercise over and over again. On each exercise the option flips from call to put or vice versa. These can be priced by introducing a price function when in the call state and another when in the put state. The Black–Scholes partial differential equation is solved for each of these, subject to certain optimality constraints.

Index amortizing rate swap is just as a vanilla swap, an agreement between two parties to exchange interest payments on some principal, usually one payment is at a fixed rate and the other at a floating rate. However, in the index amortizing rate swap the size of the principal decreases, or amortizes, according to the value of some financial quantity or index over the life of the swap. The level of this principal may be determined by the level of an interest rate on the payments dates. Or the principal may be determined by a non-fixed income index. In the first example we would only need a fixed-income model, in the second we would also need a model for this other quantity, and its correlation with interest rates. In an index amortizing rate swap the principal typically can amortize on each payment date. On later payment dates this principal can then be amortized again, starting from its current level at the previous payment date and *not* based on its original level. This makes this contract very path dependent. The contract can be priced in either a partial differential equation framework based on a one- or two-factor spot-rate based model, or using Monte Carlo simulations and a LIBOR market-type model.

Interest rate swap is a contract between two parties to exchange interest on a specified principal. The exchange may be fixed for floating or floating of one tenor for floating of another tenor. Fixed for floating is a particularly common form of swap. These instruments are used to convert a fixed-rate loan to floating, or vice versa. Usually the interval between the exchanges is set to be the same as the tenor of the floating leg. Furthermore, the floating leg is set at the payment date before it is paid. This means that each floating leg is equivalent to a deposit and a withdrawal of the principal with an interval of the tenor between them. Therefore all the floating legs can be summed up to give one deposit at the start of the swap's life and a withdrawal at maturity. This means that swaps can be valued directly from the yield curve without needing a dynamic model. When the contract is first entered into the fixed leg is set so that the swap has zero value. The fixed leg of the swap is then called the par swap rate and is a commonly quoted rate. These contracts are so liquid that they define the longer-maturity end of the yield curve rather than vice versa.

Inverse floater is a floating-rate interest-rate contract where coupons go down as interest rates go up. The relationship is linear (up to any cap or floor) and *not* an inverse one.

Knock-in/out option are types of barrier option for which the payoff is contingent on a barrier level being hit/missed before expiration.

LIBOR-in-arrears swap   is an interest rate swap but one for which the floating leg is paid at the same time as it is set, rather than at the tenor later. This small difference means that there is no exact relationship between the swap and bond prices and so a dynamic model is needed. This amounts to pricing the subtle convexity in this product.

Lookback option   is a path-dependent contract whose payoff depends on the maximum or minimum value reached by the underlying over some period of the option's life. The maximum/minimum may be sampled continuously or discretely, the latter using only a subset of asset prices over the option's life. These contracts can be quite expensive because of the extreme nature of the payoff. There are formulæ for some of the simpler lookbacks, under the assumption of a lognormal random walk for the underlying and non-asset-dependent volatility. Otherwise they can be valued via finite-difference solution of a path-dependent partial differential equation in two or three dimensions, or by Monte Carlo simulation.

Mortgage Backed Security (MBS)   is a pool of mortgages that have been securitized. All of the cash flows are passed on to investors, unlike in the more complex CMOs. The risks inherent in MBSs are interest rate risk and prepayment risk, since the holders of mortgages have the right to prepay. Because of this risk the yield on MBSs should be higher than yields without prepayment risk. Prepayment risk is usually modelled statistically, perhaps with some interest rate effect. Holders of mortgages have all kinds of reasons for prepaying, some rational and easy to model, some irrational and harder to model but which can nevertheless be interpreted statistically.

Outperformance option   is an option where the holder gets the best performing out of two or more underlyings at expiration. This option can be valued theoretically in a lognormal

random walk, constant parameter world, since it is not path
dependent and there is a closed-form solution in terms of a
multiple integral (in the same number of dimensions as there
are underlyings). This amounts to a numerical quadrature
problem which is easily achieved by Monte Carlo or quasi
Monte Carlo methods. The theory may be straightforward but
the practice is not since the price will depend on the correlations between all of the underlyings, and these parameters
are usually quite fickle.

Parisian option is a barrier option for which the barrier feature
(knock in or knock out) is only triggered after the underlying
has spent a certain prescribed time beyond the barrier. The
effect of this more rigorous triggering criterion is to smooth
the option value (and delta and gamma) near the barrier to
make hedging somewhat easier. It also makes manipulation of
the triggering, by manipulation of the underlying asset, much
harder. In the classical Parisian contract the 'clock' measuring the time outside the barrier is reset when the asset
returns to within the barrier. In the Parisian contract the
clock is not reset but continues ticking as long as the underlying is beyond the barrier. These contracts are strongly path
dependent and can be valued either by Monte Carlo simulation or by finite-difference solution of a three-dimensional
partial differential equation.

Pass through is a security which collects payments on various underlying securities and then passes the amounts on
to investors. They are issued by Special Purpose Vehicles
and can be made to avoid appearing on balance sheets. This
achieves a variety of purposes, some rather nefarious.

Passport option is a call option on the trading account of
an individual trader, giving the holder the amount in his
account at the end of the horizon if it is positive, or zero
if it is negative. For obvious reasons they are also called
perfect trader options. The terms of the contract will specify

what the underlying is that the trader is allowed to trade, his maximum long and short position, how frequently he can trade and for how long. To price these contracts requires a small knowledge of stochastic control theory. The governing partial differential equation is easily solved by finite differences. Monte Carlo would be quite difficult to implement for pricing purposes. Since the trader very quickly moves into or, more commonly, out of the money, the option is usually hedged with vanilla options after a while.

Put option is the right to sell the underlying stock. See the 'Call option' since comments about pricing methodology, embedded features, etc., are equally applicable. Deep out-of-the-money puts are commonly bought for protection against large downward moves in individual stocks or against market crashes. These out-of-the-money puts therefore tend to be quite expensive in volatility terms, although very cheap in monetary terms.

Quanto is any contract in which cash flows are calculated from an underlying in one currency and then converted to payment in another currency. They can be used to eliminate any exposure to currency risk when speculating in a foreign stock or index. For example, you may have a view on a UK company but be based in Tokyo. If you buy the stock you will be exposed to the sterling/yen exchange rate. In a quanto the exchange rate would be fixed. The price of a quanto will generally depend on the volatility of the underlying and the exchange rate, and the correlation between the two.

Rainbow option is any contract with multiple underlyings. The most difficult part of pricing such an option is usually knowing how to deal with correlations.

Range note is a contract in which payments are conditional upon an underlying staying within (or outside) a specified range of values.

Ratchet is a feature that periodically locks in profit.

Repo is a repurchase agreement. It is an agreement to sell some security to another party and buy it back at a fixed date and for a fixed amount. The price at which the security is bought back is greater than the selling price and the difference implies an interest rate called the repo rate. Repos can be used to lock in future interest rates.

Reverse repo is the borrowing of a security for a short period at an agreed interest rate.

Straddle is a portfolio consisting of a long call and a long put with the same strike and expiration. Such a portfolio is for taking a view on the range of the underlying or volatility.

Strangle is a portfolio of a call and a put, the call having a higher strike than the put. It is a volatility play like the straddle but is cheaper. At the same time it requires the underlying to move further than for a straddle for the holder to make a profit.

STRIPS stands for Separate Trading of Registered Interest and Principal of Securities. The coupons and principal of normal bonds are split up, creating artificial zero-coupon bonds of longer maturity than would otherwise be available.

Swap is a general term for an over-the-counter contract in which there are exchanges of cash flows between two parties. Examples would be an exchange of a fixed interest rate for a floating rate, or the exchange of equity returns and bond returns, etc.

Swaption is an option on a swap. It is the option to enter into the swap at some expiration date, the swap having predefined characteristics. Such contracts are very common in the fixed-income world where a typical swaption would be on a swap of fixed for floating. The contract may be European so that the swap can only be entered into on a certain date, or American in which the swap can be entered into before a certain date or Bermudan in which there are specified dates on which the option can be exercised.

Total Return Swap (TRS)   is the exchange of all the profit or loss from a security for a fixed or floating interest payment. Periodically, one party transfers the cash flows plus any positive value change of a reference asset to the other party, this includes interest payments, appreciation, coupons, etc., while the other party pays a fixed or floating rate, probably with some spread. The difference between a total return swap and a default swap is that a default swap simply transfers credit risk, by reference to some designated asset whereas a total return swap transfers all the risks of owning the designated asset. Total return swaps were among the earliest credit derivatives. TRSs existed before default swaps, but now default swaps are the more commonly traded instruments. The maturity is typically less than the maturity of the underlying instrument. A TRS therefore provides a means of packaging and transferring *all* of the risks associated with a reference obligation, including credit risk. TRSs are more flexible than transactions in the underlyings. For example, varying the terms of the swap contract allows the creation of synthetic assets that may not be otherwise available. The swap receiver never has to make the outlay to buy the security. Even after posting collateral and paying a high margin, the resulting leverage and enhanced return on regulatory capital can be large.

Ultras   give a multiple of an index's performance on a daily basis, and that multiple can be positive or negative. Suppose you have an ultrashort giving a multiple of minus two and suppose that the returns on an index over a week are 2%, 3%,

−1%, 2% and −3%. The ultrashort would then have a value given by the compounding of −4%, −6%, 2%, −4% and 6%.

Variance swap is a swap in which one leg is the realized variance in the underlying over the life of the contract and the other leg is fixed. This variance is typically measured using regularly spaced data points according to whatever variance formula is specified in the term sheet. The contract is popular with both buyers and sellers. For buyers, the contract is a simple way of gaining exposure to the variance of an asset without having to go to all the trouble of dynamically delta hedging vanilla options. And for sellers it is popular because it is surprisingly easy to statically hedge with vanilla options to almost eliminate model risk. The way that a variance swap is hedged using vanillas is the famous 'one over strike squared rule.' The variance swap is hedged with a continuum of vanilla options with the quantity of options being inversely proportional to the square of their strikes. In practice, there does not exist a continuum of strikes, and also one does not go all the way to zero strike (and an infinite quantity of them).

The volatility swap is similar in principle, except that the payoff is linear in the volatility, the square root of variance. This contract is not so easily hedged with vanillas. The difference in prices between a volatility swap and a variance swap can be interpreted via **Jensen's Inequality** as a convexity adjustment because of volatility of volatility. The VIX volatility index is a representation of SP500 30-day implied volatility inspired by the one-over-strike-squared rule.

Chapter 11

Popular Quant Books

*T*he following are the dozen most popular quant books in the wilmott.com bookshop since December 2001.

Paul Wilmott Introduces Quantitative Finance, Second Edition by Paul Wilmott

'The style is pedagogical and yet very lively and easygoing. As only great teachers can, Wilmott makes even the most obtuse mathematics seem easy and intuitive.' Marco Avellaneda

Publisher John Wiley & Sons Ltd
Publication date 2007
Format Paperback + CD
ISBN 9780470319581

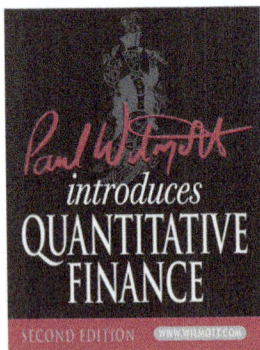

An introductory text for students based on the three-volume research-level book *PWOQF2*, see below. The book covers much of the foundation material for students approaching the subject from an applied mathematician's perspective. There are chapters on derivatives, portfolio management, equity

and fixed income, as well as the numerical methods of Monte Carlo simulation, the binomial method and finite-difference methods.

Paul Wilmott on Quantitative Finance, Second Edition by Paul Wilmott

'*Paul Wilmott on Quantitative Finance*, Second Edition, is even better than his unsurpassed First Edition. He combines the insights of an incisive theorist with his extensive practical experience. His teaching style is clear and entertaining. I recommend the book to everyone in the "quant" community, from beginner to expert, both for learning and for reference.' Ed Thorp

Publisher John Wiley & Sons Ltd
Publication date 2006
Format Hardback, three volumes in slip case, + CD
ISBN 9780470018705

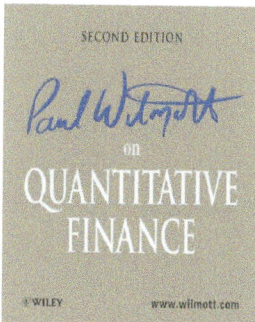

A research-level book containing the tried and trusted techniques, the analysis of models and data, and cutting-edge material. Contains models and research that cannot be found in other textbooks.

Advanced Modelling in Finance Using Excel and VBA by Mary Jackson and Mike Staunton

Publisher John Wiley & Sons Ltd
Publication date 2001
Format Hardback + CD
ISBN 9780471499220

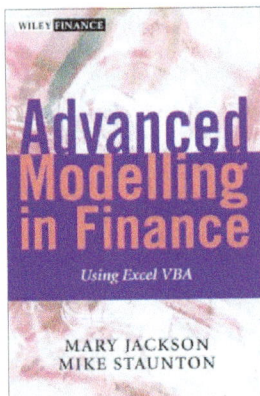

The book adopts a step-by-step approach to understanding the more sophisticated aspects of Excel macros and VBA programming, showing how these programming techniques can be used to model and manipulate financial data, as applied to equities, bonds and options. The book is essential for financial practitioners who need to develop their financial modelling skill sets as there is an increase in the need to analyse and develop ever more complex 'what if' scenarios.

Option Valuation under Stochastic Volatility by Alan Lewis

'This exciting book is the first one to focus on the pervasive role of stochastic volatility in option pricing. Since options exist primarily as the fundamental mechanism for trading volatility, students of the fine art of option pricing are advised to pounce.' Peter Carr

Publisher Finance Press
Publication date 2000
Format Paperback
ISBN 0967637201

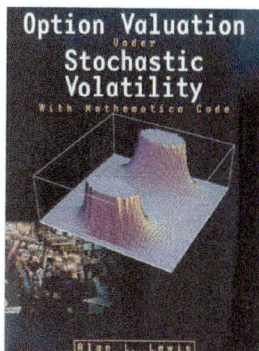

This book provides an advanced treatment of option pricing for traders, money managers, and researchers. Providing largely original research not available elsewhere, it covers the new generation of option models where both the stock price and its volatility follow diffusion processes.

These new models help explain important features of real-world option pricing that are not captured by the Black–Scholes model. These features include the 'smile' pattern and the term structure of implied volatility. The book includes Mathematica code for the most important formulæ and many illustrations.

The Concepts and Practice of Mathematical Finance by Mark Joshi

'Mark Joshi's work is one of the most thoughtful books in applied finance I know. It is both intuitive and mathematically correct and it deals with very deep concepts in derivatives pricing while keeping the treatment simple and readily understandable.' Riccardo Rebonato

Publisher Cambridge University Press
Publication date 2003
Format Hardback
ISBN 0521823552

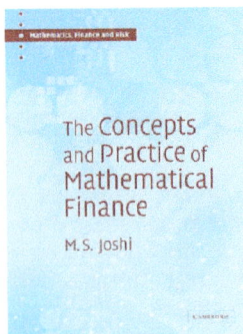

Uniquely, the book includes extensive discussion of the ideas behind the models, and is even-handed in examining

various approaches to the subject. Thus, each pricing problem is solved using several methods. Worked examples and exercises, with answers, are provided in plenty, and computer projects are given for many problems. The author brings to this book a blend of practical experience and rigorous mathematical background, and supplies here the working knowledge needed to become a good quantitative analyst.

C++ Design Patterns and Derivatives Pricing by Mark Joshi

'This book is thought-provoking and rewarding. Even for the less experienced programmer, the presentation is readily accessible, and the coded examples can be directly used to solve real-life problems.' *Journal of the American Statistics Association*, Ana-Maria Matache

Publisher Cambridge University Press
Publication date 2004
Format Hardback
ISBN 0521832357

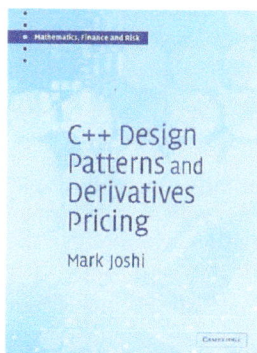

Design patterns are the cutting-edge paradigm for programming in object-oriented languages. Here they are discussed, for the first time in a book, in the context of implementing financial models in C++.

Assuming only a basic knowledge of C++ and mathematical finance, the reader is taught how to produce well-designed, structured, re-usable code via concrete examples. Each example is treated in depth, with the whys and wherefores of the chosen method of solution critically examined.

Heard on the Street by Timothy Crack

Publisher Timothy Crack
Publication date 2008
Format Paperback
ISBN 0970055269

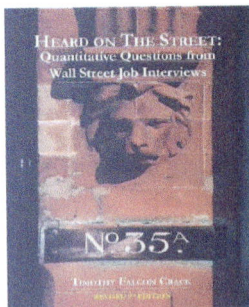

The book contains over 170 quantitative questions collected from actual investment banking, investment management, and options trading job interviews. The interviewers use the same questions year after year and here they are! These questions come from all types of interviews (corporate finance, sales and trading, quantitative research, etc.), but they are especially likely in quantitative capital markets job interviews.

The questions come from all levels of interviews (undergraduate, MBA, PhD), but they are especially likely if you have, or almost have, an MBA. The questions cover pure quantitative/logic, financial economics, derivatives, and statistics. Each quantitative question in the book is accompanied by a very detailed solution and by helpful advice.

The latest edition also includes about 125 non-quantitative actual interview questions.

Monte Carlo Methods in Finance by

Peter Jäckel

'Few expert practitioners also have the academic expertise to match Peter Jäckel's in this area, let alone take the trouble to write a most accessible, comprehensive and yet self-contained text.' Carol Alexander

Publisher John Wiley & Sons Ltd
Publication date 2002
Format Hardback
ISBN 9780471497417

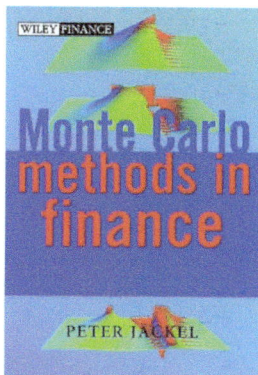

Monte Carlo Methods in Finance adopts a practical flavour throughout, the emphasis being on financial modelling and derivatives pricing. Numerous real-world examples help the reader to foster an intuitive grasp of the mathematical and numerical techniques needed to solve particular financial problems. At the same time, the book tries to give a detailed explanation of the theoretical foundations of the various methods and algorithms presented.

Credit Derivatives Pricing Models by Philipp Schönbucher

'Philipp Schönbucher is one of the most talented researchers of his generation. He has taken the credit derivatives world by storm.' Paul Wilmott

Publisher John Wiley & Sons Ltd
Publication date 2003
Format Hardback
ISBN 9780470842911

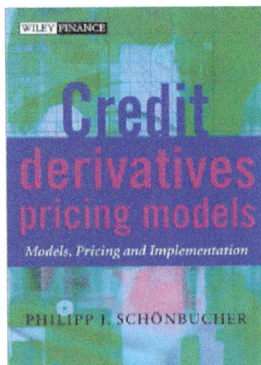

Credit Derivatives Pricing Models provides an extremely comprehensive overview of the most current areas in credit risk modeling as applied to the pricing of credit derivatives. As one of the first books to uniquely focus on pricing, this title is also an excellent complement to other books on the application of credit derivatives. Based on proven techniques that have been tested time and again, this comprehensive resource provides readers with the knowledge and guidance to effectively use credit derivatives pricing models.

Principles of Financial Engineering by Salih Neftci

'This is the first comprehensive hands-on introduction to financial engineering. Neftci is enjoyable to read, and finds a natural balance between theory and practice.' Darrell Duffie

Publisher Academic Press
Publication date 2004
Format Hardback
ISBN 0125153945

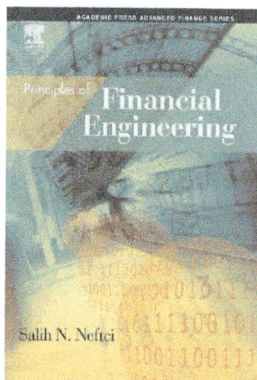

On a topic where there is already a substantial body of literature, Salih Neftci succeeds in presenting a fresh, original, informative, and up-to-date introduction to financial engineering. The book offers clear links between intuition and underlying mathematics and an outstanding mixture of market insights and mathematical materials. Also included are end-of-chapter exercises and case studies.

Options, Futures, and Other Derivatives by John Hull

Publisher Prentice Hall
Publication date 2008
Format Paperback
ISBN 0136015891

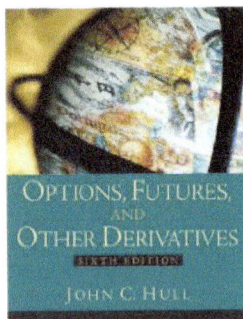

For advanced undergraduate or graduate business, economics, and financial engineering courses in derivatives, options and futures, or risk management. Designed to bridge the gap between theory and practice, this successful book continues to impact the college market and is regarded as 'the bible' in trading rooms throughout the world. This edition has been completely reworked from beginning to end to improve presentation, update material, and reflect recent market developments. Though nonessential mathematical material has been either eliminated or moved to end-of-chapter appendices, the concepts that are likely to be new to many readers have been explained carefully, and are supported by numerical examples.

The Complete Guide to Option Pricing Formulas by Espen Gaarder Haug

'The truth of the matter is that if I am being so positive about this book, it's because I know for a fact that it has saved lives more than once.' Alireza Javaheri

Publisher McGraw-Hill Professional
Publication date 2007
Format Hardback
ISBN 0071389970

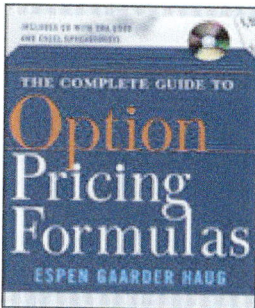

When pricing options in today's fast-action markets, experience and intuition are no longer enough. To protect your carefully planned positions, you need precise facts and tested information that has been proven time and again.

The Complete Guide to Option Pricing Formulas is the first and only authoritative reference to contain every option tool you need, all in one handy volume: Black–Scholes, two asset binomial trees, implied trinomial trees, Vasicek, exotics.

Many important option-pricing formulæ are accompanied by computer code to assist in their use, understanding, and implementation.

Chapter 12

The Most Popular Search Words and Phrases on Wilmott.com

*T*he following are some of the most common search words or phrases on wilmott.com, and a few comments on each. If other people want to know about these, then maybe you should too.

American option   An option which can be exercised at any time of the holder's choosing prior to expiration. See page 464.

Arbitrage   Arbitrage is the making of a totally riskless profit in excess of the risk-free rate of return. See page 27.

Asian option   An option whose payoff depends on the average value of the underlying asset over some time period prior to expiration. See page 464.

Asset swap   The exchange of two investments, or the cash flows to those investments, between two parties.

Barrier option   An option which either comes into being or becomes worthless if a specified asset price is reached before expiration. See page 465.

Base correlation   A correlation used in a CDO model to represent the relationship between all underlyings from zero up to a given detachment point. For example, the 0–3% and a 3–6% tranches are separate instruments but between them one can price a 0–6% tranche and so back out an implied correlation from 0–6%, that is the base correlation. See page 469.

Basket   A collection of financial instruments. In a basket option the payoff depends on the behaviour of the many underlyings. See page 466.

Bermudan swaption   An option to enter into a swap that may be exercised on any of a specified number of dates.

C++   An enhanced version of the C programming language developed by Bjarne Stroustrup in 1983. The enhancements include classes, virtual functions, multiple inheritance, templates, etc.

Calibration   Determining parameters (possibly state and time dependent) such that one's theoretical prices match traded prices. Also called fitting. This is a static process using a snapshot of prices. Calibration does not typically involve looking at the dynamics or time series of the underlying. See page 203.

Callable   A contract which the issuer or writer can buy back (call). The amount he has to pay and the dates on which he can exercise this right will be specified in the contract.

Cap   A fixed-income contract paying the holder when the underlying interest rate exceeds a specified level. See page 468.

CDO   A Collateralized Debt Obligation is a pool of debt instruments securitized into one financial instrument. See page 469.

CDS   A Credit Default Swap is a contract used as insurance against a credit event. One party pays interest to another for a prescribed time or until default of the underlying instrument. See page 472.

CFA   Chartered Financial Analyst. A professional designation offered by the CFA Institute for successfully completing three examinations. The syllabus includes aspects of corporate and quantitative finance, economics and ethics.

CMS   Constant Maturity Swap is a fixed-income swap in which one leg is a floating rate of a constant maturity (from the date it is paid). A convexity adjustment is required for the pricing of these instruments. See page 469.

Convertible An instrument that can be exchanged for another of a different type. A convertible bond is a bond that can be turned into stock at a time of the holder's choosing. This gives an otherwise simple instrument an element of optionality. See page 471.

Convexity Related to the curvature in the value of a derivative (or its payoff) with respect to its underlying. A consequence of **Jensen's Inequality** for convex functions together with randomness in an underlying is that convexity adds value to a derivative. A positive convexity with respect to a random underlying or parameters increases the derivative's value, a negative convexity decreases value. In equity derivatives convexity is known as gamma.

Copula A function used to combine many univariate distributions to make a single multivariate distribution. Often used to model relationships between many underlying in credit derivatives. See page 229.

Correlation Covariance between two random variables divided by both of their standard deviations. It is a number between (and including) minus one and plus one that measures the amount of linear relationship between the two variables. Correlation is a parameter in most option-pricing models in which there are two or more random factors. However, the parameter is often highly unstable.

CQF Certificate in Quantitative Finance, a part-time qualification offered by Wilmott and 7city Learning which teaches the more practical aspects of quantitative finance, including modelling, data analysis, implementation of the models and, crucially, focuses on which models are good and which aren't.

Default probability The probability of an entity defaulting or going bankrupt. A concept commonly used in credit risk modelling where it is assumed that default is a probabilistic concept, rather than a business decision. Pricing credit instruments then becomes an exercise in modelling probability of default, and recovery rates. See page 448.

Delta The sensitivity of an option to the underlying asset. See page 78.

Digital An option with a discontinuous payoff. See page 472.

Dispersion The amount by which asset, typically equity, returns are independent. A dispersion trade involves a basket of options on single stocks versus the opposite position in an option on a basket of stocks (an index).

Duration The sensitivity of a bond to an interest rate or yield. It can be related to the average life of the bond.

Exotic A contract that is made to measure, or bespoke, for a client and which does not exist as an exchange-traded instrument. Since it is not traded on an exchange it must be priced using some mathematical model. See pages 459–482.

Expected loss The average loss once a specified threshold has been breached. Used as a measure of Value at Risk. See page 52.

Finite difference A numerical method for solving differential equations wherein derivatives are approximated by differences. The differential equation thus becomes a difference equation which can be solved numerically, usually by an iterative process.

Gamma The sensitivity of an option's delta to the underlying. Therefore it is the second derivative of an option price with respect to the underlying. See page 79.

GARCH Generalized Auto Regressive Conditional Heteroskedasticity, an econometric model for volatility in which the current variance depends on the previous random increments.

Hedge To reduce risk by exploiting correlations between financial instruments. See page 77.

Hybrid An instrument that exhibits both equity and fixed-income characteristics, and even credit risk. An example would be a convertible bond. Pricing such instruments requires knowledge of models from several different areas of quantitative finance.

Implied Used as an adjective about financial parameters meaning that they have been deduced from traded prices. For example, what volatility when put into the Black–Scholes formula gives a theoretical price that is the same as the market price? This is the implied volatility. Intimately related to calibration.

Lévy A probability distribution, also known as a stable distribution. It has the property that sums of independent identically distributed random variables from this distribution have the same distribution. The normal distribution is a special case. The Lévy distribution is of interest in finance because returns data matches this distribution quite well. See page 383.

LIBOR London Interbank Offered Rate. An interest rate at which banks offer to lend funds to other banks in the London wholesale money market. It is quoted at different maturities.

Being a standard reference rate it is often the underlying interest rate in OTC fixed-income contracts.

Market maker Someone who gives prices at which he will buy or sell instruments, in the hope of making a profit on the difference between the bid and offer prices. They are said to add liquidity to the market.

MBS A Mortgage Backed Security is a pool of mortgages that have been securitized. See page 477.

Mean reversion The returning of a quantity to an average level. This is a feature of many popular interest rate and volatility models, which may exhibit randomness but never stray too far from some mean.

Monte Carlo A name given to many methods for solving mathematical problems using simulations. The link between a probabilistic concept, such as an average, and simulations is clear. There may also be links between a deterministic problem and a simulation. For example, you can estimate π by throwing darts at a square, uniformly distributed, and counting how many land inside the inscribed circle. It should be $\pi/4$ of the number thrown. To get six decimal places of accuracy in π you would have to throw approximately 10^{12} darts, this is the downside of Monte Carlo methods, they can be slow.

Normal distribution A probability distribution commonly used to model financial quantities. See page 219.

PDE Partial differential equation, as its name suggest an equation (there must be an 'equals' sign), involving derivatives with respect to two or more variables. In finance almost all PDEs are of a type known as parabolic, this includes the famous heat or diffusion equation. See page 22.

Quantlib Definition taken from www.quantlib.org: 'QuantLib is a free/open-source library for modelling, trading, and risk management in real-life.'

Quanto Any contract in which cash flows are calculated from an underlying in one currency and then converted to payment in another currency. See page 479.

Regression Relating a dependent and one or more independent variables by a relatively simple function.

Risk The possibility of a monetary loss associated with investments. See page 38.

Risk neutral Indifferent to risk in the sense that a return in excess of the risk-free rate is not required by a risk-neutral investor who takes risks. To price derivatives one can imagine oneself in a world in which investors are risk neutral. Options are then priced to be consistent with the market prices of the underlying and future states of the world. This is because the risk premium on the stock is already incorporated into its current price, and the price of risk for the option and its underlying should be the same. Working in a risk-neutral world is a shortcut to that result. See page 109.

SABR An interest rate model, by Pat Hagan, Deep Kumar, Andrew Lesniewski and Diane Woodward, that exploits asymptotic analysis to make an otherwise intractable problem relatively easy to manage. See page 446.

Skew The slope of the graph of implied volatility versus strike. A negative skew, that is a downward slope going from left to right, is common in equity options.

Smile The upward curving shape of the graph of implied volatility versus strike. A downward curving profile would be a frown.

Sobol' A Russian mathematician responsible for much of the important breakthroughs in low-discrepancy sequences, now commonly used for simulations in finance. See page 240 and www.broda.co.uk.

Stochastic Random. The branch of mathematics involving the random evolution of quantities usually in continuous time commonly associated with models of the financial markets and derivatives. To be contrasted with deterministic.

Structured products Contracts designed to meet the specific investment criteria of a client, in terms of market view, risk and return.

Swap A general term for an over-the-counter contract in which there are exchanges of cash flows between two parties. See page 492.

Swaptions An option on a swap. They are commonly Bermudan exercise. See page 480.

VaR Value at Risk, an estimate of the potential downside from one's investments. See pages 42 and 52.

Variance swap A contract in which there is an exchange of the realized variance over a specified period and a fixed amount. See page 482.

Volatility The annualized standard deviation of returns of an asset. The most important quantity in derivatives pricing. Difficult to estimate and forecast, there are many competing models for the behaviour of volatility. See page 162.

Yield curve A graph of yields to maturity versus maturity (or duration). Therefore a way of visualizing how interest rates change with time. Each traded bond has its own point on the curve.

Esoterica
And finally, some rather more exotic word or phrase searches, without any descriptions:

Art of War; *Atlas Shrugged*; Background check; Bloodshed; Bonus; Deal or no deal; Death; Depression; Drug test; Female; Gay; How to impress; James Bond; Lawsuit; Lonely; Sex; Suit; Test; The; Too old

From this final list one should be able to build up a personality profile of the typical quant.

Chapter 13

Brainteasers

*T*he following Brainteasers have been taken from wilmott.com. They are all the type of questions you could easily face during a job interview. Some of these questions are simple calculation exercises, often probabilistic in nature reflecting the importance of understanding probability concepts, some have a 'trick' element to them, if you can spot the trick you can solve them, otherwise you will struggle. And some require lateral, out-of-the-box, thinking.

The Questions

Russian roulette   I have a revolver which holds up to six bullets. There are two bullets in the gun, in adjacent chambers. I am going to play Russian roulette (on my own!), I spin the barrel so that I don't know where the bullets are and then pull the trigger. Assuming that I don't shoot myself with this first attempt, am I now better off pulling the trigger a second time without spinning or spin the barrel first?

(Thanks to pusher.)

Matching birthdays   You are in a room full of people, and you ask them all when their birthday is. How many people must there be for there to be a greater than 50% chance that at least two will share the same birthday?

(Thanks to baghead.)

Another one about birthdays   At a cinema the manager announces that a free ticket will be given to the first person in the queue whose birthday is the same as someone in line who has already bought a ticket. You have the option of getting in line at any position. Assuming that you don't know anyone else's birthday, and that birthdays are uniformly distributed throughout a 365-day year, what position in line gives you the best chance of being the first duplicate birthday?

(Thanks to amit7ul.)

Biased coins You have n biased coins with the kth coin having probability $1/(2k+1)$ of coming up heads. What is the probability of getting an odd number of heads in total?
(Thanks to FV.)

Two heads When flipping an unbiased coin, how long do you have to wait on average before you get two heads in a row? And more generally, how long before n heads in a row.
(Thanks to MikeM.)

Balls in a bag Ten balls are put in a bag based on the result of the tosses of an unbiased coin. If the coin turns up heads, put in a black ball, if tails, put in a white ball. When the bag contains ten balls hand it to someone who hasn't seen the colours selected. Ask them to take out ten balls, one at a time with replacement. If all ten examined balls turn out to be white, what is the probability that all ten balls in the bag are white?
(Thanks to mikebell.)

Sums of uniform random variables The random variables x_1, x_2, $x_3, \ldots$ are independent and uniformly distributed over 0 to 1. We add up n of them until the sum exceeds 1. What is the expected value of n?
(Thanks to balaji.)

Minimum and maximum correlation If X, Y and Z are three random variables such that X and Y have a correlation of 0.9, and Y and Z have correlation of 0.8, what are the minimum and maximum correlation that X and Z can have?
(Thanks to jiantao.)

Airforce One One hundred people are in line to board Airforce One. There are exactly 100 seats on the plane. Each passenger has a ticket. Each ticket assigns the passenger to a specific seat. The passengers board the aircraft one at a time. GW is the first to board the plane. He cannot read, and does not know which seat is his, so he picks a seat at random and pretends that it is his proper seat.

The remaining passengers board the plane one at a time. If one of them finds their assigned seat empty, they will sit in it. If they find that their seat is already taken, they will pick a seat at random. This continues until everyone has boarded the plane and taken a seat.

What is the probability that the last person to board the plane sits in their proper seat?
(Thanks to Wilbur.)

Hit-and-run taxi There was a hit-and-run incident involving a taxi in a city in which 85% of the taxis are green and the remaining 15% are blue. There was a witness to the crime who says that the hit-and-run taxi was blue. Unfortunately this witness is only correct 80% of the time. What is the probability that it was indeed a blue car that hit our victim?
(Thanks to orangeman44.)

Annual returns Every day a trader either makes 50% with probability 0.6 or loses 50% with probability 0.4. What is the probability the trader will be ahead at the end of a year, 260 trading days? Over what number of days does the trader have the maximum probability of making money?
(Thanks to Aaron.)

Dice game You start with no money and play a game in which you throw a dice over and over again. For each throw, if 1 appears you win $1, if 2 appears you win $2, etc. but if 6 appears you lose all your money and the game ends. When is the optimal stopping time and what are your expected winnings?
(Thanks to ckc226.)

100 kg of berries   You have 100 kg of berries. Ninety-nine percent of the weight of berries is water. Time passes and some amount of water evaporates, so our berries are now 98% water. What is the weight of berries now?

Do this one in your head.
   (Thanks to NoDoubts.)

Urban planning   There are four towns positioned on the corners of a square. The towns are to be joined by a system of roads such that the total road length is minimized. What is the shape of the road?
   (Thanks to quantie.)

Closer to the edge or the centre?   You have a square and a random variable that picks a random point on the square with a uniform distribution. What is the probability that a randomly selected point is closer to the centre than to the edge?
   (Thanks to OMD.)

Snowflake   Start with an equilateral triangle. Now stick on to the middle of each side equilateral triangles with side one third of the side of the original triangle. This gives you a Star of David, with six points. Now add on to the sides of the six triangles yet smaller triangles, with side one third of the 'parent' triangle and so on *ad infinitum*. What are the perimeter and area of the final snowflake?
   (Thanks to Gerasimos.)

The doors   There are 100 closed doors in a corridor. The first person who walks along the corridor opens all of the doors. The second person changes the current state of every second door starting from the second door by opening closed doors and closing open doors. The third person who comes along changes the current state of every third door starting from the third door. This continues until the 100th person. At the end how many doors are closed and how many open?

(Thanks to zilch.)

Two thirds of the average   Everyone in a group pays $1 to enter the following competition. Each person has to write down secretly on a piece of paper a number from 0 to 100 inclusive. Calculate the average of all of these numbers and then take two thirds. The winner, who gets all of the entrance fees, is the person who gets closest to this final number. The players know the rule for determining the winner, and they are not allowed to communicate with each other. What number should you submit?

(Thanks to knowtorious and the *Financial Times*.)

Ones and zeros   Show that any natural number has a multiple whose decimal representation only contains the digits 0 and 1. For example, if the number is 13, we get $13 \times 77 = 1001$.

(Thanks to idgregorio.)

Bookworm   There is a two-volume book set on a shelf, the volumes being side by side, first then second. The pages of each volume are two centimetres thick and each cover is two millimetres thick. A worm has nibbled the set, perpendicularly to the pages, from the first page of the first volume to the last page of the second one. What is the length of the path he has nibbled?

(Thanks to Vito.)

Compensation   A number of quants are at dinner, and start discussing compensation. They want to calculate the average compensation among themselves, but are too embarrassed to disclose their own salaries. How can they determine the average compensation of their group? They do not have pens or paper or any other way of writing down their salaries.

(Thanks to Arroway.)

Einstein's brainteaser   There are five houses of five different colours. In each house lives a person of a different nationality. Those five people drink different drinks, smoke cigarettes of a different brand and have a different pet. None of them has the same pet, smokes the same cigarette or drinks the same drink.

We know:

- The Englishman lives in the red house.
- The Swede has a dog as a pet.
- The Dane drinks tea.
- The green house is on the left of the white one.
- The person who lives in the green house drinks coffee.
- The person who smokes Pall Mall raises birds.
- The owner of the yellow house smokes Dunhill.
- The man who lives in the house that is in the middle drinks milk.
- The Norwegian lives in the first house.
- The man who smokes Blends lives next to the one who has cats.
- The man who raises horses lives next to the one who smokes Dunhill.
- The man who smokes Bluemaster drinks beer.
- The German smokes Prince.
- The Norwegian lives next to the blue house.
- The man who smokes Blends is neighbour of the one who drinks water.

Question: Who has the fish?
   (Thanks to NoDoubts.)

Gender ratio   A country is preparing for a possible future war. The country's tradition is to send only males into battle and so they want to increase the proportion of males to females in the population through regulating births. A law is passed that requires every married couple to have children and they must continue to have children until they have a male.

What effect do you expect this law to have on the makeup of the population?

(Thanks to Wilbur.)

Covering a chessboard with dominoes   You have a traditional chessboard, eight by eight square. From a single diagonal, any diagonal, you remove two squares. The board now has just 62 squares. You also have 31 domino tiles, each of which is conveniently the same size as two of the chessboard squares. Is it possible to cover the board with these dominoes?

(Thanks to alphaquantum.)

Aircraft armour   Where should you reinforce the armour on bombers? You can't put it everywhere because it will make the aircraft too heavy. Suppose you have data for every hit on planes returning from their missions, how should you use this information in deciding where to place the armour reinforcement?

(Thanks to Aaron.)

Hanging a picture   You have a framed picture with a string attached to it in the usual manner. You have two nails on the wall. The problem is to try to hang the picture on the wall such that if you remove either one of the nails then the frame falls down.

(Thanks to wannabequantie.)

Ages of three children   A census taker goes to a house, a woman answers the door and says she has three children. The census taker asks their ages and she says that if you multiply their ages, the result is 36. He says he needs more info so she tells him that the total of their ages is the address of the building next door. He goes and looks, then comes back and says he still needs more information. She tells him that she won't answer any more questions because her eldest child is sleeping upstairs and she doesn't want to wake him.

What are the children's ages?
   (Thanks to tristanreid.)

The Monty Hall problem You are a contestant on a gameshow, and you have to choose one of three doors. Behind one door is a car, behind the others, goats. You pick a door, number 2, say, and the host, who knows what is behind each door, opens one of the other two doors, number 3, say, and reveals a goat. He then says to you, 'Do you want to change your mind, and pick door number 1?' Should you?

Ants on a circle You have a circle with a number of ants scattered around it at distinct points. Each ant starts walking at the same speed but in possibly different directions, either clockwise or anticlockwise. When two ants meet they immediately change directions, and then continue with the same speed as before. Will the ants ever, simultaneously, be in the same positions as when they started out?
   (Thanks to OMD.)

Four switches and a lightbulb Outside a room there are four switches, and in the room there is a lightbulb. One of the switches controls the light. Your task is to find out which one. You cannot see the bulb or whether it is on or off from outside the room. You may turn any number of switches on or off, any number of times you want. But you may only enter the room once.
   (Thanks to Tomfr.)

Turnover In a dark room there is a table, and on this table there are 52 cards, 19 face up, 33 face down. Your task is to divide the cards into two groups, such that in each group there must be the same number of face up cards. You can't switch on a light, ask a friend for help, all the usual disalloweds. Is this even possible?
   (Thanks to golftango and Bruno Dupire.)

Muddy faces   A group of children are playing and some of them get mud on their foreheads. A child cannot tell if he has mud on his own forehead, although he can see the mud on the foreheads of any other muddy children. An adult comes to collect the children and announces that at least one of the children has a dirty forehead, and then asks the group to put up their hand if they know that they have mud on their forehead. How can each child determine whether or not their forehead is muddy without communicating with anyone else?

(Thanks to weaves.)

The Oracle at Delphi   On January 1st you go to the Oracle at Delphi who tells you the opening and closing prices of a small non-dividend-paying stock every trading day for the rest of the year. Every opening price is the same as the closing price the day before. You have a 0.5% one-way transaction cost in buying or selling the stock, and can buy every day at the opening price and sell every day at the closing price...if you choose. On the last day of the year you must not own the stock. What is the best you can do, having this perfect foresight? Every day you can buy stock at the opening price if you don't own it, and sell stock at the closing price if you do own it. Keep the problem simple, no leveraging, no short selling, no options or futures, etc.

(Thanks to cdmurray80.)

Miss Moneypenny   You need to hire a secretary. There are n possible candidates to interview and you want to find the best, the most talented. The problem is that there is great demand for secretaries, so if you want to make sure that you get one you'll have to offer her the job on the spot. Once she walks out of the door she's gone. You start interviewing candidates one after the other, they can all be ranked, so this one is better than that, or that one is worse than another, etc. There are no ties. But the order in which they are interviewed is random. What is the best strategy for maximizing the probability of getting the best secretary?

Pirate puzzle   There are 10 pirates in a rowing boat. Their ship has just sunk but they managed to save 1,000 gold doubloons. Being greedy bastards they each want all the loot for themselves but they are also democratic and want to make the allocation of gold as fair as possible. But how?

They each pick a number, from 1 to 10, out of a hat. Each person in turn starting with number 1, decides how to divvy up the loot among the pirates in the boat. They then vote. If the majority of pirates approve of the allocation then the loot is divided accordingly, otherwise that particular pirate is thrown overboard into the shark-infested sea. In the latter case, the next pirate in line gets his chance at divvying up the loot. The same rules apply, and either the division of the filthy lucre gets the majority vote or the unfortunate soul ends up in Davy Jones's locker.

Question, how should the first pirate share out the spoils so as to both guarantee his survival and get a decent piece of the action?

The Answers

Russian roulette

I have a revolver which holds up to six bullets. There are two bullets in the gun, in adjacent chambers. I am going to play Russian roulette (on my own!), I spin the barrel so that I don't know where the bullets are and then pull the trigger. Assuming that I don't shoot myself with this first attempt, am I now better off pulling the trigger a second time without spinning or spin the barrel first?

(Thanks to pusher.)

Solution

This is a very typical, simple probability Brainteaser. It doesn't require any sophisticated or lateral thought. Just pure calculation.

Whenever you spin the barrel you clearly have a two in six, or one in three chance of landing on a chamber containing a bullet.

If you spin and pull the trigger on an empty chamber, what are the chances of the next chamber containing a bullet? You are equally likely to be at any one of the four empty chambers but only the last of these is adjacent to a chamber containing a bullet. So there is now a one in four chance of the next pull of the trigger being fatal. Conclusion is that you should *not* spin the barrel. After surviving two pulls of the trigger without spinning the barrel the odds become one in three again, and it doesn't matter whether you spin or not (at least it doesn't matter in a probabilistic sense). After surviving that 'shot' it becomes fifty-fifty and if you are successful four times in a row then the next shot will definitely be fatal.

Matching birthdays

You are in a room full of people, and you ask them all when their birthday is. How many people must there be for there to be a greater than 50% chance that at least two will share the same birthday?

(Thanks to baghead.)

Solution
This is a classic, simple probability question that is designed to show how poor is most people's perception of odds.

As with many of these type of questions it is easier to ask what are the chances of two people *not* having the same birthday? So suppose that there are just the two people in the room, what are the chances of them not having the same birthday? There are 364 days out of 365 days that the second person could have, so the probability is 364/365. If there are three people in the room the second must have a birthday on one of 364 out of 365, and the third must have one of the remaining 363 out of 365. So the probability is then $364 \times 363/365^2$. And so on. If there are n people in the room the probability of no two sharing a birthday is

$$\frac{364!}{(365-n)!365^{n-1}}.$$

So the question becomes, what is the smallest n for which this is less than one half? And the answer to this is 23.

Another one about birthdays

At a cinema the manager announces that a free ticket will be given to the first person in the queue whose birthday is the same as someone in line who has already bought a ticket. You have the option of getting in line at any position. Assuming that you don't know anyone else's birthday, and that birthdays are uniformly distributed throughout a 365-day year, what position in line gives you the best chance of being the first duplicate birthday?

(Thanks to amit7ul.)

Solution
This is solved by an application of Bayes' theorem.

$$\text{Prob}(A \cap B) = \text{Prob}(A|B)\,\text{Prob}(B).$$

You need to calculate two probabilities, first the probability of having the same birthday as someone ahead of you in the queue given that none of them has a duplicate birthday, and second the probability that none of those ahead of you have duplicate birthdays. If there are n people ahead of you then we know from the previous birthday problem that the second

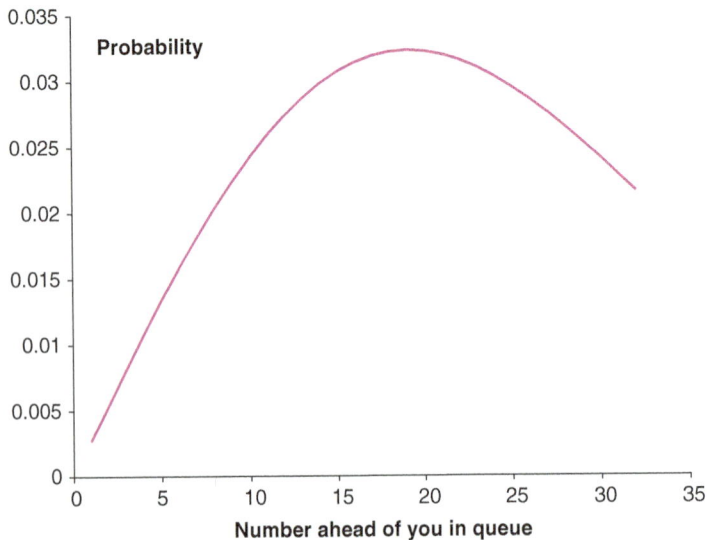

Number ahead of you in queue

probability is

$$\frac{364!}{(365-n)!365^{n-1}}.$$

The first probability is simply $n/365$. So you want to maximize

$$\frac{n\,364!}{(365-n)!365^n}.$$

This is shown as a function of n above. It is maximized when $n = 19$ so you should stand in the 20th place. This maximizes your chances, but they are still small at only 3.23%.

Biased coins

You have n biased coins with the kth coin having probability $1/(2k+1)$ of coming up heads. What is the probability of getting an odd number of heads in total?

(Thanks to FV.)

Solution

I include this as a classic example of the induction method. Use p_n to denote the required probability.

After $n-1$ tosses there is a probability p_{n-1} that there have been an odd number of heads. And therefore a probability of $1 - p_{n-1}$ of there having been an even number of heads. To get the probability of an odd number of heads after another toss, n in total, you multiply the probability of an odd number so far by the probability of the next coin being tails and add this to the product of the probability of an even number and the probability of getting a head next:

$$p_n = p_{n-1}\left(1 - \frac{1}{2n+1}\right) + (1 - p_{n-1})\frac{1}{2n+1}.$$

This becomes

$$p_n = p_{n-1}\frac{2n-1}{2n+1} + \frac{1}{2n+1}.$$

Now we just have to solve this difference equation, with the starting value that before any tossing we have zero probability of an odd number, so $p_0 = 0$. If we write $p_n = a_n/(2n + 1)$ then the difference equation for a_n becomes the very simple

$$a_n = a_{n-1} + 1.$$

The solution of this with $a_0 = 0$ is just n and so the required probability is

$$p_n = \frac{n}{2n + 1}.$$

Two heads

When flipping an unbiased coin, how long do you have to wait on average before you get two heads in a row? And more generally, how long before n heads in a row.

(Thanks to MikeM.)

Solution

It turns out that you may as well solve the general problem for n in a row. Let N_n be the number of tosses needed to get n heads in the row. It satisfies the recursion relationship

$$N_n = \frac{1}{2}(N_{n-1} + 1) + \frac{1}{2}(N_{n-1} + 1 + N_n).$$

This is because with probability $\frac{1}{2}$ we get the required head, and with probability $\frac{1}{2}$ we get a tail and will have to start the whole thing anew. Therefore we obtain

$$N_n = 2N_{n-1} + 2.$$

This has solution

$$N_n = 2^{n+1} - 2.$$

This means six tosses on average to get two heads in a row.

Balls in a bag

Ten balls are put in a bag based on the result of the tosses of an unbiased coin. If the coin turns up heads, put in a black ball, if tails, put in a white ball. When the bag contains ten balls hand it to someone who hasn't seen the colours selected. Ask them to take out ten balls, one at a time with replacement. If all ten examined balls turn out to be white, what is the probability that all ten balls in the bag are white?

(Thanks to mikebell.)

Solution

This is a test of your understanding of conditional probability and Bayes' theorem again. First a statement of Bayes' theorem.

$$\text{Prob}(A|B) = \frac{\text{Prob}(B|A)\text{Prob}(A)}{\text{Prob}(B)}.$$

Prob(A) is the probability of A, without any information about B, this is unconditional probability. Prob($A|B$) means probability of A with the extra information concerning B, this is a conditional probability.

In the balls example, A is the event that all of the balls *in* the bag are white, B is the event that the balls *taken out of* the bag are all white. We want to find Prob($A|B$).

Clearly, Prob(A) is just $\frac{1}{2}^{10} = 0.000976563$. Trivially Prob($B|A$) is 1. The probability that we take ten white balls out of the bag is a bit harder. We have to look at the probability of having n white balls in the first place and then picking, after replacement, 10 white. This is then Prob(B). It is calculated as

$$\sum_{n=0}^{10} \frac{10!}{n!(10-n)!} \frac{1}{2^{10}} \left(\frac{n}{10}\right)^{10} = 0.01391303.$$

And so the required probability is $0.000976563/0.01391303 = 0.0701905$. Just over 7%.

Sums of uniform random variables

The random variables $x_1, x_2, x_3, \ldots$ are independent and uniformly distributed over 0 to 1. We add up n of them until the sum exceeds 1. What is the expected value of n?

(Thanks to balaji.)

Solution
There are two steps to finding the solution. First what is the probability of the sum of n such random variables being less than 1. Second, what is the required expectation.

There are several ways to approach the first part. One way is perhaps the most straightforward, simply calculate the probability by integrating unit integrand over the domain in the upper right 'quadrant' between the point $(0, 0, \ldots, 0)$ and the plane $x_1 + x_2 + \cdots + x_n = 1$. This is just

$$\int_0^1 \int_0^{1-x_1} \int_0^{1-x_1-x_2} \cdots \int_0^{1-x_1-x_2-\ldots-x_{n-1}} 1 \; dx_n \ldots dx_3 \, dx_2 \; dx_1.$$

After doing several of the inner integrals you will find that the answer is simply $\frac{1}{n!}$.

From this it follows that the probability that the sum goes over 1 for the first time on the nth random variable is

$$\left(1 - \frac{1}{n!}\right) - \left(1 - \frac{1}{(n-1)!}\right) = \frac{n-1}{n!}.$$

The required expectation is the sum of $n(n-1)/n! = 1/(n-2)!$ from 2 to infinity, or equivalently the sum of $1/n!$ for n zero to infinity. And this is our answer, e.

Minimum and maximum correlation

If X, Y and Z are three random variables such that X and Y have a correlation of 0.9, and Y and Z have correlation of 0.8, what are the minimum and maximum correlation that X and

Z can have?

(Thanks to jiantao.)

Solution

The correlation matrix

$$\begin{pmatrix} 1 & \rho_{XY} & \rho_{XZ} \\ \rho_{XY} & 1 & \rho_{YZ} \\ \rho_{XZ} & \rho_{YZ} & 1 \end{pmatrix}$$

must be positive semi-definite. A bit of fooling around with that concept will result in the following constraints

$$-\sqrt{(1 - \rho_{XY}^2)(1 - \rho_{YZ}^2)} + \rho_{XY}\rho_{YZ} \leq \rho_{XZ} \leq \sqrt{(1 - \rho_{XY}^2)(1 - \rho_{YZ}^2)} + \rho_{XY}\rho_{YZ}.$$

For this particular example we have $0.4585 \leq \rho_{XZ} \leq 0.9815$. It is interesting how small the correlation can be, less than one half, considering how high the other two correlations are. Of course, if one of the two correlations is exactly 1 then this forces the third correlation to be the same as the other.

Airforce One

One hundred people are in line to board Airforce One. There are exactly 100 seats on the plane. Each passenger has a ticket. Each ticket assigns the passenger to a specific seat. The passengers board the aircraft one at a time. GW is the first to board the plane. He cannot read, and does not know which seat is his, so he picks a seat at random and pretends that it is his proper seat.

The remaining passengers board the plane one at a time. If one of them finds their assigned seat empty, they will sit in it. If they find that their seat is already taken, they will pick a seat at random. This continues until everyone has boarded the plane and taken a seat.

What is the probability that the last person to board the plane sits in their proper seat?

(Thanks to Wilbur.)

Solution
First of all let me say that the President is now BO, not GW, but then the gag about not being able to read wouldn't work. This problem sounds really complicated, because of all the people who could have sat in the last person's seat before their turn. Start by considering just two people, GW and you. If GW sits in his own seat, which he will do 50% of the time, then you are certain to get your allocated seat. But if he sits in your seat, again with 50% chance, then you are certain to not get the right seat. So *a priori* result, 50% chance. Now if there are three people, GW either sits in his own seat or in your seat or in the other person's seat. The chances of him sitting in his own seat or your seat are the same, and in the former case you are certain to get your correct seat and in the latter you are certain to not get it. So those two balance out. If he sits in the other person's seat then it all hinges on whether the other person then sits in GW's seat or yours. Both equally likely, end result 50–50 again. You can build on this by induction to get to the simple result that it is 50–50 whether or not you sit in your allocated seat.

Hit-and-run taxi

There was a hit-and-run incident involving a taxi in a city in which 85% of the taxis are green and the remaining 15% are blue. There was a witness to the crime who says that the hit-and-run taxi was blue. Unfortunately this witness is only correct 80% of the time. What is the probability that it was indeed a blue car that hit our victim?

(Thanks to orangeman44.)

Solution
A classic probability question that has important consequences for the legal and medical professions.

Suppose that we have 100 such incidents. In 85 of these the taxi will have been green and 15 blue, just based on random selection of taxi colour. In the cases where the taxi was green the witness will mistakenly say that the car is blue 20% of the time, i.e. 17 times. In the 15 blue cases the witness will correctly say blue 80% of the time, i.e. 12 times. So although there were only 15 accidents involving a blue taxi there were 29 reports of a blue taxi being to blame, and most of those (17 out of 29) were in error. These are the so-called false positives one gets in medical tests.

Now, given that we were told it was a blue taxi, what is the probability that it was a blue taxi? That is just 12/29 or 41.4%.

Annual returns

Every day a trader either makes 50% with probability 0.6 or loses 50% with probability 0.4. What is the probability the trader will be ahead at the end of a year, 260 trading days? Over what number of days does the trader have the maximum probability of making money?

(Thanks to Aaron.)

Solution

This is a nice one because it is extremely counterintuitive. At first glance it looks like you are going to make money in the long run, but this is not the case.

Let n be the number of days on which you make 50%. After 260 days your initial wealth will be multiplied by

$$1.5^n \, 0.5^{260-n}.$$

So the question can be recast in terms of finding n for which this expression is equal to 1:

$$n = \frac{260 \ln 0.5}{\ln 0.5 - \ln 1.5} = \frac{260 \ln 2}{\ln 3} = 164.04.$$

The first question then becomes: What is the probability of getting 165 or more 'wins' out of 260 when the probability of a 'win' is 0.6? The answer to this standard probability question is just over 14%.

The average return per day is

$$1 - \exp(0.6\ln 1.5 + 0.4\ln 0.5) = -3.34\%.$$

The probability of the trader making money after one day is 60%. After two days the trader has to win on both days to be ahead, and therefore the probability is 36%. After three days the trader has to win at least two out of three, this has a probability of 64.8%. After four days, he has to win at least three out of four, probability 47.52%. And so on. With an horizon of N days he would have to win at least $N\ln 2/\ln 3$ (or rather the integer greater than this) times. The answer to the second part of the question is therefore three days.

As well as being counterintuitive, this question does give a nice insight into money management and is clearly related to the **Kelly criterion**. If you see a question like this it is meant to trick you if the expected profit, here $0.6 \times 0.5 + 0.4 \times (-0.5) = 0.1$, is positive with the expected return, here -3.34%, negative.

Dice game

You start with no money and play a game in which you throw a dice over and over again. For each throw, if 1 appears you win \$1, if 2 appears you win \$2, etc. but if 6 appears you lose all your money and the game ends. When is the optimal stopping time and what are your expected winnings?
(Thanks to ckc226.)

Solution

Suppose you have won an amount S so far and you have to decide whether to continue. If you roll again you have an expected winnings on the next throw of

$$\frac{1}{6} \times 1 + \frac{1}{6} \times 2 + \frac{1}{6} \times 3 + \frac{1}{6} \times 4 + \frac{1}{6} \times 5 - \frac{1}{6} \times S = \frac{15 - S}{6}.$$

So as long as you have less than 15 you would continue.

The expected winnings is harder.

You will stop at 15, 16, 17, 18 and 19. You can't get to 20 because that would mean playing when you have 15, and throwing a 5. So we must calculate the probabilities of reaching each of these numbers without throwing a 6. At this point we defer to our good friend Excel. A simple simulation of the optimal strategy yields an expected value for this game of $6.18.

100 kg of berries

You have 100 kg of berries. Ninety-nine percent of the weight of berries is water. Time passes and some amount of water evaporates, so our berries are now 98% water. What is the weight of berries now?

Do this one in your head.
    (Thanks to NoDoubts.)

Solution

The unexpected, yet correct, answer is 50 kg. It seems like a tiny amount of water has evaporated so how can the weight have changed that much?

There is clearly 1 kg of solid matter in the berries. If that makes up 2% (100 less 98%) then the total weight must be 50 kg.

Urban planning

There are four towns positioned on the corners of a square. The towns are to be joined by a system of roads such that the total road length is minimized. What is the shape of the road?

(Thanks to quantie.)

Solution
One is tempted to join the towns with a simple crossroad shape but this is not optimal. Pythagoras and some basic calculus will show you that the arrangement shown in the figure is better, with the symmetrically placed crosspiece in the middle of the 'H' shape having length $1 - 1/\sqrt{3}$ if the square has unit side. Obviously there are two such solutions.

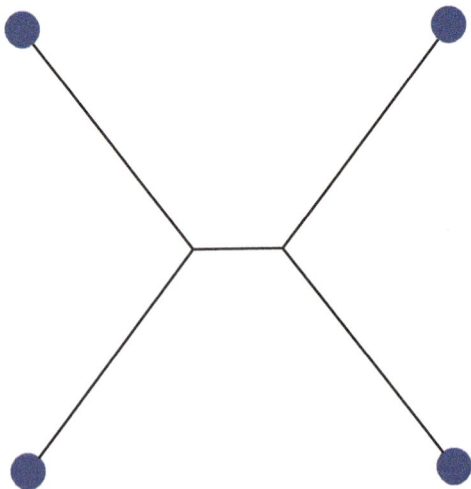

Closer to the edge or the centre?

You have a square and a random variable that picks a random point on the square with a uniform distribution. What is the probability that a randomly selected point is closer to the centre than to the edge?

(Thanks to OMD.)

Solution

Many people will think that the required probability is the same as the probability of landing in the circle with diameter half the side of the square. But this is not the case. The line separating closer to centre from closer to edge is a parabola. The answer is

$$\left(-1 + \sqrt{2}\right)^2 + \frac{2}{3}\left(3 - 2\sqrt{2}\right)^{3/2}.$$

Snowflake

Start with an equilateral triangle. Now stick on to the middle of each side equilateral triangles with side one third of the side of the original triangle. This gives you a Star of David, with six points. Now add on to the sides of the six triangles yet smaller triangles, with side one third of the 'parent' triangle and so on *ad infinitum*. What are the perimeter and area of the final snowflake?

(Thanks to Gerasimos.)

Solution

First count how many sides there are as a function of number of iterations. Initially there are three sides, and then 3×4. Every iteration one side turns into four. So there will be 3.4^n after n iterations. The length of each side is one third what it was originally. Therefore after n iterations the perimeter will be

$$\left(\frac{4}{3}\right)^n$$

multiplied by the original perimeter. It is unbounded as n tends to infinity.

The area increases by one third after the first iteration. After the second iteration you add an area that is number of sides multiplied by area of a single small triangle which is one ninth of the previously added triangle. If we use A_n to be the area after n iterations (when multiplied by the area of initial triangle) then

$$A_n = A_{n-1} + \frac{1}{3}\left(\frac{4}{9}\right)^{n-1}.$$

So

$$A_n = 1 + \frac{1}{3}\sum_{i=0}^{\infty}\left(\frac{4}{9}\right)^i = \frac{8}{5}.$$

The final calculation exploits the binomial expansion.

This is the famous Koch snowflake, first described in 1904, and is an example of a fractal.

The doors

There are 100 closed doors in a corridor. The first person who walks along the corridor opens all of the doors. The second person changes the current state of every second door starting from the second door by opening closed doors and closing open doors. The third person who comes along changes the current state of every third door starting from the third door. This continues until the 100th person. At the end how many doors are closed and how many open?

(Thanks to zilch.)

Solution
This is a question about how many divisors a number has. For example the 15th door is divisible by 1, 3, 5 and 15. So it will be opened, closed, opened, closed. Ending up closed.

What about door 37? Thirty-seven is only divisible by 1 and 37. But again it will end up closed. Since only squares have an odd number of divisors we have to count how many squares there are from 1 to 100. Of course, there are only 10.

Two thirds of the average

Everyone in a group pays $1 to enter the following competition. Each person has to write down secretly on a piece of paper a number from 0 to 100 inclusive. Calculate the average of all of these numbers and then take two thirds. The winner, who gets all of the entrance fees, is the person who gets closest to this final number. The players know the rule for determining the winner, and they are not allowed to communicate with each other. What number should you submit?

(Thanks to knowtorious and the *Financial Times*.)

Solution
This is a famous economics experiment, which examines people's rationality among other things.

If everyone submits the number 50, say, then the winning number would be two thirds of 50, so 33. Perhaps one should therefore submit 33. But if everyone does that the winning number will be 22. Ok, so submit that number. But if everyone does that . . . You can see where this leads. The stable point is clearly 0 because if everyone submits the answer 0 then two thirds of that is still 0, and so 0 is the winning number. The winnings get divided among everyone and there was no point in entering in the first place.

In discussions about this problem, people tend to carry through the above argument and either quickly conclude that 0 is 'correct' or they stop the inductive process after a couple of iterations and submit something around 20. It may be that the longer people have to think about this, the lower the number they submit.

This is a nice problem because it does divide people into the purely rational, game-theoretic types, who pick 0, and never win, and the more relaxed types, who just pick a number after a tiny bit of thought and do stand a chance of winning.

Personal note from the author: The *Financial Times* ran this as a competition for their readers a while back. (The prize was a flight in Concorde, so that dates it a bit. And the cost of entry was just the stamp on a postcard.)

I organized a group of students to enter this competition, all submitting the number 99 as their answer (it wasn't clear from the rules whether 100 was included). A number which could obviously never win. The purpose of this was twofold, (a) to get a mention in the paper when the answer was revealed (we succeeded) and (b) to move the market (we succeeded in that as well).

There were not that many entries (about 1,500 if I remember rightly) and so we were able to move the market up by one point. The *FT* printed the distribution of entries, a nice exponentially decaying curve with a noticeable 'blip' at one end! The winner submitted the number 13.

I didn't tell my students this, but I can now reveal that I secretly submitted my own answer, with the purpose of winning... my submission was 12. Doh!

Ones and zeros

Show that any natural number has a multiple whose decimal representation only contains the digits 0 and 1. For example, if the number is 13, we get $13 = 1001$.

(Thanks to idgregorio.)

Solution
Consider the $n + 1$ numbers 1, 11, 111, 1111, etc. Two of them will be congruent modulo n. Subtract the smaller one from the bigger one. You will get a number containing only 0's and 1's.

Bookworm

There is a two-volume book set on a shelf, the volumes being side by side, first then second. The pages of each volume are two centimetres thick and each cover is two millimetres thick. A worm has nibbled the set, perpendicularly to the pages, from the first page of the first volume to the last page of the second one. What is the length of the path he has nibbled?

(Thanks to Vito.)

Solution
Just four millimetres. Think about where the first page of the first volume and the last page of the second volume will be relative to each other.

Compensation

A number of quants are at dinner, and start discussing compensation. They want to calculate the average compensation among themselves, but are too embarrassed to disclose their own salaries. How can they determine the average compensation of their group? They do not have pens or paper or any other way of writing down their salaries.

(Thanks to Arroway.)

Solution

One of the quants adds a random number to his salary. The total he then whispers to his neighbour on the right. This person adds his own salary to the number he was given, and whispers it to the person on his right. This continues all around the table until we get back to the first quant who simply subtracts his random number from the total and divides by the number of quants at the table. That is the average compensation of the group.

Einstein's brainteaser

There are five houses of five different colours. In each house lives a person of a different nationality. Those five people drink different drinks, smoke cigarettes of a different brand and have a different pet. None of them has the same pet, smokes the same cigarette or drinks the same drink.

We know:

- The Englishman lives in the red house.
- The Swede has a dog as a pet.
- The Dane drinks tea.
- The green house is on the left of the white one.
- The person who lives in the green house drinks coffee.
- The person who smokes Pall Mall raises birds.
- The owner of the yellow house smokes Dunhill.
- The man who lives in the house that is in the middle drinks milk.
- The Norwegian lives in the first house.
- The man who smokes Blends lives next to the one who has cats.
- The man who raises horses lives next to the one who smokes Dunhill.
- The man who smokes Bluemaster drinks beer.
- The German smokes Prince.
- The Norwegian lives next to the blue house.

• The man who smokes Blends is neighbour of the one who drinks water.

Question: Who has the fish?
(Thanks to NoDoubts.)

Solution
This was a question posed by Einstein who said that 98% of people can't solve it. More likely 98% of people can't be bothered. And in these days of Su Doku, the percentage of people who can solve it will be higher.

Oh, and the answer is the German.

(*Historical note*: Smoking was something that the poor and the uneducated used to do. For an explanation of the process, see Newhart, R. 'Introducing tobacco to civilization': 'What you got for us this time, Walt...you got another winner for us? Tob-acco...er, what's tob-acco, Walt? It's a kind of leaf, huh...and you bought eighty tonnes of it?!!...Let me get this straight, Walt...you've bought eighty tonnes of leaves?...This may come as a kind of a surprise to you Walt but...come fall in England, we're kinda upto our...It isn't that kind of leaf, huh?...Oh!, what kind is it then...some special kind of food?...not exactly?...Oh, it has a lot of different uses...Like...what are some of the uses, Walt?...Are you saying "snuff," Walt?...What's snuff?...You take a pinch of tobacco...(ha ha ha)...and you shove it up your nose...(ha ha ha)...and it makes you sneeze?...(ha ha ha)...Yeh, I imagine it would, Walt! Hey, Goldenrod seems to do it pretty well over here! It has other uses though, huh?...you can chew it!...Or put it in a pipe!...or you can shred it up...and put it in a piece of paper...(ha ha ha)...and roll it up...(ha ha ha)...don't tell me, Walt, don't tell me...(ha ha ha)...you stick it in your ear, right? (ha ha ha)...Oh!...between your lips!...Then what do you do, Walt?...(ha ha ha)... you set fire to it!...(ha ha ha) Then what do you do,

Walt?...(ha ha ha)...You inhale the smoke, huh!...(ha ha ha) You know, Walt...it seems you can stand in front of your own fireplace and have the same thing going for you!")

Gender ratio

A country is preparing for a possible future war. The country's tradition is to send only males into battle and so they want to increase the proportion of males to females in the population through regulating births. A law is passed that requires every married couple to have children and they must continue to have children until they have a male.

What effect do you expect this law to have on the makeup of the population?

(Thanks to Wilbur.)

Solution
A bit of a trick question, this, and open to plenty of interesting discussion.

The obvious answer is that there is no effect on the gender ratio. However, this would only be true under certain assumptions about the distribution of the sexes of offspring among couples. Consider a population in which each couple can only ever have boys or only ever have girls. Those who have boys could stop after one child, whereas those who have girls can never stop having children, with the end result being more girls than boys. (Of course, this might not matter since the goal is for there to be more males, there is no requirement on the number of females.) And if there is any autocorrelation between births this will also have an impact. If autocorrelation is 1, so that a male child is always followed by a male, and a female by a female, then the ratio of males to females decreases, but with a negative correlation the ratio increases.

Covering a chessboard with dominoes

You have a traditional chessboard, eight by eight square. From a single diagonal, any diagonal, you remove two squares. The board now has just 62 squares. You also have 31 domino tiles, each of which is conveniently the same size as two of the chessboard squares. Is it possible to cover the board with these dominoes?

(Thanks to alphaquantum.)

Solution

No, since a domino always occupies a white and a black square! If you remove two from the same diagonal then they will have the same colour, leaving you with 32 of one colour and 30 of the other, so it is impossible to cover two squares.

Aircraft armour

Where should you reinforce the armour on bombers? You can't put it everywhere because it will make the aircraft too heavy. Suppose you have data for every hit on planes returning from their missions, how should you use this information in deciding where to place the armour reinforcement?

(Thanks to Aaron.)

Solution

The trick here is that we only have data for aircraft that survived. Since hits on aircraft are going to be fairly uniformly distributed over all places that are accessible by gunfire one should place the reinforcements at precisely those places which appeared to be unharmed in the returning aircraft. They are the places where hits would be 'fatal.' This is a true Second World War story about the statistician Abraham Wald who was asked precisely this.

Hanging a picture

You have a framed picture with a string attached to it in the usual manner. You have two nails on the wall. The problem is to try and hang the picture on the wall such that if you remove either one of the nails then the frame falls down.

(Thanks to wannabequantie.)

Solution
Here's one solution:

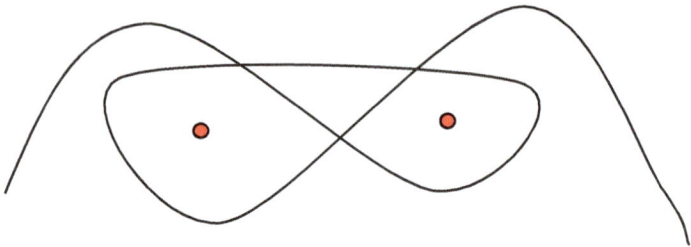

It's quite simple to 'mathematize' this problem as follows. Use x to denote wrapping once around the first nail in the clockwise direction, with x^2 meaning wrap the string around the first nail twice and, crucially, x^{-1} means wrapping anti-clockwise around the first nail. Similarly y etc. for the second nail. To solve this problem you need an expression involving products of x's and y's and their inverses which is not the identity (for the 'identity' means no wrapping and the picture falls!) but such that when either the x or the y are replaced with the identity (i.e. removed!) the result becomes the identity! (You have that multiplication by the identity leaves x and y unchanged, that $x\,x^{-1} = x^{-1}\,x = 1$, that $x\,y \neq y\,x$ and that $1^{-1} = 1$.)

One such solution is $x\,y\,x^{-1}\,y^{-1}$. Check the maths and then draw the picture.

The above picture is represented by $x\,y^{-1}\,x^{-1}\,y$.

Ages of three children

A census taker goes to a house, a woman answers the door and says she has three children. The census taker asks their ages and she says that if you multiply their ages, the result is 36. He says he needs more info so she tells him that the total of their ages is the address of the building next door. He goes and looks, then comes back and says he still needs more information. She tells him that she won't answer any more questions because her eldest child is sleeping upstairs and she doesn't want to wake him.

What are the children's ages?
(Thanks to tristanreid.)

Solution
First suitably factorize 36: (1,1,36), (1,4,9), (1,2,18), (1,3,12), (1,6,6), (2,3,6), (2,2,9), (3,3,4).

When the census taker is unable to decide from the information about nextdoor's house number we know that nextdoor must be number 13, because both (1,6,6) and (2,2,9) add up to 13. All of the other combinations give distinct sums. Finally the mother refers to the 'eldest child,' and this rules out (1,6,6) because the two older children have the same age. Conclusion the ages must be 2, 2 and 9.

Caveat: (1,6,6) is technically still possible because one of the six-year olds could be nearing seven while the other has only just turned six.

The Monty Hall problem

You are a contestant on a gameshow, and you have to choose one of three doors. Behind one door is a car, behind the others, goats. You pick a door, number 2, say, and the host, who knows what is behind each door, opens one of the other two doors, number 3, say, and reveals a goat. He then says to you, "Do you want to change your mind, and pick door number 1?"

Should you?

Solution
This is a classic question and is based on the real-life American gameshow called *Let's Make a Deal*.

Assuming that you prefer cars to goats then the correct thing to do is change door. (There is a twist though, to be explained at the end.) However, as you will probably know if you ever watch a magic show, people are more often than not reluctant to change their minds for reasons to do with belief in fate, and possible regret. (If you choose the wrong door and don't change then that was fate, it just wasn't your lucky day. If you choose correctly and then change then it is your 'fault.')

Some people think the answer to this question is counterintuitive. I don't. But let's do the maths anyway.

Suppose you don't change door. The probability of you having already picked the correct door remains at one in three. It's easy to see this, just imagine that you didn't hear the gameshow host, or you had your eyes closed when being given the option to change.

That leaves a probability that if you change to the only other possible remaining door, the probability is two thirds. Therefore change.

You can also argue as follows, assuming the car is behind door 1:

- You pick door 1. Host opens one of the other doors, it doesn't matter which. You change. You lose.

- You pick door 2. Host must open door 3, because the car is behind door 1! You change, and win.
- You pick door 3. Host must open door 2, because the car is behind door 1. You change, and win.

Hence the odds.

And now the twist. Imagine the following scenario. You are going for a quant interview. You are doing well, and the interviewer casually says 'Have you heard of the Monty Hall problem?' You reply that you have. The interviewer picks up three paper cups and a coin. He asks you to turn away while he puts the coin under one of the cups. 'Ok, you can look now. We are going to play a little game. If you can find the coin I will give you a job.' Fantastic, you think, knowing Monty Hall you are confident of a two thirds chance of getting the job!

'Pick a cup.' You pick cup number 1.

What happens next is subtle.

The interviewer lifts up cup number 2 to reveal nothing. 'Would you like to change your mind?' Of course, you would! So you say yes, the interviewer lifts up cup number 3 to reveal . . . nothing! You leave unemployed.

That was one scenario. It happens one third of the time. There is another scenario though. Go back to when you picked cup number 1. And without any comment, the interviewer picks up that cup, and beneath it, nothing! That happens two thirds of the time, and again no job.

Do you see what happened? The interviewer was only playing Monty Hall when it was to his advantage to do so. When you pick the wrong cup initially, as you will more often than not, then it's not Monty Hall! After all, the interviewer didn't say you were going to play the Monty Hall game, he only asked if you'd heard of it. Subtle, but it cost you the job.

This is related to a true story of a friend of mine, a very clever person, going for a job to work for a household-name quant. My friend was asked about Monty Hall by a quant who only knew the basics of the problem, but my friend knew about the game-theory aspects. An argument ensued and my friend did not get the job, despite clearly being brighter than the interviewer!

Ants on a circle

You have a circle with a number of ants scattered around it at distinct points. Each ant starts walking at the same speed but in possibly different directions, either clockwise or anticlockwise. When two ants meet they immediately change directions, and then continue with the same speed as before. Will the ants ever, simultaneously, be in the same positions as when they started out?

(Thanks to OMD.)

Solution
What are the chances of that happening? Surely all that bouncing around is going to shuffle them all up. Well, the answer, which you've probably now guessed, is that, yes, they do all end up at the starting point. And the time at which this happens (although there may be earlier times as well) is just the time it would take for one ant to go around the entire circle unhindered. The trick is to start by ignoring the collisions, just think of the ants walking through each other. Clearly there will then be a time at which the ants are in the starting positions. But are the ants in their *own* starting positions? This is slightly harder to see, but you can easily convince yourself, and furthermore at that time they will also be moving in the same direction they were to start with (this is not necessarily true of earlier times at which they may all be in the starting positions).

Four switches and a lightbulb

Outside a room there are four switches, and in the room there is a lightbulb. One of the switches controls the light. Your task is to find out which one. You cannot see the bulb or whether it is on or off from outside the room. You may turn any number of switches on or off, any number of times you want. But you may only enter the room once.

(Thanks to Tomfr.)

Solution

The trick is to realize that there is more to the bulb than light.

Step one: turn on switches 1 and 2, and go and have some coffee. Step two: turn off 1 and turn on 3, then go quickly into the room and touch the lamp.

It is controlled by switch 1 if it is hot and dark, 2 if it is hot and light, 3 if it is cold and light, 4 if it is cold and dark.

Turnover

In a dark room there is a table, and on this table there are 52 cards, 19 face up, 33 face down. Your task is to divide the cards into two groups, such that in each group there must be the same number of face-up cards. You can't switch on a light, ask a friend for help, all the usual disalloweds. Is this even possible?

(Thanks to golftango and Bruno Dupire.)

Solution

An elegant lateral thinking puzzle, with a simple solution.

Move *any* 19 cards to one side and turn them all over. Think about it!

The use of an odd number, 19 in this case, can be seen as either a clue or as a red herring suggesting that the task is impossible.

Muddy faces

A group of children are playing and some of them get mud on their foreheads. A child cannot tell if he has mud on his own forehead, although he can see the mud on the foreheads of any other muddy children. An adult comes to collect the children and announces that at least one of the children has a dirty forehead, and then asks the group to put up their hand if they know that they have mud on their forehead. How can each child determine whether or not their forehead is muddy without communicating with anyone else?

(Thanks to weaves.)

Solution
If there is only one child with mud on his forehead he will immediately know it because all of the other children are clean. He will therefore immediately raise his hand.

If there are two children with muddy foreheads they will not immediately raise their hands because they will each think that perhaps the adult is referring to the other child. But when neither raises his hand both will realize that the other is thinking the same as he and therefore both will raise their hands.

Now if their are three muddy children they will follow a similar line of thinking but now it will take longer for them all to realize they are muddy. And so on for an arbitrary number of muddy children.

To make this work we really need something to divide time up into intervals, a bell perhaps, because no doubt not all children will be thinking at quite the same speed!

The Oracle at Delphi

On January 1st you go to the Oracle at Delphi who tells you the opening and closing prices of a small non-dividend-paying stock every trading day for the rest of the year. Every opening price is the same as the closing price the day before. You have a 0.5% one-way transaction cost in buying or selling the stock, and can buy every day at the opening price and sell every day at the closing price...if you choose. On the last day of the year you must not own the stock. What is the best you can do, having this perfect foresight? Every day you can buy stock at the opening price if you don't own it, and sell stock at the closing price if you do own it. Keep the problem simple, no leveraging, no short selling, no options or futures, zero interest rate, etc.

(Thanks to cdmurray80.)

Solution
We must determine at the start of each day whether to buy if we are neutral, stay neutral or sell if we are long, and do so in a way that maximizes our wealth. How hard can that be? Approached correctly this is a straightforward problem in 'dynamic programming.'

Before we start, one trivial observation: Days of consecutive gains/losses may as well be treated as a single day, so that the stock effectively goes up, down, up, down, etc., on consecutive days.

Introduce some symbols:

$L_i =$ The maximum wealth you can have at the end of day i, given that you must hold the stock at the end of day i

and

$N_i =$ The maximum wealth you can have at the end of day i, given that you must be neutral at the end of day i.

Now imagine that we have found the optimal strategy up to and including day $i - 1$. At the end of that day either you own the stock or you don't. What should we do on day i? If we are long on day $i - 1$ then we either stay long or sell (losing on transaction costs in the process). If we are neutral on day $i - 1$ then we either stay neutral or go long (losing on transaction costs in the process). Optimization is then achieved simply by looking at which of the alternatives is better. If we end up long on day i we can only have got there from two states, long already, or flat the day before and have just bought:

$$L_i = \max((1 + R_i)L_{i-1}, (1 - k)(1 + R_i)N_{i-1})$$

where R_i is the return over day i and k is the transaction cost, 0.5% in this example. This simply asks which is better out of staying long or selling and going flat.

Similarly

$$N_i = \max(N_{i-1}, (1 - k)L_{i-1}).$$

The following image may be of some help in understanding this.

The above is easily coded up, as a simple loop, you just need to add the initial conditions that $L_0 = 0$ and $N_0 = 1$, representing the initial wealth, and then the final result is $\max(N_M, (1 - k)L_M)$, where M is the total number of days.

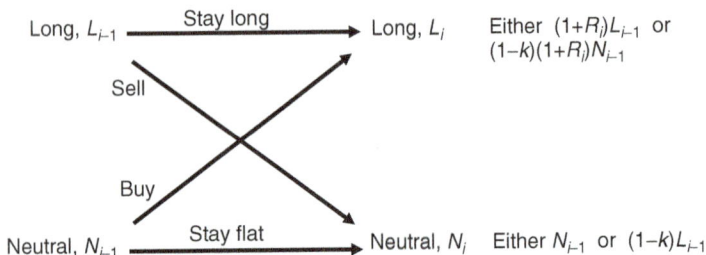

Miss Moneypenny

You need to hire a secretary. There are n possible candidates to interview and you want to find the best, the most talented. The problem is that there is great demand for secretaries, so if you want to make sure that you get one you'll have to offer her the job on the spot. Once she walks out of the door she's gone. You start interviewing candidates one after the other, they can all be ranked, so this one is better than that, or that one is worse than another, etc. There are no ties. But the order in which they are interviewed is random. What is the best strategy for maximizing the probability of getting the best secretary?

Solution

This problem is known in mathematical circles as the Secretary Problem, the Marriage Problem, the Sultan's Dowry problem, etc.

The best strategy is first to interview a number applicants with no intention of accepting any of them, call this number $m < n$. Then continue interviewing the rest one by one and then offer the job to the next one that is better than all of the ones previously interviewed, i.e. better than all the first m candidates that you interviewed but rejected out of hand. This is an example of an optimal stopping problem (not dissimilar to the problem of when to exercise an American option!). The question then becomes how many to interview, i.e. what is m?

Let's suppose that you have interviewed and rejected the first m applicants. You now interview the $(m + 1)$th. You will accept this one if she is better than the first m. What is the probability that the $(m + 1)$th applicant is the best out of all n? This one is easy. The probability that this is the best applicant is the same as any one being the best, i.e. $1/n$.

What is the probability of choosing candidate $m + 2$ and her turning out to be the best of all? This is harder because you have to have rejected candidate $m + 1$ as being worse than the first m *and* candidate $m + 2$ has to be the best of all. Well, the probability of $m + 2$ actually being the best out of all candidates is still $1/n$ but she will only being offered the job if the best applicant out of the first $m + 1$ is also the best applicant out of the initial rejected m. Now that's easy. Imagine lining up the $m + 1$ rejected applicants in order of increasing talent from left to right, what is the probability that the very best of these is not at the right-hand end? Just $m/(m + 1)$. So the probability of candidate $m + 2$ being the best and being accepted is $\frac{m}{n(m+1)}$.

Next what is the probability of choosing candidate $m + 3$ and her turning out to be the best? Again we have the $1/n$ probability of her being the best. And the probability of the previous best being in the first m out of the total rejected $m + 2$ is $m/(m + 2)$. So the required probability is $\frac{m}{n(m+2)}$.

Keep going in this vein, and add up all the probabilities to find that the probability of hiring the best applicant using this strategy is

$$\frac{m}{n}\left(\frac{1}{m} + \frac{1}{m+1} + \frac{1}{m+2} + \cdots + \frac{1}{n-1}\right).$$

And this is what we have to maximize!

If $n = 3$ then $m = 1$, i.e. interview the first applicant with no intention of accepting. And then start interviewing with the intention of accepting. This gives you a probability of 0.5 of choosing the best.

If $n = 4$ then $m = 1$. This gives you a probability of 11/24 of choosing the best.

If $n = 5$ then $m = 2$. This gives you a probability of 13/30 of choosing the best.

The secretary question is often posed with the extra '...for n large....' What is the optimal stopping time as $n \to \infty$?

The probability of success can be written as

$$\frac{m}{n}\left(\sum_{i=1}^{n-1}\frac{1}{i} - \sum_{i=1}^{m-1}\frac{1}{i}\right).$$

Since

$$\lim_{n\to\infty}\left(\sum_{i=1}^{n}\frac{1}{i}\right) = \gamma, \text{ the Euler constant, } 0.57722\ldots$$

the probability of success can be approximated for large n (and assuming that m is also large) by

$$-\frac{m}{n}\ln\left(\frac{m}{n}\right).$$

The maximum of this is easily found by differentiating with respect to m/n and we find in the limit of large n that $m = n/e$ where e. So you should interview a fraction $1/e$ of all candidates before contemplating hiring anyone!

Pirate puzzle

There are 10 pirates in a rowing boat. Their ship has just sunk but they managed to save 1,000 gold doubloons. Being greedy bastards they each want all the loot for themselves but they are also democratic and want to make the allocation of gold as fair as possible. But how?

They each pick a number, from 1 to 10, out of a hat. Each person in turn starting with number 1, decides how to divvy up the loot among the pirates in the boat. They then vote. If the majority of pirates approve of the allocation then the

Frequently Asked Questions in Quantitative Finance

loot is divided accordingly, otherwise that particular pirate is thrown overboard into the shark-infested sea. In the latter case, the next pirate in line gets his chance at divvying up the loot. The same rules apply, and either the division of the filthy lucre gets the majority vote or the unfortunate soul ends up in Davy Jones's locker.

Question: how should the first pirate share out the spoils so as to both guarantee his survival and get a decent piece of the action?

Solution
This is obviously one of those questions where you have to work backwards, inductively, to the solution for 10 pirates. Along the way we'll see how it works for an arbitrary number of pirates.

Let's start with two pirates, with 1,000 doubloons to share. Pirate 2 gets to allocate the gold. Unless he gives it all to Pirate 1 the vote will be 50:50 and insufficient to save him. Splash! We are assuming here that an equal split of votes isn't quite enough to count as a majority. So he gives Pirate 1 the entire hoard, and prays that he lives. (Of course, Pirate 1 could say hard luck and dump Pirate 2 overboard and still keep the money.)

Now on to the three-pirate case. In making his allocation Pirate 3 must consider what would happen if he loses the vote and there are just two pirates left. In other words, he should make his allocation so that it is preferred to the next scenario by sufficient numbers of pirates to ensure that he gets a favourable vote.

Pirate 3 allocates 1,000 to himself and nothing to the others. Obviously Pirate 3 will vote for this. And so will Pirate 2, if he votes against in the hope of getting some loot he will find himself in the two-pirate situation...in which case he could easily end up over the side.

Pirate 3	Pirate 2	Pirate 1
	0	1000
1000	0	0

Now to four pirates. Pirate number 3 is not going to vote for anything number 4 says because he wants Pirate 4 in the deep. So there's no point in giving him any share at all. Pirates 2 and 1 will vote for anything better than the zero they'd get from the three-pirate scenario, so he gives them one each and 998 to himself.

Pirate 4	Pirate 3	Pirate 2	Pirate 1
		1000	0
	1000	0	0
998	0	1	1

With five pirates similar logic applies. Pirate 4 gets zero. Then Pirate 5 needs to get two votes from the remaining three pirates. What is the cheapest way of doing this? He gives one to Pirate 3 and two to either of Pirates 2 and 1. Pirate 5 gets the remaining 997.

Pirate 5	Pirate 4	Pirate 3	Pirate 2	Pirate 1
			1000	0
		1000	0	0
	998	0	1	1
997	0	1	2 / 0	0 / 2

Pirate 6 needs four votes to ensure survival, his own plus three others. He'll never get Pirate 5 so he needs three votes from Pirates 4, 3, 2 and 1. Pirate 4 is cheap, he only needs 1 doubloon. But how to get two votes from the remaining Pirates 3, 2 and 1?

There are clearly several options here. And we are going to have to think carefully about the actions of the Pirates when faced with uncertainty.

Imagine being Pirate 2 when Pirate number 6 is allocating the gold. Suppose he gives you zero, what do you do? You may as well vote against, because there is a chance that on the next round you will get two doubloons. If Pirate 6 gives you two doubloons you should vote in favour. Things cannot be improved on the next round but may get worse. If given one doubloon now, what should you do? Next round you will either get zero or two. A tricky choice. And a possibly personal one.

But it is up to Pirate 6 to make sure you are not faced with that tricky decision which may result in his expulsion from the boat.

The conclusion is that Pirate 6 should give two doubloons to any of Pirates 3, 2 and 1. It doesn't matter which.

Pirate 6	Pirate 5	Pirate 4	Pirate 3	Pirate 2	Pirate 1
				1000	0
			1000	0	0
		998	0	1	1
	997	0	1	2 / 0	0 / 2
995	0	1	2 / 2 / 0	2 / 0 / 2	0 / 2 / 2

On Pirate 7's turn he will give zero to Pirate 6, one to Pirate 5 and two to any of Pirates 4 down to 1, again it doesn't matter which two, they will both now vote in his favour.

Pirate 7	Pirate 6	Pirate 5	Pirate 4	Pirate 3	Pirate 2	Pirate 1
					1000	0
				1000	0	0
			998	0	1	1
		997	0	1	2 / 0	0 / 2
	995	0	1	2 / 2 / 0	2 / 0 / 2	0 / 2 / 2
995	0	1	Two doubloons to any two of these four			

Now we settle down into a rhythm. Here's the entire allocation table.

Pirate 10	Pirate 9	Pirate 8	Pirate 7	Pirate 6	Pirate 5	Pirate 4	Pirate 3	Pirate 2	Pirate 1
								1000	0
							1000	0	0
						998	0	1	1
					997	0	1	2 / 0	0 / 2
				995	0	1	2 / 2 / 0	2 / 0 / 2	0 / 2 / 2
			995	0	1	Two doubloons to any two of these four			
		993	0	1	Two doubloons to any three of these five				
	993	0	1	Two doubloons to any three of these six					
991	0	1	Two doubloons to any four of these seven						

This Brainteaser is particularly relevant in quantitative finance because of the backward induction nature of the solution. This is highly reminiscent of the binomial model in which you have to calculate today's option price by working backwards from expiration by considering option prices at different times.

Another of these backward induction types is the famous Brainteaser, the unexpected hanging. In this problem we have a prisoner who has been condemned to be executed in ten days' time and an unusually considerate executioner. The executioner wants the prisoner to suffer as little mental anguish as possible during his last days and although the prisoner knows that sometime in the next ten days he will be executed he doesn't know when. If the executioner can surprise him then the prisoner will be able to enjoy his last few days, at least relatively speaking. So, the executioner's task is to wake the prisoner up one morning and execute him but must choose the day so that his visit was not expected by the prisoner.

Let's see how to address this problem by induction backwards from the last of the ten days. If the prisoner has not been executed on one of the first nine days then he goes to bed that night in no doubt that tomorrow he will be woken by the executioner and hanged. So he can't be executed on the last day, because it clearly wouldn't be a surprise. Now, if he goes to bed on the night of the eighth day, not having been executed during the first eight days then he knows he can't be executed on the last day because of the above, and so he knows that he must be executed tomorrow, day nine. Therefore it won't be a surprise and therefore the execution can't happen on the ninth day either. We have ruled out the last two days, and by working backwards we can rule out every one of the ten days.

On day four the prisoner is awoken by the executioner, and hanged. Boy, was he surprised!

Where did our backward induction argument go wrong? Ok, now I can tell you that this brainteaser is called the unexpected hanging *paradox*. There have been many explanations for why the prisoner's logic fails. For example, because the prisoner has concluded that he can't be hanged, then to surprise him is rather simple.

Chapter 14

Paul & Dominic's Guide to Getting a Quant Job

*I*f you enjoyed this book, and are looking for a job in quantitative finance, you might be interested in *Paul & Dominic's Guide to Getting a Quant Job*. To whet your appetite there follows the opening sections of the first version of this famous guide. For details on how to get the full guide in its latest version email paul@wilmott.com.

Introduction

This guide is for people looking for their first or second job in Quant Finance, the theory being that after a few years you ought to know most of this stuff.

Making a difference   If the hiring process is working well, the people seen by the bank will be roughly the same quality and from comparable backgrounds. Thus you need to stand out in order to win. We speak to a lot of recruiting managers, and we find that the difference between the one who got the job, and the person who came second is often very small for the employer, but obviously rather more important for you.

You have to walk a line between standing out, and not seeming too much for them to handle.

Understand the process   Interviewing people is a major industry all by itself, multiply the number of applicants by the number of interviews they attend and you sometimes wonder how any useful work ever gets done. Certainly this thought occurs to interviewers on a regular basis. They want it to end, soon, and although it is important to get the right people almost no one enjoys the process, and this is made worse by the fact that >80% of the work is wasted on those you never hire. Thus a core objective must be to make life as easy for the interviewer as possible. This means turning up on time, but not too early, being flexible on interview times, and trying to be pleasant.

What you need to prove

- You are smart
- You can work with people
- You can get things done
- You can manage yourself and your time
- You are committed to this line of work.

Kissing frogs   Like trying to find a prince by kissing frogs, you have to accept that it is rare for your first attempt to succeed, so you must be prepared for a long haul, and to pursue multiple options at the same time. This means applying to several banks, and not being deterred by failure to get into a particular firm.

Writing a CV

A CV is not some passive instrument that simply tells a recruiter why he should interview you, it also to some extent sets the agenda for the questions you will get when he meets you. Thus it is important to choose what you disclose as a balance between what you think he wants and the areas in which you are confident in answering questions.

Read the job specification   You should think of how you can present your skills and experience so as to be as close a match as possible. At one level this might sound obvious, but you should be aware that in many banks your CV will not be read by the hiring manager at all. Although at P&D we've actually done this stuff, it is often the case that CVs are filtered by people with little or no skills in finance. Often they resort to looking for keywords. Thus you should not rely upon the interviewer working out that if you have done subject X, you must have skills Y and Z. If you believe those skills are critical for this job, then make sure this can easily be spotted. Read the specification carefully, and if it specifically asks for a skill or experience, then include whatever you can to illustrate your strengths. If you believe particular skills to be critical, mention them in your covering letter as well (or if you believe the headhunter is especially dim).

Make sure you can be contacted   Make sure your contact details are reliable and that you regularly monitor the relevant email account(s) and telephones. It is sad when someone's CV shows great promise, but he doesn't respond in time to be interviewed. If you are at university, be aware that your current email address may stop working soon after you complete your course. GMail is to be preferred over Yahoo for a personal email address.

Get it checked   Have your CV and covering letter proofread by a native English speaker. This is important because people really do judge your ability by how you express yourself. Quant Finance is an international sport, with speakers of every language, and the ability to communicate difficult ideas is important, and if you can't get the name of your university correct, it makes one wonder if you can explain your views on jump diffusion. Also CVs use a particular style of English, which is subtly different from the one you learned in school. As there are a lot more applicants than jobs, the early stages are optimized to filter out those who stand no chance of getting in. Thus you must take considerable care to make sure you don't fail at an early stage because of trivial errors.

Covering letter   In your covering email, mention where you saw the advertisement and, importantly, which job you are applying for. If you don't say which job you are applying for, you are relying upon the person receiving your application to guess correctly. That does not always happen, and the larger the firm, the lower the probability, and at the very least it makes their lives harder, which is not the way to start the relationship.

A good format for a covering letter is to respond to the job specification point by point. State your ability to handle each item, together with why you think you can do it. This makes your CV more digestible, and shows that you are serious about the application.

Opinion is divided about whether you should have some 'statement of intent.' If you can think of something useful to say here, by all means put it, but be aware that a lot of new entrants to the market 'want to pursue a career in finance with a leading firm.'

Above we emphasize getting your CV checked, and this applies especially to the covering letter. Some managers discard the CV unread if the letter is sloppy.

Fonts and layout   Some things oN YOUR cv are important, and you may want tO draw their attention to them. Do not do this excessively. It is really irritating. The only time breaking THIS rule has worked to our knowledge was a hardcore programmer who learned the POstscript language that PCs use to talk directly to printers and he developed A program that printed his CV as concentric spirals of text in varying size. Viewed on screen it would slowly spin. YES, Dominic hired him.

If you're not prepared to spend at least a month learning reverse Polish notation, use a standard template. (Stick to two main font families, a sanserif, such as Arial, for large headings, and a serif font, such as Times, for main body text.)

PDF   Make a PDF if possible. These have a more professional feel than Word documents, they do not have virus problems (yet) and they retain original fonts and layout. Whatever software you use, print it out to make sure that what you see is really what you get. Perhaps view on, and print from, another PC to double check.

Name   Give your document a name that will be meaningful to the recruiter. Call it YourNameHere.pdf and not CV.pdf in the spirit of making it easier for the recruiter. It's not nice to have a large number of files with the same name, and it's actually quite easy to get your CV written over by the CV by someone else who also called it CV.

Dates   Make sure your dates 'join up' as much as possible. Some people in the recruitment process worry about gaps.

Be honest   If you claim skills in some area, it's a good bet that you will be asked questions about it. The CV should be a fair and positive statement of what you have to offer. No one expects you to share your history of skin diseases, but you'll be expected to back the talk with action.

Show that you can do things   By this point in your life you've soaked up a lot of information, and acquired skills, which is, of course, good. But a big question in the inquisitor's mind is whether you can translate this into real actions that are finished, complete and correct. One can pass most exams by getting answers wrong, but by showing good working, and an understanding of the principles. However, banks aren't really all that happy if you lose a pile of money by getting 'nearly' the right answer, where you put a minus when it should have been a plus. They like to see projects where you've started, worked to a goal and completed without having to have your hand held. This is a big reason why they like PhDs since it's a powerful argument that you can complete things. However, if you're going for a PhD-level job, you still have to beat others who have reached that level.

Projects completed are good, and you should be prepared to answer questions on them. The people who interview you will often have your sort of academic background, so these questions may be deep.

You may have changed direction in your career, and you should be prepared to answer why you made any given choice. It is important to be able to show that you didn't just 'give up' on an area when it got tough.

Interests and hobbies   Several of the people you meet will want to understand what sort of personality you have, or indeed whether you actually have one.

In finance you spend more of your waking hours with your colleagues than the person you marry, so it is good to present yourself as interesting as well as smart. They all want to feel you can work with others, so the cliché of 'reading, walking and listening to music,' doesn't really cut it. Certainly you shouldn't fake an interest in something, but do try to find something with which you can speak with a little passion. One candidate had somehow acquired a formal qualification in stage combat. Although it's relatively rare for quants to need to fight each other with swords, it's the sort of thing that catches people's eyes, and can make a crucial difference. It also gives the non-specialist people who you will meet something they can talk to you about.

Last job first   In your CV your most recent/current employment should stand out and be relevant to the job for which you are applying. Someone reading your CV may never get beyond this one piece of information. Make sure your dates are correct. As part of the pre-employment screen at most banks, they check your past employment, and people have had offers withdrawn because of mistakes on this.

Paul & Dominic   When applying to P&D, we also like to see a simple list of the various skills you have acquired, together with some estimate of how good you are. If you're new to QF then it won't be obvious which are most important, that's our job, so include as many as possible.

Multiple CVs   Finally, there is no reason why you should have only one CV. Presumably your entire life doesn't fit on two pages, so you can turn out a variety that each emphasize different aspects of your experience and education. You may take this as an exercise to work out the optimal number of variants, and you will quickly find out that it is not one. This is made more acute by the fact that failed CVs get little if any feedback. Think of it as shooting in the dark. If you don't hear a scream when you fire in one direction, you aim somewhere else.

Finding banks   In this document, we use the term 'bank' for the firm you want to work for. It is of course the case that quants work for many types of outfit, including brokers, the government, hedge funds, insurers, thrifts, consultancies, building societies, and in the case of P&D, for a headhunting firm. The wilmott.com website mentions any number of firms, and before you approach anyone it's good to do a few searches so that you know the nature of the target.

If you're still linked with your college then it has many resources to help you. Most have a careers office with directories of banks, and they will have some contacts with banks in that country. The library will have directories, and of course there is Google and Yahoo! for getting a list of targets. All large firms have entry-level programmes of some form, and you can relatively easily find a good number to apply for. At this stage numbers are important, since the ratio of new entrants to the market to jobs is quite high.

Interviews

Be prepared Before you go for the interview, find out the names of the people you are seeing, and do a Google on their name, as well as the bank/business unit you are joining. Try to avoid the error made by one candidate who could not understand why the interviewer was so interested in one part of her thesis. The candidate had quoted papers by the interviewer, but somehow managed to fail to connect the interviewer's name with the paper.

Be confident Almost no one at banks actually enjoys interviewing people; some even see it as a form of punishment. That means they only interview you if there's a good chance they will want to hire you. Most people who are considered for any job never even get a first interview.

Be punctual This shouldn't need saying. If you can't be on time for your interview how can they expect you to put in 12-hour days? If you are going to be late (and assuming it was unavoidable), telephone ahead with an accurate ETA. The best strategy is to schedule having a coffee before the interview, a little caffeine and sugar may well help, and this is a useful time buffer. Probably the worst bit about being late is not what it does to the interviewer, but what it does to you. The idea is to present yourself as cool, smart and in control. If you've been stressed out dealing with transport you knock a few points off your performance.

Set traps Although some questions are set in advance, most interviewers like to drill down based upon your answers. Thus you should try to mention areas where you feel confident in answering hard questions. This is best done subtly, by phrases like 'this is quite like X, but the answer is Y,' where X is a bastion of your competence; or by saying thoughtfully 'this isn't like X at all," if you feel you are being drawn into an area where you will sink.

Show you can do things We mention this in the CV section, and here's a chance to 'casually' drop in things you've done that show you can dig in and finish the job. It's OK to mention problems you overcame, and the lessons you learned from initial difficulties. Good managers are sceptical of people who claim to glide effortlessly through life, and don't want to be there when such a person hits a rock. Practical ability is therefore something that you will need to demonstrate a little more than theory. You wouldn't have reached this point if you didn't have a respectable record for absorbing theory, so the next step is to see if you can apply what you've learned. When asked your motivation for moving into finance, it's worth asking yourself if this is a reason.

Questions for the interviewer It is a good idea to have a question thought out in advance – it makes you look interested in the position. You have two objectives when they ask if you have questions for them.

Getting the message across A question can be a good way of bringing in things you want them to know, or to emphasize a point you want them to remember. You can ask the importance of your experience in MC, C++ or PDEs to the work you'd be doing. This gets the message across, either as a reminder or to bring it to their notice.

Find out more about the job Good questions are on the direction for the team over the next year, and how your work would help them to get where they want to be. It shows interest, and may give a better insight into what you really will be doing. Although they are interviewing you, it is also the case that they are selling the job to you, since they want you to accept if they offer. So it's up to you to work out whether it's a good job or not.

Remember, do not ask things that you should already know. You should discuss the job and the bank as much as you can with your recruiting consultant ahead of the interview and consult websites and any recruitment brochures. You don't want to give the interviewer the impression that you aren't interested enough in their bank to find out about it before the interview. Interviewers often say that this is the thing that really irritates them most at interviews. Instead, it is good to preface a question with a statement about some achievement that the bank is proud of (i.e. talks at length about their website or on recruitment materials) e.g. 'I know your office won the International Finance Press Award for Being a Bank last year, but could you tell me...'

Appearance

Good clothes   It is entirely possible, in your interview process, that every person you meet is not wearing a suit; some may not have shaved. That doesn't make it wise for you to turn up in 'smart casual.' How you look is not a big deal for quants, you're being paid to think. However, some people do get remembered for the wrong reason, and it can undermine your application a little. You should feel comfortable, and if that means a bit of perfume or good cufflinks then that's fine, but see below.

Neatness is good   More important than colour of cloth or design of tie, is the general impression of being in control of how you look. This means wearing it well, and being ordered in your appearance. It is worth checking this before you go into the bank.

Colours Black is the new black. White is nice for shirts and for no other visible item of clothing. Shoes should be clean and preferably black for men, and muted tones for women. A particular issue for women is the poor workmanship in most of their shoes. Do not attempt to walk long distances in new shoes that hurt your feet so badly they bleed (we know one person who stained the carpet with her blood). Make sure your clothes fit – badly fitting clothes do not look presentable and if your trousers are too tight you (and everyone else) will find this distracts from the matter at hand. There are some complexions that are generally complemented by certain colours, and apparently in some circles 'brown' is seen as a colour for your clothing. It is not; it merely says things about you that are never said to your face.

Dark blue is good as well.

Ties are best boring, novelty is bad.

Another reason for white shirts is that they don't show sweat, some colours do this terribly and it's not the image you want to project. A good shirt doesn't crease badly in wear.

Jewellery This will never help you get a job, no matter how expensive or fashionable. Thus if you have any doubt at all, don't wear it. If you're female and you have some brooch or bracelet, that's fine, but there's no upside for a man at all in bling. Cufflinks of course are fine, as long as they are not 'novelty' – you have no idea as to the sense of humour your interviewer may have; he may not have one at all. Some banking people spend quite appalling amounts on their watches, so don't even try to compete.

Perfume and aftershave Feel free to smell nice, but make sure that it's not too strong.

Make-up   The following is for women. If you're a male reader, you really should not be reading this paragraph and we are rather concerned that you are. Unless you really never wear make-up, a small amount is a good idea. Again, this gives the impression that you are making an effort and will possibly counter the deadening effect of all the monochrome clothing you are wearing. It should be discreet (i.e. no bright colours) and presentable rather than intending to make you look prettier. There are jobs that you can obtain by being attractive, but they are rarely fun and never intellectually rewarding. Any make-up should always be well applied – if you can't get eyeliner on straight, don't put it on, and never wear nail polish if there is any chance it will chip before the interview.

What People Get Wrong

Zeroth law of holes   When you find yourself in a hole, stop digging. You will be asked questions for which you can't think of any answer at all. Some interviewers make the questions harder until that point is reached. The trick is to cut your losses. With any luck they will just move on, unless it's a critical topic. Of course if it's critical then it's game over anyway. What you must avoid is wasting time wandering like the lost spirit of ignorance over a vast formless expanse of your incompetence. A good response is to look them in the eye after a little thought, then simply say 'Don't know, sorry.'

The exception to this are the 'all the tea in China' questions where you are asked to estimate some quantity like the number of bull testicles consumed by McDonald's customers per year. You aren't expected to know the answer to these, indeed knowing it would seem rather strange. They want to see how well you can estimate an unknown quantity and how you think.

But the biggest hole catches people who get very nervous when things go wrong. This is about the most negative personality defect you might have in a bank. When you realize you've said something dumb, stop, say something like 'let me think about that for a second,' and correct yourself. Make the pause work for you. Think the answer through, and show that you are capable of recovering. Remember that no one can talk about things at the edge of their competence for 4–5 hours without saying something silly. You don't have to be defect free, but self-knowledge and recovery will score you vital points.

Sleep regularly, sleep often Probably the most common error we've seen is not getting enough sleep the night before. As we said earlier, the difference between you and your competitors is tiny, and losing a small percentage of your thinking ability through being tired has an exponential effect on your probability of getting a job. Hours in a bank can be quite hard, so it's really not a good idea to mention feeling tired. Not only will they not be impressed, but if you get drawn into a conversation about how it degrades your performance it won't end well. Conversely, a cup of coffee doesn't do any harm, but we have seen people who clearly had drunk rather too much, and it didn't work well for them.

Make eye contact You need to make sure you look at your interrogators, they can smell fear. No need to stare at them, just remind yourself to look at them when they or you are speaking.

Apply for the right job You may feel you are a unique individual, and an obvious match for the job. Sadly, that often turns out not to be the case. If you are applying for a job called 'Henchman to Assistant Quant's Minion—PD0701067,' then do try to include that in your application, prominently. If you don't include this, then you are critically dependent upon whoever opens your application guessing.

Don't send a blue CV   Just don't, OK?

Barbarians   The word barbarian comes from the ancient Greeks who took anyone who didn't speak Greek as making 'bar bub bar' noises, like a drunk Homer Simpson, not Barbarian as in the icy commanding tones of Governor Schwarzenegger. Although Dr Simpson has enjoyed careers as an astronaut, rock star and nuclear engineer, few of us would hire him as a quant. It's important to get the right balance between gushing at people so fast that they have trouble following you, or being too quiet. You should try to practise looking at the reaction of people talking to you, and if the interviewer is clearly trying to move on, you usually should accept that. If you think of the conversation style used when first meeting someone you find attractive, you won't go far wrong. (Just remember it's a first date.)

It is also the case that no one wants to discriminate against those who aren't English speakers. This is good, but means that if you aren't understood they may just skip over what you say, rather than pass comment on your accent. This is especially true when having a telephone interview where you will not get visual feedback, and the sound quality is degraded.

Read your CV   Make sure that your CV is correct. A surprisingly large number have dates that are clearly wrong, or that by accident give the wrong impression. These worry interviewers a lot, and if your dates don't match, this can lose you an offer when they do the basic background check on all employees. Also read it to work out which questions it might provoke them to ask, 'Why did you pick X?,' 'I see you've done a lot of Y, here's a hard question about it.'

Mobile phone interviews   We're old people (>35), and thus sometimes use quaint phone technology which involves long wires physically connecting us to a huge ancient Unix computer miles away (yes, we still use miles). A typical quant has done enough physics to know that you can actually talk down copper wires rather than a 1 mm thick cell phone that has more processing capacity than its owner.

Sadly, the quality of cell phone speech is hideously degraded, and on many systems you can't both talk at the same time. This is occasionally awkward when both speakers have the same first language, but if both have English as a second language neither comes out of the conversation impressed with the other.

Do not attempt to do a phone interview on a cell phone.

Focus   Forging a rapport with the interviewer is a good thing, but some interviews drift off topic as the people involved chat. However, there is a time budget for each interview, and most managers have specific objectives in checking your ability. If they don't get covered it can hurt your progress to the next stage. Although it is the interviewer's responsibility to get things done, it's your problem if he doesn't. This is where the politeness we mention elsewhere is important. When you feel that time is moving against you, ask to make sure that everything he needs to know is covered.

Asking questions   Actually there are stupid questions. Bad questions are ones which embarrass the interviewer, or force him into a corner; that's his job, not yours. Do not try to score points off the interviewer; either you fail and look silly, or worse still, you succeed. It's a bad idea to bring up any screw-ups that the bank has been involved in, or where the manager has to admit that he hasn't read your CV.

Buzzwords   Your interrogator will often come from a similar background to you, but even within maths and physics there are many specializations that are mutually incomprehensible. You're just emerging from a discipline where you think in terms of these names and equations and it's easy to emit a stream of noises that your interviewer can barely understand. It's actually worse if he is from a similar background, since he may feel embarrassed to ask what you actually mean. You lose points here. But it is generally polite to enquire about the background of your audience when asked to explain some part of your work. This both shows consideration, and prevents you making this error.

Show some market insight This doesn't mean you have to know the ticker symbols of all SP500 stocks, but it does mean you should be able to comment on the reliability of models, what are their common pitfalls and how the quant and the trader might communicate about this. If you can quantify some practical phenomenon that is rarely discussed in academic literature then you will impress. (*Tip:* Because banks are often delta hedging, everything usually boils down to gamma and/or volatility.)

It is also worth reading *The Economist* before the interview. Some interviewers are keen to see if you have awareness of the world in general. *The Economist* may disturb some people since it covers other countries and has no astrology column or coverage of golf.

Brainteasers There are several different types of brainteasers you might get asked, all designed to test how your mind works under pressure, and to try to gauge how smart you are, rather than how much you have learned.

- **Straightforward calculation**. *Example:* How many trailing zeros are there in 100 factorial?
- **Lateral thinking**. *Example:* Several coworkers would like to know their average salary. How can they calculate it, without disclosing their own salaries?
- **Open to discussion**. *Example:* What's the probability that a quadratic function has two real roots?

- **Off the wall**. *Example:* How many manhole covers are there within the M25?

Work through the Brainteaser Forum on wilmott.com. You can practice for IQ tests, and the more you do, the better your score. Brainteasers are no different. And you'd be surprised how often the same questions crop up.

It's worth having a few numbers at your fingertips for the 'manhole covers.' One manager recently told us in rather despairing tones of the stream of candidates who didn't have even a rough approximation to the population of the country they were born and educated in. Several put the population of Britain between 3 and 5 million (it's around 60 million). A good trick when 'estimating' is to pick numbers with which it is easy to do mental arithmetic. Sure you can multiply by 57, but why expose yourself to silly arithmetic errors.

In many types of question, the interviewer wants to hear your train of thought, and has simply no interest in the actual answer. Thus you need to share your thoughts about how you get to each stage. You also should 'sanity check' your answers at each step, and make sure he is aware that you're doing it. This is a soft skill that's very important in financial markets where the money numbers you are manipulating are rather larger than your credit card bill.

At entry level we also see people being asked what we call 'teenage maths.' You've probably been focusing on one area of maths for some years now, and to get this far you've probably been good at it. However, some banks will ask you to do things like prove Pythagoras' theorem, calculate π to a few decimal places, or prove that the sum of N numbers is $N(N + 1)/2$. That last fact being surprisingly useful in brainteasers.

Be polite   Your mother told you this would be important one day, this is the day. 'Please,' 'thank you,' and actually looking as if you are listening are good things. Fidgeting, playing with your tie, or looking like you'd rather be somewhere else aren't polite. Standing when people come into the room is good. Occasionally you will find it appropriate to disagree, this is good, but get in the habit of using phrases like 'I'm not sure if that's the case, perhaps it is....'

You can't just wake up one day and be polite on a whim. (*Hint:* 'Pretty Woman' is fiction, we know this for a fact.) Without practice, it may even come over as sarcasm. In some languages 'please' and 'thank you' are implied in the context of the sentence, and that habit can spill over into English. Break that habit, break it now.

Practise sounding positive about things.

Of the things you can change between now and your interview, this one may have the biggest payback. If you've been doing calculus for a decade, you aren't going to improve much in a week. However, you become better at presenting yourself as someone who's easy to work with.

This is so important because your team will spend more waking hours together than most married couples, and senior people want to know you will 'fit in.' Like much of this whole process it's a game. No one really cares if you have a deep respect for your fellow man, but if you can emulate it well under pressure it's a difference that makes no difference.

Be true to yourself   You are selling yourself, so obviously you will be putting a positive spin on things. However, this is a career, not a job. If you feel the job may really not be what you want, then it's important that you think that through. If in the interview you hear something that sounds bad, ask about it. This does not have to be confrontational; you can use phrases like 'How does that work out in practice?' and 'What sort of flexibility is there to choose the work?' when told you're going to be counting buttons for the first six months.

Do not sound as if you work for Accenture   Even if you do work for Accenture or Arthur Andersen, you don't want to sound like you do. Avoid the sort of management speak that resembles Dilbert cartoons. A common type of interview question is of the form: 'You find that something has gone terribly wrong, what would you do about it.' An Accenture answer is 'I would see it as a challenge that would allow me to work as a good team player, as part of the global synergy'; or perhaps you might respond 'I will grasp the opportunity to show excellent leadership in integrity' which is interview suicide.

This part may sound quite silly, but there is a growing trend for some universities to have formal coaching in interview technique. In theory this should be very useful. In theory. The real practice is rather scary. It frustrates interviewers a lot to be faced with an obviously bright candidate who parrots clichés that some consultant has fed into him. We say at the beginning that you need to stand out, and given that the people you are competing with may well include people from your institution, it does you very little good.

By all means listen to these people, but take it with a pinch of salt. When you know little about the process, it's easy to give too much weight to the few things you get told.

Interview overlap   It is tempting to schedule lots of interviews as closely together as possible, because travel does eat into your budget. You should be very conservative about the amount of time you allow for each interview. It's not easy to get a manager to speed up his process because you want to get across town to talk to one of his competitors. The worry about time, just like lateness, can reduce your effectiveness, so make sure this doesn't come up.

To find out more about this quant-job guide please send either of us an email (Dominic Connor, dominic@pauldominic.com, or Paul Wilmott, paul@wilmott.com).

Index

Index compiled by Terry Halliday